Socialist Modern

Socialist Modern

East German Everyday Culture and Politics

Katherine Pence
and Paul Betts
EDITORS

THE UNIVERSITY OF MICHIGAN PRESS

Ann Arbor

Published in the United States of America by
The University of Michigan Press
Manufactured in the United States of America
♾ Printed on acid-free paper

2011   2010   2009   2008   4   3   2   1

A CIP catalog record for this book is available from the British Library.

Library of Congress Cataloging-in-Publication Data

Socialist modern : East German everyday culture and politics / Edited
    by Katherine Pence and Paul Betts.
        p   cm. — (Social history, popular culture, and politics in
    Germany)
    Includes index.
    ISBN-13: 978-0-472-09974-0 (cloth : alk. paper)
    ISBN-10: 0-472-09974-4 (cloth : alk. paper)
    ISBN-13: 978-0-472-06974-3 (pbk. : alk. paper)
    ISBN-10: 0-472-06974-8 (pbk. : alk. paper)
        1. Germany (East)—Social life and customs.   2. Politics and
    culture—Germany (East)   3. Socialism and society.   4. Popular
    culture—Germany (East)   I. Pence, Katherine, 1968–   II. Betts, Paul,
    1963–

    DD287.3.S63   2007
    943'.1087—dc22   2007035405

*Dedicated to the memory and
spirit of Daphne Berdahl (1964–2007)*

Contents

Introduction

Katherine Pence and Paul Betts

The reunification of Germany in 1989, known popularly as the *Wende,* may have put an end to the experiment in East German communism, but its historical assessment is far from over. In many ways this was a predictable by-product of the Wende itself, which abruptly released German history from its cold war confines. With it came a lively transatlantic discussion about the meaning of the past for reunified Germany. While this discussion has largely been inspired by the pressing need to take stock of the country's changed place in a brave new world of post–cold war geopolitics, a pronounced uncertainty about how to interpret Germany's historical role within the broader drama of the past century has also fueled the debate.[1] Even if one might detect an assumption that German history is somehow coterminous with the century's more general "crisis of classical modernity," the framework for interpretation is wider than ever. For many observers, this is all the more unsettling given that the long-familiar narratives of modern German history—nationalism, socialism, and even liberalism—seemed to have lost much of their once-formidable explanatory power, driving idealism and even popular appeal.[2] No sooner had the Berlin Wall been dismantled than historians began to reassess Germany's twentieth century from fresh post–cold war perspectives. This has been delicate business, to be sure, as many of these post-1989 debates have been quite contentious and public, particularly concerning reconsiderations of the role of ordinary Germans in the Nazi regime and the Final Solution. For example, controversies over Daniel Goldhagen's thesis that masses of Germans in the 1930s were "willing executioners" during the Nazi regime, the 1995 Hamburg exhibition exposing crimes of the average Wehrmacht soldier, the opening of Berlin's Jewish museum in 1999, and the construction of the Berlin Holocaust memorial all dramatically underscore the high political stakes involved in reconfiguring Germany's troubled past.[3]

But while the ongoing process of "coming to terms with the past"[4] in unified Germany has focused a good deal of attention on the Third Reich's "brown heritage," it is really the Germany Democratic Republic's (GDR) own "red legacy" that has had more of an immediate impact on residents of the "New Germany." The popular uproar over the crude rendering of GDR history in the mass media has indicated just how sensitive and vital this past was—and is—for ex-GDR citizens. Given the radical and rapid transformation of East Germany after 1989, it was no surprise that interpretations of GDR history assumed real political gravity from the very outset. Decisions about the hiring and firing of individuals and the closing of institutions, and the more general reckoning with the role of the secret police (Stasi) in public life, for instance, turned on interpretations of complicity and collusion in the former GDR, as did the high-profile trials of former leaders Erich Honecker and Egon Krenz, Stasi chief Erich Mielke, and border guards accused of human rights violations. When the Stasi archives were opened, many East Germans were also shocked to discover that their friends and loved ones had been spying on them as informal collaborators of the Stasi.[5] Little wonder, then, that the GDR past has been the subject of intense political and even moral anguish, what historian Konrad Jarausch has described as an "ideological contest for the soul of the country."[6]

Yet the relevance of the GDR past went well beyond the courtroom and dramatic spy stories. Even after the fall of the Berlin Wall, Germans apparently still felt separated by a "mental wall" of deep-seated East-West antagonism. Since the transformation of East German economy and infrastructure largely was absorbed by the Federal Republic of Germany (FRG), rather than any negotiated "third way" settlement, hostility erupted between reunified Germans who continued to define themselves and each other according to cultural differences. Westerners and Easterners derisively have called each other "Wessies" and "Ossies," as the 1990s witnessed acrimonious cultural wars over the place and value of the GDR in reunified Germany. After a brief period in which East Germans thronged to "Test the West," disillusionment with reunification often led to defensive and even nostalgic memories of their lost social and cultural world.[7] The GDR state may be long dead, but its past is still very much alive. As the historian Corey Ross summarized: "For millions of ordinary Germans it [the East German past] forms a crucial part of their own biographies and identities. For political elites, its legacies still strongly affect the German economy and inform the political culture of the unified state. For intellectuals, it represented the end of a particular utopia and a failed alternative to liberal-capitalist democracy."[8]

That the GDR past would look different in Düsseldorf and Dresden is obvious enough. But the striking thing, perhaps, is that histories of the GDR have not done much to produce reconciliation and narrative consensus, as the antagonism between the former cold war rivals has amply shown that there were definite limitations to national unity that Germans hoped to affirm and celebrate. So intractable has been this mental Berlin Wall that many German histories written after 1989 dispensed altogether with myths of common culture and national solidarity in favor of addressing the seemingly more pressing issue at hand, namely, the roots of German-German difference.[9]

In part this accounts for the tremendous output of new histories of the GDR since 1990, made possible by the opening of state and Party archives after 1989. The mountain of newly available files demonstrates one aspect of the way in which the GDR was a uniquely modern state. Using the tools of the modern bureaucracy and police apparatus, the state monitored the East German population and logged records of their participation and protests in vast archives. Literally hundreds of monographs, ethnographies, documentaries, exhibitions, and memoirs have taken up various dimensions of East German history in light of these new sources. They have worked to trace the regime's dizzying collapse, to recount the country's lost social networks and cultural lifeworlds, and to chronicle the mixed and sometimes destructive effects of the Wende upon many East German citizens. Early predictions that the whole history of the GDR would soon sink into oblivion—as Stefan Heym famously surmised—as a mere "footnote of world history"[10] have proven premature and off the mark. For if nothing else, the unexpected persistence of cold war separatism has made plain that cultural—even more so than economic—reunification would be neither seamless nor uncontested, as older cold war identities have in many ways outlasted the country's forty-year political division.

Since 1989 there have been shifting trends in scholarly interest and inquiry about the GDR past. For example, much of the early post-Wende research was driven by the desire to uncover the very relationship between power and resistance, complicity and consent. A large proportion of 1990s historiography was framed by the Bundestag's Enquete Commission, a high-profile parliamentary body set up to investigate the "history and con-sequences of the socialist dictatorship in Germany" in order to identify and eliminate the GDR's apparent illiberalism. In the course of its tenure from 1992 to 1998, the commission oversaw numerous public hearings, culmi-nating in two multivolume published reports.[11] Of particular relevance here is the way in which the commission viewed GDR life almost exclu-sively in terms of the logic of totalitarian domination: according to the report, the ruling Socialist Unity Party (SED) "deformed the life of every individual person and the entire society," using its reach to penetrate "all areas of state and society" so as to effect "the complete suppression of free-dom of opinion and the free exchange of political views in the GDR," not unlike its National Socialist predecessor.[12] Bald and often self-serving as this rendition of the GDR was, it exerted profound influence on the initial wave of post-1989 GDR histories, whose reckoning with the past often amounted to a simplistic identification of heroes, victims, and villains.[13] The 1990s abounded with popular books on the cruel exploits of the Stasi and its henchmen on the one hand and the heroic resistance of the innocent *Volk* on the other, giving rise to what Mary Fulbrook has rightly called a crude and moralizing "Checkpoint Charlie" version of GDR history.[14]

This post-Wende work in some ways remained tied to cold war–era historiography on the GDR produced in the West that focused on the repressive politics of "socialist tyranny." The end of communism has actu-ally given a new lease on life to old totalitarian theories about the GDR's hapless world of Party rule. In this vein many of the 1990s "new histories" flattened the experience of GDR society into a monochromatic, "thor-oughly ruled society" from the top down. In this approach, the state, the SED, the Stasi, and the netherworld of censors and low-level apparatchiks invariably assumed center stage. East German social life, by contrast, was painted as a "de-differentiated" and "shut-down" society,[15] one that stressed the state's successful control of the daily activities and habitus of East German citizens. In the face of state intrusion, society itself suppos-edly "withered away"[16] or retreated into "niches."[17] Although many of these studies have clearly shed new light on the former centers of GDR power, they all too infrequently ventured beyond the directives and purview of the state apparatus itself.

Such approaches were not the only scholarly treatments of the GDR before or after 1989. Besides the obviously Marxist analyses from pre-Wende GDR authors themselves, an alternative school of thought more sympathetic to the GDR emerged in the West in the 1960s and 1970s as a corrective to one-dimensional accounts of the GDR as nothing but a "Soviet protectorate,"[18] furnishing instead more benign images of the state as a noble if failed experiment in socialist modernity. Historians of this school were more concerned with evaluating the extent to which the socialist regime's promise of social emancipation and broad-based welfare lived up to its Marxist promise. New histories of the GDR have tried to forge a middle path between polarized "hard" and "soft" interpretative frameworks in order to study the GDR from less polemical ideological standpoints.[19] Recent work has offered much more complex renderings of various aspects of GDR diplomatic relations, politics, and economics.[20] Although much of this scholarship has provided important insights into the workings and limits of GDR state power and the planned economy, many accounts deal less directly with everyday life and culture. This volume aims to build on the recent historiography that has more explicitly explored a nuanced relationship between GDR state and society.

As such our volume owes much to the growing existing literature that has more concertedly interrogated East German culture and society. An early intervention that helped shift the debate was a 1994 compilation stemming from the now vast historiography on German social history (*Gesellschaftsgeschichte*) edited by Hartmut Kaelble, Jürgen Kocka, and Hartmut Zwahr, *Sozialgeschichte der DDR*. This volume moves fruitfully from a purely political vision of the so-called SED state toward more social and cultural issues such as work, citizenship, religion, gender, law, and generational conflict. Even so, its starting point is more the analysis of macrostructures and societal/institutional comparison arising from a comparative approach to dictatorship than the examination of everyday experiences within the East German state.[21] Recent years have witnessed new efforts to move beyond state-centered models to explore what Richard Bessel and Ralph Jessen call the "limits of dictatorship" in the GDR in their edited collection from 1996.[22] While their volume primarily focuses on the professions and other related social groups, their approach has inspired subsequent research coming out of the Zentrum für Zeithistorische Forschung in Potsdam that has fanned out in a number of directions.[23] Much of this has fruitfully extended the pioneering work of Lutz Niethammer, Alf Lüdtke, and others in the field of oral history and "everyday life history," or *Alltagsgeschichte*. Lüdtke's concept of *Eigensinn* (which one might translate as "a sense of one's interests"), which addresses how everyday citizens assert their subjectivity and make meaning in their own immediate social worlds, has proven a useful tool for understanding the possibilities for individual action and autonomy.[24] One influential essay collection edited by Thomas Lindenberger, entitled *Herrschaft und Eigen-Sinn in der Diktatur,* explicitly takes up the very interplay of state power and individual subjectivity from a variety of vantage points. In his introduction, Lindenberger calls attention to local contexts in which citizens made sense of the state in which they lived through myriad acts of will and resistance. As such this approach combines the study of dictatorship with the insights from cultural studies.[25] Another volume published in Germany with similar goals examines the role of workers in the GDR.[26] In English, *Dictatorship as Experience,* edited by Konrad Jarausch, neatly moves beyond one-sided analyses of the GDR stuck either within outdated totalitarian models or "nostalgic" interpretations of the regime as a noble failed tragedy, laying bare the contradictions and complexity of GDR life by looking beneath the "uniformity of dictatorship."[27] Another recent collection, Patrick Major and Jonathan Osmond's *The Workers' and Peasants' State: Communism and Society in East Germany under Ulbricht, 1945–1971,* profitably builds upon this newer work, offering an assortment of wide-ranging essays on the very meaning of society in the GDR during its first two critical decades of existence.[28] More recently, David Crew's 2003 edited collection, *Consuming Germany in the Cold War,* focuses on the comparative development of postwar German consumer societies, indicating the extent to which consumption became a key cold war battleground of East-West conflict.[29]

Our *Socialist Modern* volume, too, is an attempt to move beyond the conceptual divide between politics at the state level and the culture of everyday life in order to bring into better perspective the specific contours of the GDR's "socialist modernity." It hopes to bridge popular experience and politics in a way that maintains subjective agency and highlights the complex relationship between everyday citizens and the GDR state. It is inspired by the insights of Alltagsgeschichte, as well as by recent work in the fields of cultural studies and anthropology, which have helped show how state and society interact and influence each other in a more dynamic relationship.[30] In this sense, our volume amply illustrates Ralph Jessen's claim that the GDR was never a fully "shut-down society,"[31] despite the SED's reach and grip on power; indeed, as the contributors to our volume make clear, GDR society may have been a severely circumscribed field of interaction, but it was still characterized by a surprising amount of conflict and texture.[32]

Where our volume is distinctive, however, is its emphasis on exploring the ways in which the GDR was fundamentally modern. This may strike some readers as odd, given that the GDR was often characterized as anything but a modern society. One of the problems in post–cold war conceptualizations of modernity is a common tendency to equate modernity with triumphant liberal capitalism. This is in many ways an extension of an older Western cold war logic, which often characterized state socialism as essentially a culture of surveillance, privation, economic mismanagement, and colorless lifestyles. West German critic Hans Magnus Enzensberger summed it up for many when he caustically remarked that "real existing socialism" was "the highest stage of underdevelopment."[33] The "rush to unity" in 1989 seemed only to confirm these old cold war stereotypes. The well-publicized day trips of wide-eyed East Berliners feverishly spending their "welcome money" on West German bananas, cigarettes, and VCRs apparently substantiated long-standing cold war images of East German bankruptcy, unfreedom, and consumer want.[34] No one would deny the significance of such consumer tourism as an early expression of political liberation. It is also clear that the GDR, like its socialist neighbors, suffered from relatively calcifying economic stagnation by the 1970s and 1980s. However, these economic problems were only one element of the story of what defined the state's modernity.

Indeed, there was a more serious ideological sleight of hand at work in these popular renditions. Such logic of backwardness effectively reversed Marx's schema of history, in which socialism, the modern vanguard, would eventually succeed capitalism. The 1989 Eastern bloc revolutions seemed to imply that the very idea of socialism, as judged by the forms of its "neo-absolutist" political world and shabby material culture, was in essence unmodern. Once socialism had been subtly removed from modernity in this manner, it became easy to reread the events of 1989 as simply a desire to be modern—in this case, Western. Modernity, once inseparable from the telos of socialism, now returned as its nemesis. It was in this context that East German history was reworked as a descriptive ethnography about the "land that time forgot."[35] Such views were put on permanent display of East and West German history at Bonn's "House of History" or the Leipzig Forum of Contemporary History, examined in Daphne Berdahl's essay here, where these former cold war rivals are contrasted largely in terms of material output and commodity cultures.[36] Even if some have tried to confront this crude formulation by celebrating East German cultural life as less materialistic and more noble in its austere simplicity than that of the West, the pseudo-anthropology of modernity/

unmodernity still shapes some scholarly constructions of German-German historical difference.[37]

Our volume is not intended to engage with the debate on these terms but rather to broaden the idea and understanding of modernity itself. It neither attempts to assess how the GDR ranks on a spectrum ranging from backward to modern nor tries to measure how "sufficiently" or "successfully" modernized it ultimately was. Instead, we prefer to approach the problem differently: what did modernity mean in East Germany, particularly in the way it shaped the relationship between socialist state and society?

In so doing, we hope to shift the way modernity is assessed from the achievement of particular standards of industrialization or political structures to an examination of the commitment to a full reshaping of society. No doubt the regime featured many hallmarks of what we take as modern: a premium on rapid industrialization, mass organization of society, a vast security and police apparatus, a developed welfare state, and a collective ideology, among others. Many important studies have investigated the GDR's struggles to implement its modernizing goals of political or diplomatic power[38] and economic transformation within the planned economy[39] through collectivization of agriculture,[40] technological change,[41] and industrialization.[42] These works examine modernization at crucial levels of policy and illuminate the roots of some of the major crises, such as the 1953 uprising and the Berlin crisis during 1958–61.[43]

Yet the whole question of modernity ran much deeper than that. After all, it was precisely the regime's more comprehensive project of social engineering that qualified it as fundamentally modern, one that set its sights on the full-scale makeover of the state, society, material culture, and citizens alike. Of course, the definition of society as a secular object of scrutiny and experimentation has been a crucial aspect of modern politics ever since the Enlightenment. But it took on radical expression in the wake of World War I, and it was this feverish will to social reconstruction—that is, politics in the subjunctive tense—that wed the Weimar and Nazi periods, even if the ends of their particular vision of modernity differed so dramatically. As Peter Fritzsche noted, interwar Germany played host to sundry dreams of breathless social engineering that were powered by "the apprehension of the malleable: the dark acknowledgment of the fragility and impermanence of the material world allied with the conviction that relentless reform could steady collapsing structures."[44] The point is that this spirit of experimentation and reconstruction did not die with the Nazis. Both East German socialism and West German welfare capitalism took part in actively working to reconstruct society often through government policy. Such visions were perhaps most zealously continued—albeit with different means and ends than the Nazis—with East Germany's project to build a shiny new socialist republic atop the ruins of fascism. Indeed, as some contributors discuss, GDR politics—at least until the mid-1970s—was fueled by the "Enlightenment dream" of the mutability and even perfectibility of its citizenry, one that then justified relentless reform, education measures, and paternal supervision. In this sense, the particular political and economic form that the society took, be it liberal or conservative, or even whether it succeeded or not, is less a measure of its modern substance than the undertaking to radically recast society anew.

No less significant were the ways in which East German society was culturally modern. In fact, it is striking to note how much of the debate about GDR modernity has focused largely on the spheres of economics and politics. With a few exceptions,[45] to a surprising degree culture is often left out of the general discussion and standard historiographical overviews, at best confined to a section appended at the end of larger edited collections. This is unfortunate, not least because—as many of the contributors in this volume show—the sphere of culture played host to many of these tensions of modernity over the decades. Microhistories and oral histories of life in the GDR, along with analyses of conflicts within state organizations, the media, and even the Party itself, have also worked to dispel the image of a single-mindedly dictatorial state exerting unrelenting domination over its citizens.[46] Certainly the role of repression and the erasure of civil liberties must not be downplayed. But it is crucial to uncover the spaces for agency of "ordinary" people, which had a decisive effect on the formation of Party policy and the state. To this end, influential concepts like Eigensinn have helped to show the ways that everyday citizens constructed meaning in their own immediate social worlds[47] and devised various "imagined communities" that were not limited to state ideologies and organizations.[48] Even the socialist command economy, which has been a major arena of scholarly scrutiny, became a key cultural field upon which East-West conflicts were fought out and where new notions of selfhood were articulated, as recent studies of consumer culture have shown.[49]

To get at these issues, the study of GDR society cannot be limited to top-down transformative efforts by state and Party but should also examine the experience of the "modern" in everyday life and popular culture. Thus this volume focuses less on avant-garde modernity within elite culture than on culture as lived experience and habitus.[50] In this regard, popular music, fashion, consumption, and film are particularly telling sources for exploring the individual articulation of East German identities and informal structures of sociability, especially since Soviet-type societies largely did away with civil society and a classical public sphere, which liberal theorists have long viewed as fundamental to the formation of modern selfhood.[51] By examining everyday cultures in arenas such as work, consumption, domesticity, and youth subcultures, a more complex picture of the relationship between a modernizing state and its citizenry emerges. Erica Carter and a number of historians and ethnologists of East German consumption have made a particularly strong case for the consumer economy as the "source of core values for the nation" and "fantasy object of collective identification."[52] A recent volume of essays on material culture throughout the Eastern bloc also examines modernity across the Sovietized world by focusing on style and consumption to show "how the material realities of what has been described as 'real existing socialism' were appropriated and negotiated in everyday life."[53] What these observations make plain is that the sphere of economics was never limited to production quotas and the politics of provisions but rather gave form to a host of "cultural" questions about identity, allegiance, and even nationhood. The relationship between individual identities articulated in the realm of culture and the state's project of building modern socialism is one of the key themes of this book. Taking more seriously the collective desires, fantasies, or "dreamworlds"[54] of the GDR population may also help to illuminate why cultural differences between East and West have been so trenchant after 1989.

Our *Socialist Modern* volume takes this question of cultural identity as its starting point, presenting case studies of GDR social and cultural history that shed new light on the relationship between state-level politics and the culture of everyday life. By focusing on modernity, this volume hopes to avoid facile comparisons to the Third Reich or Stalinism that can limit the contextual frameworks for understandng the GDR's meaning. The diverse case studies gathered here show just how fundamentally modern the GDR was and, in so doing, help link the GDR to longer trajectories of German history and more global reconsiderations of what is modern.

Socialist Modern as "Alternative Modernity"

Investigating the relationship between GDR state and society goes right
to the heart of the meaning of modernity itself, especially in connection
with the German context. As is well known, modernity has been defined
and redefined by a number of theorists over the years. Those who have
tried to classify modernity often list a number of economic, cultural, and
political elements emerging from eighteenth-century Europe. These modern characteristics include breaks with tradition; the rise of capitalism and
the nation-state; rapid urbanization, industrialization, and commercial-
ization; rationalization and scientific efficiency; secularization, artistic
innovation, and cultural radicalization; the development of the welfare
state;[55] the evolution of a public sphere,[56] civil society, and the mobilization of mass publics; as well as increasing democratization according to
Enlightenment-based values of citizenship. Not least, Max Weber, Michel
Foucault, and others have identified dark sides of modern society as an
"iron cage" beset with technologies of surveillance and discipline;[57]
bureaucratization, racism, and imperialism; cultural despair or anxiety;[58]
and at worst the industrial organization and implementation of mass
killing and genocide.[59]

This checklist approach to defining modernity contains obvious limitations and paradoxes. For one thing, how many of these characteristics
does a society need in order to be considered modern? How does one categorize complex societies in which "traditional" forces still compete with
"modern" ones? Postcolonial theorists, for their part, have significantly
pointed out how these standards of conceptualizing modernity end up uni-
versalizing an experience of modernization that was actually particular to
the European context.[60] Central to their inquiries is the question, How
might understandings of modernity differ once we move beyond the conceptual framework of the liberal West? Such questions touch on issues of
both historical explanation and self-identity. As Frederic Jameson has
remarked, modernity consists less of set categories or standards of development than of "the stories we tell ourselves and others about it."[61]

With these issues in mind, we propose to approach the GDR as an
"alternative modernity," what is known in German as *Gegenmoderne.*
Admittedly, this is not so easy, especially since it requires thinking beyond
an eighteenth-century political vocabulary of the liberal state—including
the separation of economy, politics, and society; a distant relationship
between citizen and state; the rule of law; as well as a participatory public

sphere and empowered citizenship—that still shapes our perceptions and judgments of illiberal entities of all stripes. In the case of the GDR, one is faced with a historical world that is inherently difficult to describe: a nonsocial society, a depoliticized polity, a nonpublic public sphere.[62] Nevertheless, the structural features of the economy, social life, and gender relations, as well as the look and styling of East German material culture, may be seen as aspects of the GDR's distinctive alternative modernity, as the contributors suggest in various ways.

The concept of alternative modernity has become a hallmark of recent postcolonial and subaltern studies. Less well known, however, is that such vocabulary also has its roots in the 1920s, to the extent that Soviet communism and Italian fascism very much saw themselves as alternative modernities to the more famous liberal variant.[63] Lenin's followers in the Soviet Union, for example, even believed communism to be a higher stage of modernity.[64] Indeed, the interwar "clash of ideologies" in many ways pivoted on contending notions of whose modernity would succeed in inheriting the earth.[65] The cold war, and in particular the 1960s doctrine of superpower detente and peaceful coexistence, reinforced the idea of the Soviet Union as the developed world's alternative modernity to the West.

Yet it is postcolonial studies that have forever shattered this "bipolar" and Eurocentric scheme of modernity itself. In fact, terms such as *multiple modernities,*[66] *modernity at large,*[67] or *alternative modernities*[68] in the plural have been devised precisely to free the study of modernity in "peripheral" settings like Asia and Latin America from normative standards set by the European "metropole."[69] By looking at modernity from vantage points outside Europe, these critics have worked to debunk the assumption that modernization evolves along similar paths pioneered and exported by Western Europe with "cultural homogeneity" as a result.[70] The Eurocentric model, they argue, had justified a paternalist or imperialist view of the "developing world" as backward and "*not yet* civilized enough to rule themselves."[71] To this end, Dipesh Chakrabarty, Arjun Appadurai, and others have made the case for local studies of the experience of modernity elsewhere that expose "multiple genealogies" of uneven development across the globe.[72] As Chakrabarty put it, "The idea is to write into the history of modernity the ambivalences, contradictions, the use of force, and the tragedies and the ironies that attend it."[73]

In this case, it may seem paradoxical and even ironic to use these critiques of Eurocentric modernization theories to analyze the case of East Germany, which is squarely at the center of Europe. Indeed, from the perspective of India or Latin America, European socialism and capitalism may appear as two sides of the same modernization coin. After all, the argument has been made many times that the bitter antagonism between the Soviet Union and the liberal West over much of the twentieth century may be best characterized as a family squabble among Europeans about the true legacy of the Enlightenment ideals of freedom and justice. And yet, postcolonial theories of alternate modernities are very useful in rethinking socialist modernity beyond the overburdened comparison with Western capitalist norms of development. If nothing else, this perspective helps reposition GDR history in more global frameworks of analysis.[74] It not only draws attention to the role of the GDR as a colony itself of the Soviet Union but also reminds us that socialist states like the GDR once served as inspiring models of alternative development for decolonizing nations that sought to sidestep a Western liberal modernity plagued by retrograde assumptions of third world "backwardness."[75]

That said, East Germany's alternative modernity still has a more specific meaning, given that it developed in direct dialogue with Western liberalism in general and West Germany in particular. If taken seriously, it behooves historians to pay closer attention to the manner in which East Germany, like its East Bloc neighbors, sought to engineer a superior alternative to the liberal West. Just because we know the end of the story should not deter us from revisiting this dashed "dreamworld" of East German socialism and to rescue its evaluation from what E. P. Thompson famously called the "condescension of posterity." After all, there is much to learn in the way that Eastern European states delivered advanced forms of welfare, a break from traditional gender roles, and a distinctly modern socialist culture, to say nothing of massive investment in industrialization and the mass mobilization of its citizenry. The darker sides of this modernity such as the bureaucracy and the vast reaches of the police and surveillance state also need to be given attention as aspects of the GDR's modernity. Ina Merkel in particular has profitably applied this term to sketch out the contours of GDR consumer culture.[76] This leitmotif of social engineering resonates throughout this book. From various perspectives, this volume chronicles the GDR's desire and struggle to fulfill these promises of a "socialist modern."

Another important subject of analysis is the interplay of ongoing tradition and conservatism in GDR life even as it cast the regime as supremely modern. In some ways the construction of modernity entailed reconfiguration of older ideals or practices into what Alf Lüdtke calls "specific amalgams" of old and new. Despite the regime's overall claim to have produced a break with the past starting with the so-called zero hour of 1945, numerous continuities were perpetuated either within official doctrine and policy or within society. At times, for example, the state invoked traditional and even patriotic vernacular German concepts that had premodern origins, such as "German quality work" and "honorable labor," even if they were exploited for the modern ends of raising productivity, cultivating loyalty, and quelling potential shop-floor discontent.[77] Although official policy toward youth and gender was progressive, the implementation of this progressivism was not consistent, and the general population's conservative attitudes toward youth and gender relations provided further evidence of the persistence of tradition in key spheres of GDR social life.[78] In other ways, "traditional" institutions like the churches took on new significance as sources of resistance to and critique of the regime in the absence of other sites of autonomous civil society. As one sociologist has noted, what particularly exercised the Lutheran Church at the time "was the GDR's integration into a modernization project that in their eyes represented a threat to peace, was ecologically costly, and anti-humane."[79] The emergence of the GDR's peace and ecological movements—to which the leading GDR literary figures and intellectuals lent their impassioned support—in many ways grew out of these religiously inspired "critiques of civilization" (*Zivilisationskritik*) from the early 1980s.[80] That the main sources of criticism against the state now came from the so-called defenders of tradition—in this case, the churches and the ecological movement—may seem at first to point up the failure of the GDR's grand modernization campaign to eliminate vestiges of bourgeois culture. Nonetheless, these trenchant "civilization critiques" actually sprang from the strong sentiment that the GDR had become *too* modernized and that more traditional elements—Christian faith, love of nature, and so forth—had to assert themselves in the face of a decidedly antitraditional state. For this reason, it is much too cavalier to suggest that the regime ultimately collapsed as a result of its "deficits of modernization," since it was precisely the scale and success of GDR modernization that spurred such passionate criticism and agitation in the first place.

How tradition and modernity collided in the hothouse conditions of GDR social politics is one of the key subthemes of the book.[81] That does not mean that all of the contributors are in agreement about the nature and achievement of the GDR's alternative modernity. Some find evidence of modernity in seemingly unexpected places, whether in GDR sexual mores, models of clinical psychology, or desire to travel. Others chronicle its contradictions by examining the recasting of decidedly old-fashioned work attitudes and prejudices toward foreigners. Still others make the point that modern is hardly synonymous with good and progressive, insomuch as modernity can subjugate as much as it frees. For the purposes of this book, the concept of "socialist modern" has been deliberately left open to interpretation and the contributors have drawn their own conclusions based on their individual topics. That there is no single storyline to socialist modern and that its outcomes are often at odds and ambiguous is the whole point and the very impetus behind collecting essays on the topic.

Germany's Modern?

Contested interpretations of German modernity are nothing unique to GDR historiography. This volume situates GDR history within this long-standing debate. Disagreement over the idea of a German "special path" or *Sonderweg* raised the question of Germany's development in a way that has significantly transformed the field since the 1960s. Historians like Hans-Ulrich Wehler and Jürgen Kocka, building on Anglo-American social science scholarship from the 1950s and 1960s, reasserted the concept of the Sonderweg by interpreting the political history of the Kaiserreich as an illiberal defense of an aristocratic, antimodern elite out of step with the country's rapid industrial modernization. In their estimation, this development anticipated the Nazi dictatorship a generation later.[82] Critics David Blackbourn and Geoff Eley challenged the idea that Wilhelmine political culture connoted the persistence of "backward" antimodern attitudes; in their eyes, Imperial Germany was a distinctly bourgeois—and thus modern—political culture. In so doing, they took issue with the longstanding Sonderweg thesis of a direct path from Bismarck to Hitler built on the apparent "democratic deficit" of German exceptionalism.[83] If nothing else, this discussion pointed out the problems with measuring modernity according to the yardstick of an idealized model of British, American, or French liberalism and as such questioned the very concepts of "backward" and "modern" themselves. Much of this same logic has informed conflicting assessments of the Weimar Republic as well. Scholars have long tended to judge Germany's first experiment in parliamentary democracy in terms of a failed socialist revolution, inadequate democratic structures, unintegrated militant elites, and dangerous illiberal holdovers from the prewar era. To be sure, there has also been a formidable literature on the Weimar Republic as a "laboratory of modernity," especially in terms of its fascination with Fordism, rationalization, modern sex and gender politics, progressive welfare policies, and unparalleled avant-garde cultural achievement.[84] Even so, the centrality of Weimar's failure to uphold democracy—and with it Germany's peculiar weakness of liberal modernity—has long shaped general accounts of the period.[85]

Overshadowing these various debates about German modernity is the case of Nazi Germany and the Final Solution. There has been a protracted debate among historians and social scientists for decades about whether and to what extent Nazi Germany—to say nothing of the Final Solution itself—can be counted as modern.[86] Some historians and social scientists have construed ideologies of antimodernism and preindustrial traditions as the root of Nazi success.[87] Others viewed the Third Reich and the Shoah as essentially a deviant or backward step from modern German political development. On another side of the debate, historians have interpreted the horrors of Hitler and the Holocaust as in fact the very epitome of modernity itself. In the mid-1960s David Schoenbaum and Ralf Dahrendorf, for example, suggested that the Third Reich's modernizing thrust helped create the conditions—often despite its own intentions and propaganda—for the more individual-oriented consumer society of 1950s West Germany.[88] A generation later Zygmunt Bauman suggested Nazism was not an aberrant exception to a modern rational world but rather "the rational world of modern civilization that made the Holocaust thinkable."[89] Detlev Peukert elaborated on how the Nazi techniques of rule and the Final Solution encompassed modernity as a technologized, highly bureaucratic form of genocide, underpinned by scientific theories of shaping the people's community through eugenics.[90] As a result, such historians in the 1980s treated the Third Reich as less the midwife of 1950s "liberalism" than as an alternative form of modernity itself.[91] While it would be misleading to claim that the concept of Nazi modernity enjoys full consensus,[92] the thesis has clearly gained more and more acceptance among scholars on both sides of the Atlantic.[93] This dark side of modernity encompassed by this aggressive dictatorial society has come to frame the debates about German modernity in all its contexts, particularly in the case of the so-called second dictatorship, the GDR. In linking these regimes, debates over whether Nazism constituted modernity have by extension led to questions of whether to define the GDR as modern. In this sense, the repressive political culture of the GDR, like the Third Reich, has led to a historiographical pairing of these dictatorial regimes as heirs to what some in the Sonderweg debate have seen as Germany's central "failure to create a 'modern society.' "[94]

Both post-1945 German states sought to build their rival republics as stable democracies and thriving economies that they defined in most ways in very different terms except for the conviction that they were both unquestionably modern. Yet the repressiveness and collapse of the GDR have prompted historians to revisit this question of German exceptionalism and antimodernity. The complexity in analyzing GDR modernity can be seen in the way that the influential historian Jürgen Kocka has defined the East German state as a "modern dictatorship." Under this definition Kocka identifies a variety of ways that this socialist state was modern, particularly from a top-down perspective, including its bureaucratic administration; mass mobilization; a single mass party with claims to absolute control; land reform, industrialization, and increased mobility; an all-encompassing ideology; as well as ruptures with tradition in terms of family and gender relations. He notes how scholars have often seen the GDR more self-evidently as a dictatorship than as a modern state. Even though his terminology asserts GDR modernity, however, he still qualifies and questions this modernity by identifying the GDR's ultimate fate as "a state that lagged behind the FRG and the superior West in terms of modernity" and by pointing to "modernization deficits vis-à-vis the Federal Republic."[95] What became clear, he admitted, was that judgments about the regime's modernity closely depended on the perspective of the observer and on the points of comparison. As Corey Ross neatly put it:

> Compared to the Third Reich or other Soviet satellite states, the GDR's oft-cited level of gender equality, high degree of industrialization, emphasis on technology and science and high degree of secularization seem relatively modern. But when considered alongside the Federal Republic and other "western" societies, the GDR appears relatively unmodern, even antimodern, in view of the weak tertiary sector of employment, the low degree of mass consumption and technical innovation, and most importantly the "primacy of politics" over all basic economic, political and social institutions.[96]

Such a comparative approach has thus created nettlesome problems in evaluating the GDR on its own terms. As Kocka himself conceded: "A comparison of historical modernity seldom leads to simple results, but rather more often to conclusions that are qualified with such statements as 'on the one hand . . . but on the other hand.'"[97]

By coupling the Nazi and SED states as twentieth-century Germany's two dictatorships, both appear as heirs to what proponents of the Sonderweg thesis have seen as Germany's older historical inability to develop a progressive and stable modern society. This historiographical turn is part of a larger post–cold war renaissance in totalitarianism theory, as twentieth-century history in general—and Eastern European history in particular—has been commonly reinterpreted from the normative vantage point of exposing the defects and shortcomings of liberalism's enemies.[98] The result is that the old "special path" thesis has sometimes enjoyed a strange new lease on life. In some accounts, the SED and Stasi play a role parallel to that of the landowning aristocratic Junker elites in earlier assessments of the Wilhelmine period; both serve as agents desperately trying to hold back the tide of modernization.[99] East German sociologist Wolfgang Engler summed up this position when he argued that the SED wanted "modern life without modern citizens."[100] In this way, the reinvigorated Sonderweg thesis within GDR historiography no longer idealizes foreign liberal states as the measure of misdevelopments but rather those very German regimes against which the GDR always defined itself: the Third Reich and the FRG. So whereas the "special path" thesis may have diminished if not been largely discredited as a model for studying Wilhelmine, Weimar, or even Nazi Germany, it has been surprisingly alive and well in some GDR studies, so much so that German historians of late make no bones about rehabilitating the Sonderweg term to describe GDR history as a "special kind of modern dictatorship" plagued by a monstrous "democratic deficit" and antiliberal culture in some respects helps to rehabilitate the idea of a German Sonderweg.[101] Ironically, the old political logic used to explain the historical peculiarities of Germany's political development even as a divided nation has remained very much intact.

The other major point of comparison for the GDR has been the FRG. The role of West Germany looms large in the course of GDR history, and it would be naive to ignore the comparison or interconnection between the two German cold war states. Many GDR citizens did indeed look to the "Golden West" as a mecca of fashion, prosperity, and progress, not to mention civil liberties. For this reason, the SED was in a clear antagonistic relationship with its neighbor, blaming Western "saboteurs" and those who fled to the West for many of the GDR's problems, even though the GDR economy was simultaneously dependent on imports from the FRG. The SED also competed explicitly with its Western counterpart, most bombastically in Party chair Walter Ulbricht's 1958 overblown claim that the GDR's "primary economic task" would be to surpass the West in per capita consumption by 1961. GDR engineers and planners gauged their own successes by measuring and comparing specific economic, social, or political achievements, such as levels of productivity, rate of technological innovation, or percentage of women integrated into the workforce. Historical assessments of GDR modernity have often evaluated the state in similar terms. Therefore, measuring GDR modernity against the experience of the FRG in some ways actually reflects the SED's own obsession with West German developments. As Jeffrey Kopstein has suggested, "In setting up capitalist modernity as the yardstick against which it measured itself, rather than defining a 'yardstick' of its own, communism was doomed to live in capitalism's shadow."[102] Certainly the GDR fell behind the FRG in numerous aspects of economic development, and these deficits contributed greatly to the worst aspects of the regime—such as material shortages and police repression—as well as to its ultimate demise. However, understanding the GDR as a *modern* state does not mean that its assessment should be limited by these terms of analysis based on measuring specific achievements of *modernization*. Rather, it might be more fruitful if one worked to understand the role of this competition and race for progress and prosperity itself as a major constituent of what made German socialism modern.

But there is more at stake in this comparative model of GDR history. One of the dangers in this conceptualization of the GDR as the "second German dictatorship" is the facile perpetuation of cold war paeans to Western superiority. As Hanna Schissler stated in her introduction to a volume on West German cultural history,

> Reexamining the German past under the auspices of two dictatorial trajectories, Nazism and Communism, automatically validates West Germany and makes western Germans into judges and eastern Germans into the object of what westerners have embraced since the 1960s: a better 'coming to terms with the past,' as the stereotypical formula goes. The absorption of East Germany validates the modernist superiority of the West German model (meaning its Westernization, Americanization, democratization) and inflates the model out of proportion. It nourishes illusions about the possibility of renewed West German master narratives, be they West Germany as a

success story or the model of Westernization as the necessary (if not inevitable) consequence of the Nazi past and now, in fact, of two German pasts.[103]

In this case, Schissler is pleading for a closer examination of West German society, on the grounds that "[t]he hegemonic structures of this (West German) reexamination of the two dictatorial German pasts in the service of the assimilation of the ex-GDR clearly stand in the way of a thorough reexamination of West Germany as history."[104] Her call to study West Germany also elicits a more nuanced examination of East Germany so as to arrive at a better understanding of the interrelated history of cold war Germany that does not fall prey to shopworn occidental triumphalism.[105]

This volume hopes to prompt reconsideration of East German socialism as modern. Comparative approaches will still be crucial to this endeavor, but the types and purposes of comparison can take new forms. Future research might fruitfully bring in more varied points of comparison, such as the United States and other Western states, the Soviet Union, the other Socialist bloc states, China, and other countries around the world, such as decolonizing nations. This greater variety of comparisons might yield alternative understandings of how modernity was manifested in the GDR, especially since East Germany's economy was a beacon of modernity within the socialist world in the 1960s. Instead of using comparisons with other German regimes like the Third Reich or the FRG as the sole measure of East German levels of progress or backwardness, different types of questions might be raised about ways that each regime engaged in the ubiquitous project of transforming society to forge modernity with both positive/liberating and negative/repressive effects. Such investigations might help broaden current assessments of the role of socialism in the development of global forms of modernity more generally. In an approach that mirrors Alf Lüdtke's analysis of GDR reconfigurations of "quality work," Engler has offered an ironic counterargument to more deterministic views of socialist modernity's failure, contending that the GDR's pre-Fordist work culture forced improvisation and that its perennially "decentered" economic life has prepared ex-GDR citizens to adjust rapidly to post-Fordism and a globalized production culture. In his view, East Germans—unlike their West German counterparts, who were still wedded to Fordism and the West German way of doing things in the 1970s and 1980s—were thus natural postmodernists, as the "rearguard suddenly became the avant-garde."[106] Such perspectives are of course a minority position; but Lüdtke and Engler at least call attention to the possibility of other approaches besides more normative ideas of progress and development.

The essays in this volume have been collected as case studies for rethinking what was modern about the GDR. These cases purposefully focus on aspects of society and culture that evolved in relationship to the state rather than on macroeconomic structures or internal state politics, in hopes that these fields of inquiry might invigorate discussions of socialist modernity. This group of essays does not claim to provide coverage of all aspects of GDR life but offers compelling profiles of some key aspects of socialist culture, some of which have only recently been taken up as topics of historical inquiry, such as sexuality, psychology, race relations, interior design, and tourism. The collection cannot hope to give a single thesis defining such a complex question as socialist modernity. Instead, the diverse approaches to the subject presented here offer material for an ongoing discussion of socialism's modernity, sometimes thinking through such previously proposed categories as "modern dictatorship" or "welfare dictatorship." These terms for discussing modernity are employed, however, not as a route to targeting deficits or successes of that modernity but as a reappraisal of the often messy and contradictory process of remaking one particular postfascist socialist society.

Organization

To present the diversity of approaches and topics concerning the question of socialist modernity, we have arranged our volume around three themes: selves, belonging, and desires. We deliberately avoided assigning conventional thematic headings based on sociological categories like women, the church, workers, and intellectuals but rather have elected to group the essays within more provocative headings so as to encourage broader vistas of inquiry. Each rubric speaks to the interface between state and society within socialism's alternative modernity over the decades.

The contributions to the volume look at changes in the modern project of constructing socialism throughout the entire history of the GDR, starting with its foundation in 1949. Some of the essays focus more on specific decades, while others span the life of the regime. As a whole, the essays show some of the shifting aspects of modern life under the administrations of both SED Party chairs, Walter Ulbricht (1949–71) and Erich

Honecker (1971–89). Several of the essays focus on the 1950s before the building of the Berlin Wall in 1961. This period is often viewed as a transitional era when the regime invested optimism and funds in economic planning and productivism to overcome the shortages of the immediate postwar period. Ulbricht aimed to implement this transition most aggressively through campaigns to build socialist industry and collectivized agriculture in 1952 and again in 1958. Essays that focus on this period demonstrate some of the tensions within society that emerged as a result of this radical effort at societal transformation; these conflicts erupted in the uprising of June 1953 and also played a major role in the building of the Berlin Wall.

After the borders had been sealed, the contours of the project to create socialist modernity shifted in the 1960s with the implementation of the New Economic System, which allowed for greater economic flexibility and ushered in a relative period of prosperity and cultural vibrancy. However, in this decade and the 1970s, the project of building modern socialism would continue to be a struggle as SED goals were thwarted by groups like noncompliant youth who had their own visions of modern selfhood. The volume's essays focus less explicitly on the 1980s, a decade in which the problems of the regime became insurmountable and many lost faith in things promised by the regime. Still, until the regime's fall in 1989, the programs for crafting modernity, evolving throughout the life of the GDR, continued to animate the regime and provided a context for the daily experience of its populace. The Trabant car became an icon of the contradictory nature of this development; when it appeared on the market in 1958 it embodied the pinnacle of modern technology, design, and equal access to prosperity. But when GDR industry still produced the same model in the 1980s, it encapsulated both the fierce adherence to socialist modernity at its most optimistic at the dawn of the 1960s and ultimately its greatest problems increasingly evident two decades later: pollution, an overbureaucratized economy, dogmatic inflexibility, and political naïveté.[107] For this reason, the Trabant has remained both a hated and beloved symbol prominent in the post-Wende memories of the GDR's complex modern landscape. The volume's essays explore these contradictory aspects of modern culture throughout the GDR's forty years of existence, culminating in an exploration of the popular memory of the regime through memorializations and exhibitions.

While these essays all examine socialist modernity through the relationship between state and society in some way, they do so using very different types of sources and from different angles. Some investigate official discourses employed by authorities within the regime—such as sex thera-pists, psychologists, or designers—to scrutinize or mold society. Others look at the relationship between state policies and institutions like schools or the police and average citizens who were their targets, such as students or criminals. In other essays, sources like letters to state authorities, sur-veys of public opinion, or oral interviews yield voices "from below" of people such as housewives or foreign exchange students, who articulated their relationship to the state in these texts. As a whole, these varied approaches add pieces to the puzzle of how historians can analyze individ-ual subjectivity of GDR citizens marking out spaces for agency and auton-omy within a largely paternalistic, coercive, and didactic regime.

The first section, "Selves," addresses the dynamic relationship between self and society, part of which concerns the ambiguous interplay of public and private. The historical interface of public and private has been another ongoing subject of debate in the modern context, but one that is especially complicated in the case of socialism, since the regime worked in many ways to dissolve the distinction in order to integrate pri-vate citizens fully into the community. The GDR state intruded aggres-sively into private life through modern institutions of scientific investiga-tion, surveillance, propaganda, and mass organization. This section of the volume is interested in the question of how this interplay between private selves and public institutions and policy took place in this context and what meaning private lives had for the regime and the population. These essays explore various meanings of private selves ranging from psychology to sexuality, domesticity to travel. Greg Eghigian opens the section with a study of perhaps the most intimate aspect of the self: the individual psy-che. He examines how the discipline of psychology and public policy inves-tigated and defined the socialist personality. In particular he uses psycho-logical definitions of deviance to demonstrate how socialist selves intersected with political ideology. Next, Dagmar Herzog analyzes the way that various people in the GDR hoped to form a sexual culture as an alternative to that practiced in Western capitalist societies. In it she looks at the state's attempt to formulate a specific socialist morality and the ways that individuals "carved out their own freedoms" through private interpersonal relations. From there Paul Betts focuses on domestic interi-ors, showing how the state's growing preoccupation with the domestic sphere was part of a larger campaign to strengthen socialist culture at home. Alon Confino closes the section by considering tourism and travel ironically via the most prominent symbol of the GDR as a repressive regime: the secret police. In his essay, Confino uses the archival file of one woman who used her status as an informant for the Stasi as a way to travel to foreign countries and eventually to West Germany, where her desire for travel meshed with her romantic desire for a West German lover. She was clearly complicit in the GDR's repressive system of surveillance, and yet this system also afforded her a measure of freedom that she in turn used to flee from the GDR for fulfilment of her private wishes. As such, his study offers a window into the everyday tensions between individual desire and social control. The focus on a single life course also reveals how individuals cannot easily be categorized as victims or perpetrators.

The second section, "Belonging," takes up the state's effort to target particular groups for disciplining and socialization, as well as a means of building a strong normative "socialist community." The essays in this section examine the shifting ways that the regime or society defined individuals and groups as insiders or outsiders. For example, SED leaders put faith in the generation of youth born in 1949 and schooled in the virtues of socialism as the basis for building socialism. In the first essay, Dorothee Wierling explores the tensions between state educators and rebellious youth who failed to conform to this utopian vision. As she demonstrates, postwar children of relative prosperity strayed from the ideals held by their war-scarred parents and thus became a constant source of concern and suspicion. The question of belonging was even more complicated in the case of racial difference.[108] Young-Sun Hong's essay examines a particular group of foreigners living in the GDR, the trainees from newly independent African countries who hoped to learn medicine in East Germany. Given socialism's claim to eliminating racism, part of the enterprise of the GDR was a supposed egalitarian integration of all races. Hong shows how the GDR hoped to establish itself as an anti-imperialist partner in solidarity with decolonizing third world countries, using its advanced system of medicine and "hygienic modernity" as part of its mission of solidarity with African countries. However, the real experience of students in East Germany revealed the continuation of German racial prejudice manifested in segregation of nonwhite students and their relegation to menial positions. Hong raises questions of belonging by examining the limits to the GDR's ability to integrate minorities domestically and the problems the GDR faced in working to establish foreign relations within the concert of nations globally. In contrast to the cases of youth or minorities, Thomas Lindenberger looks at those elements in GDR society who were by definition meant to be excluded from the ideal socialist community.

What is interesting in his account is precisely how these threatening elements were defined; social scientists, criminologists, and the GDR state itself used the category "asocial" as a key marker of outsiders within the GDR. As the state worked to mold ideal socialist citizens, asocial East Germans were seen as their mirror image. Although the asocial element in the GDR might have been formally limited to those who shirked work or didn't cooperate with state-sponsored activities, these underclass asocials were seen as the fertile ground for potential criminality that could endanger the GDR's delicate social fabric. Lastly, Alf Lüdtke examines the consummate GDR insider seen as the builder of socialism: the male laborer. In a classic essay that originally appeared in the popular German press, he offers a suggestive treatment of how popular images elevated the male worker to the status of a hero committed to traditional values of German "quality work." His nuanced approach addresses not only popular culture's depictions of GDR masculinity but also individual workers' varied articulations of Eigensinn, which served as both an extension of and resistance to the state's modernization crusade. This profile of the laborer demonstrates how the regime's attention to this iconic figure inherently celebrated a normative path toward belonging in socialist society.

As East Germans worked to establish an identity distinct from the West, their utopian vision was bound up with the mobilization of contradictory desires. Both the proximity and distance from the West heightened the role of desire in the crafting of socialist selves, as the West increasingly became a taboo object of longing. The third section, "Desires," addresses the complex nexus of fantasy and desire that animated GDR citizens in their everyday lives. Since material goods often gave shape to these longings and imaginaries, the essays in this section revolve around issues of consumption and material culture. They suggest how problems of shortage in the GDR did not limit consumers to a fixation on base needs; rather, citizens articulated desires for fashionability, comfort, and progress toward a happier future through this iconic world of commodities, not least during periods of shortage. The first author in this section, Judd Stitziel, focuses on East Germans' desire for a highly fetishized commodity that was also a basic necessity: clothing. Stitziel explores how the yearning for attractive clothing was often at variance with the constraints of the planned economy and the limited fashion industry in the GDR. His analysis affords insight into the variety of compensatory practices, such as sewing, undertaken to fulfill unmet desire for goods not available on the market. Katherine Pence's essay, too, examines the desire for a better material standard of living as an increasingly central focus of the regime's promises of modernity. She explores the links between modern planning for prosperity and progressive visions of emancipation for women, who were most concerned with consumer problems in everyday life. The conjunction of private needs or desires and state politics emerges in her analysis of demands made on the state by GDR housewives, and Party functionary Elli Schmidt as their representative, on the eve of the June 17, 1953, uprising. The context of this major crisis accentuated the evolving dynamic among consumers' efforts to provide for their families, the ways they situated themselves in the socialist community, and claims they made on the state to deliver promises of prosperity. Ina Merkel follows with an examination of the GDR's efforts to mold consumer desires through specifically socialist advertising and to monitor them with market research. She reflects on the recent trend of *Ostalgie* to show how conceptions of prosperity and shortage continue to inform GDR identity. Instead of concentrating on nostalgia for socialist kitsch, her essay discusses the "inner logic of socialist society" through the lens of advertising and market research, two cultural fields that both shaped and scrutinized GDR consumer citizens. Her anthropological analysis of socialist consumer culture discards the misnomer "shortage society" to describe the GDR and instead reconsiders the planned economy's mixed record in creating a viable alternative of modernity. The anthropologist Daphne Berdahl picks up the theme from a postreunification perspective, recounting as she does the dramatic ways that the GDR has figured in popular memory since 1989. She specifically looks at the debate over the legacy of the GDR as manifested in two exhibitions on GDR material culture. Her analysis reveals among other things how these exhibitions recast citizens of the former East German states as outsiders within reunified Germany. Her essay is a fitting end to the volume, since these museums raise the question of how the culture of "Ossis" can and should be integrated into the broader history and national identity of the New Germany.

All told, the wide-ranging thematic scope of the volume is designed to raise new questions and to test hypotheses about the everyday practices of socialist modernity in the GDR. In so doing, the volume will hopefully stimulate continued interdisciplinary research on East Germany. What unites all the essays is the question of how the very tensions around socialist modernity shaped the views, memories, and actions of East Germans over four decades. As such, the goal of the volume is not only to move beyond a crude totalitarian model but also to reconsider the whole history of the GDR from a more imaginative interpretative framework. Examining the German experiment in socialism as an "alternative modernity" will perhaps help retrieve "real existing socialism" from the "dustbin of history."[109] Through such an approach, we hope that this volume not only will afford a fruitful addition to the analysis of East Germany and socialist states but perhaps may contribute in some way to the larger, ongoing debate on the nature of modernity in Germany and the twentieth century more generally.

NOTES

We would like to thank those who read and gave useful comments on drafts of this chapter, including Bonnie Anderson, Dolores Augustine, Marion Berghahn, Rebecca Boehling, Renate Bridenthal, Jana Bruns, Jane Caplan, Belinda Davis, Atina Grossmann, Amy Hackett, Maria Hoehn, Young-Sun Hong, Marion Kaplan, Jan Lambertz, Molly Nolan, Molly O'Donnell, Nancy Reagin, Julia Sneeringer, and Corey Ross. Thanks also to the anonymous readers who offered useful suggestions for revisions to the volume.

1. Andrei S. Markowits and Simon Reich, *The German Predicament: Memory and Power in the New Europe* (Ithaca, 1997); Geoff Eley, "The Unease of History: Settling Accounts with the East German Past," *History Workshop Journal* 57 (2004): 175–201.

2. Konrad H. Jarausch and Michael Geyer, *Shattered Past: Reconstructing German Histories* (Princeton, 2003), esp. part I.

3. Geoff Eley, ed., *The "Goldhagen Effect": History, Memory, Nazism—Facing the German Past* (Ann Arbor, 2000); Hamburg Institute for Social Research, ed., *The German Army and Genocide: Crimes against War Prisoners, Jews, and other Civilians, 1939–1944* (New York, 1999); Brian Ladd, *The Ghosts of Berlin: Confronting German History in the Urban Landscape* (Chicago, 1997); and Jan-Werner Müller, *Another Country: German Intellectuals, Unification and National Identity* (New Haven, 2000).

4. Charles Maier, *The Unmasterable Past: History, Holocaust, and German National Identity* (Cambridge, MA, 1988). For an insightful account of the Wende itself, see Charles Maier, *Dissolution: The Crisis of Communism and the End of East Germany* (Princeton, 1997).

5. Timothy Garton Ash, *The File: A Personal History* (New York, 1997).

6. Konrad Jarausch, "Beyond Uniformity: The Challenge to Historicizing the GDR," in *Dictatorship as Experience: Towards a Socio-Cultural History of the GDR,* ed. Konrad Jarausch (New York, 1999), 5.

7. Ina Merkel, "From a Socialist Society of Labor into a Consumer Society? The Transformation of East German Identities and Systems," in *Envisioning Eastern Europe: Postcommunist Cultural Studies,* ed. Michael D. Kennedy (Ann Arbor, 1994), 60ff. See also Daphne Berdahl, "(N)ostalgie for the Present: Memory, Longing and East German Things," *Ethnos* 64, no. 2 (1999): 192–211; and Paul Betts,

"Twilight of the Idols: East German Memory and Material Culture," *Journal of Modern History* 72 (September 2000): 731–65.

8. Corey Ross, *The East German Dictatorship: Problems and Perspectives in the Interpretation of the GDR* (London, 2002), 3.

9. Jonathan Grix and Paul Cooke, eds., *East German Distinctiveness in a Unified Germany* (Birmingham, 2002); and Patrick Stevenson, *Language and German Disunity: A Sociolinguistic History of East and West Germany, 1945–2000* (Oxford, 2002).

10. Quoted in Peter Bender, *Unsere Erbschaft: Was war die DDR—was bleibt von ihr?* (Hamburg, 1992), 155.

11. *Materialien der Enquete Kommission "Aufarbeitung von Geschichte und Folgen der SED-Diktatur in Deutschland im Deutschen Bundestag,"* 18 vols. (Baden-Baden, 1995); and *Materialien der Enquete-Kommission "Überwindung der Folgen der SED-Diktatur im Prozess der deutschen Einheit,"* 13 vols. (Baden-Baden, 1999).

12. The excerpts are taken from A. James McAdams, *Judging the Past in Unified Germany* (Bloomington, 2001), 113.

13. Peter Barker, ed., *The GDR and Its History: Rückblick und Revision: Die DDR im Spiegel der Enquete-Kommissionen* (Amsterdam and Atlanta, 2000).

14. Mary Fulbrook, "Reckoning with the Past: Heroes, Victims and Villains in the History of the German Democratic Republic," in *Rewriting the German Past: History and Identity in the New Germany,* ed. Reinhard Alter and Peter Monteath (Atlantic Highlands, 1997), 175–96.

15. This view is the main thesis of Sigrid Meuschel, *Legitimation und Parteiherrschaft: Zum Paradox von Stabilität und Revolution in der DDR* (Frankfurt, 1992).

16. Ibid.

17. Günter Gaus, *Wo Deutschland Liegt: Eine Ortsbestimmung* (Hamburg, 1983).

18. David Childs, *The GDR: Moscow's German Ally* (London, 1983).

19. Jarausch, "Beyond Uniformity," 3–14.

20. For a discussion of recent literature, see Ross, *East German Dictatorship.* Some earlier works have also provided more nuanced approaches to society and the economy, such as Rainer Karlsch, *Allein bezahlt? Reparationsleistungen in der SBZ/DDR, 1945–1953* (Berlin, 1993); and Wolfgang Zank, *Wirtschaft und Arbeit in Ostdeutschland, 1945–1949: Probleme des Wiederaufbaus in der sowjetischen Besatzungszone Deutschlands* (Munich, 1987).

21. See the introduction in Hartmut Kaelble, Jürgen Kocka, and Hartmut Zwahr, eds., *Sozialgeschichte der DDR* (Stuttgart, 1994), 9–14.

22. Richard Bessel and Ralph Jessen, eds., *Die Grenzen der Diktatur: Staat und Gesellschaft in der DDR* (Göttingen, 1996).

23. Some of the work from this center's groups of scholars includes Patrice G. Poutrus, *Die Erfindung des Goldbroilers: Über den Zusammenhang zwischen Herrschaftssicherung und Konsumentwicklung in der DDR* (Cologne, 2002); and André Steiner, *Die DDR-Wirtschaftsreform der sechziger Jahre. Konflikt zwischen Effizienz und Machtkalkül* (Berlin, 1999).

24. Alf Lüdtke, ed., *The History of Everyday Life: Reconstructing Historical Experiences and Ways of Life* (Princeton, 1995).

25. Thomas Lindenberger, ed., *Herrschaft und Eigen-Sinn in der Diktatur: Studien zur Gesellschaftsgeschichte der DDR* (Cologne, 1999).

26. Peter Hübner and Klaus Tenfelde, eds., *Arbeiter in der SBZ-DDR* (Essen, 1999).

27. Jarausch, "Beyond Uniformity," 3–16.

28. Patrick Major and Jonathan Osmond, eds., *The Workers' and Peasants' State: Communism and Society in East Germany under Ulbricht, 1945–1971* (Manchester, 2002).

29. David Crew, ed., *Consuming Germany in the Cold War* (Oxford, 2003).

30. Daphne Berdahl, *Where the World Ended: Re-Unification and Identity in the German Borderland* (Berkeley, 1999), as well as John Borneman, *After the Wall: East Meets West in the New Berlin* (New York, 1991), 5. See also his *Belonging in the Two Berlins: Kin, State, Nation* (Cambridge, 1992).

31. Ralph Jessen, "Die Gesellschaft im Sozialismus: Probleme einer Sozialgeschichte der DDR," *Geschichte und Gesellschaft* 21 (1995): 96–110.

32. Thomas Lindenberger, "Everyday History: New Approaches to the History of the Post-War Germanies," in *The Divided Past: Rewriting Post-War German History*, ed. Christoph Klessmann (Oxford, 2001), 44–89.

33. Hans Magnus Enzensberger, *Political Crumbs*, trans. Martin Chalmers (London, 1990 [1982]), 35–52.

34. Marc Fischer, *After the Fall: Germany, the Germans and the Burdens of History* (New York, 1995), 144.

35. Martin Ahrends, "The Great Waiting, or the Freedom of the East: An Obituary for Life in Sleeping Beauty's Castle," in *When the Wall Came Down: Reactions to German Reunification*, ed. Harold James and Marla Stone (New York, 1992), esp. 158–60.

36. Deutsches Historisches Museum, ed., *Einigkeit und Recht und Freiheit: Wege der Deutschen, 1949–1999* (Reinbek bei Hamburg, 1999).

37. Ilja Srubar, "War der reale Sozialismus modern? Versuch einer strukturellen Bestimmung," *Kölner Zeitschrift für Soziologie und Soziopsychologie* 43 (1991): 415–32, and, more generally, Zbiegniew Brzezinski, *The Grand Failure: The Birth and Death of Communism in the 20th Century* (New York, 1989).

38. Hope Harrison, *Driving the Soviets Up the Wall: Soviet East-German Relations, 1953–1961* (Princeton, 2003); William Glen Gray, *Germany's Cold War: The Global Campaign to Isolate East Germany, 1949–1969* (Chapel Hill, 2003).

39. Peter C. Caldwell, *Dictatorship, State Planning, and Social Theory in the German Democratic Republic* (New York, 2003).

40. Arnd Bauerkämper, ed., *"Junkerland in Bauernhand"? Durchführung, Auswirkungen und Stellenwert der Bodenreform in der Sowjetischen Besatzungszone* (Stuttgart, 1996); and Arnd Bauerkämper, *Ländliche Gesellschaft in der kommunistischen Diktatur: Zwangsmodernisierung und Tradition in Brandenburg, 1945–1963* (Cologne, 2002).

41. Raymond G. Stokes, *Constructing Socialism: Technology and Change in East Germany, 1945–1990* (Baltimore, 2000); Karin Zachmann, *Mobilisierung der Frauen. Technik, Geschlecht und Kalter Krieg in der DDR* (Frankfurt, 2004).

42. Corey Ross, *Constructing Socialism at the Grass-Roots: The Transformation of East Germany, 1945–65* (London, 2000).

43. Many new books have appeared recently on these crises, especially the June 1953 uprising. For example, see Torsten Diedrich, *Waffen gegen das Volk. Der Aufstand vom 17. Juni 1953* (Munich, 2003); and Michael Lemke, *Die Berlin Krise 1958 bis 1963: Interessen und Handlungsspielräume der SED im Ost-West-Konflikt* (Berlin, 1995).

44. Peter Fritzsche, "Nazi Modern," *Modernism/Modernity* 3, no. 1 (January 1996): 12.

45. Peter Becker and Alf Lüdtke, eds., *Akten, Eingaben, Schaufenster. Die DDR und ihre Texte. Erkundungen zu Herrschaft und Alltag* (Berlin, 1997).

46. A number of important studies have begun this type of analysis: Dorothee Wierling, *Geboren im Jahr Eins: Der Jahrgang 1949 in der DDR. Versuch einer Kollektivbiographie* (Berlin, 2002); Lutz Niethammer, Alexander von Plato, and Dorothee Wierling, eds., *Die volkseigene Erfahrung: Eine Archäologie des Lebens in der Industrieprovinz der DDR* (Berlin, 1991); and Stefan Wolle, *Die heile Welt der Diktatur: Alltag und Herrschaft in der DDR 1971–1989* (Berlin, 1998).

47. Lüdtke, *The History of Everyday Life;* Jan Palmowski, "Between Conformity and Eigen-Sinn: New Approaches to GDR History," *German History* 20 (2002): 494–502.

48. Benedict Anderson, *Imagined Communities: Reflections on the Origin and Spread of Nationalism* (London, 1983).

49. Ina Merkel, "Consumer Culture in the GDR, or How the Struggle for Antimodernity Was Lost on the Battleground of Consumer Culture," in *Getting and Spending: European and American Consumer Societies in the 20th Century,* ed. Susan Strasser, Charles McGovern, and Matthias Judt (New York, 1998), 281–300; and Katherine Pence, "'You as a Woman Will Understand': Consumption, Gender and the Relationship between State and Citizenry in the GDR's Crisis of 17 June 1953," *German History* 19, no. 2 (2001): 218–52. Donna Harsch's work on the inner conflicts of the state and party from a gendered perspective is an important example of this approach. See her "Approach/Avoidance: Communists and Women in East Germany, 1945–9," *Social History* 25, no. 2 (May 2000): 156–82; and *Revenge of the Domestic: Women, the Family, and Communism in the German Democratic Republic* (Princeton, 2007).

50. Pierre Bourdieu, *Outline of a Theory of Practice* (Cambridge, 1977).

51. Jürgen Habermas, *The Structural Transformation of the Public Sphere: An Inquiry into a Category of Bourgeois Society* (Cambridge, MA, 1991).

52. Erica Carter, *How German Is She? Postwar West German Reconstruction and the Consuming Woman* (Ann Arbor, 1997), 5, 21; and, more generally, Michael Wildt, *Am Beginn der "Konsumgesellschaft": Mangelserfahrung, Lebenshaltung, Wohlstandshoffnung in Westdeutschland in den fünfziger Jahren* (Hamburg, 1994); Paul Betts, *The Authority of Everyday Objects: A Cultural History of West German Industrial Design* (Berkeley, 2004); Rainer Gries, *Produkte als Medien: Kulturgeschichte der Produktkommunikation in der Bundesrepublik und der DDR* (Leipzig, 2003); Annette Kaminsky, *Kaufrausch: Die Geschichte der ostdeutschen Versandhäuser* (Berlin, 1998); Neue Gesellschaft für Bildende Kunst, ed., *Wunderwirtschaft: DDR-Konsumkultur in den 60er Jahren* (Cologne, 1996); and Jonathan R. Zatlin,"Ausgaben und Eingaben: Das Petitionsrecht und der Untergang der DDR," *Zeitschrift für Geschichtswissenschaft* 10 (1997): 902–17; and Jonathan R.

Zatlin, *The Currency of Socialism: Money and Political Culture in East Germany* (New York, 2007).

53. David Crowley and Susan E. Reid, "Style and Socialism: Modernity and Material Culture in Post-War Eastern Europe," in *Style and Socialism: Modernity and Material Culture in Post-War Eastern Europe,* ed. Susan E. Reid and David Crowley (Oxford, 2000), 4.

54. The attempt to build socialism was a modern "dreamworld" in a Benjaminian sense: an "expression of a utopian desire for social arrangements that transcend existing forms." Susan Buck-Morss, *Dreamworld and Catastrophe: The Passing of Mass Utopia in East and West* (Cambridge, MA, 2000), xi.

55. Young-Sun Hong, *Welfare, Modernity and the Weimar State, 1919–1933* (Princeton, 1998); George Steinmetz, *Regulating the Social: The Welfare State and Local Politics in Imperial Germany* (Princeton, 1993).

56. Habermas, *The Structural Transformation of the Public Sphere.*

57. Michel Foucault, *Discipline and Punish: The Birth of the Prison* (New York, 1979).

58. Anson Rabinbach, *The Human Motor: Energy, Fatigue, and the Origins of Modernity* (New York, 1990); Sigmund Freud, *Civilization and Its Discontents,* trans. James Strachey (New York, 1989).

59. Zygmunt Bauman, *Modernity and the Holocaust* (Ithaca, 1989); Detlev J. K. Peukert, *Inside Nazi Germany: Conformity, Opposition, and Racism in Everyday Life* (New Haven, 1982), esp. 243ff.

60. Dipesh Chakrabarty, *Provincializing Europe: Postcolonial Thought and Historical Difference* (Princeton, 2000).

61. In Christopher Pendergast's discussion of Frederic Jameson, "Codeword Modernity," *New Left Review* 24 (November–December 2003), 95–111.

62. Marc Garcelon, "The Shadow of the Leviathan: Public and Private in Communist and Post-Communist Society," in *Public and Private in Thought and Practice: Perspectives on a Grand Dichotomy,* ed. Jeff Weintraub and Krishan Kumar (Chicago, 1997), 303–35.

63. Richard Stites, *Revolutionary Dreams: Utopian Vision and Experimental Life in the Russian Revolution* (Oxford, 1989); Ruth Ben-Ghiat, *Fascist Modernities, Italy 1922–1945* (Berkeley, 2001).

64. Odd Arne Westad, *The Global Cold War: Third World Interventions and the Making of Our Times* (Cambridge, 2005), 40; see also David L. Hoffmann, *Stalinist Values: The Cultural Norms of Soviet Modernity, 1917–1941* (Ithaca, 2003), 7–10.

65. Mark Mazower, *Dark Continent: Europe's Twentieth Century* (New York, 1998).

66. Shmuel N. Eisenstadt, "Multiple Modernities," *Daedalus* 129, no. 1 (winter 2000): 1–30.

67. Arjun Appadurai, *Modernity at Large: Cultural Dimensions of Globalization* (Minneapolis, 1996).

68. Dilip Parameshwar Gaonkar, *Alternative Modernities* (Durham, 2001).

69. Dipesh Chakrabarty, *Habitations of Modernity: Essays in the Wake of Subaltern Studies* (Chicago, 2002).

70. Arif Dirlik, "Modernity as History: Post-revolutionary China, Globaliza-

tion and the Question of Modernity," *Social History* 27, no. 1 (January 2002): 20. A classic statement is Eric R. Wolf, *Europe and the People without History* (London and Berkeley, 1982).

71. Chakrabarty, *Provincializing Europe,* 8

72. Appadurai, *Modernity at Large,* 2.

73. Dipesh Chakrabarty, "Provincializing Europe: Postcoloniality and the Critique of History," *Cultural Studies* 6, no. 3 (October 1992): 337–57.

74. A good effort to approach the GDR comparatively is David Childs, Thomas A. Baylis, and Martin Rueschemeyer, eds., *East Germany in Comparative Perspective* (London, 1989).

75. Vivian Schelling, "Introduction: Reflections on the Experience of Modernity in Latin America," in *Through the Kaleidoscope: The Experience of Modernity in Latin America,* ed. Vivian Schelling (London, 2000), 12; and Brigitte H. Schulz, "The Politics of East-South Relations: The GDR and Southern Africa," in Childs, Baylis, and Rueschemeyer, *East Germany in Comparative Perspective,* 209–31.

76. Merkel, "Consumer Culture in the GDR," 281. It should be noted that although translated in this article as "antimodernity" the term used by Merkel is *Gegenmoderne,* which actually refers to an alternative form of modernity opposed to the West.

77. Alf Lüdtke, "'Helden der Arbeit': Mühen beim Arbeiten: Zur missmutigen Loyalität von Industriearbeitern in der DDR," in *Sozialgeschichte der DDR,* ed. Kaelble, Kocka, and Zwahr, 188–213.

78. On youth policy and resistance see Alan McDougall, *Youth Politics in East Germany: The Free German Youth Movement, 1946–1968* (Oxford, 2004); and Uta G. Poiger, *Jazz, Rock, and Rebels: Cold War Politics and American Culture in a Divided Germany* (Berkeley, 2000). On continuity in gender roles see Ina Merkel, . . . *Und Du, Frau an der Werkbank: Die DDR in den 50er Jahren* (Berlin, 1990).

79. Detlef Pollack, "Modernization and Modernization Blockages," in *Dictatorship as Experience,* ed. Jarausch, 36. On the East German leadership's blindness toward ecological concerns see Arvid Nelson, *Cold War Ecology: Forests, Farms, and People in the East German Landscape, 1945–1989* (New Haven, 2005).

80. Peter Wensierski and Wolfgang Büscher, eds., *Beton ist Beton: Zivilisationskritik aus der DDR* (Hattingen, 1981); and Michael Schenkel, "Die Öffentlichkeit der künstlerischen Literatur: Fortschritt- und Modernitätskritik in der DDR-Literatur," in *Gesellschaftliche Differenzierung und Legitimätsverfall des DDR-Sozialismus: Das Ende des anderen Weges in der Moderne,* ed. Winfried Thaa (Tübingen, 1992), 303–89.

81. See Alf Lüdtke's essay for further discussion of the idea of "specific amalgams" reconfiguring older ideas or practices within the new context of the GDR.

82. Hans-Ulrich Wehler, *Deutsche Gesellschaftsgeschichte* (Munich, 1987); Thomas Nipperdey, "Probleme der Modernisierung in Deutschland," in *Nachdenken über die deutsche Geschichte,* ed. Thomas Nipperdey (Munich, 1986), 44–64.

83. David Blackbourn and Geoff Eley, *The Peculiarities of German History: Bourgeois Society and Politics in Nineteenth-Century Germany* (Oxford, 1984). For a more recent reappraisal of how Blackbourn and Eley's theories shaped and con-

tinue to influence understandings of German modernity, see Geoff Eley and James Retallack, eds., *Wilhelminism and Its Legacies: German Modernities, Imperialism, and the Meanings of Reform, 1890–1930* (Oxford, 2003).

84. Mary Nolan, *Visions of Modernity: American Business and the Modernization of Germany* (New York, 1994); Adelheid von Saldern, *The Challenge of Modernity: German Social and Cultural Studies, 1890–1960* (Ann Arbor, 2002); Atina Grossman, *Reforming Sex: The German Movement for Birth Control and Abortion Reform, 1920–1950* (New York, 1995); Kathleen Canning, "Claiming Citizenship: Suffrage and Subjectivity in Germany after the First World War," in *Gender History in Practice: Historical Perspectives on Bodies, Class, and Citizenship,* ed. Kathleen Canning (Ithaca, 2006), 212–38; Katharina von Ankum, ed., *Women in the Metropolis: Gender and Modernity in Weimar Culture* (Berkeley, 1997).

85. Peter Fritzsche, "Did Weimar Fail?" *Journal of Modern History* 68, no. 3 (September 1996): 629–56. See also Martin H. Geyer's *Verkehrte Welt. Revolution, Inflation und Moderne: München 1914–1924* (Munich, 1998).

86. The most balanced assessment of the key positions is still Ian Kershaw, *The Nazi Dictatorship: Problems and Perspectives of Interpretation* (London, 1985).

87. For an outline of the debate around this contentious issue, see Geoff Eley, "What Produces Fascism: Preindustrial Traditions or a Crisis of the Capitalist State?" in *Radical Perspectives on the Rise of Fascism in Germany, 1919–1945,* ed. Michael N. Dobkowski and Isidor Wallimann (New York, 1989), 69–99.

88. Ralf Dahrendorf, *Society and Democracy in Germany* (Garden City, 1967); and David Schoenbaum, *Hitler's Social Revolution: Class and Status in Nazi Germany, 1933–1939* (Garden City, 1966).

89. Bauman, *Modernity and the Holocaust,* 13.

90. Detlev J. K. Peukert, "The Genesis of the 'Final Solution' from the Spirit of Science," in *Nazism and German Society, 1933–1945,* ed. David F. Crew (London, 1994), 274–99.

91. Detlev J. K. Peukert, *Max Webers Diagnose der Moderne* (Göttingen, 1989). See also Ronald Smelser, *Robert Ley: Hitler's Labor Front Leader* (New York, 1988); and Peter Reichel, *Der schöne Schein des Dritten Reiches: Faszination und Gewalt des Faschismus* (Munich, 1991). Peukert's *Inside Nazi Germany* can be read this way as well, though his conclusion very much asserts the connection between 1940s and 1950s West Germany (see esp. 236–49). Needless to say, such an interpretation was—and still is—quite delicate, not least because it has been at times used to downplay the centrality of racism within Nazi Germany's radical project to build a new state and society. The controversy sparked by the 1991 publication of Rainer Zitelmann and Michael Prinz's edited volume, *Nationalsozialismus und Modernisierung* (Darmstadt, 1991), much of which resulted in the volume's overall tendency to discuss Nazi social policy divorced from racist politics, underscored the high stakes of the modernity debate.

92. Influential rebuttals of the modernization thesis include Jens Alber, "Nationalsozialismus und Modernisierung," *Kölner Zeitschrift für Soziologie und Sozialpsychologie* 41 (June 1989): 346–65; and Norbert Frei, "Wie modern war der Nationalsozialismus?" *Geschichte und Gesellschaft* 19 (1993): 367–87.

93. Paul Betts, "The New Fascination with Fascism: The Case of Nazi Modernism," *Journal of Contemporary History* 37, no. 4 (October 2002): 541–58.

94. Blackbourn and Eley, *Peculiarities*, 73.

95. Jürgen Kocka, "The GDR: A Special Kind of Modern Dictatorship," in *Dictatorship as Experience*, ed. Jarausch, 19–21. See too Bernd Faulenbach, "Überwindung des 'deutschen Sonderweges'? Zur politischen Kultur der Deutschen seit dem Zweiten Weltkrieg," *Aus Politik und Zeitgeschichte* B5 (1998): 11–23.

96. Ross, *East German Dictatorship*, 30.

97. Jürgen Kocka, ed., *Historische DDR-Forschung* (Berlin, 1992), 25f.

98. Wolfgang Wippermann, *Totalitarismustheorien: Die Entwicklung der Diskussion von den Anfängen bis Heute* (Darmstadt, 1997); Alfons Soellner, Ralf Walkenhaus, and Karin Wieland, eds., *Totalitarismus: Eine Ideengeschichte des 20. Jahrhunderts* (Berlin, 1997); and Abbott Gleason, *Totalitarianism: The Inner History of the Cold War* (New York, 1995). For a recent critique of totalitarianism theories and a call for studies that bridge state and society in the GDR see Mary Fulbrook, "Putting the People back In: The Contentious State of GDR History," *German History* 24, no. 4 (2006): 608–20.

99. Lutz Niethammer, "The German *Sonderweg* after Unification," in *Rewriting the German Past*, ed. Alter and Monteath, 129–51.

100. Wolfgang Engler, *Die Ostdeutschen: Kunde von einem verlorenen Land* (Berlin, 2000), 61.

101. Jürgen Kocka, "The GDR: A Special Kind of Modern Dictatorship," 23.

102. Jeffrey Kopstein, *The Politics of Economic Decline in East Germany, 1945–1989* (Chapel Hill, 1997), 196.

103. Hanna Schissler, "Introduction: Writing about 1950s West Germany," in *The Miracle Years: A Cultural History of West Germany, 1949–1968*, ed. Hanna Schissler (Princeton, 2001), 5.

104. Ibid.

105. The same point is made by Eric D. Weitz, *Creating German Communism, 1890–1990: From Popular Protests to Socialist State* (Princeton, 1997), 393.

106. Wolfgang Engler, *Die Ostdeutschen als Avant-Garde* (Berlin, 2002), 73–82. Alf Lüdtke's contribution to this volume, which is a revised and translated version of an article that appeared in 2000 in the *Frankfurter Allgemeine Zeitung*, was first to point to the advantages that workers gained through their experience of developing their own patterns of "quality work" that allowed them both to deal with production problems creatively during the GDR and to adapt to changing market conditions after 1989. Alf Lüdtke, "Bei der Ehre packen: Männer und 'ihre' Arbeit in Ost- und Westdeuschland," *Frankfurter Allgemeinen Zeitung*, May 20, 2000, 3.

107. Jonathan Zatlin, "The Vehicle of Desire: The Trabant, the Wartburg, and the End of the GDR," *German History* 15, no. 3 (1997): 358–80.

108. Jan C. Behrends, Thomas Lindenberger, and Patrice G. Poutrus, eds., *Fremde und Fremd-Sein in der DDR: Zu historischen Ursachen der Fremdenfeindlichkeit in Ostdeutschland* (Berlin, 2003); Peter Monteath, "The German Democratic Republic and the Jews," *German History* 22, no. 3 (2004): 448–68.

109. Charity Scribner, *Requiem for Communism* (Cambridge, MA, 2003).

Selves

Homo Munitus

The East German Observed

Greg Eghigian

In 1990, the East German psychoanalyst Hans-Joachim Maaz published *Der Gefühlsstau* (Congested Feeling), a psychological portrait of the recently collapsed German Democratic Republic (GDR) and its citizens.[1] His book quickly became a best-seller, going through eight editions in two years and cited extensively—both positively and critically—by academics, journalists, and public intellectuals. Maaz followed up a year later with *Das gestürzte Volk* (The Overturned People), in which he attempted to assess the psychological costs and problems associated with reunification for East Germans.[2]

In these works, Maaz holds Stalinism chiefly responsible for the Communist Party authoritarianism and state control that, through constant, institutionalized fear, repressed people both civically and psychologically. State security (the Stasi), schools, the health-care system, churches, and parents, Maaz contends, conspired to "protect" children and adults by enforcing official ideals and ridiculing all forms of deviance and authentic expression.[3] The pathological nature of East German society, thus, resulted in a "deformation of character." The East German personality suffered from a "deficiency syndrome": deprived of everything from good service to clean air to unconditional love, East Germans invariably blocked instinctive emotional responses and often channeled them into dysfunctional outlets, such as overeating, drinking, smoking, and watching television. "We were," Maaz sums up, "as walled in emotionally as our country was blocked off physically from the outside world by the Berlin Wall."[4]

If East German society had created a nation of neurotic personalities, the fall of the Berlin Wall, Maaz argues, did nothing to undermine such psychopathologies. While the concrete edifice of the Berlin Wall was demolished, a "psychological wall" remained in the minds of East Germans. The heady days of 1989 and early 1990, marked by civic activism, political courage, spontaneity, creativity, enthusiasm, and honesty, were soon replaced by a wave of anxiety and childishness: anxiety, in the form of the fear of freedom, change, uncertainty, and loss; childishness, in the expression of the infantilizing desire to be taken care of and in placing unrealistic hope on the paternalistic policies of Helmut Kohl and a beneficent West Germany.[5] Thus, to Maaz's thinking, the deformation of East German personalities under the communist regime has carried over into postcommunist society, where easterners remain psychologically submissive and manipulable.

Together, these two highly impressionistic books accomplished two things. First, they helped popularize a project of the human sciences in Germany that continues to this day: the study of East German perceptions, self-perceptions, identities, and values. Second, Maaz laid out a set of questions and arguments that became a reference point for future psychological and sociological investigations. Since 1990, psychologists, psychiatrists, ethnographers, social scientists, historians, and journalists inside and outside Germany have debated the veracity of the claim that a psychological Stalinism ultimately fashioned a "deformed Ossi."[6]

Investigations into the frame of mind of *Ossis* (eastern Germans) and, to some extent as well, *Wessis* (western Germans) have been motivated by two overriding interests. One has been to assess the accuracy of, and ultimately to revise, stereotypical characterizations East and West Germans have commonly attributed to one another.[7] In addition, many see such research as a corrective to the Federal Republic's reunification policy, which they criticize for operating according to a behaviorist model of human subjectivity that assumes a naive, mechanistic view of East Germans, with little or no curiosity about their inner worlds.[8]

All together, three kinds of data have figured prominently in researching East German subjectivity: psychological tests, surveys and polls, and interviews. The results—contradictory and controversial as they sometimes have been—have shown there to be persistent differences between Ossis and Wessis in their espoused values, self-perceptions, cognitive processes, social interactions, life goals, and general sense of satisfaction. Psychologists, for instance, using personality and problem-solving tests, have found that Germans from the east tend to react to quandries and crisis situations by adopting an axiomatic approach, that is, arriving at a solution deductively, attempting to reduce uncertainty to a unifying explanation, and remaining short-sighted in focus, though tactically flexible.[9] This has been taken by some as confirmation of the relatively passive and unadventurous nature of the Ossi personality. Harry Schröder and Heiner Keupp have seen in the nostalgia, the idealization of the "opposition" against the former regime, and the denial of the processes of change so prevalent in the east during the early 1990s, a general lack of responsibility and critical distance rooted in the conformism of the GDR.[10] A much-cited study conducted by the Department of Psychology at the University of Trier in 1991 added some empirical support to this view. After administering a battery of psychodiagnostic tests, researchers generally found East Germans to be, on the one hand, more nervous and insecure, self-controlled, loyal to principle, and norm oriented, and, on the other, less spontaneous, desirous of new experiences, and autonomous than their western counterparts.[11]

It is not only psychologists who acknowledge such differences. Studies have also shown that Ossis perceive themselves to be different from Wessis. In response to tests designed to assess self-perception, those in the east in 1994 tended to describe themselves as more socially open, self-critical, contemplative, and disciplined than Germans in the West.[12] Wolf Wagner and Stefan Hradil, encountering similar results, have found East Germans to be self-consciously more traditional, more proletarian, and more moralistic in their outlooks on life relative to West Germans.[13] Summing up ten years of research on the subject, Elmar Brähler and Horst-Eberhard Richter note that East Germans are apt to define themselves in terms of four *P*s: "they portray themselves as more passive, more pessimistic, more paranoid, and more pacifistic" than West Germans.[14]

East German reactions to reunification and its aftermath have also been seen as indicative of a distinctly Ossi mentality. Surveys have consistently shown that the rapid disintegration of political, social, and economic infrastructures in the east promoted a widespread sense of insecurity among easterners that has translated into a durable set of political values oriented around economic growth, job security, and law and order.[15] And while indications are that, over time, Germans in the east and west are drawing ever closer together in the values they espouse, the former have differentiated themselves by continuing to place a premium on family, work, safety, and the state.[16] Identifying themselves more strongly with personal and intimate relationships than their western counterparts,[17] Ossis have come to be described as materialists trapped in a postmaterialist society, discontent with their public, yet largely content with their private, lives.[18]

Both scholars and everyday Germans since 1989, therefore, appear to agree with Maaz that the Berlin Wall was replaced by a more insubstantial, yet equally effectual, object: a "wall in the mind" (*Mauer im Kopf*) that has undermined the unification of German identities. Some attribute Ossi perceptions, attitudes, and values to the socialization of East Germans under the communist regime.[19] Others, however, believe the differences between Eastern and Western mentalities have more to do with the fact that East Germans have had to carry most of the burden of grappling with the socioeconomic dislocation, cultural anomie, and life crises that have attended the *Wende*.[20] In either case, most analysts have understood the Ossi as a qualitatively distinct type of personality, one stamped by authoritarianism, dependence, disruption, and fear.[21]

What is striking here is how most observers see the East German as "the problem" to be understood, with West German norms of individualism, consumerism, and achievement serving as the default standard for evaluation.[22] More specifically, both the figures of "the East German" and of "the Ossi" have been depicted as suffering from a literal or figurative psychopathology rooted in the demise of an illegitimate political and social order. As Thomas Ahbe has pointed out, this characterization has often involved equating socialism with fascism. Germans in the east, so the story goes, are and were "inner fascists," having lived under a "psychical Stalinism" that perpetuated Nazi forms of petty bourgeois conformity and then transformed itself into authoritarian political sentiments after 1989.[23] Comparisons with the aftermath of World War II are perhaps to be expected, especially given the fact that both postwar and post-GDR Germans had to renarrativize their lives around the themes of loss, destruction, guilt, victimization, and collaboration.[24]

But there is something different in this wave of research on the East German and the Ossi than simply a return of the image of "the authoritarian personality" or the brainwashed or inherently fascist German.[25] In this most recent literature, the East German personality is defined by its lack of any number of psychological characteristics and resources that its western counterpart possesses. East Germans are emplotted as fragile, insecure subjects, unused to autonomy, flexibility, and choice, and now thrown into an equally fragile, insecure postmodern world of risks.[26] Those interested in tracing the origins of this vulnerability typically find it in the controlling and condescending paternalism of the governing Socialist Unity Party (SED). Largely cut off from outside influences and shielded from choices by the SED's "welfare dictatorship" (*Fürsorgediktatur*),[27] East Germans apparently fled into their own private niches, while preserving a public face of ritualistic conformity.[28] The East German self, thus, is seen as one forged by a shortage of goods, a paucity of reliable information, an inadequate education, and an empty public life.[29] Even in those cases where Ossis are associated with having more than Wessis, this "more" remains rooted in a history of having "less."[30] If those in the east are more proletarian, more sociable, more German, and more conservative in their outlook than those in the West, it is because they have been less free, less independent, less cosmopolitan, and less enlightened than their western counterparts. Any change in lifestyles or frames of mind among those in the east is generally chalked up to an "erosion" of the old order due to the allure of individualizing trends from the West (*Westdrall*).[31]

Thus, we arrive at a bifurcated image of German subjectivity, with West and East Germans and Wessis and Ossis serving as opposing referents for one another and each characterized by a set of relatively stable attributes (see table 1). Not only do these characterizations—admittedly, ones that are widely accepted as true among Germans themselves—perpetuate the idea of two distinct types of people, but they also split into two the psychology of the East German. The very ideal types that define the poles of analysis are projected onto, or, more accurately, *in*to, the very objects of investigation. Both the "East German" of the past and the present-day "Ossi" are seen as divided personalities, cut off from experiences, ambitions, desires, feelings, and ways of thinking to which they were, are, and must invariably be drawn. One could hardly be more explicit in turning the Berlin Wall from a concrete structure into a psychological barrier.

All this represents nothing short of a historically new way of imagining the modern human being. To be sure, it is an understanding with ties to the notion of the totalitarianized Soviet individual, or *homo sovieticus,* as it has been called.[32] But it is something more than that, in that it has as its center of gravity the metaphor of a wall or walls. Let us call this new image of personhood *homo munitus* (the sheltered, defended human). From the Latin infinitive verb *munire,* meaning "to fortify, guard, defend, secure, protect, or shelter," the perfect passive participle *munitus* has political connotations and is also related to *moenia,* meaning "defensive and city walls, ramparts, or fortifications." The term also has a secondary meaning of making open or passable a way or road, since building a road in the ancient world was conceived as a process of building up or fortifying a passage.[33] Over the past decade and a half, social scientists, policymakers, journalists, public intellectuals, and average Germans have all helped cast the East German and the Ossi in the guise of homo munitus: people historically repressed and denied access to happiness by the walls and overly protective political system ostensibly designed to defend them.

But is homo munitus an invention of post-1989 Germans? Hardly. The image of the sealed off, deprived, and underdeveloped East German dates back to the 1950s and some of the earliest Western representations of life in the GDR.[34] Homo munitus, therefore, has a history predating the Berlin Wall. But from where does it come? Those critical of the image of the deformed Ossi have pointed exclusively to West German ethnocentrism for perpetuating this view.[35] Yet many who hold this view of East Germans are themselves Ossis.

Homo munitus is not merely an import from the West. It has a history in East Germany as well, one that is itself entangled in the history of the modern individual. It remains a popular misconception that communism had no interest in the individual as such. On the contrary, social scientists, psychologists, physicians, educators, and policymakers in the GDR were

TABLE 1.   Features and Characteristics Attributed to Germans

West German and Wessis	East Germans and Ossis
Powerful	Powerless
Multiplicity	Uniformity
Individualism	Conformism
Society	Community
Freedom of expression	Suppression of expression
Authenticity and revelation	Repression and concealment
Independence	Dependence
Spontaneity	Planning
Play	Work
Inductive	Deductive
Strategic	Tactical
Creative	Formulaic
Active	Passive
Adult	Child
Prosperity	Scarcity
Postmaterialist	Materialist
Realists	Idealists
Security	Insecurity
Risk embracing	Risk aversive
Aggressive	Pacifistic
Content	Discontent
Autarky	Welfare
Doing	Contemplating
Modern	Traditional

preoccupied with the inner workings of the East German. Convinced that socialist society could only work if human psychology was also reconstructed, the SED turned to the human sciences for answers. The result was a vast literature and an array of policies concerned with making sense of and dealing with deviance. It is here that we find the figure of homo munitus articulated explicitly, as East German public institutions engaged in that most modern of projects: the medical and scientific management of normality and abnormality.[36] Homo munitus, a creature born of the cold war, is a view of the human psyche ultimately rooted in the modern political hope of social reform.

The Individual as Ideological Bulwark

During the years of Soviet occupation (1945–49) and most of the 1950s, East German understandings of the individual and human subjectivity were stamped by the radical political, social, and economic changes going on in Germany. As German communist exiles from Moscow, led by Walter Ulbricht, returned to Germany after the war and quickly established the dominance of the SED, they took the lead in casting the fledgling GDR (founded in 1949) as a socialist bulwark against an imperialist West and a U.S.-allied West Germany.[37] From the beginning, then, Party and state officials conceived the reconstruction of East Germany in highly ideological, bifurcated terms.[38] Building a socialist society was to be a revolutionary project inspired by the Soviet Union, informed by Marxism-Leninism, and planned and directed by the Communist Party and the state. Since, however, Germans were presumably burdened by the legacy of fascism and the influence of American imperialism, the GDR would have to be ever vigilant in defending the socialist project against those reactionary forces—both inside and outside the country—determined to undermine it.

Science and technology occupied a prominent place in the SED's reconstruction plans. In part, this had to do with a long-standing German tradition of state sponsorship of research and development.[39] The Party's faith in science and technology, however, was also informed by its conviction, rooted in the intellectual history of Marxism-Leninism, that society followed natural laws of development and that its own ideology was inherently scientific.[40] Already by the First Five-Year Plan (1951–55), Party and state leaders understood the building of a socialist state not only as a political project but also as a social scientific project, requiring the skills of scholars, scientists, and engineers.[41] This vision of science and technology as essential elements in the rational construction of East German infrastructure and society was eventually given its ad hoc Marxist-Leninist justification with the publication of Gerhard Kosel's *Productive Force Science* in 1957.[42]

That said, officials remained deeply suspicious about the East German intelligentsia throughout the late 1940s and 1950s. Earlier, professionals such as doctors, psychiatrists, neurologists, and engineers had joined the Nazi Party in significant numbers—as many as 50 percent of all physicians were card-carrying members of the party by 1945—and over the course of the 1950s, they represented a disproportionately large group among those fleeing the GDR into the Federal Republic.[43] As had been the case in West Germany, after an initial phase of de-Nazification, Soviet and East German administrators found it necessary to retain many highly skilled personnel who had been active during the Third Reich in key postwar positions and institutions. Adopting a "policy of alliance" (*Bündnispolitik*) with the bourgeois intelligentsia, the regime sought to stem the emigration tide westward by giving academics a stake in the new order.[44]

Party officials, however, continued to harbor grave doubts about the political reliability and loyalty of the country's experts. In response, the planning of scientific research was centralized, Soviet and natural scientific models privileged, and the influence of the Communist Party at all levels secured. The result was not so much a routine of political interference in scientific work but rather the emergence of a peculiarly politicized style of scientific practice, one engaged in by functionaries and researchers alike: Party dogma and scientific knowledge were to be defended and protected from fractious and corrupting influences (*Parteilichkeit*); ideologically acceptable "lines" of questioning and thinking were prescribed; knowledge was treated as cumulative, not dialectical, its growth reciprocally linked to the "development" of socialism; and, thus, "deviations" from sanctioned lines of inquiry were to be rooted out and their proponents "educated" (*parteierzogen*) to abandon their position.[45]

The form of official scientific discourse and that of the prevailing political discourse thereby mirrored one another, both emphasizing the defense of the party line's projection of the development of socialist knowledge and a socialist society. And just as the intelligentsia did not always behave in the ways the SED hoped, so too the general population in East Germany did not always behave as "planned."[46] Jurists, police, and Party officials generally chalked up crime and everyday resistance to reactionary elements inside and outside the GDR as well as to an insufficient "political consciousness" among East Germans.[47] By the second half of the 1950s, Party leaders began attacking the problem by embarking on a concerted plan to rear a new generation of "decent and respectable human beings" (*wohlanständige Menschen*). The educational system was reformed and oriented toward raising party activists and so-called comprehensively developed personalities *(allseitig entwickelte Persönlichkeiten)*.[48] Conventional stereotypes about the public role of women were called into question, as the state and Party glorified and encouraged women's equal access to jobs and careers.[49] Eventually, "new" rules of everyday decency and discipline were publicized, culminating in July 1958 with Walter Ulbricht's announcement of "The Ten Commandments for the New Socialist Person."[50]

Individuals and their subjectivities thereby assumed a surprisingly conspicuous place in the politics and science of the nascent, self-avowedly collectivist GDR. In the decade and a half following World War II, a host of experts and practitioners from the legal, forensic, psychological, and pedagogical sciences and from medicine, psychiatry, psychotherapy, public policy, and social services became involved in monitoring, assessing, and managing individuals who, in one form or another, deviated from official ideals of behavior. As with scientific practice in general, this field of scientific, policy, and rehabilitative work should not be construed simply as a direct response to party-political mandates. Rather, it needs to be understood as a set of concerns, investigations, and remedies coproduced at the same time as politics and policies and simultaneously informed by German policy, legal, and scholarly traditions; Marxist-Leninist theory; and Soviet scholarship.[51]

Take, for example, the study and handling of juvenile delinquency following World War II. Since the late 1920s, Germany had adopted a largely punitive approach to juvenile delinquency that stressed the institutional confinement of difficult and "wayward" youth.[52] The breakdown of normal social structures in Germany that accompanied the war and its aftermath, however, dissolved this system and brought with it the rise of gangs and a wave of violent crime, theft, vandalism, and black marketeering in which young people—and, in particular, young men—were increasingly involved.[53] Under these circumstances, authorities and social service professionals in the Soviet Occupied Zone clamored to reestablish a comprehensive, custodial system of youth welfare, this time built around a more clinical approach. Already in early 1946, demands were being made to establish "therapeutic-pedagogical counseling centers" (*heilpädagogische Beratungsstellen*) for juvenile delinquents in Berlin, to be run by pedagogues, psychotherapists, and psychiatrists trained in depth psychology.[54] Experts in the field informed local officials that a combination of "character" deficiencies, family separation, and wartime and postwar anxieties was responsible for placing many young people on a path toward a "criminal career" (*Verbrecherlaufbahn*).[55]

By the end of 1947, "psychological counseling centers" (*Nervenberatungsstellen*) had been established in every district in Berlin, and soon investigators were using the sites to conduct research on the impact of the war on children. Beginning in May 1951, researchers began examining and interviewing eighth graders in Berlin-Malchow for signs of, among other things, poor hygiene, anxiety, depression, dysfunctional family life, unruliness, and speech impediments.[56] Walter Ulbricht himself took a personal interest in the project and enjoined his minister of health to fully back the initiative.[57] The results of this and other studies conducted by local health offices led the psychological counseling centers to press authorities to develop a more seamless network of closed, transitional, and outpatient facilities to monitor and supervise the "premorbid personality" of at-risk youths. "It is understandable," as one report put it, "that the same questions are always raised in the seminars we hold with parents about difficulties in rearing, the call for medical advice and assistance regarding the disturbed mental development of the child, problems of discipline, [and] the many deviations and lapses [*Abwegigkeiten und Entgleisungen*]."[58] Within a year, however, the project in Malchow was plagued by infighting, as some physicians involved in the study began reporting back to Ulbricht that their efforts to apply Pavlovian models and methods were being actively opposed by colleagues trained in depth psychology.[59]

The case of juvenile delinquency and youth welfare demonstrates the extent to which the human sciences, public policy, communist ideology, and concerns over deviance mutually reinforced one another to shape the specter of "wayward youth" in the 1940s and 1950s. The investigation and administration of other forms of deviance at the time, such as mental illness, alcoholism, and antisocial and criminal conduct, followed a similar pattern.[60] It was medical, scientific, and social service experts, along with parents and average citizens, who encouraged the SED and the state—not the other way around—to take a more active role in the surveillance of East German youth. Appealing both to German policy traditions and to mainstream trends in international psychiatry and psychology, researchers, therapists, and policy experts clamored for a therapeutic, preventive, and comprehensive approach toward juvenile delinquents. This resonated well among Party functionaries, who held it to be the task of the newly found state, according to the leader of the Free German Youth in 1949, "to educate the young generation to love and be loyal to the German Democratic Republic."[61] Once the SED took a direct interest in matters, Marxism-Leninism and party politics became yet another resource to mobilize and obstacle around which to navigate.[62]

East German preoccupations with deviant behavior in the first decade and a half after World War II reveal something else as well. They show that, as was the case elsewhere in postwar Europe, understandings of normality and abnormality were being actively reconstructed along with political and economic infrastructures.[63] The rise and fall of National Socialism, war, mass death and destruction, and the sudden elevation of new elites and new ideologies: this relatively quick succession of profound political events compelled Germans from all walks of life to rehistoricize identities and renarrativize life histories.

While academic work on this subject in postwar West Germany stressed the victimization of refugees, evacuees, and POWs,[64] in East Germany assessing the state of the self was publicized in a more forward-looking manner, as part of the SED's ambition to impart a new socialist consciousness in its citizens. As Dietfried Müller-Hegemann (1910–89), a longtime communist and the psychiatrically trained director of the university clinic in Leipzig, argued, fascism had deformed not only social conditions but also the human psyche. Thus, socialism required the assistance of the human sciences to "reshape" subjectivities. In his psychological postmortem of National Socialism entitled *Toward the Psychology of the German Fascist,* Müller-Hegemann held that the Nazis and the Third Reich were made possible by, and in turn reinforced, an existential anxiety, a civic docility, and an interpersonal aggressiveness rooted in Prussian authoritarianism. Hitler himself, according to Müller-Hegemann, was a product of this depersonalizing conditioning that undermined a community sensibility. An inhibited weakling and a self-pitying failure growing up in a petty bourgeois family and a martial society, Hitler never fully developed as a person (*Fehlentwicklung*), becoming an unsociable, frustrated, do-nothing who channeled his impotence into an all-encompassing faith in authority, obedience, and war.[65]

Müller-Hegemann's portrait of Hitler, of course, was meant to be

more than a psychobiogaphy of the dictator. It represented the first concerted scholarly effort to merge psychology and Marxism-Leninism in
order to assess the political mentality of the (East) German people. In
doing so, the image of the underdeveloped Hitler notably accomplishes
two things. For one, it neatly separates the ideals, social relations, and
worldviews associated with recent German political history from those of
the GDR, thereby emphasizing the promise of a revolutionary new way of
being a person. At the same time, Müller-Hegemann's Hitler is a mirror
image of the prevailing picture of the East German delinquent at this time.
By associating the Nazi leader with the same kinds of developmental problems, antiquated outlooks, and antisocial behaviors researchers and
officials attributed to juvenile delinquents, Müller-Hegeman effectively
linked youth deviance in East Germany to the specter of fascism. Everyday nonconformity, thus, appeared to carry with it the potential for social
ruin.

The East German At Risk: Reforming the Deviant in the Sixties

What is so striking about early East German images of the human psyche
is how they mirror images of Communist Party doctrine, state policy, and
scientific knowledge. As noted earlier, ideology, policies, and science were
all believed to advance cumulatively, arriving at official "lines" that then
had to be defended against subversions and corruptions. Human subjectivity was widely portrayed as operating in the same manner. The obsession with and policing of borders and behavior in the early GDR, therefore, derived not only from cold war fears and communist paternalism but
also from a very peculiar epistemology. The East German of the 1950s was
understood in mostly cognitive terms, as a subject who required education, rearing, and consciousness raising and needed to be protected from
dangerous diversions and detours.

Just as this view of the East German subject had begun to crystallize,
sweeping changes in the Soviet Union following Stalin's death prompted a
series of reforms affecting policy and science throughout communist
Europe. Debates within party and scholarly circles in the USSR beginning
in 1954 resulted in a reorganization of the Soviet Academy of Sciences in
1961. The effect of this change was a reversal of the conventional Stalinist
relationship between science and ideology. The principle of "partymind-

edness" (*partiynost'*) in science was formally dropped, and it now became the task of ideologues "to adapt their interpretations, at least superficially, by incorporating the lessons of the newest scientific achievements" rather than vice versa.[66]

At first glance, the building of the Berlin Wall in 1961 would appear to be evidence that the post-Stalinist "thaw" was not felt in the GDR. But it must be kept in mind that Party leaders saw the Wall as a precondition for realizing the goals of socialism. Thus, it was none other than Walter Ulbricht who, in the early 1960s, initiated a comprehensive reform of the country's economic, legal, health care, and education systems. The New Economic System (1963–69), first outlined by the SED in June 1963, hailed "scientificness" (*Wissenschaftlichkeit*), technical innovation, greater openness and creativity, and expert know-how as the keys to unlocking the full productive potential of the people. To this end, a new generation of engineers, social scientists, psychologists, psychiatrists, physicians, jurists, and social workers were recruited to advance "actually existing socialism" in the 1960s.[67] Thus, while the closing of the border appeared to Western observers as a sign of the SED's final abandonment of progressive change, inside the GDR it marked the beginning of a period of experimentation and enthusiasm within the human sciences that lasted well into the 1970s.

Fields once categorically dismissed as "bourgeois" were reborn. Empirical sociology, for instance, was officially reestablished by 1964, following a number of international conferences for Eastern European social scientists and with the backing of the SED. In the words of Kurt Hager, the director of the Ideological Commission of the Central Committee, sociological research was justified on the grounds that it "made a contribution to the political leadership and management activities of the Party and the state."[68] Programs and research centers were quickly built up, recruiting academics and staff from existing institutes and departments of philosophy, political economy, modern history, pedagogy, psychology, Marxism-Leninism, hygiene, and even musicology. Using standard methods and tools, such as surveys, questionnaires, experiments, and observation, studies focused on two basic themes: factors affecting the productivity of workers and promoting the education and activism of young people.[69] By the late 1960s, the Politburo took it upon itself to formally sanction these methods and lines of questioning. "Central Research Plans of Marxist-Leninist Social Science" in 1968 and 1972 made "the development of the worker class and the growth of its role in society" the ultimate goal of all empirical sociology. To this end, social group formation, political and consumer attitudes, and patterns of social behavior all became objects of investigation.[70]

Psychology was another field reinvigorated in the 1960s. After Stalin's death, Pavlovian theory's virtual monopoly over psychological research in the USSR was broken, allowing researchers to express alternatives to the Pavlovian view that had seen subjects as largely passive objects of material conditions.[71] While the "pavlovization" of psychology had met with only mixed results in East Germany,[72] the new intellectual climate and the Berlin Wall made it possible for psychologists there to organize themselves nationally for the first time, founding the Society for Psychology in the GDR in 1962. Subsequent conventions of the society in 1964 and 1968 extolled "psychology as a socially productive force," whose recognized fields of specialization—cybernetics, psychophysics and perception, work and engineering psychology, clinical psychology, pedagogical psychology, social psychology, and forensic psychology—would augment worker proficiency and contribute to the development of "the socialist human community" (*sozialistische Menschengemeinschaft*).[73]

Psychology also appeared well suited to grapple with a growing public concern. The participation of young people in the unrest of 1953, the large numbers of them that fled to the West, and their receptiveness to American popular culture led East German officials to see the young as one of the principal risks to national security.[74] A marked rise in the crime rate around 1960, something widely attributed to juvenile delinquents, reinforced anxieties.[75] For the SED, which represented itself as a parental figure in the lives of East German youth, the key to addressing these issues lay in more effective rearing and education.[76] The historical association of German psychological institutes with pedagogical applications of their research made psychology a logical ally in reforming young people.

As a result, there was a wave of research on children and pedagogy during the 1960s. At the University of Jena, the psychologists Hans Hiebsch (1922–90) and Manfred Vorwerg (1933–89) established a research program and formal curriculum in pedagogical psychology.[77] In Berlin, Hans-Dieter Schmidt (Humboldt University, 1963–92) directed the study of developmental psychology, wedding cybernetics, and evolutionary theory with behavioral, cognitive, and Gestalt psychologies. His book *General Developmental Psychology,* published in 1970, became the standard East German textbook in the field.[78] By decade's end, the Ministry of Public Education and the Office for Youth Affairs had become intimately involved in promoting and coordinating pedagogical psychology in the

GDR, successfully centralizing teacher training, research planning, and publication outlets.[79]

The renaissance in the human sciences of learning and childhood fed and was reciprocally influenced by a sweeping change in the general conceptualization of subjectivity in the GDR. With the rebirth of empirical social science came efforts to operationalize formerly abstract ideals of the self. Inspired by the international preoccupation with "personality," policymakers, psychologists, and educators in the years 1965–75 took up and revamped the Marxist-Leninist concept of "the socialist personality."[80] Shaping "comprehensively developed socialist personalities" became a prominent catchphrase in virtually all East German reform plans at the time. As the vice president of the Academy of Pedagogical Sciences in the GDR expressed it at a major conference in 1972, the task was to promote "personality qualities such as mental flexibility, adherence to principle and courage, decisiveness, inexhaustible thirst for knowledge, discipline, industriousness, conscientiousness, considerateness, thoroughness, and dependability."[81]

Nowhere did the transformative power of the socialist personality appear more promising than when it came to women. In the sixties, the SED and the state made the integration of women into the "scientific-technological revolution" of East German society a high priority. Social scientific studies found a glaring underrepresentation of women in high-skill jobs and leadership positions and largely attributed this to backward attitudes and values among both men and women.[82] Change, reformers believed, could only be achieved through simultaneously altering the "objective" and "subjective" conditions under which women worked. This meant, on the one hand, publicizing images of accomplished, working women.[83] At the same time, women were treated as projects to be "developed," as the state enlisted enterprises, officials, schools, and universities in a campaign to enhance the training and hiring of aspiring women.[84] Together, the science of and the policies for developing "socialist female personalities" were offered as the catalysts for not only changing women's roles in the workplace but also modifying family relations and gender stereotypes.[85]

The new notion of the socialist personality, thus, retained many of its utopian features, invoking the promise of a bold, collectivist, egalitarian, and politically energized consciousness that was expected to accompany advanced socialism. At the same time, however, it invested the individual with a more complicated psychology than earlier philosophical formulations. Renouncing a psychodynamic view of the self, East German theorists of the socialist personality understood it as the product of interaction between an individual's constitutional dispositions and the social conditions under which he or she is raised. In actively engaging the outside world, the human being learned how to be a social being, as external influences were internalized. Biological and psychological development were portrayed as then unfolding progressively in stages that were more or less universal. The trope of "development" is what, therefore, presumably linked the ontogenetic development of the individual with the phylogenetic development of socialist society. And by the early 1970s, the theories of child and pedagogical psychologists such as Hiebsch, Vorwerg, Schmidt, Walter Friedrich, and Adolf Kossakowski had become canonical reading for ideologues and social scientists alike.[86]

In this manner, the human sciences in East Germany arrived at a novel view of human personality, one that assumed the natural emergence of hard work, cooperation, duty, discipline, responsibility, and activity as an individual matured. Such a perspective necessarily had a direct impact on prevailing images of deviance. Similar to other fields, criminology and forensic psychiatry were given a new lease on life in the 1960s, providing a venue for legal scholars, psychologists, psychiatrists, pedagogues, and policymakers to establish the new social and legal parameters of abnormality.[87] Led by the clinician Hans Szewczyk, the influential head of the Department of Forensic Psychiatry and Psychology at the Charité Hospital in Berlin, the Society for Psychiatry and Neurology beginning in 1963 established a special section dedicated to the study of forensic issues.[88] This provided the institutional support for the systematic study of antisocial and criminal conduct.

By 1970, studies were finding not only a high degree of recidivism among criminals but also a strong correlation between criminal and antisocial behavior on the one hand and lazy work habits, poor upbringing, underachievement in school, and alcohol abuse on the other.[89] The talk now was of "risk factors" (Gefährdungen) associated with such things as hooliganism, assault, robbery, sexual assault, and murder. For the state, therefore, the key to fighting crime rested in prevention, early detection, and reeducation. To this end, beginning in 1962, psychiatrists consulted in criminal cases were enjoined to speak directly to the motives and reform potential of the perpetrator in their reports.[90] As Hans Szewczyk explained it in 1966, having abandoned the stimulus-response model of human psychology in favor of a milieu theory, social services and legal

institutions required a new method of observation and record keeping—
one attuned to the deviant's "ability to understand his actions and to steer
his own will appropriately"—in order to single out potential repeat
offenders.[91]

This more psychologically curious form of surveillance was coupled
with broadening the jurisdiction of youth detention centers. So-called
Homes for Social Support (*Heime für soziale Betreuung*) had existed in the
GDR since the late 1950s, designed to house youthful offenders and "asocials." In 1960, there were twenty homes of this sort, with 847 beds. Of
these, 825 were filled by individuals who had been committed there invol-
untarily. Though institutionally part of the criminal justice system, the
homes seemed to offer a ready-made venue for realizing the dream of therapeutic rehabilitation. Thus, beginning in 1961, an effort was made to use
the facilities to house fewer actual convicts and more "at-risk" individuals. The result was a pronounced decrease in the number of male residents
previously convicted of a crime, from 78 percent in 1961 to only 21 percent
in 1964.[92] The ubiquitous Hans Szewczyk, with the support of officials in
the Ministry for Health, became the chief spokesman for this move away
from punishment and toward the therapeutic, arguing that social and
health services personnel directly supervise the homes and that the latter
be treated as clinical facilities offering psychiatric and psychotherapeutic
support.[93]

Care and Control: The Sciences of Deviance in the 1970s and 1980s

By the time Erich Honecker officially replaced Walter Ulbricht as head of
the SED and the East German state in May 1971, a new vision of the
deviant had emerged in the GDR, one looking surprisingly similar to that
found in Western Europe. Inspired in part by social psychiatry, community mental health, and decarceration movements, East German researchers, clinicians, and policymakers in the 1960s very deliberately
turned to psychiatric and psychotherapeutic knowledge and language.
This led them to emphasize psychological and family, rather than ideological, influences that set individuals on a path toward antisocial behavior. The leitmotiv of "development," thus, linked the social and economic
advancement of the socialist state with the unfolding life history of the
individual: here, ontogeny was supposed to recapitulate phylogeny. The

result was an expansion of the jurisdiction of social and health services within both the criminal justice system and East German society in general.

We should not lose sight of the fact, however, that the care and concern expressed in this wave of social reformism also carried with them a mind-set of suspicion and an obsession with defending political ambitions. By making the arrested psychological development of the individual the key to understanding deviance, the human sciences and public policy placed a premium on observing, registering, screening, and redirecting human beings and their behavior. Simply put, as prevention assumed a greater importance, ever more mundane forms of deviance could be seen as politically dangerous. One of the more pointed examples of this came in the summer of 1973, as preparations were being made for the Tenth World Festival of Youth and Students meeting in East Berlin. In an effort to remove from the streets "all negatively appearing persons who might damage our image," the Ministry of Interior, the state prosecutor's office, the police, and youth welfare apprehended hundreds of drug addicts, alcoholics, prostitutes, and homeless persons and committed them to psychiatric facilities throughout the GDR.[94] Few, if any, of these individuals met the criteria for involuntary commitment.

While clinicians and social services were finding themselves wrapped up in the ideological work of the SED, state security in the seventies and eighties showed a growing interest in the work of the human sciences. As talk of reform came and went in the 1960s and relations between West and East Germany thawed in the 1970s, the Stasi experienced a phase of unprecedented growth in the years 1961–82.[95] Under Erich Honecker and Erich Mielke (head of the Stasi), state security sought to expand the network of reliable "unofficial collaborators" (*inoffizielle Mitarbeiter*) within the population by using the most modern technologies of surveillance and subversion. Here, as they did in education, criminal justice, and social work, officials placed a premium on identifying and steering specific personality types.[96] To this end, academic fields such as psychology, pedagogy, sociology, and psychiatry and their practitioners were used in Stasi training centers to establish a new human science, "operative psychology," whose ultimate goal was to exploit and subvert human weaknesses in the service of overtly political goals.[97]

The creeping invasiveness of state security in the last decade and a half of the GDR was, among other things, a response to domestic reforms and détente. As geographical and discursive boundaries opened up, particularly after Mikhail Gorbachev's introduction of glasnost in 1985,

Mielke understood the Stasi as a shield against a new wave of international and domestic threats to socialist society. But at the same time that security concerns were occupying a more prominent place in policy-making circles, images of nurturing, kindness, and protection also assumed a higher profile in public life.[98] In what was dubbed the new *Muttipolitik* of the 1970s, the SED reasserted the value of domesticity, family, and motherhood as a response to falling birthrates and a stagnant economy.[99] In the process, the language and policies of maternalism helped revivify ideals of humanism and social activism, all of which had been linked with one another in East German social welfare discourse since the 1950s.[100]

The ethos of caring (*Fürsorge*), even when coupled with policing and security, appears to have reinforced an increasingly individualistic and psychological outlook among East Germans.[101] It also created an alternative space for more mundane, less ideological scientific and clinical projects. In this regard, the place of psychology and social science in the National People's Army (Nationale Volksarmee, or NVA) is illustrative. Established in 1956, the NVA had very little engagement with the psychological sciences until 1966, when the first officers, at the invitation of Hans Hiebsch, were sent to the University of Jena to formally study academic psychology. By 1968, an independent Institute for Military Pedagogy and Military Psychology was founded at the Friedrich Engels Military Academy in Dresden, providing institutional support for work in the field.[102] Soon thereafter, army and air force officers began conducting research for dissertations and diplomas in psychology.

Without question, Party and military ideology strongly inflected military psychology studies. But since academic advisers insisted on a measure of scientific rigor and findings remained accessible only to approved readers, the authors of these reports and dissertations by and large relied on internationally recognized methods and data to explore a number of vexing problems. A 1978 study, for instance, showed how family problems and "abnormal personality structure" contributed to suicides in the military.[103] Psychodiagnostic tests were administered to explore job aptitude and explain the surprisingly high incidence of foreign-object swallowing in the jails of the armed services.[104] Yet another study in 1988 assessed the importance of psychotherapy in "stabilizing [the] self-esteem and sense of security" of functionally disturbed pilots.[105] In fact throughout the 1980s, the NVA showed a consistent interest in employing the social sciences to investigate family dynamics, job satisfaction, and attitudes toward the state among soldiers.[106]

Thus, even when administrators and researchers were motivated by security concerns, an ethos of care and a genuine psychological curiosity often displaced ideological dogma. This had something to do, of course, with the tutelary nature of the East German state, a "welfare dictatorship"[107] whose raison d'être was mobilizing the comprehensive welfare of its citizens. But something else was at work here as well. By the late 1970s and 1980s, social care as such had become associated with the methods and approaches of the human sciences. *They* represented the "soft" line in contrast to the "hard" line of ideologues and police.[108] Psychology, psychiatry, psychotherapy, social work, sociology, pedagogy, social policy, criminal justice, youth assistance: all had become wrapped up in one another, and this at a time when East German intellectual life was more open than ever to international influences.

This did not escape the notice of hard-liners. Already in the late 1960s, for instance, as criminal law and health policy in the GDR were being reconstructed, the psychosocial approach to crime advocated by reformers—conceptualizing the actions of perpetrators as expressions of pathologies and stressing treatment instead of punishment—often met with reserve, even hostility, from justice and law enforcement officials. Like their counterparts in the West, many prosecutors and police officials began to publicly and privately suggest that psychiatry and psychotherapy were pushing courts to be too lenient in their handling of violent and hardened offenders.[109]

The genie could not be put back in the bottle, however. The human sciences were there to stay, and by the mid-1980s intellectual and methodological innovations were taking notions of deviance into new directions. This can best be seen in the understanding and treatment of sex criminals. Like other deviants in the GDR, rapists and sexual molesters had been seen in the 1950s as individuals with backward, bourgeois attitudes toward self-gratification and responsibility.[110] This began to change in the 1960s, as psychiatrists successfully argued that sex crime be seen as the result of a psychopathology, of a perverse drive or warped personality within the perpetrator nurtured by a dysfunctional milieu.[111] Then, in the late 1970s and 1980s, psychodiagnostic and intelligence tests, originally repudiated in East Germany, were reintroduced into clinical and pedagogical practice.[112] Tests such as the Minnesota Multiphasic Personality Inventory, the Multiple Choice Vocabulary Test, the Freiburg Personality Inventory, the Freiburg Aggression Questionnaire, and the Gießen Test were administered to sex offenders in the hopes of profiling perpetrators still at large and providing an empirical basis for determining the likelihood that a sex offender would commit another offense after release.[113]

This new wave of research reconstructed its human subjects—and, in turn, its notions of sexuality, the criminal, and the self—based on a different set of terms from those that had been in currency over the previous decades. Whereas earlier forensic psychiatrists had been drawn to a delinquency model that sought the truth about the sex criminal "inside" him through a case history approach, East German psychodiagnosticians in the 1980s aimed at measuring the offender's cognitive skills, interpersonal styles, and habitual ways of thinking. Batteries of tests exploring multiple variables at once might be administered whose results could be graphically depicted. The psychologist ultimately searched for patterns or clusters of responses that could then be compared to standardized results. In the process, a new, more decentered image of the self emerged: this was a "flatter," less essentializing view of human subjectivity that treated personality no longer as the inner core of a person but as a convenient shorthand for the sum and form of an individual's interactions and habits.

All of this opened up new possibilities for making sense of sex offenders, who now could be categorized based on their lifestyles rather than on their clinical diagnoses. And as the behavior of perpetrators began to be treated less as "symptoms," the sexuality attributed to them changed as well. Sexuality took on new meaning as "a social and communicative phenomenon," and the sex criminal's problem was relocated, situated not in an abnormal sexual drive but instead in a diminished ability to express sexual desires in socially appropriate ways.[114] Here, then, in the last years of the regime, were signs of the first real break with the view of personality that had come to dominate the East German human sciences.

As historians like Stephen Kotkin have argued, communism was always more than just a set of doctrines and policies; it was also a moral universe that provided a language for understanding what an individual could and should be.[115] As I have attempted to show, East German researchers and policymakers developed a very peculiar notion of human beings grounded in a marriage of Marxism-Leninism and the twentieth-century human sciences. By around 1970, a consensus (or better put, an official line) had emerged around the idea that the inner workings of the individual were the result of interaction between a linear psychological development on the one hand and a reinforcing or corrupting milieu on the other. While rejecting the essentializing worldview of National Socialism, this perspective all but elided questions of inter- and intrapersonal conflict and autonomous self-expression. In the East German human sciences, the self was and remained a highly politicized object designed for mobilization.

That said, however, there is no reason to dismiss the human sciences in the GDR as cynical tools of a Machiavellian state. Quite the contrary, it was a modern idealism—the promise of scientific knowledge, economic development, and social progress—that inspired the figure of homo munitus. And while this discourse eventually rang hollow for most East Germans, it rooted homo munitus in a long-standing and accepted ethos of humane concern. By enlisting the social and psychological sciences in the service of social reform, then, policymakers in the GDR embarked on a quintessentially modern project, one characteristic of most advanced industrial societies in the twentieth century.[116]

If anything connects East German and postunification opinions about those living in the east, it is the association of the East German with being deficient, fragile, even primitive. Researchers, politicians, social services, and clinicians in both East and reunified Germany have been remarkably similar in their characterizations of the deviant East German as a person fearfully out of step with political events of the day. Voices of discontent, criminal violence, and psychiatric problems, more often than not, have been chalked up to a lack of keeping up, itself a function of a woefully inadequate upbringing. Even before the construction of the Berlin Wall, the idea was there that East Germans had barriers inside their public, private, and mental lives that threatened to foil attempts to develop them into upstanding socialist personalities. The presence of the Berlin Wall after 1961 only reinforced this idea, providing a concrete reality for the already circulating metaphor.[117]

It must be acknowledged that not everyone has shared this more or less "official" view of East Germans. A counterdiscourse existed among East Germans—and continues to exist today among those living in the east—according to which East Germans, far from being socially damaged and out of step, were and are blessed with a healthier, more authentic mentality than their western counterparts.[118] This way of thinking and talking about East German distinctiveness appears to have existed side by side with the official versions of the self, in the niches of everyday life in the GDR. Rejecting prevailing ideals of a socially constructed and mobilized personality, a great many East Germans appear to have embraced an essentialist identity, rooted in bourgeois notions of privacy, family, and religion.[119] The degree to which this counterdiscourse and more publicly acceptable understandings of East German subjectivity influenced one another remains to be seen.

It also must be added that, to some extent, the features attributed to the East German deviant predate even the GDR and the cold war. Recriminations of laziness, whining, and atavism, for instance, play on older German stereotypes about Jews, welfare recipients, "asocials," and colonized peoples. But there is something significantly different about how East Germans and Ossis have been seen. It lies in the way in which the human sciences before and after 1989 have portrayed them not as parasites but as victims. East Germans, so the story goes, were and are not entirely responsible for their plight, since they were victims of sensory deprivation, cut off from positive influences, be they work collectives or Western democracy or a capitalist work ethic.

The figure of homo munitus, then, is not solely the concoction of patronizing Wessis. It is an image of the East German propagated by East Germans as well, seeing human beings as products of their environment, requiring security and guidance in order to unleash and rescue their full potential. In this sense, then, twentieth-century liberalisms, communisms, and even fascisms had much more in common than is often thought: the idea and ideal of the reformable human being.

NOTES

1. Hans-Joachim Maaz, *Der Gefühlsstau: Ein Psychogramm der DDR* (Berlin: Argon, 1990), translated and published in English as *Behind the Wall: The Inner Life of Communist Germany* (New York and London: Norton, 1995). All citations that follow are from the English edition.

2. *Das gestürzte Volk: Die verunglückte Einheit* (Berlin: Argon, 1991).

3. Maaz, *Behind the Wall,* 13–14, 20–49.

4. Maaz, *Behind the Wall,* 59–79; quote is from 79.

5. Maaz, *Behind the Wall,* 169–70; *Das gestürzte Volk,* 34–52, 86.

6. The now vast literature on this subject can be found online in "The Bibliography of German Unity" at www.wiedervereinigung.de. As of September 2006, the bibliography, first made available online in 1999, had some fifty-two thousand citations and continues to grow.

7. Wessis, for instance, commonly criticize Ossis for being overly deferential to paternalistic authority and lacking in initiative, openness, self-reliance, and a sense of individuality. Those from the east frequently counter by claiming that those in the west are generally arrogant, egotistical, competitive, and unable to share their feelings or admit their failings. Rainer Zoll, ed., *Ostdeutsche Biographien: Lebenswelt im Umbruch* (Frankfurt a.M.: Suhrkamp, 1999), 9.

8. Gisela Trommsdorff and Hans-Joachim Kornadt, "Innere Einheit im

vereinigten Deutschland? Psychologische Prozesse beim sozialen Wandel," in *Die Transformation Ostdeutschlands: Berichte zum sozialen und politischen Wandel in den neuen Bundesländern,* ed. Hans Bertram and Raj Kollmorgen (Opladen: Leske + Budrich, 2001), 379–80; Heiner Keupp and Hans-Jürgen Wirth, "Vorwort," in *Abschied von der DDR* [*Psychosozial* 45, 14 (1991)], ed. Heiner Keupp and Hans-Jürgen Wirth (Hembach: Psychologie Verlagsunion, 1991), 3.

9. Stefan Strohschneider, ed., *Denken in Deutschland: Vergleichende Untersuchungen in Ost und West* (Bern: Hans Huber, 1996). Wessis, by contrast, tend to be anecdotal in their approach to problems, learning by doing and adopting a feedback strategy, remaining open to new evidence and the complexity and flux of a situation.

10. Harry Schröder, "Zur psychologischen Vergangenheitsbewältigung der DDR-Bürger nach der Wende," in *Abschied von der DDR,* ed. Keupp and Wirth, 23–29; Heiner Keupp, "Umbruch in der DDR—Spurensuche in einer Korrespondenz," in *Abschied von der DDR,* ed. Keupp and Wirth, 34–47.

11. Peter Becker, Klaus-Dieter Hänsgen, and Elisabeth Lindinger, "Ostdeutsche und Westdeutsche im Spiegel dreier Fragebogentests," *Trierer Psychologische Berichte* 18, no. 3 (1991).

12. Elmar Brähler and Horst-Eberhard Richter, "Deutsche Befindlichkeiten im Ost-West Vergleich: Ergebnisse einer empirischen Untersuchung," *Aus Politik und Zeitgeschichte* B40–41 (1995): 13–20.

13. Wolf Wagner, "'Deutscher, proletarischer und moralischer': Unterschiede zwischen Ost- und Westdeutschland und ihre Erklärung," in *Deutsch-deutsche Vergleiche: Psychologische Untersuchungen 10 Jahre nach dem Mauerfall,* ed. Hendrik Berth and Elmar Brähler (Berlin: Verlag für Wissenschaft und Forschung, 1999), 53–69; Stefan Hradil, "Die Modernisierung des Denkens: Zukunftspotential und 'Altlasten' in Ostdeutschland," *Aus Politik und Zeitgeschichte* B20 (1995): 3–15.

14. Elmar Brähler and Horst-Eberhard Richter, "Ost- und Westdeutsche—10 Jahre nach der Wende," in *Deutsch-deutsche Vergleiche,* ed. Berth and Brähler, 24.

15. Claudia Dalbert, "Psychisches Wohlbefinden und Persönlichkeit in Ost und West: Vergleich von Sozialisationseffekten in der früheren DDR und der alten BRD," *Zeitschrift für Sozialisationsforschung und Erziehungssoziologie* 13 (1993): 82–94.

16. Bernhard Christoph, "Weiter deutliche Zufriedenheitsdifferenzen zwischen Ost und West trotz Annäherung in manchen Bereichen: Zur Entwicklung des subjektiven Wohlbefindens in der Bundesrepublik 1990–2000," *Informationsdienst Soziale Indikatoren* 28 (2002): 11–14; Rolf Reißig, *Die gespaltene Vereinigungsgesellschaft: Bilanz und Perspektiven der Transformation Ostdeutschlands und der deutschen Vereinigung* (Berlin: Dietz, 2000), 70–90; Roland Habich, Heinz-Herbert Noll, and Wolfgang Zapf, "Subjektives Wohlbefinden in Ostdeutschland nähert sich westdeutschem Niveau: Ergebnisse des Wohlfahrtssurveys 1998," *Informationsdienst Soziale Indikatoren* 22 (1999): 1–6.

17. Elmar Brähler, Jörg Schumacher, and Martin Eisemann, "Das erinnerte elterliche Erziehungsverhalten im Ost-West-Vergleich und seine Beziehung zur aktuellen Befindlichkeit," in *Sozialistische Diktatur und psychische Folgen: Psycho-*

analytisch-psychologische Untersuchungen in Ostdeutschland und Tschechien, ed. Ingrid Kerz-Rühling and Tomas Plänkers (Tübingen: Edition Diskord, 2000), 91–118; Volker Hielscher, "Arbeitsorientierung in Ostdeutschland," in *Ostdeutsche Biographien,* ed. Zoll, 125–39; Rainer Zoll, "Zur Lebenswelt in der DDR," in *Ostdeutsche Biographien,* ed. Zoll, 248–54

18. Thomas Gensicke, "Deutschland am Ausgang der neunziger Jahre: Lebensgefühl und Werte," *Deutschland Archiv* 31 (1998): 19–36. On postmaterialism, see the work of Ronald Inglehart, most recently his edited volume, *Human Values and Social Change* (Leiden and Boston: Brill, 2003).

19. Internationale Erich-Fromm-Gesellschaft, *Die Charaktermauer: Zur Psychoanalyse des Gesellschafts-Charakter in Ost- und Westdeutschland* (Göttingen and Zürich: Vandenhoeck & Ruprecht, 1995); Michael Schmitz, *Wendestress: Die psychosozialen Kosten der deutschen Einheit* (Berlin: Rowohlt, 1995); Detlef Österreich, *Autoritäre Persönlichkeit und Gesellschaftsordnung. Der Stellenwert psychischer Faktoren für politische Einstellungen: Eine empirische Untersuchung von Jugendlichen in Ost und West* (Weinheim: Juventa, 1993); Harry Schröder, "Staatliche Repression und psychische Folgen (DDR-Bürger in der Wende)," *Gruppendynamik* 21 (1990): 341–56.

20. See, for instance, Daphne Berdahl, *Where the World Ended: Re-Unification and Identity in the German Borderland* (Berkeley: University of California Press, 1999); Ralf Schwarzer and Matthias Jerusalem, eds., *Gesellschaftlicher Umbruch als kritisches Lebensereignis. Psychosoziale Krisenbewältigung von Übersiedlern und Ostdeutschen* (Weinheim and Munich: Juventa, 1994); Gisela Trommsdorff, "Psychologische Probleme bei den Transformationsprozessen in Ostdeutschland," in *Psychologische Aspkete des sozio-politischen Wandels in Ostdeutschland,* ed. Gisela Trommsdorff (Berlin and New York: Walter de Gruyter, 1994), 19–42; Dalbert, "Psychisches Wohlbefinden."

21. There are some, however, who have argued that the evidence shows there are no discernible personality differences between eastern and western Germans. See, for instance, Gerhard Schmidtchen, *Wie weit ist der Weg nach Deutschland? Sozialpsychologie der Jugend in der postsozialistischen Welt* (Opladen: Leske + Budrich, 1997).

22. David Clarke, "Representations of the East German Character since Unification," *Debatte* 10 (2002): 51–71; Reißig, *Die gespaltene Vereinigungsgesellschaft,* 63.

23. Thomas Ahbe, "Predigt auf den Marktplätzen oder Das Karussell der psychologisierenden Gesellschaft," *Forum Kritische Psychologie* 30 (1992): 51–74. On looking at the GDR as a petty bourgeois society, see Rudolf Woderich, "Mentalitäten im Land der kleinen Leute," in *Abbruch und Aufbruch: Sozialwissenschaften im Transformationsprozeß—Erfahrungen, Ansätze, Analysen,* ed. Michael Thomas (Berlin: Akademie, 1992), 76–90.

24. Walter Giere, *Schwindel im Kopf: Zur Opfermentalität von Lehrern und Lehrerinnen der ehemaligen DDR* (Wiesbaden: Hessische Landeszentrale für politische Bildung, 1992); Stefan Busse, "Täter, Opfer, Helden—Perspektiven von Schuld," *Forum Kritische Psychologie* 27 (1991): 48–67. On these themes in postwar Germany, see Greg Eghigian, "Der Kalte Krieg im Kopf: Ein Fall von Schizo-

phrenie und die Geschichte des Selbst in der sowjetischen Besatzungszone," *Historische Anthropologie* 11 (2003): 101–22; Robert Moeller, *War Stories: The Search for a Usable Past in the Federal Republic of Germany* (Berkeley: University of California Press, 2001); Elizabeth Heineman, *What Difference Does a Husband Make? Marital Status in Nazi and Postwar Germany* (Berkeley: University of California Press, 1999).

25. Michael R. Marrus, *The Nuremberg War Crimes Trial, 1945–1946: A Documentary History* (Boston and New York: Bedford, 1997); Tony Kushner, *The Holocaust and the Liberal Imagination: A Social and Cultural History* (Oxford and Cambridge, MA: Blackwell, 1994); T. W. Adorno, Else Frenkel-Brunswik, Daniel J. Levinson, and R. Nevitt Sanford, *The Authoritarian Personality* (New York: Harper, 1950).

26. It is no coincidence that many studies make direct reference to the ideas of Ulrich Beck. See, for instance, Ulrich Beck, *Risk Society: Towards a New Modernity* (London: Sage, 1992).

27. Konrad H. Jarausch, "Care and Coercion: The GDR as Welfare Dictatorship," in *Dictatorship as Experience: Towards a Socio-Cultural History of the GDR,* ed. Konrad H. Jarausch (New York and Oxford: Berghahn, 1999), 47–69.

28. Günter Gaus, *Wo Deutschland liegt* (Munich: Deutscher Taschenbuch Verlag, 1983).

29. Heinz Hennig, "Der Mensch im Spannungsfeld zwischen Mangel und Konsum: Psychische Krankheit als Kritik an der Konsumgesellschaft," in *Ossis und Wessis: Psychogramm deutscher Befindlichkeiten [Psychosozial* 59, 18 (1995)], ed. Hans-Jürgen Wirth (Gießen: Psychosozial-Verlag, 1995), 59–70; Irene Misselwitz, "Zur Identität der DDR-Bürger: Eine erste Gedankensammlung," in *Abschied von der DDR,* ed. Keupp and Wirth, 31–33; Winfried Hammann, "Die Mentalitätsdifferenz zwischen Ost- und Westdeutschen," in *Abschied von der DDR,* ed. Keupp and Wirth, 51–57.

30. See, for instance, Wagner, "'Deutscher, proletarischer und moralischer'"; Woderich, "Mentalitäten im Land der kleinen Leute"; Thomas Koch, "'Hier ändert sich nie was!' Kontinuitäten, Krisen und Brüche ostdeutscher Identität(en) im Spannungsfeld zwischen 'schöpferischer Zerstörung' und nationaler Re-Integration," in *Abbruch und Aufbruch,* ed. Thomas, 319–34.

31. See, for instance, the essays on youth and leisure in Günter Burkart, ed., *Sozialisation im Sozialismus: Lebensbedingungen in der DDR im Umbruch,* special issue *of Zeitschrift für Sozialisationsforschung und Erziehungssoziologie* (Weinheim: Juventa, 1990).

32. Anna Krylova, "The Tenacious Liberal Subject in Soviet Studies," *Kritika* 1 (2000): 119–46; Mikhail Geller, *A Cog and the Wheel: The Development of Homo Sovieticus* (New York: Knopf, 1988); Aleksander Zinoviev, *Homo Sovieticus* (Boston: Atlantic Monthly Press, 1985).

33. I wish to thank Daniel Berman for his thoughts and suggestions on the various meanings of the term *munitus.*

34. Ingrid M. Schenk, "Scarcity and Success: The East According to the West during the 1950s," in *Pain and Prosperity: Reconsidering Twentieth-Century Ger-

man History, ed. Paul Betts and Greg Eghigian (Stanford: Stanford University Press, 2003), 160–77.

35. David Clarke, for example, blames neoliberalism for stereotypes about East German character. See Clarke, "Representations."

36. Michel Foucault, *Discipline and Punish: The Birth of the Prison* (New York: Vintage, 1995) and *The History of Sexuality: An Introduction, Vol. 1* (New York: Vintage, 1990).

37. Michael Lemke, "Foreign Influences on the Dictatorial Development of the GDR, 1949–1955," in *Dictatorship as Experience: Towards a Social-Cultural History of the GDR,* ed. Konrad H. Jarausch (New York and Oxford: Berghahn, 1999), 91–107; Eric D. Weitz, *Creating German Communism, 1890–1990* (Princeton: Princeton University Press, 1997), 311–56.

38. Klaus Schroeder, *Der SED-Staat: Partei, Staat, und Gesellschaft, 1949–1990* (Munich: Carl Hanser, 1998), 115–19.

39. Raymond G. Stokes, *Constructing Socialism: Technology and Change in East Germany, 1945–1990* (Baltimore and London: Johns Hopkins University Press, 2000), 37.

40. Manfred Bierwisch, "Wissenschaft im realen Sozialismus," *Kursbuch* 101 (1990): 112–23; Peter Altner and Günter Kröber, eds., *KPD und Wissenschaftsentwicklung, 1919–1945* (Berlin: Dietz, 1986).

41. Hansgünter Meyer, "Wissenschaftspolitik, Intelligenzpolitik: Das Personal für Wissenschaft, Forschung, und Technik in der DDR," in *Intelligenz, Wissenschaft, und Forschung in der DDR,* ed. Hansgünter Meyer (Berlin and New York: Walter de Gruyter, 1990), 1–51.

42. Gerhard Kosel, *Produktivkraft Wissenschaft* (Berlin: Verlag Die Wirtschaft, 1957).

43. Greg Eghigian, "Was There a Communist Psychiatry? Politics and East German Psychiatric Care, 1945–1989," *Harvard Review of Psychiatry* 10 (2002): 364–68; Anna-Sabine Ernst, *"Die beste Prophylaxis ist der Sozialismus": Ärzte und medizinische Hochschullehrer in der SBZ/DDR, 1945–1961* (Münster and New York: Waxmann, 1997); Monika Renneberg and Mark Walker, eds., *Science, Technology, and National Socialism* (Cambridge and New York: Cambridge University Press, 1994).

44. Mitchell G. Ash, "Verordnete Umbrüche—Konstruierte Kontinuitäten: Zur Entnazifizierung von Wissenschaftlern und Wissenschaften nach 1945," *Zeitschrift für Geschichtswissenschaft* 43 (1995): 903–23; Meyer, "Wissenschaftspolitik," 16.

45. Andreas Malycha, "Frost nach dem Tauwetter: Wissenschaft und Politik in der DDR in den fünfziger Jahren," *Deutschland Archiv* 35 (2002): 237–52; Mitchell G. Ash, "Wissenschaft, Politik, und Modernität in der DDR: Ansätze zu einer Neubetrachtung," in *Wissenschaft und Politik: Genetik und Humangenetik in der DDR (1949–1989),* ed. Karin Weismann, Peter Kröner, and Richard Toellner (Münster: LIT, 1997), 1–25; Hubert Laitko, "Wissenschaftspolitik," in *Die SED— Geschichte—Organisation—Politik: Ein Handbuch,* ed. Andreas Herbst, Gerd-Rüdiger Stephan, and Jürgen Winkler (Berlin: Dietz, 1997), 405–20.

46. Corey Ross, *Constructing Socialism at the Grass-Roots: The Transformation of East Germany, 1945–1965* (New York: St. Martin's Press, 2000).

47. Bundesarchiv Berlin Lichterfelde (hereafter BArch), DP1, VA/5873, Bezirksgericht Suhl in Meiningen, 2. Strafsenat, Strafsache gegen F. B., Beschluß, 4 February 1959; B. Gertig and R. Schädlich, *Lehrbuch für Kriminalisten: Die allgemeinen Verfahren und Arbeitsmethoden der Kriminalistik* (Berlin: Verlag für Fachliteratur der Volkspolizei, 1955), 3; Heinz Hoffmann, "Entscheidend ist das politische Bewußtsein," *Die Volkspolizei* 3 (1950): 2–3.

48. John Rodden, *Repainting the Little Red School House: A History of Eastern German Education, 1945–1995* (New York: Oxford University Press, 2002), 44–110.

49. Gesine Obertreis, *Familienpolitik in der DDR 1945–1980* (Opladen: Leske Verlag & Budrich, 1986), 48–88, 140–70.

50. Anna-Sabine Ernst, "Vom 'Du' zum 'Sie': Die Rezeption der bürgerlichen Anstandsregeln in der DDR der 1950er Jahre," *Mitteilungen aus der kulturwissenschaftlichen Forschung* 16, no. 33 (1993): 190–209.

51. On the idea of the "coproduction" of knowledge, politics, and the social order, see Sheila Jasanoff, "Beyond Epistemology: Relativism and Engagement in the Politics of Science," *Social Studies of Science* 26 (1996): 393–418.

52. Edward Ross Dickinson, *The Politics of German Child Welfare from the Empire to the Federal Republic* (Cambridge, MA: Harvard University Press, 1996); Marcus Gräser, *Der blockierte Wohlfahrtsstaat: Unterschichtsjugend und Jugendfürsorge in der Weimarer Republik* (Göttingen: Vandenhoeck & Ruprecht, 1995); Elizabeth Harvey, *Youth and the Welfare State in Weimar Germany* (Oxford: Oxford University Press, 1993); Detlev Peukert, *Grenzen der Sozialdisziplinierung: Aufstieg und Krise der deutschen Jugendfürsorge von 1878 bis 1932* (Cologne: Bundverlag, 1986).

53. Karl S. Bader, *Soziologie der deutschen Nachkriegskriminalität* (Tübingen: J. C. B. Mohr, 1949).

54. Landesarchiv Berlin (hereafter LAB), C Rep. 118, Nr. 116, Dr. Käte Busch, "Stellungnahme zu dem von Herrn Staubesand dem Magistrat Berlin eingereichten Vorschlag," 24 February 1946, 68–70.

55. LAB, C Rep. 118, Nr. 710, Dr. med. Gräfe, "Organisation der Fürsorge für jugendliche Psychopathen," Organisation der Geisteskranken- und Psychopathen-Fürsorge und ihre Therapie, 22–23 November 1946, 378–82, and Dr. H. W. Janz, "Psychopathologische Erfahrungen aus der Kriegs- und Nachkriegszeit," 22–23 November 1946, 398–414; LAB, C Rep. 118, Nr. 116, Paul Strehl an Geschke und Jendretzky, 24 September 1945, 1.

56. BArch, DQ 1/5574, Bericht der Beratungsstelle für Nerven- und Gemütskranke des Gesundheitsamtes Weißensee bez. der Reihenuntersuchungen in der 8. Grundschule Berlin-Malchow, 16 January 1952.

57. BArch, DQ 1/5574, Gotsche, Stellvertreter des Ministerpräsidenten, Sekretariat Ulbricht an Minister für Gesundheit Steidle, 6 June 1952.

58. BArch, DQ 1/5574, "Denkschrift überreicht von den 8. Beratungsstelle für Nerven- und Gemütskranke der Gesundheitsämter/Bezirksämter von Groß-Berlin" an Magistrat von Groß-Berlin, Abt. Gesundheitswesen, 17 November 1952.

59. BArch, DQ 1/5574, Dr. Anne-Marie Schnell an Walter Ulbricht, 1 June 1953.

60. Space does not permit me to discuss these examples at length, but records of the Health and Social Welfare Department of the city of Berlin and of the national Ministry of Health do reveal a similar story.

61. Peter Skyba, *Vom Hoffnungsträger zum Sicherheitsrisiko: Jugend in der DDR und Jugendpolitik der SED, 1949–1961* (Cologne: Böhlau, 2000), 61.

62. On seeing politics and ideology as resources, see Mitchell G. Ash, "Wissenschaftswandel in Zeiten politischer Umwälzungen: Entwicklungen, Verwicklungen, Abwicklungen," *NTM: Internationale Zeitschrift für Geschichte und Ethik der Naturwissenschaften, Technik, und Medizin* 3 (1995): 1–21.

63. Richard Bessel and Dirk Schumann, eds., *Life after Death: Approaches to a Cultural and Social History of Europe during the 1940s and 1950s* (New York: Cambridge University Press, 2003).

64. Svenja Goltermann, "Psychisches Leid und herrschende Lehre: Der Wissenschaftswandel in der westdeutschen Psychiatrie der Nachkriegszeit," in *Akademische Vergangenheitspolitik: Beiträge zur Wissenschaftskultur der Nachkriegszeit*, ed. Bernd Weisbrod (Göttingen: Wallstein, 2002), 263–80, and "Verletzte Körper oder 'Building National Bodies': Kriegsheimkehrer, 'Krankheit,' und Psychiatrie in der westdeutschen Nachkriegsgesellschaft, 1945–1955," *WerkstattGeschichte* 24 (1999): 83–98; Frank Biess, "Survivors of Totalitarianism: Returning POWs and the Reconstruction of Masculine Citizenship in West Germany, 1945–1955," in *The Miracle Years: A Cultural History of West Germany, 1949–1968*, ed. Hanna Schissler (Princeton and Oxford: Princeton University Press, 2001), 57–82.

65. Dietfried Müller-Hegemann, *Zur Psychologie des deutschen Faschisten* (Rudolstadt: Greifenverlag, 1955).

66. Konstantin Ivanov, "Science after Stalin: Forging a New Image of Soviet Science," *Science in Context* 15 (2002): 317–38; quote is from 318.

67. Monika Kaiser, "Reforming Socialism? The Changing of the Guard from Ulbricht to Honecker during the 1960s," in *Dictatorship as Experience*, ed. Jarausch, 325–39; Mitchell G. Ash, "Wissenschaft, Politik, und Modernität in der DDR: Ansätze zu einer Neubetrachtung," in *Wissenschaft und Politik: Genetik und Humangenetik in der DDR, 1949–1989*, ed. Karin Weisemann, Peter Kröner, and Richard Toellner (Münster: Lit, 1997), 1–25; Jeffrey Kopstein, "Ulbricht Embattled: The Quest for Socialist Modernity in the Light of New Sources," *Europe-Asia Studies* 46 (1994): 597–615; Jörg Roesler, "Die Wirtschaftsreform der DDR in den sechziger Jahren: Einstieg, Entwicklungsprobleme, und Abbruch," *Zeitschrift für Geschichtswissenschaft* 38 (1990): 979–1003.

68. Peter Christian Ludz, "Soziologie und empirische Sozialforschung in der DDR," in *Studien und Materialien zur Soziologie der DDR* (Sonderheft 8 Kölner Zeitschrift für Soziologie und Sozialpsychologie), ed. Peter Christian Ludz (Cologne and Opladen: Westdeutscher Verlag, 1964), 327–418; quote is from 337.

69. Ibid.

70. Ina Merkel, *Utopie und Bedürfnis: Die Geschichte der Konsumkultur in der DDR* (Cologne: Böhlau, 1999), 133–50; Heinz Niemann, *Hinterm Zaun. Politische*

Kultur und Meinungsforschung in der DDR: Die geheimen Berichte an das Politbüro der SED (Berlin: Edition Ost, 1995); Horst Laatz, *Klassenstruktur und soziales Verhalten: Zur Entstehung der empirischen Sozialstrukturforschung in der DDR* (Cologne: Wissenschaft und Politik, 1990). Quote is from Laatz, *Klassenstruktur,* 13.

71. David Joravsky, *Russian Psychology: A Critical History* (Oxford and Cambridge: Basil Blackwell, 1989), 445–63; Manfred Thielen, *Sowjetische Psychologie und Marxismus: Geschichte und Kritik* (Frankfurt a.M. and New York: Campus, 1984), 153–76.

72. Stefan Busse, "'Von der Sowjetwissenschaft lernen': Pawlowismus und Psychologie," *Psychologie und Geschichte* 8 (1998): 150–73.

73. Joachim Siebenbrodt, ed., *Bericht über den 2. Kongreß der Gesellschaft für Psychologie in der DDR* (Berlin: Deutscher Verlag der Wissenschaften, 1969); Vorstand der Gesellschaft für Psychologie in der DDR, ed., *Psychologie als gesellschaftliche Produktivkraft: Bericht über den 1. Kongreß der Gesellschaft für Psychologie in der DDR vom 21.–23. Mai 1964 in Dresden* (Berlin: Deutscher Verlag der Wissenschaften, 1965).

74. Uta G. Poiger, *Jazz, Rock, and Rebels: Cold War Politics and American Culture in a Divided Germany* (Berkeley: University of California Press, 2000); Skyba, *Vom Hoffnungsträger;* Dorthee Wierling, "Die Jugend als innerer Feind: Konflikte in der Erziehungsdiktatur der sechziger Jahre," in *Sozialgeschichte der DDR,* ed. Hartmut Kaelble, Jürgen Kocka, and Hartmut Zwahr (Stuttgart: Klett-Cotta, 1994), 404–25.

75. Gerrit Bratke, *Die Kriminologie in der Deutschen Demokratischen Republik und ihre Anwendung im Bereich der Jugenddelinquenz: Eine zeitgeschichtlich-kriminologische Untersuchung* (Münster: Lit, 1999), 36, 116–25. As Thomas Lindenberger points out, *Rowdytum* was seen as the chief problem in this regard. See his pioneering work on the subject in *Volkspolizei: Herrschaftspraxis und öffentliche Ordnung im SED-Staat, 1952–1968* (Cologne, Weimar, and Vienna: Böhlau, 2003), 367–443.

76. Dorothee Wierling, "Über die Liebe zum Staat—der Fall der DDR," *Historische Anthropologie* 8 (2000): 236–63.

77. Kitty Dumont, *Die Sozialpsychologie der DDR: Eine wissenschaftshistorische Untersuchung* (Frankfurt a.M.: Peter Lang, 1999), 77–129.

78. Hans-Dieter Schmidt, *Allgemeine Entwicklungspsychologie* (Berlin: Deutscher Verlag der Wissenschaften, 1970).

79. Hans-Dieter Schmidt, "Erziehungsbedingungen in der DDR: Offizielle Programme, individuelle Praxis, und die Rolle der Pädagogischen Psychologie und Entwicklungspsychologie," in *Sozialisation und Entwicklung von Kindern vor und nach der Vereinigung,* ed. Gisela Trommsdorff (Opladen: Leske + Budrich, 1996), 15–171, esp. 128–30.

80. Before this, the term had been used mostly by Marxist-Leninist philosophers and party ideologues. On the history of the concept of personality in general, see Giovanni Pietro Lombardo and Renato Foschi, "The Concept of Personality in 19th-Century French and 20th-Century American Psychology," *History of Psychology* 6 (2001): 123–42; David G. Winter and Nicole B. Barenbaum, "History of

Modern Personality Theory and Research," in *Handbook of Personality: Theory and Research*, ed. Lawrence A. Pervin and Oliver P. John (New York and London: Guilford Press,1999), 3–27.

81. Karl-Heinz Günther, "Begrüßungsansprache," in *Psychologische Probleme der Entwicklung sozialistischer Persönlichkeiten*, ed. Akademie der Pädagogischen Wissenschaften der DDR and Akademie der Pädagogischen Wissenschaften der UdSSR (Berlin: Volk und Wissen, 1972), 9.

82. Horst Laatz, "Vom Klassenkampf zur individuellen Wertorientierung: Zur Entwicklung der soziologischen Frauenforschung in der DDR von 1960 bis 1980," in *Qualifikationsprozesse und Arbeitssituation von Frauen in der Bundesrepublik Deutschland und in der DDR*, ed. Dieter Voigt (Berlin: Duncker & Humblot, 1989), 175–200.

83. Gunilla-Friederike Budde, "'Tüchtige Traktoristinnen' und 'schicke Stenotypistinnen': Frauenbilder in den deutschen Nachkriegsgesellschaften—Tendenzen der 'Sowjetisierung' und 'Amerikanisierung'?" in *Amerikanisierung und Sowjetisierung in Deutschland 1945–1970*, ed. Konrad Jarausch and Hannes Siegrist (Frankfurt and New York: Campus, 1997), 243–73; Irene Dölling, "Gespaltenes Bewußtsein—Frauen- und Männerbilder in der DDR," in *Frauen in Deutschland 1945–1992*, ed. Gisela Helwig and Hildegard Maria Nickel (Berlin: Akademie, 1993), 23–52.

84. Gunilla-Friederike Budde, "Women's Policies in the GDR in the 1960s/1970s: Between State Control and Societal Reaction," in *State Policy and Gender System in the Two German States and Sweden, 1945–1989*, ed. Rolf Torstendahl (Uppsala: Uppsala University, 1999), 199–217.

85. Susanne Diemer, *Patriarchalismus in der DDR: Strukturelle, kulturelle, und subjektive Dimensionen der Geschlechterpolarisierung* (Opladen: Leske & Budrich, 1994), 58–72. As Budde points out, however, even during this phase of activism in East German women's policy, women continued to be seen as categorically different from men as physical and reproductive beings. See Gunilla-Friederike Budde, "Der Körper der 'sozialistischen Frauenpersönlichkeit': Weiblichkeits-Vorstellungen in der SBZ und frühen DDR," *Geschichte und Gesellschaft* 26 (2000): 602–28.

86. Hans-Dieter Schmidt, "Erziehungsbedingungen in der DDR"; Adolf Kossakowski, "Die pädagogische Psychologie der DDR im Spannungsfeld zwischen kindorientierter Forschung und bildungspolitischen Forderungen," in *Pädagogik in der DDR*, ed. Ernst Cloer and Rolf Wernstedt (Weinheim: Deutscher Studien Verlag, 1994), 205–18; Harry Dettenborn and Hans-H. Fröhlich, *Psychologische Probleme der Täterpersönlichkeit* (Berlin: Deutscher Verlag der Wissenschaften, 1971).

87. Christian Rode, *Kriminologie in der DDR* (Freiburg i.B.: Max-Planck-Institut für ausländisches und internationales Strafrecht,1996), 25–74.

88. "Symposion über aktuelle Fragen der Gerichtspsychiatrie in der Charité, Berlin, am 8. und 9. März 1963," *Psychiatrie, Neurologie, und medizinische Psychologie* 16 (1964): 120–25.

89. Heinz Blüthner, *Die soziale und kriminelle Gefährdung sowie die darin eingeschlossenen asozialen Verhaltensweisen und ihre Überwindung im Prozeß der*

Kriminalitätsbekämpfung und -vorbeugung (Potsdam-Babelsberg: Deutsche Akademie für Staats- und Rechtswissenschaft "Walter Ulbricht," 1970).

90. Hans Szewczyk, "Die künftigen Aufgaben des Psychiaters in der Rechtspflege," in *Die Gerichtspsychiatrie in der neuen Rechtspflege,* ed. Hans Szewczyk (Jena: Gustav Fischer, 1964), 23–36.

91. Hans Szewczyk, "Die Begutachtung der Zurechnungsfähigkeit," *in Die Begutachtung und Behandlung erwachsener und jugendlicher Täter,* ed. Hans Szewczyk (Jena: Gustav Fischer, 1966), 29–64.

92. BArch, DQ 1/6033, Ministerium für Gesundheit, Abt. Sozialwesen, Richter. "Die Durchführung von Aufgaben der Gefährdeten-Fürsorge auf dem Gebiete des Sozialwesens," 9 June 1966. The percentage of female residents previously convicted of a crime also declined, from 70 percent to 45 percent, during this time.

93. BArch, DQ 1/6033, Hans Richter, Ministerium für Gesundheit, Abt. Sozialwesen, 24 August 1966; Hans Szewczyk, "Zur Frage der Prophylaxe, Forschung, Erziehung, Behandlung, und Rehabilitation von gefährdeten, fehlentwickelten, und kriminellen Jugendlichen," 16 May 1966.

94. Brandenburgisches Landeshauptarchiv (hereafter BLHA), Rep. 601, Nr. 2653, Gemeinsame Beratung über weitere Maßnahmen der Bekämpfung von Asozialität und debilen Personen, 6 June 1973. For more on this episode, see Sonja Süß, *Politisch mißbraucht? Psychiatrie und Staatssicherheit in der DDR* (Berlin: Ch. Links, 1999), 523–34.

95. Jens Gieselke, *Mielke-Konzern: Die Geschichte der Stasi, 1945–1990* (Stuttgart and Munich: Deutsche Verlags-Anstalt, 2001), 72–73. The number of those working for the Stasi rose from 20,000 in 1961 to 81,500 in 1982.

96. Matthias Wanitschke, *Methoden und Menschenbild des Ministeriums für Staatssicherheit der DDR* (Cologne: Böhlau, 2001), 187–88.

97. Sandra Pingel-Schliemann, *Zersetzen: Strategie einer Diktatur* (Berlin: Robert-Havemann-Gesellschaft, 2003); Jörn Mothes, Gundula Fienbork, Rudi Pahnke, Renate Ellmenreich, and Michael Stognienko, eds., *Beschädigte Seelen: DDR-Jugend und Staatssicherheit* (Bremen: Edition Temmen, 1996); Klaus Behnke and Jürgen Fuchs, eds., *Zersetzung der Seele: Psychologie und Psychiatrie im Dienste der Stasi* (Hamburg: Rotbuch, 1995).

98. Sebastian Pfau and Burkhard Raue, "Sozialistisches Menschenbild und Familienleitbilder in der DDR: Traum vom neuen Menschen," www.ddr-fernsehen.de/8familienserien/familienleitbilder.pdf.

99. Dorothee Wierling, "Das weiblich-proletarische Tüchtigkeitsideal der DDR," in *Arbeiter in der SBZ-DDR,* ed. Peter Hübner and Klaus Tenfelde (Essen: Klartext, 1999), 831–48; Diemer, *Patriarchalismus,* 72–82.

100. Gunilla-Friederike Budde, "Heldinnen der Arbeit: Öffentliche Fremd- und Selbstdarstellungen von Arbeiterinnen in der DDR der 50er und 60er Jahre," in *Arbeiter in der SBZ-DDR,* ed. Hübner and Tenfelde, 849–66.

101. See, for instance, in the case of women, Donna Harsch, "Society, the State, and Abortion in East Germany, 1950–1972," *American Historical Review* 102 (1997): 53–84; Laatz, "Vom Klassenkampf."

102. Wilfried Reuter, *Militärpsychologie in der DDR* (Herbolzheim: Centaurus, 2000), 23–35.

103. Bundesarchiv-Militärarchiv Freiburg (hereafter BAM), VA-01/39851, Bernd-Joachim Gestewitz, "Zur Erkennung, Behandlung, und militärmedizinischen Begutachtung selbstmordgefährdeter Armeeangehöriger," PhD diss., Wissenschaftlicher Rat der Ernst-Moritz-Arndt Universität Greifswald, 1978.

104. BAM, VA-01/40202, Marlen Schneider, "Zur Persönlichkeit von Fremdkörperschluckern im Straf- und Untersuchungshaftvollzug aus klinisch-psychologischer Sicht," PhD diss., Wissenschaftlicher Rat der Militärmedizinischen Akademie, 1987; BAM, VA-01/39985, Bernd Koppatz, "Die Häufigkeit neurologisch-psychiatrischen Erkrankungen und Störungen bei Wehrpflichtigen in einem Motor-Schützenregiment unter besonderer Berücksichtigung der psycho-vegetativen Syndrome," PhD diss., Wissenschaftlicher Rat der Militärmedizinischen Akademie, 1982; BAM, VA-01/40253–54, Maria Louise-Stoll, "Auswahl Psycho-Diagnostischer Methoden zur Ermittlung der Eignung von PALR-Schützen," PhD diss., Wissenschaftlicher Rat der Ernst-Moritz-Arndt Universität Greifswald, 1975.

105. BAM, VA-01/40093, Ernst Peper, "Untersuchungen zur Einführung der Psychotherapie in die medizinische Betreuung des fliegenden Personals der Nationalen Volksarmee und der Grenztruppen der DDR," PhD diss., Wissenschaftlicher Rat der Militärmedizinischen Akademie, 1988.

106. Dagmar Pietsch, "Motivation des Wehrdienstes," in *Rührt Euch! Zur Geschichte der Nationalen Volksarmee der DDR,* ed. Wolfgang Wünsche (Berlin: Edition Ost, 1998), 391–411.

107. Jarausch, "Care and Coercion," 59.

108. The ways in which distinctions between "soft" and "hard" lines were recognized as such by East Germans in the GDR is something largely neglected in present-day debates over the extent to which East Germany was a "soft" or "subtle" form of totalitarianism. On the notion of the GDR as "soft" or "subtle" totalitarianism, see Pingel-Schliemann, *Zersetzen;* Hubertus Knabe, "'Weiche' Formen der Verfolgung in der DDR: Zum Wandel der repressiven Strategien in der Ära Honecker," *Deutschland Archiv* 30 (1997): 709–19; Clemens Vollnhals, "Das Ministerium für Staatssicherheit: Ein Instrument totalitärer Herrschaftsausübung," in *Sozialgeschichte der DDR,* ed. Kaelble, Kocka, and Zwahr , 498–518.

109. BArch, DP 3/1194, Generalstaatsanwaltschaft, Abt. Jugendkriminalität an Ministerium für Gesundheitswesen, 24 June 1974; Joachim Schlegel, "Zu Problemen der wirksamen Bekämpfung von vorsätzlichen Körperverletzungen, Rowdytum, und gewaltsamen Sexualdelikten," *Neue Justiz* 26 (1972): 663–69; Siegfried Wittenbeck, "Strafzumessung bei gewaltsamen begangenen Sexualdelikten," *Neue Justiz* 26 (1972): 684–87, and "Probleme der Strafzumessung," *Neue Justiz* 23 (1969): 264–71.

110. See, for instance, Gerhard Feix, *Die Bekämpfung von Sexualverbrechen an Kindern* (Berlin: Verlag des Ministeriums des Innern, 1961).

111. Heinz Ulrich, "Die Sexualdelikte des älteren Mannes," in *Kriminalität der Frau—Alterskriminalität—Psychiatrische Begutachtungsfragen im Zivilrecht,* ed.

Hanns Schwarz (Jena: Gustav Fischer, 1971), 87–91; Hans Szewczyk and Ingrid Dreschler, "Untersuchungen von Alterssittlichkeitstätern," in *Kriminalität der Frau*, ed. Schwarz, 93–100; F. Barylla, "Zur Klinik und forensischen Psychiatrie der Pädophilie," *Psychiatrie, Neurologie, und medizinische Psychologie* 17 (1965): 217–21.

112. Lothar and Helga Sprung, "Geschichte der Psychodiagnostik in der Deutschen Demokratischen Republik—Ausbildung, Weiterbildung, Forschung, Praxis," *Psychologie und Geschichte* 7 (1995): 115–40.

113. Eckhard Littmann, "Zur Persönlichkeitsstruktur forensisch begutachteter Sexualstraftäter," in *Kriminalpsychologie und Kriminalpsychopathologie*, ed. Heide-Ulrike Jähnig and Eckhard Littmann (Jena: Gustav Fischer, 1985), 147–65; Heide-Ulrike Jähnig, "Psychiatrische Beiträge bei der Ermittlung von Sexualdelikten," in *Kriminalpsychologie*, ed. Jähnig and Littmann, 130–46; Eckhard Littmann, "Ergebnisse psychodiagnostischer Untersuchungen forensisch-psychologisch und -psychiatrisch begutachteter Straftäter," *Psychiatrie, Neurologie, und medizinische Psychologie* 33 (1981): 734–43.

114. Michael Heim and Joachim Morgner, "Der pädophile Straftäter," *Psychiatrie, Neurologie, und medizinische Psychologie* 37 (1985): 107–12; H.-H. Fröhlich, "Die Sexualkriminalität im Blickwinkel menschlicher Sexualität und sexueller Norm," *Kriminalitstik und forensische Wissenschaften* 41 (1980): 43–54; J. Morgner, "Exhibitionistische sexuelle Fehlentwicklungen," *Kriminalistik und forensische Wissenschaften* 30 (1977): 105–8. Quote is from Morgner, "Exhibitionistische," 105.

115. Stephen Kotkin, *Magnetic Mountain: Stalinism as a Civilization* (Berkeley: University of California Press, 1995).

116. See Greg Eghigian, Andreas Killen, and Christine Leuenberger, eds., *The Self as Project: Politics and the Human Sciences in the Twentieth Century*. Vol. 22, *Osiris* (Chicago: University of Chicago Press, 2007).

117. Christine Leuenberger, "Constructions of the Berlin Wall: How Material Culture Is Used in Psychological Theory," *Social Problems* 53 (2006): 18–37.

118. I wish to thank Moritz Föllmer and Rüdiger Graf for raising this issue with me.

119. Albrecht Göschel, *Kontrast und Parallele—Kulturelle und politische Identitätsbildung ostdeutscher Generationen* (Stuttgart, Berlin, and Cologne: W. Kohlhammer, 1999). This appears to have been the case throughout Eastern Europe. See Katherine Verdery, *What Was Socialism and What Comes Next?* (Princeton: Princeton University Press, 1996), 61–82.

East Germany's Sexual Evolution

Dagmar Herzog

There was no sexual revolution in East Germany. Unlike West Germany, where the mid- to late 1960s saw a liberalization of the social and cultural landscape so dramatic that to many observers it seemed as though it had happened virtually overnight, East Germany experienced a far more gradual evolution of sexual mores. By the late 1960s, West Germany had been inundated by the commodification of sex in every facet of existence—from highly sexualized advertising to easily available hard-core pornography, from a constant stream of news reportage about sexual matters to sex enlightenment films and curricula and a culturewide discussion of nudity, adultery, and group sex. Market-driven voyeurism had become an inescapable part of everyday life in the West. By contrast—and although East Germany entered a period of sexual conservatism in the 1950s and the first half of the 1960s in many respects comparable to the sexual conservatism of West Germany in those years—there were already in the 1950s notable elements of liberality in East Germany that had no parallel in West Germany. These early liberal aspects of East German culture would have a decisive impact on the subsequent trajectory of sexual politics in the decades that followed.

In what did this liberality consist? One major difference between East and West Germany in the 1950s was not so much the extent of female labor force participation, although it was indeed somewhat higher in the East (since also in the West women worked outside the home to supplement the family's income while in the East there were still numerous women, especially in the older generations, who were solely housewives). Rather, the difference lay in the combination of institutional structures and strong rhetorical support in the East, which made women's work for wages not only possible but also much less guilt inducing. The double burden of

71

work for wages and household chores (or rather triple burden, if one added the demands of political participation in party- or workplace-linked organizations) did cause East German women in the course of the 1950s to retreat to more part-time work. But there is no question that the psychological misery induced in so many West German women in the 1950s (and also later) by the idealization of faithful, home-bound femininity and self-sacrificing wifehood and motherhood was much less evident in the East. East German women were continually told that they should improve and develop themselves through further studies, and men were enjoined to support this. Indeed, already in the 1950s, East German men were expressly encouraged to participate in housework and child rearing, a suggestion unthinkable in 1950s West Germany (where the message from the government and popular magazines alike was that a wife's whole purpose was to create a warm and nurturing home for her husband and children and to tend to her husband's little psychic wounds after his stressful day feeling underappreciated at work). The idea that a man might be the househusband and care for the baby and assist his wife through her studies was familiar enough in the East already in the mid-1950s that one author approvingly noted the phenomenon had become so prevalent a part of the landscape that one could "already recognize a certain type."[1]

Beyond these economic and social factors, there were also the Socialist Unity Party (SED) regime's clear stances in defense of both premarital heterosexual activity and unwed motherhood. West Germany too had technically abolished legal discrimination against illegitimate children. But in the East, a push to end social discrimination and the culture of shame surrounding illegitimacy was a genuine government objective. In the West, by contrast, with its officially Christianized political culture under Christian Democratic Union (CDU) auspices, shaming was standard. Moreover, although in West and East Germany alike premarital heterosexual intercourse was practiced by a large majority of the population, West Germany in the 1950s and early 1960s saw a major campaign against premarital sex. This campaign was not only promoted by the Protestant and Catholic churches through sermons and sex advice tracts running into millions of copies. Christian perspectives also informed government policy, teacher education, and school curricula, and popular West German magazines too reinforced the idea that good girls did not permit premarital sex and that a gentlemanly young man should respect this. Girls were told that, if a boy really loved them, he would wait until the wedding day; the idea that girls might have desires of their own was simply not considered. Far from being a trivial matter, the postwar Western campaign to clean up German sexual mores was a core element in securing West German Christianity's antifascist moral authority, for during the Third Reich sexual matters had formed a main focus of conflict between the Nazis and the Catholic Church in particular and Nazis had continually ridiculed Christian prudery and opposition to premarital heterosexuality.

In the officially secularized East, by contrast, sex was not a main site for managing the legacies of Nazism because the East secured its antifascist status above all by emphasizing its anticapitalism. While fully aware of Nazism's encouragements to premarital sexual activity, the SED felt no particular need to break with this legacy, since it was congruent with popular values, which simply saw sex as the customary way to express love.[2] Instead, the main concern in the East was to show citizens that socialism provided the best conditions for lasting and happy love. (In fact, Eastern authors frequently pointed out that sexual relationships really were more love based and hence honorable in the East than in the West specifically because under socialism women did not need to "sell" themselves into marriage in order to support themselves.) In the East, discussion of sex was seen not so much as a means for mastering the past but rather as a means for orienting people toward the future—a future that was declared to be always already in the making and that required all citizens' engaged participation. Socialism, it was constantly stressed, was steadily en route to perfection. And no sex advice text in the East was complete without reference either to the idea that only socialism provided the context for the most loving and satisfying marriages or to the notion that a couple's commitment to and struggle on behalf of socialism would enhance their romantic relationship.

While a number of East German doctors in the 1950s and 1960s counseled against premarital sex and/or cautioned that the East German government's support for illegitimate children should not be interpreted as direct encouragement to bear children out of wedlock, the overwhelming message from the government and from advice writers was that premarital heterosexual activity was both natural and normal. Medical doctor Hanns Schwarz, for example, in an SED-sponsored sex advice lecture delivered more than forty times throughout the East between 1952 and 1959 (and circulated in hundreds of thousands of copies), criticized promiscuity but otherwise energetically endorsed premarital sex and rejected "moralistic preachments" against it. "Sensuality," he told his listeners, "can be something glorious and positive" and should not be "branded as a sin by uptight people [*Mucker*]." All that mattered, according to Schwarz (as he revealed his heteronormativity), was that this sensual activity should occur between "two people of the opposite sex who in addition to physical attraction to each other are emotionally entwined, have similar ways of looking at the world and have shared interests."[3] And in a book published in 1959, Schwarz again described sex as "the quintessence of being alive." Moreover, unlike more conservative East German writers who unreflectingly collapsed intercourse with reproduction, Schwarz declared forthrightly that "we as free people know that intercourse does not just serve the propagation of the human race, but also furthers pleasure very significantly."[4] A similar message was communicated by the medical doctor Rudolf Neubert's *Das neue Ehebuch* (The New Marriage Book), the single most popular East German advice book in the late fifties and early sixties. Although Neubert thought it advisable for teenagers between the ages of fourteen and eighteen to avoid "regular [*regelmässigen*] intercourse" (even as he was rather unclear what he meant by "regular"), he was completely in favor of premarital intercourse for the nineteen-to-twenty-five-year-old set. "No one," he announced confidently, "will take moral offense if these matured people also love each other in the bodily sense." And this generosity extended also to nonmarital pregnancies. In Neubert's opinion, there was no need to rush into marriage. For as long as the child was "conceived and received in love, it is completely irrelevant when the parents marry."[5]

By the early 1960s, a government statement formalized the view that love made premarital sex permissible. The SED's memorandum on youth (*Jugendkommuniqué*) formulated in 1963 stated that "every true love between two young people deserves candid respect" and implicitly instructed parents and grandparents that they should be understanding of young couples' loving relationships also when these turned sexual. The German Democratic Republic's (GDR) gender egalitarianism and practice of coeducation, together with the incontrovertible fact that young people were simply experiencing puberty at an earlier age than previous generations had, it was held, made support for young love both sensible *and* ethical. The "morality of the convent" was anathema; "prohibitions, prudery, secrecy and punishment" were inappropriate. Romantic happiness was inspiring and life enhancing. "True love belongs to youth the way youth belongs to socialism," the memorandum announced, and "To be socialist is to help young people toward life-happiness and not to create tragedies." At the same time, the memorandum emphasized, the government was definitely not advocating indiscriminate sexual experimentation. Love relationships, it advised, should be "deep" (*tief*) and "clean" (*sauber*).[6]

Yet despite the SED's consistent commitment to female economic independence and professional advancement and despite its apparent acceptance of premarital heterosexual intercourse, the GDR in the 1950s and 1960s also developed a distinctively socialist and in many ways quite oppressive brand of sexual conservatism. What needs to be grasped, in short, as the 1963 memorandum's language already implies, is the double quality of the messages sent about sex in the 1950s and 1960s. There was in numerous texts, in all the sympathy expressed for the inevitability of pre- marital sex, nonetheless a strongly normative expectation that this sex would be entered into in the context of a relationship heading toward mar- riage and that ideally sexual relations would not start until "psychological maturity" had been attained. Numerous advice writers expended consid- erable energy emphasizing the importance of delaying the onset of sexual relations until this "psychological maturity" was evident, even as they var- iously associated this term with the capability for long-term commitment, a willingness to become parents in case contraceptives failed, or the attain- ment of a certain level of education and hence the capacity for economic independence from one's own parents.

A fundamentally conservative attitude was also powerfully evident in the SED's notions of socialist virtue, the suspicion that private bliss might draw citizens away from socialism rather than toward it and a generalized skepticism about the pursuit of pleasure as potentially depoliticizing. This, then, was the grounds for hectoring injunctions that lasting happiness was only possible when human beings involved themselves in political struggle. As, for example, divorce court judge Wolfhilde Diehrl put it in 1958 in her especially tendentious attack on pleasure seeking, "there is no fulfillment of existence in an idyll set apart from human society," and although she conceded that "a healthy marital life is generally not possible without the harmony of bodily union" she nonetheless drew on the authority of exam- ples from her work encountering unhappy couples to argue that excessive sexual activity caused severe psychological and physiological damage. "An unmastered indulgence [*ein unbeherrschtes Geniessen*], a perpetual stimulation of the nerves so that pleasure can be achieved [*ein ständiges Aufpeitschen der Nerven zur Erreichung der Wollust*] and dissipation [*Aus- schweifungen*] in sexual life," Diehrl declared in her frequently reprinted book, "rob people of joy, tension and strength, drive them to perversities, cause bad moods and satiation. Such people show apathy in their dealings with others, enervation, indifference for one's own tasks and the problems of society." And to prove that lack of social concern also hurt the individual, Diehrl reinforced her point with a frightening tale of a couple that had so much sex right after they were married that they became physically ill and also turned against each other. Only by redirecting them to their social responsibilities, she asserted, was the marriage rescued.[7]

Normativity made itself aggressively felt in other ways as well, as the recurrent rhetorical emphasis on "clean" relationships implied not only sexual fidelity but also a rejection of homosexuality. East German advice writers throughout the 1950s and 1960s did not only deem homosexuality a perversion, pathology, or deviance. They also often replicated the predominant Nazi analyses of homosexuality as they either asserted that most homosexuality resulted from seduction during the adolescent phase when sexual orientation was not yet fixed on the opposite sex and/or associated homosexuality with mental deficiency and crime.[8] In his book for young teens, for example, the oft-reprinted *Die Geschlechterfrage* (The Question of the Sexes), Rudolf Neubert pretended to be sensitive to the small minority of "true" homosexuals when he stated that homosexuality was sometimes caused by a "deformation of the inner glands" (*Missbildung der inneren Drüsen*) and went on to say that "these people are to be pitied just as much as those born with any other deformation." But Neubert also observed that even these congenital cases should be treated with hormone preparations, surgery (transplantation of "glandular tissue"), and above all psychotherapy (or, as he indicatively defined it, "pedagogic influencing by the doctor"). In addition, like Nazis before him and like so many in West and East Germany in the 1950s, Neubert insisted that, while the number of true homosexuals was small, the number of those seduced in youth was larger. Yet even as he announced that homosexuality occurred primarily among "pleasure-addicted progeny of rich families" or "asocial elements from other social strata," Neubert also assured readers that the incidence of homosexuality was far less frequent in a "young, constructively developing" society like the GDR than it was in (presumably capitalist) societies in a state of "dissolution."[9]

In 1957, the SED quietly instructed police and judges no longer to prosecute or imprison adult men engaged in consensual homosexual activity, and this certainly marked an important contrast to the ongoing coordinated criminalization, replete with police raids and prison sentences, in West Germany.[10] And in 1968 the GDR abolished Paragraph 175, one year ahead of the Federal Republic of Germany's (FRG) modification of the law. Yet at the same time, a newly introduced law, Paragraph 151, under the guise of "protection of youth," criminalized same-sex activity for *both* men and women if it occurred between someone over the age of eighteen and someone under the age of eighteen. SED officials strenuously sought to avoid the topic of homosexuality altogether, in a double inability to acknowledge that homosexuality existed at all in a socialist society and to acknowledge that there could be within socialism "marginal" groups of any sort that could not be integrated seamlessly into the social whole.[11] Throughout the 1960s, what little was written about homosexuality continued to treat it as a "perversion." This, for example, was the term chosen by Gerhard and Danuta Weber in their popular advice book *Du und ich* (You and I)—the advice book most frequently consulted by East German youth in the mid- to late 1960s—as they advised young women not to marry homosexual men.[12] And since the SED was always apprehensive and anxious to keep from international attention any empirical data that could possibly be used against socialism by its "enemies," it was no surprise that research that was able to demonstrate an especially low incidence of youth homosexual activity in the GDR was published.[13] The official tendencies to denigrate homosexuality and attempt to steer youth away from it and above all to force youth caught in homosexual encounters to undergo coercive psychotherapy remained disturbing features of East German life throughout the 1950s and 1960s and well into the 1970s.[14]

Meanwhile, and all through the 1950s and 1960s, East German sex advice writers also struggled to find imaginative arguments for frightening young people away from "too early" heterosexual activity. In the gynecologist Wolfgang Bretschneider's view, for instance, premarital intercourse should preferably be avoided altogether, and in his advice book for parents of teens he provided a battery of arguments against it. For example, he argued that premarital intercourse could disrupt the proper psychological maturation process. He not only felt compelled to point out that, although the GDR had equalized the status of illegitimate with legitimate children, it was nonetheless exceedingly difficult to parent a child alone but also strategically argued that the contraception that would likely be used to prevent unwed motherhood tended in almost all cases to inhibit sensation, and he warned readers that this inhibition of sensation in turn could cause lasting sexual dysfunction. He further said that long-standing use of contraceptives could cause female infertility. Moreover, he declared, the "abnormal" locations in which most premarital intercourse occurred—park benches, courtyard corners, behind the bushes—and the accompanying anxieties about fear of discovery were not well suited to the development of female sexual responsiveness in particular (even as else-where he downplayed the importance of that responsiveness and declared that female orgasm really was not as important as many women seemed to think it was). At the same time, Bretschneider also adopted, with only the slightest modification, ideas from the Swiss Protestant (and devout Christian) advice writer Theodor Bovet, whose writings were enormously influential in 1950s West Germany. For example, Bretschneider's recom-mendations to men to help them distract themselves from the desire to indulge in masturbation were lifted directly from Bovet. And Bretschnei-der's ideas about the deleterious impact of masturbation on the potential for marital happiness were also indistinguishable from those advanced in West German Catholic and Protestant advice writings. Girls were warned that they would have trouble transitioning from clitoral stimulation to vaginal sensation during intercourse, while boys were informed that "mas-turbation is a pitiful substitute for real love" and that "one remains stuck in oneself."[15] Socialist sexual conservatism, in short, despite the critical asides about Christian sex hostility in most East German sex advice texts, appeared quite compatible with Christian sexual conservatism.

In part, then, as noted, the conservative tendencies of the 1950s and 1960s had their source in the profoundly conventional views of the Ger-man communist leadership and the directives coming from the Soviet Union. The conservative tendencies of the 1950s and 1960s can also in part be ascribed to both the public's and the government's worries about the still fairly desperate state of the economy, and the atmosphere this created in which regime arguments about the need to concentrate energies on the basic daily task of survival could appear plausible.[16] Rationing, for exam-ple, was not ended until 1958. The "brain drain" of qualified technocratic and professional elites that continued unabated throughout the 1950s until the building of the Berlin Wall in 1961 not only increased regime paranoia but also exacerbated the difficulty of economic reconstruction after the combined devastations of wartime damage and Soviet appropriation of infrastructure, resources, and reparations payments. Basic consumer goods were frequently unavailable, and mismanagement and bad deci-sions in economic planning at the highest levels continually made produc-tion processes and their coordination uneven and unreliable.[17] The hous-ing shortage remained acute well into the 1970s—even as, fascinatingly, a marriage book published in 1972 was still able to blame this on Nazism.

(While encouraging their readers to have multichild families, the authors conceded that "there is without a doubt a contradiction between the demands of the society for larger families and the demands of families for larger living spaces." But alas, "after the terrible devastations of the fascist war our social means simply do not as yet permit us to offer every child-rich family anything like a four- or five-bedroom apartment—as much as we are making an effort to do this.")[18] Indeed, there was hardly a sex advice text written that did not refer to the problems—such as self-consciousness or inadequate privacy—caused for young couples by the inevitable need to continue living with parents even after they had married (only once a child was born did most couples have a chance at a tiny apartment of their own).

In sum, then, it is no surprise that the 1950s and at least the first half of the 1960s in East Germany have been remembered by contemporaries as the dark ages of an enforced fixation with conventionality and respectability. As one man put it, the atmosphere was "thoroughly sterile, there was very little to delight the senses."[19] There was in that era "no public discourse about many questions related to sexuality" but rather a "self-disciplining morality, unfriendly to pleasure, chaste . . . ascetic or pseudo-ascetic, uptight, interventionist," the leading East German sexologist Kurt Starke recalled in the 1990s.[20] And the prominent West German sexologist Volkmar Sigusch, who lived in East Germany until he fled to the West in 1961, said that "the climate in the East was horribly philistine [*furchtbar spiessig*]. You couldn't get more petty-bourgeois or philistine than that. Ulbricht? Honecker? They were so narrow and provincial. All the liberal, sophisticated people had gone to the West."[21] Starke and others recollect a climate of invasive surveillance of private lives and public humiliation for any departure from the expected narrow norms. This was especially true for Party members. Young people in Party-run boarding schools were forbidden from forming into couples ("*keine Pärchenbildung*"), student dormitories were monitored at night to make sure no one was having sex, and also after marriage the SED wanted its functionaries to maintain stable and conformist arrangements.[22] If married functionaries had extramarital affairs or one-night stands, they were expected to confess all and publicly castigate themselves and recommit to their spouses at a Party forum.[23]

Yet at the same time, and all through the 1950s and 1960s, popular practices elicited significant regime concessions. Rates of illegal abortions, unwed teen motherhood (only at age eighteen was it legal to marry in the GDR), youthful divorces (especially among couples who had only married

because a child was on the way), and even the strains on "student mothers" struggling to juggle child care and professional development all
caused consternation in SED circles and led the regime to reevaluate its
priorities. Empirical studies ordered by the regime to assess these issues
turned up incontrovertible evidence that each was a genuine social concern.[24] The government responded, among other things, by directing doctors already in 1965 to handle abortion requests more leniently and to consider a woman's psychological well-being in addition to her physical
health. And in a law that went into effect in 1966, family, marriage, and sex
counseling centers were established throughout East Germany.[25] The
experts involved in organizing these centers and coordinating continuing
education for staff advanced some of the most progressive perspectives on
sexuality in the GDR; they forged strong ties to the International Planned
Parenthood Federation and sponsored conferences on sexuality, which
received respectful international notice. In turn, the issues that brought
individuals and couples to these centers in ever-rising numbers—above all
worries about contraception and about sexual dissatisfaction within marriages—again created opportunities for professionals concerned with sexual matters to persuade the government that more expansive research,
public education, and therapeutic services were needed.[26]

The second half of the 1960s saw a strong oscillation between conservative and liberal perspectives. On the one hand there were texts that
explicitly reacted against what they found to be a too value-neutral tendency in early 1960s empirical studies and tried to find novel arguments for
a return to sexual conservatism. (In this vein, for instance, experts warned
of the deleterious impact especially on females of a sexual encounter experienced in a relationship not heading toward marriage; used the idea that
the female capacity for orgasm during coitus might be an acquired skill
that took some practice as a reason to put off sex until a marriage partner
had been found; or even declared outright that females under the age of
twenty were simply unlikely to achieve sexual satisfaction so it was best
not to try.)[27] On the other hand in these years an increasing effort to present the GDR as a desirable site for young romance was also evident.
Sometimes both tendencies were combined, as for example when Heinrich
Brückner proudly published his finding that more youth in the GDR than
in the FRG felt that premarital abstinence was physically possible, even as
he was also pleased to find that GDR youth had more sexological savvy
than their Western counterparts.[28] A similar combination could be found
in Klaus Trummer's 1966 advice book for young teens. While parents and

teachers should never advance "the moral views of the convent," too early intercourse would disturb an individual's psychological and intellectual development. At the same time, love was definitely better in the East, because "how people live together here is no longer determined by the laws of capitalism ('everyone is only looking out for himself')" and "love is not a commodity."[29]

Indeed, the comparison between East and West became a major motif in East German writings on sex after the mid-1960s—even as West Germans increasingly ignored the East. (This was an interesting departure from the powerful role anticommunist rhetoric had played in the West in the 1950s, as the West had sought to justify its efforts on behalf of female subordination and confinement within the domestic realm through constant rhetorical invocations of the purported horrors of female emancipation in the GDR.) It was almost as though, now that the West was no longer the stuffy place it had once been and had started to resemble a pleasure palace in sexual terms, the East needed to stress also the sexual advantages of socialism. What was most noticeable in the efforts to disseminate a new socialist message about sex was an apparently urgent—if nonetheless also ambivalent—SED intention not to be perceived as overly puritanical.

Thus the socialist ethicist Bernd Bittighöfer in an essay on youth and love from 1966 registered approval that more and more parents in East Germany were letting go of the remnants of bourgeois "prejudices" and "inhibitions." On the one hand, Bittighöfer declared himself in favor of "the moral cleanness of our socialist way of life," and he expressly criticized the titillating material disseminated by West German radio and television. The West was, in his view, purveying "imperialist ideology," propagating "skepticism and anarchism in the realm of morality," encouraging "sexual excess" and "trivialization and brutalization of relations between the sexes," and—as he awkwardly put it—"stimulating adolescents' natural urge for recognition [*Geltung*] onesidedly in the sexual realm." Yet on the other hand, and significantly, premarital chastity was not his recommendation. This idea, he said, was "antiquated." He went on to contend that "the satisfaction of the sexual drive is . . . one of the most elementary needs of human life-expression," and he invoked August Bebel's point that those who were prevented from satisfying drives that were so "closely connected with their innermost being" would be damaged in their development. "Fulfilling love," Bittighöfer concluded, "includes sexual union" and "is an essential element in personality development and fulfilled existence."[30]

A similar kind of uncertainty marked the government's approach to sex in literature. When the Central Committee of the SED met in 1965, for instance, it considered the apparent problem that East German writers increasingly included sex scenes that were not in tune with the regime's notions of socialist morality. Rather than strictly censoring narrative representations of sexual acts and encounters (as it had done only a year earlier), the SED now declared itself in favor of sex scenes—the Party expressly did not want "prudery and prettification" (*Prüderie und Beschönigungstendenzen*). Once again, however, the message was mixed: Such scenes would only be allowed if they occurred in a proper partnership, or, if not, the narrative must in some way censure the characters' actions.[31]

In the face of the government's apparent disorientation through the sixties and into the seventies, progressive professionals concerned with sexuality, whether medical doctors or pedagogues, did their utmost to use the evidence of the populace's desires and difficulties as a wedge to influence the SED and to redirect national debate on sexual matters. Collectively, through their support for each other and through their publications, these professionals—notable among them Lykke Aresin, Peter G. Hesse, Karl-Heinz Mehlan, and Siegfried Schnabl—managed to make open discussion of sexual matters possible. Hesse was an early and eloquent advocate of more broad-based public education about contraception, rejecting worries about a declining birthrate and insisting on the "higher" morality of sex free from fear; he subsequently provided a major service by organizing and coediting a massive three-volume encyclopedia of sexological knowledge, the first of its kind in the GDR.[32] Mehlan was singularly important in the liberalization of abortion law.[33] And Aresin was enormously influential in making the Pill widely acceptable and available in the GDR. She and Schnabl were also pioneers in the treatment of sexual dysfunctions and marital disharmony; they followed the work of such American sexologists as William Masters and Virginia Johnson, and they created individual and couple therapy in the GDR. (Strikingly, it must be noted that rather than seeing these centers as potentially invasive institutions, couples flocked to them.)[34] Schnabl also conducted the theretofore largest empirical study on sexual dysfunction and sexual practices within marriage, based on interviews with and anonymous questionnaires answered by thirty-five hundred men and women. Aresin's and Schnabl's works were crucial in making issues of sexual conflict within marriages an acceptable subject for public discussion. Schnabl's sex advice book of 1969, *Mann und Frau intim* (Man and Woman Intimately), based on his research findings, became a runaway best-seller. His reassuring, no-nonsense recommendations for facilitating female orgasmic response were the centerpiece of his broader campaign to affirm the joys and the importance of heterosexual sex apart from its potential reproductive consequences.[35] By the GDR's end in 1989, this book (together with a guide on gardening) had the highest sales of any book in the nation's history.

Above all, GDR citizens plainly carved out their own freedoms. Nude bathing, for example (known as FKK, for *Freikörperkultur*), became an important part of GDR culture. Starting in the middle of the 1960s nude bathing became acceptable for growing numbers of GDR citizens, and by the 1970s full nudity was clearly the norm at GDR beaches, lakeside or oceanside. Early attempts by municipal authorities to prevent this practice were simply overridden by the adamant masses, who stripped and would not move. Nakedness for the whole family also within the home became increasingly standard practice as well, especially for that generation that had grown up together with the GDR; for their children, nudism simply became the cultural commonsense. As subsequent studies showed, homes in which parent and child nakedness were routine tended also to be those in which parents advocated progressive attitudes about sex and where there was generally warm, trusting, and open parent-child communication; this second GDR generation was raised with far more liberal and tolerant perspectives toward all aspects of sexuality.

In an interview published in 1995, the Leipzig sexologist Kurt Starke evocatively summarized the gradual transformation of the GDR's sexual culture in this way:

> At the latest in the 1970s the citizens in the GDR started to defy all kinds of possible constrictions with respect to their partner- and sexual behavior. They became FKK-fans. They birthed illegitimate children in droves. They handed in divorce papers when love had faded. They casually got involved with a coworker if they felt like it. At some point kissing couples lay on the grass in Leipzig's Clara-Zetkin-Park or female students sunbathed naked, and no police intervened. The few sex enlightenment books that appeared were not disdained but rather passed from hand to hand and by no means secretly. Often they provided the occasion for conversations between parents and their adolescent children. All of this came together with the improvement of living conditions, for example the creation of more housing;

after all, one needs a place for living and loving. . . . This process was also combined with a more positive valuation of sexuality. An affirmative attitude toward sexuality developed, very connected with family and with love. So: somehow a romantic ideal.[36]

Still, it would take another decade before the gains claimed by many in the GDR in the course of the 1970s became fully visible to all. Starke's own research—conducted under the auspices of the Center for Youth Research in Leipzig together with the center's director, Walter Friedrich, and in creative circumvention of the regime's monitoring efforts—would play no small part in helping GDR citizens see for themselves their own achievements. And by the early 1980s, when Starke published *Junge Partner* (Young Partners) and together with Friedrich published *Liebe und Ehe bis 30* (Love and Marriage until Thirty), it became manifestly apparent that East German women in particular not only had been special objects of their government's solicitude but had successfully reconfigured their private relationships as well.

Just as there had been no momentous or spectacular sexual revolution in East Germany, so too there would be no large-scale and dramatic feminist protest movement or development of a women-centered counterculture. While especially in the course of the 1980s, a number of women's organizations were founded in the GDR, their self-definition was rarely feminist. To a great extent, feminism in East Germany was simply perceived by East German women as a redundancy.

The hesitancy about feminism felt by East German women was due in no small part to the state-sponsored advantages East Germany offered them. So many of the desiderata West German feminists had to fight for in the 1970s—abortion rights, child-care facilities, economic independence, and professional respect—were things East German women by that point could largely take for granted. First-trimester abortions upon demand were legalized in 1972, an achievement never matched in the West. While West German women were continually encouraged to feel guilty if they placed their young children in daycare, and options to do so remained few and far between in any event, and while West German women constantly experienced motherhood and careers as conflicting, East German women increasingly tended to consider this combination fully manageable.

Another major impetus for the West German feminist movement was the pervasiveness of pornography and, more generally, the objectification of women's bodies in advertising and all media. Although available as contraband, pornography was illegal in the East; its distribution was severely limited. Whereas in the West, consumer capitalism functioned to a large degree via the (always distorted) representation of female sexuality, East German state socialism was not driven by this imperative. In East Germany, the populace did walk around naked, but nothing was being sold by this. Occasionally, products made in the GDR were advertised with a hint of sexual innuendo, and one popular magazine (*Das Magazin*) published a nude female centerfold every month, but these photographs were remarkably tame compared with representations in the West and generally lacked the lascivious look and the nonaverage bombshell bodies so prevalent in Western porn. Meanwhile, the heterosexual male anxieties that both funded and were fostered by the porn typically available in the West were not provoked in the same way in the East.

Yet another significant difference from the West was East Germany's state-sponsored insistence that men should respect women who were their superiors at work and that men should assist their female partners with household and child-care responsibilities. In both cases, and while the realization of these aims certainly remained imperfect, the standard set by the state had important consequences. East German women found themselves routinely in positions of authority and responsibility in work and public life. As the East German journal *Visite* (produced for Western visitors' consumption) exulted already in 1971, one-third of all judges in the GDR were female, "an impressive number that no capitalist country in the world can even approach." Every fourth school was run by a female principal. More than one thousand women were mayors—13 percent of all East German mayors (compared with less than 1 percent in West Germany). Hundreds of thousands of women held offices in unions; tens of thousands were members of production committees; thirteen hundred women were directors of industrial enterprises. And, importantly, "sociological research shows that the majority of the workers take a female as their superior just as seriously as they would a man." The journal article also emphasized that only men's help with the household and child rearing made this socialist female emancipation possible. And of course *Visite* did not fail to conclude sonorously that these amazing female achievements were no miracle but rather due to "the socialist relations of production that set free the creative forces of all people. Where the exploitation of the human being has been overcome, where the driving force of the society is no longer the striving after profit but rather the coincidence of individual and social interests, there is no ground in which egoism, self-glorification and oppression of woman could grow."[37] But for all the unwarranted self-congratulation, there was nevertheless a significant enough kernel of truth to these claims. For East Germany did develop its own distinctive standards of masculinity and femininity. The ideals propounded by the leadership were more than just empty phrases; they were also practically approximated in the daily interplay between social conditions and individual negotiations.

Importantly, socialism was cast as not just about better love but also and specifically about better sex. Indeed, meticulous and elaborate attention to intensifying female pleasure became the most significant innovation in East German sexological writing in the 1970s and early 1980s. And an emphasis on heterosexual men improving their performance in bed was strongly assimilated in East Germany.[38] When Starke and Friedrich in 1984 published *Liebe und Sexualität bis 30,* based on extensive empirical research among East German youth, they not only found that young GDR women had their first orgasm on average at the age of sixteen or seventeen—and that already 70 percent of sixteen-year-olds had orgasmic experience—but also that two-thirds of all the young women surveyed had an orgasm "almost always" during sex, with another 18 percent declaring that they had one "often." In fact, the majority of informants—female and male alike—were very satisfied with their sex lives in general (and interestingly the authors found no differences in sexual experience or happiness between the Christian minority and the atheist majority). Moreover, the authors resolutely concluded that East German social conditions—"the sense of social security, equal educational and professional responsibilities, equal rights and possibilities for participating in and determining the life of society"—were preeminently responsible for the high rates of female pleasure. "The young women of today are in general more active and more discriminating, less inhibited and reticent, expecting to have their personality and wishes honored, striving much more self-confidently for higher sexual satisfaction," and "they are accustomed to demanding happiness in love . . . and to tasting it fully." These young women started having sex earlier, they switched their partners more frequently, and they enjoyed themselves more. And Starke and Friedrich were also convinced that whatever male ambivalence was still being expressed among the somewhat older men about this new state of affairs was just a passing phase of adjustment, since they found that such ambivalence had already disappeared almost entirely within the younger generation. Precisely those young men and women who had grown up in supportive families and whose parents had been loving toward each other were the ones who were most secure in themselves and the most creative and experimental in their own love lives.[39] Nor were these conclusions contradicted by subsequent research. On the contrary, when the first comparative East-West German study of female students' sexual experiences was conducted in 1988, the results showed (to the Western scholar's amazement) that East German heterosexual women liked sex more (and experienced orgasms more frequently) than their West German counterparts.[40]

The East German experts' endless reiterations of the idea that socialism produced especially charmed conditions for mutually satisfying sex, in short, was not just a figment of their own fantasy lives. While Starke and Friedrich had also considered the introduction of the Pill as a key factor that made all this newfound female pleasure possible, the comparison with West Germany suggests that their argument about gender equality under socialism was far from insignificant. In the seventies and eighties, the West German feminist movement loudly proclaimed Western women's fury at heterosexual coital practices that left them cold, and they made men's boorish and selfish behavior in bed a major public issue. During that same era, East German women made no such accusations; instead, they simply could (and did) break up with unsatisfactory men specifically because they possessed economic independence and because theirs was a social environment that treated singlehood, including single motherhood, as acceptable and feasible—and even a social norm. (By the end of the GDR, one in three children was born out of wedlock; in the FRG it was one in ten.)[41] Once East and West German women encountered each other more frequently after the collapse of the GDR, East German women could only roll their eyes and express astonishment at many West German heterosexual women's apparent lack of satisfaction with the men in their lives and at the fuss that Western feminists continued to make about sexual practices. "Those that enjoy it don't need to talk about it in public," one East German woman in her fifties said in exasperation in the 1990s, summarizing her feelings about her first experiences with West German feminists.[42] And also in the later 1990s a forty-something formerly East German woman proudly—almost patronizingly—announced: "East-women have more fun, everybody knows that [*Ost-Frauen haben mehr Spass, das weiss jeder*]. Orgasm rates were higher in the East, all the studies show that." And then (revealing a misconception some Easterners still had about Westerners) she added: "After all, it was a proletarian society. None of this bourgeois concern with chastity until the wedding night."[43]

The collapse of the Berlin Wall in 1989 and the reunification of Germany under Western auspices in 1990 brought immediate change to the sexual culture of the East. The day after the Wall came down, the entrepreneur Beate Uhse had her staff ship truckloads of sex toys and pornography into the five East German states; supply could not keep up with demand. Pornography shops proliferated, and Easterners queued up for hours for a chance both finally to look and to purchase. "We felt like we'd been left out," one fortyish male East German librarian commented with both pathos and irony, and numerous comments made by Easterners to West German reporters suggest much the same.[44] The long lines in front of porn shops quickly became part of the standard self-congratulatory Western narrative of communism's collapse, and Western journalists gleefully seized upon each instance an East German articulated regret over a sex-commodity-deprived existence under socialism. Yet what got drowned out in these facile assumptions of Western superiority were more reflective East German voices that sought to articulate what had been valuable about East German sexual culture—as that culture itself began rapidly to dissolve.

There were indisputably gains made. It was not at all insignificant, for instance, that the collapse of East Germany helped liberalize major aspects of reunified Germany's sexual culture. While East German women's distress over the possible elimination of abortion rights was widely discussed in the media, Western feminists remained optimistic that the process of reunification might provide an opportunity for the West to adopt the more progressive East German arrangement. In large part, they were proven accurate. What resulted was a compromise; now all German women were granted first-trimester approval (standard in the East since 1972) if they agreed to preabortion counseling (as had been required in the West). Notably the process of reunification also provided the occasion for a new advance for gay rights, as—continuing a further legal liberalization implemented in the GDR in 1988—Paragraph 175 was finally abolished in all its dimensions in reunified Germany in 1994.

Yet for the most part, the former East German sexual culture found itself the object of condescending bemusement and ruthless ridicule as a cacophony of competing theories was promoted. The East German psychotherapist Hans-Joachim Maaz, for example, made a big name for himself with his book *Der Gefühlsstau: Ein Psychogramm der DDR* (Emotional Congestion: A Psychological Diagnosis of the GDR), which caricatured his former fellow citizens as emotionally repressed and sexually deprived. "The GDR was a land with widespread sexual frustration," Maaz said, seeing this deficit of Eastern life as a crucial symptom of a broader paranoia and psychic deformation induced by living under tightly controlled conditions and constant surveillance.[45] Contradictorily, others proposed that, because there had not been much else to do in the East and daily life had been so gray and monotonous, sex had emerged as a favorite pastime. Now, East Germans would have to learn to pull themselves together and acquire the work ethic necessary for success under capitalism. Rejecting as communist propaganda the notion that Eastern women's reportedly higher orgasm rates might have their source in higher levels of female economic independence, for instance, the right-wing tabloid *Bild* provided this countervailing analysis in May 1990: "Everywhere that human beings are offered nothing or very little—aside from much work and little pay—everywhere where there are few discos, restaurants, amusement parks, in other words few opportunities for entertainment—in all those places sex is practiced more frequently and more intensively."[46] Meanwhile, the East German habit of naked display at the beach was variously interpreted as quaint and odd, as a trifle disturbing, or as (misplaced) compensation for East Germans' lack of political independence. "Wasn't this FKK-cult a kind of expression of your will to freedom?" a female reporter from Hamburg asked her younger East German colleagues, a question interpreted by the *Ossis* as yet one more exemplar of Western snobbery and cluelessness.[47]

Above all, however, there was among Easterners a profound sense of loss. The flood of Western pornography effectively demolished the Eastern culture of nakedness. As West Germans rushed to stake out the beaches on the formerly East German shores of the Baltic Sea as they sought out cheap and beautiful vacation spots, they proceeded to take offense at the widespread nudity and insisted their children be spared the sight of guilelessly self-displaying *Ossis*. In effect, the West Germans achieved what the GDR police had failed to do decades earlier. Many East German women no longer felt safe going naked now that they were viewed with Western men's "pornographically schooled gaze" (*pornographisch geschulter Blick*).[48] And they did begin to cover themselves. Indicatively, too, after they had sated their initial curiosity, many *Ossis* turned away in disappointment at the poor quality and (what they saw as) lack of genuine eroticism in the Western porn products. (Already by 1995, two-thirds of the porn video shops that had opened in the formerly East German states shut their doors.)

Without a doubt, most devastating for the former East was a loss of economic security and the new idea that human worth would now be measured primarily by money. East German citizens felt enormous anxieties about the loss of jobs and social security, rising rents, and uncertain futures. Once it became clear that Germany would be reunified under Western auspices (rather than developing some mutually worked out "third path") and once the full consequences of such Westernization became apparent (it would not just mean Easterners finally acquiring Western goods and a strong currency and political freedoms but also a huge rise in unemployment and social instability), Easterners scrambled to acquire new job skills and a whole new style of comporting themselves. These developments also had incalculable consequences on sexual relations. Many long-term East German relationships went into crisis; couples first clung together despite conflicts and then crashed as they struggled with varying degrees of success to reinvent themselves under new conditions.[49]

Little wonder, then, that the disappearing sexual ethos of the GDR quickly became an especially important site for *Ostalgie*—a popular coinage that joined together *Ost* (East) and *Nostalgie* (nostalgia). "In the East the clocks ran more slowly," the East German journalist Katrin Rohnstock remembered with retrospective longing in 1995. In the West, in her view, lust for capital had replaced desire for another person. With reference to capitalism's competitive climate, she said: "Eroticism feels with its fingertips, elbows destroy that. The pressure to achieve makes human beings sick and has a negative impact on sexuality."[50] Or as another formerly East German woman phrased it, as she explained that GDR sexuality was in some respects more emancipated than that of the West: "Money played no role. In the East, sex was not for sale."[51] The East German cultural historian Dietrich Mühlberg too emphasized in 1995 that "the cost-benefit analysis" so constantly employed in human interactions in the West "was largely absent" in the East and that this inevitably affected sexual relations and partnerships as well.[52] And the Magdeburg-based sexologist Carmen Beilfuss spoke of "the difficult path of love in the market economy."[53] Throughout the 1990s, and over and over, Easterners (gay and straight alike) articulated the conviction that sex in the East had been more genuine and loving, more sensual, and more gratifying—and less grounded in self-involvement—than West German sex.[54]

Whether these memories were fully accurate or not, there is no question that the GDR's sexual culture was remarkable, for it differed not only from capitalist West Germany but also from the rest of socialist Eastern Europe. While men in other Eastern European cultures were notorious for their "socialist machismo" (their patriarchalism and misogyny existing in counterpoint to gender-egalitarian Soviet bloc rhetoric), East German men's domesticity and self-confident comfort with strong women were both legendary.[55] Prostitution hardly occurred at all in the GDR, even while it was commonplace in Warsaw and Budapest. Homosexual men were thrown into prison in the Soviet Union and Romania up until the demise of communism; this had not occurred in the GDR since 1957. The Polish Church was thoroughly homophobic; in the GDR, gays and lesbians were able to organize in the 1980s under church auspices.[56] In its rejection of prostitution and pornography, the GDR appeared prudish by Western standards. Yet precisely the absence of these two means of marketing sex allowed other liberties to flourish. The moralism and asceticism the SED tried to enforce was undermined by the very processes of secularization that the SED also fostered. In the end, there was something peculiarly *German* about East Germany, even if former East Germans did not necessarily recognize that. The easy relationships to nakedness and sexual matters had their source not least in a distinctive tradition going back to Weimar and even before.

Without a doubt, the West German sexual revolution had been perceived by the SED as a threat that needed to be countered. But the sexual liberalization in East Germany that happened from the mid-1960s on, and with growing force through the 1970s and 1980s, was *not* just an imitation of the West but took its own peculiar form not least because of a precursor liberalization that had already occurred in the otherwise gloomy 1950s and early 1960s. While in West Germany the realm of sexuality repeatedly became the site for attempts to master the past of Nazism and the Holocaust, in East Germany the emphasis was always on what was yet to come—on the constant declaration that "the future belongs to socialism," a wishful prescription pretending to be a description.[57] Only once the GDR itself was a thing of the past did sex and memory in the GDR become firmly conjoined. All through the history of the GDR, there was in the SED the never-ending hope that the populace's affections might yet be won, if only the right formula of select consumer goods and managed freedoms were found. Love and sexuality became absolutely crucial elements in this struggle to win popular approval. The majority of the populace, however, never was taken in by the endlessly announced romance of socialism itself. Instead, it was the romance for which the GDR had indeed created important preconditions but that ultimately the people had simply claimed for themselves that became the eventual site for *Ostalgie*.

NOTES

1. Rudolf Neubert, *Das neue Ehebuch: Die Ehe als Aufgabe der Gegenwart und Zukunft* (Rudolstadt: Greifenverlag, 1957), 192.

2. A valuable source on ordinary GDR citizens' attitudes about premarital sex in the 1950s are the letters collected in Hanns Schwarz, *Schriftliche Sexualberatung: Erfahrungen und Vorschläge mit 60 Briefen und Antworten* (Rudolstadt: Greifenverlag, 1959). The letters make clear that in the populace premarital heterosexual activity was simply taken as a given; it was *the* commonsense behavior in 1950s East Germany. Whenever qualms or anxieties were expressed, they had to do with masturbation, not premarital intercourse. The letters also make clear that girls and women were hardly fearful shrinking violets but rather often the active ones who willingly made overtures to men. Not only do the letter writers remark in passing on their experiences with premarital sex, but they also openly asked Schwarz for advice in resolving sexual problems they were having within nonmarital relationships.

3. Hanns Schwarz, *Sexualität im Blickfeld des Arztes: Vortrag* (Berlin: Verlag Volk und Gesundheit, 1953), 10–11.

4. Schwarz, *Schriftliche Sexualberatung,* 34, 48.

5. Neubert, *Das neue Ehebuch,* 130, 188.

6. See "Der Jugend Vertrauen und Verantwortung" (1963), in *Dokumente zur Jugendpolitik der DDR* (Berlin: Staatsverlag der DDR, 1965), 93–94; and see the discussion in Heinz Grassel, *Jugend, Sexualität, Erziehung: Zur psychologischen Problematik der Geschlechtserziehung* (Berlin: Staatsverlag der DDR, 1967), 11–12.

7. Wolfhilde Diehrl, *Liebe, Ehe—Scheidung?* (1958, 1961), reprinted in Wolfhilde Diehrl and Wolfgang Bretschneider, *Liebe und Ehe* (Leipzig: Urania, 1962), 198, 201.

8. A classic expression of all three of these assumptions can be found in Wolfgang Bretschneider, *Sexuell Aufklären—Rechtzeitig und Richtig* (Leipzig: Urania, 1956), 63–64.

9. Rudolf Neubert, *Die Geschlechterfrage: Ein Buch für junge Menschen* (Rudolstadt: Greifenverlag, 1955, 1966), 80–82.

10. See Gudrun von Kowalski, *Homosexualität in der DDR: Ein historischer Abriss* (Marburg: Verlag Arbeiterbewegung und Gesellschaftswissenschaft, 1987), 26–27; and James Steakley, "Gays under Socialism: Male Homosexuality in the GDR," *Body Politics* 29 (1976–77): 15–18.

11. The Committee of Antifascist Resistance Fighters, for example, rejected the East German physician and homosexual rights activist Rudolf Klimmer's efforts

to get homosexual victims of Nazism officially acknowledged as victims of fascism with the following words: "The overwhelming majority of surviving homosexuals are in the FRG. . . . In the rule they belonged to bourgeois or petty bourgeois strata and were hostile to the socioeconomic changes that took place in the GDR after 1945." Quoted in von Kowalski, *Homosexualität,* 26. See also Marianne Krüger-Potratz, *Anderssein Gab Es Nicht: Ausländer und Minderheiten in der DDR* (Münster: Waxmann, 1991), 2.

12. Gerhard and Danuta Weber, *Du und ich* (Berlin: Verlag Volk und Gesundheit, 1965), 102–3. On *Du und ich*'s popularity, see Werner Kirsch, *Zum Problem der sexuellen Belehrung durch den Biologielehrer* (Berlin: Verlag Volk und Wissen, 1967), 78–79.

13. For example, see Helmut Rennert, "Untersuchungen zur Gefährdung der Jugend und zur Dunkelziffer bei sexuellen Straftaten," *Psychiatrie, Neurologie und Medizinische Psychologie: Zeitschrift für Forschung und Praxis* 17, no. 10 (October 1965): 364; and Helmut Rennert, "Untersuchungen über die sexuelle Entwicklung der Jugend in der DDR," *Wissenschaftliche Zeitschrift der Universität Rostock* (Mathematisch-Naturwissenschaftliche Reihe) 17, no. 6–7 (1968): 707.

14. Conversation with L. S., 2003.

15. Bretschneider, *Sexuell Aufklären,* 40–41, 67–68, 131.

16. The widely held 1950s conviction about the need to sublimate libidinal energies into reconstruction is documented persuasively by Matthias Rothe in "Semantik der Sexualität," manuscript, 2001. Only in the 1960s, Rothe finds, did the SED—turning to the theory of "cybernetics"—consider the possibility that sex could be a source of energy rather than an energy drain.

17. See André Steiner, "Dissolution of the 'Dictatorship over Needs'?: Consumer Behavior and Economic Reform in East Germany in the 1960s," in *Getting and Spending: European and American Consumer Societies in the Twentieth Century,* ed. Susan Strasser et al. (Cambridge: Cambridge University Press, 1998), 167–85.

18. Hans-Joachim Hoffmann and Peter G. Klemm, *Ein offenes Wort: Ein Buch über die Liebe* (Berlin: Verlag Neues Leben, 1972), 175–76.

19. Conversation with L. U., 2001.

20. Kurt Starke, ". . . ein romantisches Ideal" (interview conducted by Uta Kolano), in Uta Kolano, *Nackter Osten* (Frankfurt/Oder: Frankfurter Oder Editionen/Sammlung Zeitzeugen, 1995), 83, 86.

21. Conversation with Volkmar Sigusch, 2002.

22. Starke, ". . . ein romantisches Ideal," 82–83; and conversation with Kurt Starke, 2001.

23. Conversation with L. U., 2001; Heiner Carow, ". . . da kommt niemand gegen an," in Kolano, *Nackter Osten,* 153. For the transcript of a 1967 SED shaming session, see Felix Mühlberg, "Die Partei ist eifersüchtig," in *Erotik macht die Hässlichen Schön: Sexueller Alltag im Osten,* ed. Katrin Rohnstock (Berlin: Elefanten Press, 1995), 122–43.

24. For example, see Heinz Grassel, "Studentin und Mutterschaft," *Wissenschaftliche Zeitschrift der Universität Rostock (Gesellschaftliche und Sprachwissenschaftliche Reihe)* 13 (1964): 541–47; K. Lungwitz, "Die Stabilität frühzeitig geschlossener Ehen im Spiegel der Statistik," *Neue Justiz* 19 (1965); and Karl Heinz

Mehlan, "Die Abortsituation im Weltmassstab," in *Arzt und Familienplanung: Tagungsbericht der 3. Rostocker Fortbildungstage über Probleme der Ehe- und Sexualberatung vom 23. Bis 25. Oktober 1967 in Rostock-Warnemünde* (Berlin: Verlag Volk und Gesundheit, 1968), 85–86.

25. See H. Rayner and J. Rothe, "Zur Entwicklung von Richtlinien über Arbeitsweise und Organisation des medizinischen Zweiges der Ehe- und Familienberatung (Ehe- und Sexualberatung)," in *Arzt und Familienplanung;* and Lykke Aresin, "Ehe- und Sexualberatungsstellen und Familienplanung in der DDR," in *Sexuologie in der DDR,* ed. Joachim Hohmann (Berlin: Dietz, 1991), 72–94.

26. See Siegfried Schnabl, "Die Sexualberatung bei der Anorgasmie der Frau und der Impotenz des Mannes," *Zeitschrift für ärztliche Fortbildung* 60, no. 132 (1966): 815; Lykke Aresin and M. Bahder, "25 Jahre Ehe- und Sexualberatung an der Universitäts-Frauenklinik Leipzig" (1973–74), Magnus Hirschfeld Archive, Berlin; the entry on the GDR in "Familienplanung in Europa aus persönlicher Sicht," and "Hindernisse für die Kontrazeption," both in *IPPF Europa: Regionale Informationen* 8 (1979).

27. See, for example, Grassel, *Jugend,* 110; Weber and Weber, *Du und ich,* 107.

28. See Heinrich Brückner, *Das Sexualwissen unserer Jugend, dargestellt als Beitrag zur Erziehungsplanung* (Berlin: Deutscher Verlag der Wissenschaften, 1968), 134–37; and "Hüben wie drüben," *Der Spiegel,* May 26, 1969, 72, 75.

29. Klaus Trummer, *Unter vier Augen gesagt . . . : Fragen und Antworten über Freundschaft und Liebe* (Berlin: Verlag Neues Leben, 1966), 7, 11–12.

30. Bernd Bittighöfer, *Deine Gesundheit,* June 1966, 169–71.

31. See Grassel, *Jugend,* 141, 155–56. In 1964, the SED directly censored Irmtraud Morgner's *Rumba auf einen Herbst,* among other things rejecting outright as unnecessary and inappropriate a sex scene in which an unfaithful wife appeared to be having fun; if Morgner was not willing to change her text, it would simply not be able to appear in the GDR.

32. Peter G. Hesse, *Empfängis und Empfängnisverhütung* (Berlin: Verlag Volk und Gesundheit, 1967), 39. See also *Sexuologie: Geschlecht, Mensch, Gesellschaft,* 3 vols., ed. Peter G. Hesse et al. (Leipzig: S. Hirzel, 1974–77).

33. See Donna Harsch, "Society, the State, and Abortion in East Germany, 1950–1972," *American Historical Review* 102, no. 1 (February 1997): 62–66.

34. See Lykke Aresin, "Sexologische Probleme in jungen Ehen," *Psychiatrie* 20 (1967): 3–7; Aresin and Bahder, "25 Jahre," 87; and Siegfried Schnabl, *Intimverhalten Sexualstörungen Persönlichkeit* (Berlin: Deutscher Verlag der Wissenschaften, 1972), 265.

35. See Siegfried Schnabl, *Mann und Frau intim: Fragen des gesunden und des gestörten Geschlechtslebens,* 5th ed. (Berlin: Verlag Volk und Gesundheit, 1972).

36. Starke, ". . . ein romantisches Ideal," 87–88.

37. Staatssekretariat für westdeutsche Fragen, "Das schöne Geschlecht und die Gleichberechtigung in der DDR," *Visite* 3 (1971): 17–21.

38. See on this point also Starke, ". . . ein romantisches Ideal," 94.

39. Kurt Starke and Walter Friedrich, *Liebe und Sexualität bis 30* (Berlin: Deutscher Verlag der Wissenschaften, 1984), 187, 202–3.

40. Ulrich Clement and Kurt Starke, "Sexualverhalten und Einstellungen zur Sexualität bei Studenten in der BRD und in der DDR," *Zeitschrift für Sexual-*

forschung 1 (1988): 30–44; conversations with Ulrich Clement and Kurt Starke, 2001 and 2002. See also Gunter Schmidt, "Emanzipation zum oder vom Geschlechtsverkehr," *ProFamilia Magazin,* no. 5 (1993); and Wolfgang Engler, "Nacktheit, Sexualität und Partnerschaft," *Die Ostdeutschen: Kunde von einem verlorenen Land* (Berlin: Aufbau, 1999), 271–72.

41. See Hans-Joachim Ahrendt, "Neue Aspekte der Familienplanung und Geburtenregelung in Ostdeutschland," in *Sexualität und Partnerschaft im Wandel: Jahrestagung 1991 der Gesellschaft für Sexualwissenschaft* (Leipziger Texte zur Sexualität 1, no. 1 [1992]), 6.

42. Conversation with N. U., 1997.

43. Conversation with H. N., 1998.

44. Conversation with L. U., 2001.

45. See Hans-Joachim Maaz, *Der Gefühlsstau: Ein Psychogramm der DDR* (Berlin: Argon, 1990); and Dietrich Mühlberg, "Sexualität und ostdeutscher Alltag," *Mitteilungen aus der kulturwissenschaftlichen Forschung* 18, no. 36 (1995): 10.

46. "DDR-Frauen kriegen *öfter* einen Orgasmus," *Bild,* May 30, 1990, 1.

47. Holger Kaukel, *Schweriner Volkszeitung,* October 23, 1993, quoted in Ina Merkel, "Die Nackten und die Roten: Zum Verhältnis von Nacktheit und Öffentlichkeit in der DDR," *Mitteilungen aus der kulturwissenschaftlichen Forschung* 18, no. 36 (1995): 80.

48. Conversation with Kurt Starke, 2001.

49. See Carmen Beilfuss, "'Über sieben Brücken musst Du geh'n . . .': Der schwierige Weg der Liebe in der Marktwirtschaft," in *Sexualität und Partnerschaft,* 18–27.

50. Katrin Rohnstock, "Vorwort," in *Erotik macht die Hässlichen Schön,* ed. Rohnstock, 9–10.

51. Conversation with T. T., 2001.

52. Mühlberg, "Sexualität und ostdeutscher Alltag," 20.

53. Beilfuss, "'Über sieben Brücken.'"

54. See Bert Thinius, "Vom grauen Versteck ins bunte Ghetto: Ansichten zur Geschichte ostdeutscher Schwuler," in *Schwuler Osten: Homosexuelle Männer in der DDR,* ed. Kurt Starke (Berlin: Christoph Links Verlag, 1994), 73; Starke, *Schwuler Osten,* 300–301; Kolano, *Nackter Osten;* Konrad Weller, *Das Sexuelle in der deutsch-deutschen Vereinigung: Resümee und Ausblick* (Leipzig: Forum, 1991); Werner Habermehl, ed., *Sexualverhalten der Deutschen: Aktuelle Daten, intime Wahrheiten* (Munich: Heyne, 1993), 28.

55. See Aleksandar Stulhofer, "Sexual Freedom and Sexual Health in Times of Post-Communist Transition," paper delivered at the International Academy of Sex Research, Hamburg, Germany, June 20, 2002; Katrin Rohnstock, ed., *Stiefbrüder: Was Ostmänner und Westmänner voneinander denken* (Berlin: Elefanten, 1995).

56. Kurt Starke makes these points in "Die Unzüchtige Legende vom prüden Osten," in *Erotik macht die Hässlichen schön,* ed. Rohnstock, 157. See also Eduard Stapel, "Schwulenbewegung in der DDR" (interview conducted by Kurt Starke), in Starke, *Schwuler Osten,* 91–110.

57. Diehrl, *Liebe, Ehe—Scheidung?* 199.

Building Socialism at Home
The Case of East German Interiors
Paul Betts

Recent years have witnessed growing academic interest in material culture as a particularly rewarding approach to reinterpreting the German past. New studies on monuments, architecture, museums, urban landscapes, and "commodity culture" have greatly enriched the ever-expanding field of German cultural history.[1] That Germany served as one of the twentieth century's busiest construction sites of political experimentation and utopian ventures of all stripes meant that the "built environment" was crucial for conveying new dreams of political power, place, and possibility. Two world wars, revolution, full-scale physical destruction, and cold war division only intensified the primacy of symbolic artifacts, as buildings and public spaces were enlisted by each twentieth-century regime to broadcast desired historical ruptures and restored traditions, fresh political starts as well as images of continuity.

Less well known is that the twentieth century lay great premium on the domestic interior. At first this may seem a little surprising, given that the twentieth century is commonly viewed as an "age of extremes" marked by brutal projects of social engineering that often began by doing away with the traditional boundaries between public and private. Over the decades many an observer has interpreted the state's assault on subjectivity and the private sphere as one of the defining elements of the last century. While usually associated with the Third Reich and the German Democratic Republic (GDR), these developments were also present in both the Weimar and Bonn Republics. Indeed, the private sphere and the idealized domicile were central to each German government over the course of the last century, not least because decent housing was so closely tied to political legitimacy.[2] This is particularly true of worker domiciles. Even if worker housing first emerged as a new pet issue among social reformers, architects, and city planners in the late nineteenth century, as international schemes about improving worker housing made their debut at the World Exhibition in Paris in 1867, the German reform movement did not really take wing until the 1920s. Housing then moved to the center of social politics and often served as a critical litmus test of the new Weimar welfare state until its demise in 1933. The Nazi accession to power may have announced the state's assault against Weimar modernism and its supposed "cultural bolshevik" plot to reduce the hallowed German dwelling to mass-produced "living machines," as gabled housetops and *völkisch* appliqué replaced flat roofs and unadorned surfaces in at least the Third Reich's high-profile building projects. But the ideological centrality of decent worker homes—significantly renamed the *Volkssiedlung,* or "People's Dwelling"—carried on through the 1930s, even if the Nazis never actually built as much housing as their hated predecessors.[3]

Needless to say, the massive destruction of the country during World War II assured that housing would remain a top priority in postwar social policy. Yet this went far beyond simply physical reconstruction. A key element in building a postfascist culture was the new accent placed on private life. So much so that the postwar period may even be characterized as a new "culture of privacy" in its own right, one that began by reinstating the boundaries between public and private life. This was especially the case in West Germany, where the restored nuclear family, domestic stability, and the "private virtues" of individual propriety and decency were commonly lauded as the bedrock of a postfascist social order.[4] Housing then assumed heightened significance as a symbol of peace and recovery, freedom and prosperity. The urgent need to provide shelter for the millions of refugees after 1945 further intensified the primacy of housing after the war and, in turn, the state's credibility in delivering adequate accommodations to its homeless masses.[5] The upshot was that the private sphere took on unprecedented political gravity during the postwar period, as Arendt and Habermas astutely observed. Now, whether or not this led to the vitiation of the public sphere or the ironic reversal of public and private in postwar life is debatable.[6] But what is beyond doubt is that the private realm moved to the center of social policy and public discussion in the postwar years. To be sure, the "cult of the private" played a key—and still underestimated—role in wartime life in both the Allied and Axis countries.[7] Yet it acquired new vigor and authority after 1945. This found cultural expression as well, as there was a discernible shift in aesthetic focus from the grandiose and spectacular (political pageantry, monumental building, and epic filmmaking) toward the stylization and showcasing of domestic interiors and home furnishings. While this trend was everywhere apparent in the West, it was especially commended in "re-educated" West Germany, Italy, and even Japan as manifestations of postfascist progress and liberal culture.[8]

Yet the stylization of the private sphere was equally pronounced in the GDR, even if it took place under different conditions. At first this may seem puzzling. After all, the revival of monumentalist architecture and statuary; the regularity of state pageantry; the politicization of public space and the workplace; the routine public celebration of martyred heroes; the state policing of literature and the arts; the religious iconography and pop culture memorabilia glorifying the Socialist Unity Party (SED)—together with the cultural elevation of the united "community of workers"—all underscored the kinship with a 1930s-style "aestheticization of politics" and the GDR's unwitting continuities with both Soviet and Nazi culture.[9] Nevertheless, the private sphere took on great symbolic importance there too. From the late 1940s on, the importance of the home as an emblem of personal security, socialist achievement, and postwar prosperity emerged as a primary concern in the GDR and across the Soviet Union. In each case, the much-touted "standard of living" and the visual markers of material comfort played a decisive role in the larger cold war struggle for ideological legitimacy.[10]

In recent years there has been plenty of research on GDR urban planning, workplace design, housing policy, and architectural forms. Yet we still know relatively little about the role and meaning of the private sphere in GDR life and politics. It is all the more unfortunate, given that the home played host to such powerful political dreams and desires. From the very beginning the ruling SED recognized its potential in buttressing the Party's shaky political authority, wasting little time in making decent housing and a secure domestic life its chief campaign promise to the new republic's war-weary citizenry. Already by 1946 such sentiments were enshrined in the new Wohnungsgesetz, or Housing Law, which made affordable housing a right of every socialist citizen. Not that this idea was new; in fact, the ruling SED was paying homage to this key feature of the 1919 Weimar Constitution. The Weimar heritage could be seen in other ways as well: the SED followed the lead of the interwar Social Democratic Party (SPD) and Communist Party (KPD) in making the reorganization of domestic life a vital step in raising socialist political consciousness and brokering the new "workers' and peasants' state."[11]

Cold war concerns also came into play. To a large degree this was fueled by a cold war desire to build more and better dwellings than its Western counterpart, not least because adequate worker housing was seen as a key litmus test of "people's democracy" and can-do socialism. Justification, as always, was found in Marxist ideology. The SED never tired of quoting Friedrich Engels's conclusion to his 1873 essay "The Housing Question," in which he wrote that the "housing question" was inseparable from the "social question." Only once the "capitalist contradictions" of society had been overcome, so he argued, would housing problems be truly resolved. The "true humanism of the socialist order" would then bring in its train the "well-being of people, the happiness of the nation as well as the interests of the working class and other workers."[12] Solving the housing problem was therefore interpreted as the very fruit of a centrally planned economy and socialist victory. But there was another ideological element at work. Since the revolution of the economic base had already come to pass, then—following classic Marxist theory—a new socialist *Wohnkultur,* or "domestic culture," must necessarily arise as the corresponding cultural expression of such economic transformation. Decisive here was the old chestnut of consciousness: for if it was true that the home was the citizen's first and most influential material environment, then the actual form and habitus of the home were instrumental in properly educating socialist citizens. This of course was nothing novel: many Soviet designers and ideologues grappled with similar concerns in the wake of the Russian Revolution, as did their counterparts in interwar Germany, Austria, Holland, and elsewhere.[13] Yet the stakes were higher in East Germany, especially in view of the SED's wish to rid the population of both the remnants of fascist culture and the allures of the West.

Building a model socialist culture at home was neither easy nor obvious, however. Given that socialist victory in East Germany was really born of fascist defeat and Soviet intervention, and not popular demand, and given that much of the old Weimar worker culture had been irreparably destroyed by the Nazis, the SED was left to create a new national material culture virtually from scratch. This essay aims not to rehearse Soviet cultural influences nor reiterate the heated fifties and sixties debates about what exactly constituted proper social domestic culture. Rather, it focuses on how the reform crusade largely set its sights on the home and the private sphere as targets for aesthetic and political makeover, precisely because the private sphere was identified as a critical dimension of "socialist education." The slew of housing exhibitions, interior design shows, and trade fairs, to say nothing of the symbolic authority of *Stalinallee* as a model of future socialist dwelling and urban community, all bespoke this reform spirit to reengineer both private spaces and private citizens.

The rush to rebuild housing assumed center stage in the cold war rivalry between West and East Germany, as each government used housing reconstruction to trumpet its democratic credentials and ability to meet its citizens' most pressing needs. Such propaganda tactics were especially rife in the newly formed GDR. Countless newspaper editorials, pamphlets, and books aimed to expose the false allures of the West, arguing that the apparent affluence of the West was really the privilege of the happy few. Lurid journalism about the misery of the masses in the West was never in short supply. In his oft-cited 1954 book significantly entitled *The Rental Barracks of Capitalism, Living Palaces of Socialism,* Herbert Riecke described the squalor of capitalist worker life from New York to Nuremberg. Repeatedly the connections among "dollar domination" (*Dollarherrschaft*), militarism, oppression, and domestic despair (complete with photographs) were presented as the true face of liberal capitalism. The second half of the book was then given over to extolling the virtues of socialist life in general and East German housing in particular. The high-profile East Berlin worker housing project, Stalinallee, was singled out as a "foretaste of the good life to be found in socialist residential quarters of the future," one that both "enriched and beautified everyday life."[14] In it a well-built, comfortable, and affordable dwelling was heralded as material proof of the new regime's rupture from the class-based inequalities and miserable working-class life found in "Western fascist society" and the "capitalist-imperialist" powers. In this case, the "ennoblement" of everyday life was seen as a trump card in winning over citizens to the socialist cause: "The noble traits of communist citizens, including their compassion, joy, openness to the world, love of beauty and cultivation must find appropriate cultural expression in their surrounding architecture. . . . The high task of architecture is then to ennoble the everyday life of workers, and to promote communist education about the ideals of humanism."[15]

Even so, what exactly was "socialist domestic living culture?" Was it to be a complete break from the past, or did certain traditional styles and historical influences count as positive legacies? Was GDR domestic culture only to be an imitation of Soviet models, or was there to be something fundamentally German (or, for that matter, East German) about it? Questions such as these invited great controversy over the decades, especially since the successful revolution of the economic base necessitated a revolutionized domestic life.[16] The outfitting and arrangement of domestic space were therefore both cause and effect of socialist change and stability. Given its importance, it is no surprise that this debate resonated across broad political terrain. Various viewpoints and ideological stances about "socialist lifestyle" surfaced in a wide variety of sources, ranging from government committee papers to design journals, social policy to home decoration magazines like *Kultur im Heim* (Culture in the Home).

While the politicization of housing began immediately after the cease-fire as a cherished symbol of peace and recovery, the cold war dimension was a child of the early 1950s. In fact, the East German campaign to convert housing into political capital was in no small measure a response to similar developments in West Germany. From the late 1940s onward, the American occupying government was keen to exploit housing exhibitions as a means of showcasing the "American way of life" to destitute West Germans and especially West Berliners. Already in 1949 the U.S. Office of Military Government for Germany (OMGUS) sponsored the show "So wohnt Amerika," or "How America Lives," in Frankfurt as a supposed foretaste of coming American-style modernity and future prosperity. A spate of additional housing exhibitions of idealized domestic life followed, complete with the latest consumer appliances made in America. That many of these early cold war shows were sponsored by Marshall Plan administrators makes plain the perceived connections among reconstruction, reeducation, and domestic happiness. For the East German government, the most troubling aspect of these shows was their incontestable success. It was bad enough that the West Berlin's Marshall House Pavilion of 1950—which included a model family of local actors inhabiting the space as living evidence of material comfort and democratized luxury—attracted tens of thousands of West German visitors per week. More awkward, however, was that an estimated fifteen thousand East Berliners traveled across town to see what the West had to offer.[17] The SED did not take long to realize that these shows were perhaps the most effective propaganda weapons of all and that the East German government needed to respond in kind quickly and forcefully.

This was all the more grave given the deplorable state of East German housing at the time. While precise statistics are difficult to come by, the housing situation through the 1950s was sobering: 52 percent of residences had one to two rooms only, while 31 percent included three rooms. Central heating was available in less than 3 percent of homes; only 30 percent of residences had a toilet and only 22 percent a bath. Some 11 percent of housing had been built since 1945, whereas 45 percent of GDR housing was constructed before 1900. As Christoph Klessmann has noted, the only thing that saved housing from becoming a truly explosive political issue was that the exodus of some two million East Germans to the West over the course of the 1950s opened up housing for those who stayed.[18] But even so, the regime needed to provide some sort of indication of where the future lay.

By 1950 the issue of developing a distinct vision of "socialist lifestyle" at home became a hot topic of discussion among government officials, architects, and interior designers. Much of the sound and fury grew out of the question of whether Germany's interwar modernist heritage or Soviet-style neoclassicism should be embraced as the most apt expression of "national in form, socialist in content." At this point there is no need to revisit the ideological battles between East German modernists and anti-modernists, much of which pivoted on assessing the value of the Bauhaus legacy for postwar building and design practice.[19] What was clear is that, by the early 1950s, official ideology clearly swung in favor of Soviet neo-classicism.[20] Nowhere was this more evident than in the construction of the famed Stalinallee, hailed as "Germany's first socialist street." It was the GDR's grandest and most documented housing project ever, comprising some two miles of worker housing along East Berlin's Stalinallee boulevard. The ensemble, overseen by the East Berlin architect Hermann Henselmann, perfectly captured this new postwar ideology. Paramount here was the firm rejection of Western ideas of dispersed, decentralized urban planning (as codified in the 1933 Charter of Athens) in favor of a more centralized integration of the citizen's work life and home life, production and social reproduction. As such, Stalinallee was a kind of minia-turized version of the GDR's ideal community, one that integrated residence, shopping, and communal activities in a tightly organized architectonic whole.[21] Even the use of monumental decoration, as stated in Principle 6 of the GDR's Bauakademie (Building Academy) sixteen-point program of 1950, was part and parcel of this new desire to overcome the alienation of capitalist urban life by building new "worker palaces" befitting the new citizens of a new worker state.[22]

The same went for the model domestic interior. Official ideology was plainly on display in the pronouncements during the 1951 "Battle for a New German Interior Architecture." Here the objective was to apply a more local variant of Soviet-style socialist realism to the realm of East German visual culture, most notably in the fields of painting, crafts, and architecture. Interior design was trickier, though, not least since 1930s neo-classicism offered little in the way of guidance for furniture and household prototypes. Equally worrisome was that Western modernism—often derisively called the "Bauhaus style"—was still very much present in East German material life. In one newspaper article covering the Central Committee's 1951 "Battle Against Formalism in Art and Literature" congress, the unnamed journalist reported that not only was true architecture hindered by the "so-called 'Bauhaus style' and its underlying constructivist, functionalist philosophy," but that this style was particularly pronounced in "mass-produced furniture and household utensils."[23] Yet it was not just formal pluralism—and potential cultural decadence—that prompted such concern.[24] High ideological stakes were also at issue, since remade East German interiors were to be broadcast as emblems of a victorious socialist culture and as such would help assure its uncertain citizenry that the future—despite present problems—still belonged to socialism. In this respect, the interior was viewed as vital in educating socialist citizens. SED party chairman Walter Ulbricht himself often weighed in on the debate. As a trained furniture maker, he repeatedly stressed the power of well-designed domiciles in raising "socialist consciousness." In one 1959 speech, for example, he remarked that properly designed residential architecture "will promote social life, as well as the unity of personal and societal interests. . . . The principal task is to bring family life and social life closer together. The arrangement of socialist living quarters should harmonize the inhabitant's material and cultural daily needs."[25] For him, such socialist consciousness would naturally result from bringing socialist citizens in closer contact with beauty. By this Ulbricht meant a more traditional arts and crafts style, one that patently rejected the anonymity and industrial boxiness of modernist furniture. The SED premier had made the point explicitly a few years before in his keynote speech at the two-day 1952 conference entitled "Questions of German Interior Architecture and the Design of Furniture" held at East Berlin's House of Soviet Culture, when he said that "furniture manufactured in the Bauhaus style does not correspond to the sensitivity to beauty among the new Germany's progressive human beings."[26] The main task, however, was to design and decorate homes so that dwellers "felt happy and fortunate."[27] A new domestic culture based on a distinctive national cultural tradition, so went the logic, would be both the precondition and the proud fulfillment of a new "socialist humanism."

What these ideals of "national cultural tradition" and "socialist humanism" meant changed with time. To illustrate, I would like to focus on two well-known exhibitions from the 1950s and 1960s. The first is East Berlin's "Besser Leben-Schöner Wohnen" (Living Better, Dwelling More Beautifully") exhibition from 1953. The idea of this show grew out of SED debates the year before on the specific theme of "realism and formalism" in domestic architecture and furniture design. Its aim was to help instill and popularize a new "progressive, national living culture" based on a newly celebrated "realistic interior design." The exhibition was supposed to combat the dangers of "culture-destroying formalism," while at the same time serving the "spiritual and material necessities of our workers."[28] Once again the main bugbear was the infamous Bauhaus style, whose "cult of the ugly and the immoral" was denounced for having perversely deformed postwar German architecture and industrial design in the name of the "profit-seeking economy of imperialism."[29] Such sentiments were hardly new, having been enshrined as official ideology in the "formalism debate" two years earlier when modernism was summarily condemned as a toxic and degenerative Western influence. This time, however, the stakes were much higher. For one thing, the danger went well beyond painting and literature; given the basis of industrial mass-production, these "degenerate" architectural forms were everywhere. Even worse was the fact that these mass-produced "alienated forms" had penetrated the private sphere. This was all the more perilous, since interior design supposedly determined the very form, actions, and even understanding of home life. As the director of the East German Building Academy's Research Institute for Interior Design, Jakob Jordan, put it, "the domicile and its interior design [*Innenarchitektur*] indeed play an especially active role in the development of a progressive consciousness among our workers. The necessity of a realistic orientation is a vital precondition for a new German living culture."[30]

In this instance, the way forward was to look back to tradition, which was interpreted as the very font of cultural identity, aesthetic education, and psychological ballast. As Jordan concluded, "there can therefore be no disregarding of our own national cultural heritage. Let's show each other in a dignified manner how to carry on this crusade into our consciousness, how to build a beautiful life that summons our energies for the still greater successes of our Five-Year Plan to come. In this way, we architects are helping the state to achieve its goals faster. We are consequently meeting the challenge of giving form to a new interior design style that will help develop and raise the nation's taste, while at the same time enthusing our people with new progressive ideas."[31] Design's importance thus went well beyond style wars; instead, aesthetics was viewed as instrumental in binding state and citizen.

So what did this "progressive, national living culture" and "realistic architecture" look like? Some sixty-seven thousand visitors flocked to the show to glimpse into the future and to see what the regime had on offer for its hallowed "working community." Not surprisingly the exhibition catalog began by praising Stalinallee as the guiding star for East Germany's new "domestic culture." Its harmonious "architectural ensemble" supposedly reflected "the humanism underlying our democratic order in connection with a progressive national architectural heritage."[32] Not that Stalinallee boasted a pure pedigree. It was more an admixture of old and new styles: it harked back to the more conservative architectural style of the Kaiserreich, while at the same time paying homage to the official style of postwar Soviet architecture of the early 1950s. The problem, however, was that most East German interiors were seen to be grossly at odds with this new spirit. To help bring exterior and interior into a new unity, the show's organizers mounted thirty small exhibition rooms featuring both positive and negative models from the late medieval past down to the present. As such the show functioned as a kind of history lesson of German home furnishings, one that made clear which traditions were acceptable and which were not. Each room included short commentary condemning or praising the particular style on display. *Gründerzeit* eclecticism, Jugendstil subjectivism, and above all Bauhaus functionalism invited special ire; the catalog was also not timid about singling out certain hotels and restaurants in the capital and other large East German cities as fifth column "capitalist monuments" (for example, the Dresden Hotel in Berlin) in their midst.

More interesting perhaps is the way that certain styles—namely, Schinkel neoclassicist furniture, English Chippendale, and early nineteenth-century Biedermeier—were routinely lauded for their simplicity, taste, and proportion. In fact, postwar furniture makers were encouraged to take their cues from these older styles; as figure 1 indicates, every attempt was made to draw connections between past and present—in this case, between eighteenth-century English Chippendale styling and 1950s GDR Building Academy–designed chairs, or between Biedermeier and the always celebrated reception room of East Berlin's Soviet Embassy. More traditional German *Volkskunst* and rustic styles—presumably as part of the effort to distance the GDR from Nazi "blood and soil" ideology—received scant attention. What emerged as the vaunted "realistic living culture" was to a large extent recycled models from the early 1930s, as seen in figure 2. It was a style expressly rooted in tradition, whose artisanal materials and handcrafted appearance were explicitly counterposed to the hard-edged world of steel and concrete outside. The implicit notion was that East Germany was the true guardian of German culture and tradition, not least because the Federal Republic was supposedly in the process of sacrificing its venerable national past on the altar of naked American-style economic interest and spiritless functionalism. So much so that the exhibition organizers crowed that this "new blossoming of our national living culture" will doubtlessly "win more and more friends in West Germany" as they too will appreciate the socialist republic's cultivation of Germany's common cultural heritage. To this end, the goal was to help build "a life of happiness and prosperity in a united Fatherland through the design of beautiful dwellings."[33] The irony of course was that this East German "national style" was really a makeover from selected international styles of the past and even bourgeois ones at that (i.e., Biedermeier). But such inconsistencies hardly troubled the regime overmuch, largely because such internationalism could be safely rediscovered under the umbrella of a broadly defined "socialist style." East German domestic furnishings were to be distinguished by heightened artistic value and stylistic continuity, reflecting the proud craftsmanship, *Lebensfreude,* and technical achievement allegedly characterizing socialist culture. Not that the show yielded cultural dividends. Many of the prototypes on display were unavailable to consumers; those that were were often beyond the financial reach of most citizens. Many visitors were reportedly disappointed and continued to buy some of the more modernist furniture styles if for no other reason than they were readily available and cheaper.[34] Still, the show was of great cultural importance, to the extent that it captured the Party's idealized union of classic bourgeois culture and communist private life. It was also revealing in the way that it sought to provide cultural ballast for a new republic with shallow historical roots, all the while giving form to the regime's promises of "worker palaces" and domestic comfort for all.

The second selected exhibition took place almost a decade later. This was the famed 1962 "P2 Wohnung" (P2 Dwelling) show, which signaled a dramatic shift in East German ideology and outlook. In the intervening years, virtually everything had changed. The thinly disguised threats issued from the 1953 show were heeded less and less by East German manufacturers and the public. The demonized Bauhaus style and functional forms continued apace—albeit under new monikers such as "good form"—in the

Abb. 61. Stuhl im Stile Chippendales
von Andr. Irmer, Dessau

Abb. 62. Neuschöpfung in kritischer
Verarbeitung des kulturellen Erbes,
Entwurf Deutsche Bauakademie, 1953

Fig. 1.   A Chippendale chair compared to a GDR design in 1953. (From the *Besser Leben—Schöner Wohnen* exhibition catalog, 60–61, edited by the Deutsche Bauakademie and the Ministry of Light Industry [1954].)

name of cost-cutting industrial production. This was especially true in the sphere of interior design, where Soviet models lagged behind technical developments in East German furniture production and consumer goods technology.[35] The modernist cause also enjoyed increasing patronage from new official Soviet ideology, as Khrushchev to everyone's surprise now changed tack in his 1954 speech at the Moscow University conference on Soviet architecture. In it he rejected the Stalinist penchant toward monumentalism and *Baukunst,* arguing that such expensive decorative styling ultimately hindered the construction of badly needed housing. He even went so far as to make the ironic point that Soviet architects were themselves in danger of becoming more "constructivist" than their Western enemies, in that they had unduly subordinated all considerations to outward form. Instead, Khrushchev commanded architects, engineers, and planners to modernize the East Bloc's building industry and appearance by "building better, cheaper and faster."[36] Only such a modern industrial building program, so argued the Soviet premier, could help redress the catastrophic housing situation bedeviling the Soviet Union. Many East German observers were perplexed by Khrushchev's ideological pirouette.

Fig. 2.   Inspirations for GDR interior design. (From the *Besser Leben—Schöner Wohnen* catalog, 78–79.)

Rearguard warnings about the pitfalls of such modern styles were issued by the East Berlin Bauakademie,[37] while Ulbricht himself condemned East German "technoid" domestic modernism ("black coffee cups, black souls," as he put it once) for being spiritually bankrupt.[38]

Nonetheless, the floodgates of modernization were now wide open. The changes quickly made their mark on the world of industrial architecture and housing construction. In 1958, for example, only 12 percent of new housing units were built with prefabricated components. By 1963 this figure had leapt to 63 percent.[39] Of perhaps more relevance here is that the shift also helped unleash a new crusade to make over East German interiors in this new modern style. A raft of new interior decoration and industrial design journals were founded in the mid- to late 1950s, including *Kultur im Heim* (1957) and *Form und Zweck* (1957), to serve as pacesetters for East German domestic modernism.[40]

The famed "P2" Berlin exhibition of 1962 was born of this spirit. It pivoted on a new design for East German "domestic culture"; it derived its name—P2—from the new five-story residential housing block design (fig. 3). It was fully prefabricated and standardized according to new industrial techniques and was, as one of its chief designers recalled in a 1995 interview, the realization of old Bauhaus dreams.[41] The design was publicized as a symbol of the regime's renewed commitment to improving the material life of workers, as well as further evidence of socialism's cultural prog-

Fig. 3.   Prototype of a P2 apartment building. (From the exhibition catalog *Tempolinsen und P2: Alltagskultur der DDR* [Berlin, 1996], 86.)

ress.[42] No doubt the 1961 construction of the Berlin Wall loomed in the
background, to the extent that the 1962 show aimed to stem growing internal criticism about socialism's backwardness and material misery. It was
also during the early 1960s that the SED decided to embark on its daring
experiment in "consumer socialism"—complete with state advertising
agencies, colorful product packaging, modern furniture, household decoration magazines, mail-order clearinghouses, and even state travel
bureaus—as a kind of Great Leap Forward in the modernization of GDR
material culture. Passages from Marx and Engels's *German Ideology*—in
particular the one stating that "Life however involves above all eating and
drinking, a dwelling, clothing and other things. The first historical act is
thus the production of the means to satisfy these needs"—were repeatedly
cited to illustrate the SED's firm commitment to meeting the consumer
needs and desires of its citizens.[43] Yet it was housing that held center stage
in this reform initiative, and it was this P2 design that fundamentally
remade East German domestic life. In fact, it became the standard model
of East German residential building construction from 1962 all the way

until 1990. Already by 1965 over 80 percent of all new dwellings were built along these lines.

The design's real innovation was in the interior, though. First, it explicitly rejected the Deutsche Bauakademie–inspired "realistic living culture" concept espoused at the 1953 "Living Better" show. This time there was virtually nothing about tradition or the past; even the once-obligatory references to the USSR were muted. Indeed, inspiration for these ideas actually came (albeit acknowledged only later) from Scandinavia and West Germany.[44] Special emphasis was placed on the more practical issues of the home's ground plan: it was a more integrated use of tighter spaces, including built-in bookshelves and wall units, and was also relatively open in plan, featuring large windows, central heating, and small efficient kitchens and bathrooms for its users (fig. 4). What is more, the living room was foregrounded as the real center of domestic life. Trivial as this may seem, it pays to recall that such a design represented a fundamental departure from traditional worker housing, which tended to place the enlarged kitchen (*Wohnküche*) as the worker domicile's real centerpiece (usually because it was the warmest room). The new plan reflected the idea of the home as primarily a respite of leisure and relaxation, one that put family life as the heart of socialist solidarity. Its novelty is more striking if we contrast it with the Stalinallee residences. There the worker apartment was not dominated by the living room; relatively generous space was given to the kitchen and bedrooms instead. Even more revealing is that the guiding logic of Stalinallee was one of socialist community, of a kind where housing units, common rooms, grocery stores, bookstores, sports facilities, and cafés were all integrated into a larger architectonic whole. In this case the aim was to create a semienclosed socialist world based on organized community and collectivist living.[45] In the P2 interior, by contrast, the modern technology of the large communal kitchens had been integrated into each individual apartment, while the living room was enlarged to enable family members to spend more time together. The large collective spaces (common rooms, state-run Handelsorganisation shops, etc.) were either located elsewhere or reduced in size and importance.

The P2 model was thus both a departure and a continuity with the 1953 exposition. In the 1953 show, for example, the task was not simply to educate East German citizens into bourgeois taste and style. It also featured a bourgeois conception of the home itself, one in which the home was seen as a respite of familial conviviality and repose. The world of technology, production, and rationalization was noticeably absent. There were

Fig. 4. Kitchen in a model P2 dwelling. (From NGBK, ed., *Wunder-wirtschaft: DDR-Konsumkultur in den 60er Jahren* [Cologne, 1996], 95.)

no traces of the interwar fascination with bringing Taylorist factory ethics—much of which was based on the disciplining and rationalization of the female homemaker—into the home. Indeed, housework and domestic labor—let alone its work station, the kitchen—hardly figured in this show at all. Housework, in the forms of communal laundries and kitchens, was to be taken out of the private domicile altogether. By contrast, the 1962 show marked the full-scale introduction of the world of industrial technology and rationalization into the home.[46] The socialization of household services still continued apace, but there was increasing clamor from women's groups for more labor-saving appliances to ease their double burden of work and domestic duties. This was especially pressing in light of the fact that the late 1950s witnessed the massive influx of women into the GDR workforce.[47] Such design changes were thus in large measure propelled "from below" as the state worked to address the plight of women and working families under duress.[48] Yet policy—and interior design—still assumed that women were and would be the primary homemakers. The P2 show—to say nothing of the gendered literature and advertising surrounding the exhibition—made this plain. In this sense, the 1962 show was a mixture of nineteenth-century ideology and mid-twentieth-century socialist demands and became the guiding image of GDR domesticity for decades to come.

Such a ground plan was also a boon to modern furniture designers and decorators. The small spaces made larger, representational furniture almost impossible to keep; newer styles—including Scandinavian and West German Modern—were considered more appropriate for this kind of modern living. Gone was the accent on preserving the German arts and crafts tradition or any effort to close off the dwelling from the technological world outside. Exterior and interior were again to be harmonized, but this time in the spirit of industrial modernity. But this was not just an urban phenomenon. Design and home advice journals, women's magazines (*Für Dich,* 1963), and Regional Home Advice Centers played a decisive role in popularizing East German modernism far beyond the capital.[49] Not that East German designers ever completely abandoned the 1950s rhetoric of the elevated artistic and even spiritual quality of things. While it is true that the new stress upon austerity, rationality, and functional use value was seen as the perfect expression of the larger GDR effort to create a controlled socialist consumer culture ("each according to his needs") that did not fall prey to capitalist decadence and commodity fetishism,[50] modern interior design was still seen as possessing formidable affective powers. At the Fifth German Art Exposition in 1962, for example, design moved to the forefront of the SED's crusade to modernize socialist culture. Given that design was considered an "applied art" endowed with the "spiritual qualities" that could move and win its subjects, designers were now summoned alongside writers and artists to provide new sources of affective identification with the state. As noted by East German Design Council director Martin Kelm, the new socialist designer's chief task was to "contribute to the development of the socialist lifestyle and character."[51] Such views lay behind the state's motivation to introduce more zip and excitement in socialist furniture and product design, not least because the SED feared that functionalist socialist goods looked too ascetic and cheap.[52] The explosion in the sixties of colorful plastics in GDR interiors registered the shift, as plastics were now championed as a vital element in modernizing and beautifying GDR interiors, what Ulbricht called "an essential element of the socialist cultural revolution."[53]

As a consequence, the picture of the modern socialist family relaxing together amid the latest design goods and consumer technology—as in West Germany—became a mass-produced symbol of normality, security, and prosperity in GDR lifestyle journals. Admittedly, the favorite West German image of the modern middle-class home complete with elegantly dressed (that is, nonworking) housewives and high-tech kitchens was a distinguishing self-image of the leisured, affluent West. But even here, the fifties and sixties ideals of East German home life—despite SED rhetoric about the full equality of the sexes—betrayed its own myth of the "new woman in socialism" based to a large degree upon old bourgeois assumptions of proper female behavior and duties.[54] Not only were images of the cheerful nuclear family touted as the very embodiment of happiness in East German media; women were photographed at home (and at work) in such a manner that underscored a more traditional feminine identity.[55] It was no accident either that the era saw the flowering of GDR etiquette books, which prized bourgeois morality and comportment as the bedrock of East German civility and domestic order.[56] In this way, both Germanys shared a common perception about the elective affinity of traditional family and domestic modernity as a key hallmark of postfascist culture.

However, this modernization campaign did not aim only to make over interiors; it also sought to remake private life itself. At this point I would like to shift gears somewhat in order to show how the private sphere became a central concern in the GDR more generally. For some this may seem a little puzzling at first, given that privacy was apparently another of those East German commodities forever in short supply. Indeed, private life and state socialism are generally seen as antithetical by definition, to the extent that the private person has no legal identity or political standing outside the socialist community. Privacy, so goes the logic, is the natural and exclusive offspring of liberalism, not least because privacy is theoretically grounded in individual liberty and a distant relationship between state and citizen. From this perspective, privacy in the GDR cut a poor figure. The SED's myriad surveillance techniques, best evidenced in the well-known exploits of the Stasi and its reserve army of "unofficial collaborators," only serve to dramatize the full penetration of the state into the private sphere. But I think it is misleading to interpret these well-known developments as merely proof of the absence of privacy in the GDR; for if privacy really did not exist, then the state would hardly have gone to such extraordinary lengths to investigate it. The deeper question is, rather, Why did the private sphere matter so much?

This question is crucial to understanding socialist culture more generally; yet thus far surprisingly little empirical work has been done on the topic. After all, it was precisely the state's overbearing presence itself that made a relatively private home life all the more necessary and valued among GDR citizens. As noted in a range of published recollections, this was certainly the case with the much-loved *dachas* and small country garden houses, where citizens felt freer and more private than anywhere else.[57] Yet this cherished sense of private identity was also something that people cultivated at home as well. In a world in which most social interaction was heavily monitored, the private sphere (as the East German sociologist Wolfgang Engler has asserted) functioned for many citizens as the last vestige of individuality, potential dissent, and alternative identity formation. Interviews, conversations, and questionnaires that I have conducted with dozens of East Germans about their home life have certainly borne this out.[58] Broadly speaking, the home became a place where religious conviction could be openly expressed and nurtured or where nonworker class identities—as noted in furniture and housewares betraying bourgeois or aristocratic family backgrounds—could be displayed. It was also the main location where artifacts from the West (foodstuffs, objects, and even books) were to be found. The domicile thereby acted as a semipermeable refuge from public life and prescribed collective identities, as well as giving form to more private understandings of the self. Over the decades the SED, for a variety of reasons, increasingly acknowledged the formal existence of a private sphere (one that included the protection of personal property and a well-ordered residential life) as a vital dimension of the state's social contract with its citizens. Little wonder, then, that the private sphere played host to great tension between state and citizen about the meaning and maintenance of socialist identity at home.

These housing exhibitions reflected these larger impulses. One architect affiliated with the 1953 Berlin "Living Better" exhibition, for instance, made it quite clear that this "new living culture infused with progressive elements" would go far beyond cosmetic changes. For him, it also necessitated the full dissolution of the boundary between public and private: "We know that political consciousness is for many not sufficiently developed to enable citizens to distinguish beautiful and good from ugly and bad. Such a faculty is analogous to an adopted child. Only when such material education penetrates [the citizen's] most inner being, including the world of his dreams and fantasies, only when we have fully recognized how intimately and indelibly connected the substance of life is with the form of life, will such changes bear fruit."[59] If nothing else, such statements cast these exhibitions in a slightly different light, revealing the extent to which these model interiors were also fueled by the desire to remodel the relationship between citizen and state.

Nevertheless, the enforcement of socialist domesticity was far too important to leave to urban planners, architects, and interior designers. Practically from the very beginning, the state felt it necessary to intervene more directly in people's private lives. The lack of any real avenue of unregulated popular expression—be it comparatively uncontrolled mass media, alternative culture, or of course voter choice—meant that the state was always unsure about citizen loyalty. It thus felt compelled to organize networks of intelligence, snooping, and supervision in order to scout out potential wellsprings of dissent and dissatisfaction. The home was routinely singled out as the most worrisome cell of secrecy and danger. In part this was because the home was such a crucial source of political legitimacy for the SED. Improving people's homes—and delivering ever more badly needed worker accommodations—emerged as a central plank of every SED party congress and was a perennial subject of great anxiety. Complaints about domestic life and in particular problems associated with the dwelling—such as poor heating, leaky roofs, shoddy construction, and overdue repairs—served as the primary source of dissatisfaction among East German written complaints (*Eingaben*) every year and across every region, outstripping complaints about travel restrictions and workplace discontent in every instance.[60]

Such agitation increased dramatically in the wake of the June 16–17 uprising, as the state became ever more sensitive to all forms of citizen unhappiness. With it came redoubled efforts to step up the surveillance of private life. A good deal of this was linked to the perceived (and sometimes real) threat of Western espionage, as reports of American spy activities were routinely published in East German newspapers.[61] One of the earliest incursions in the private sphere was the so-called *Hausbuch,* or "housebook," program. While this initiative started in the early 1950s, it was expanded considerably after 1953. In this case, every GDR citizen was required to register all house guests in a Hausbuch kept by an elected

housing supervisor, significantly named the *Hausvertrauensmann*. It not
only enabled the authorities to keep track of who was entertaining visitors
(especially foreign ones) on a regular basis; it also helped create a new
cadre of so-called confidence men (and they were nearly 90 percent men) to
keep tabs on building tenants. Not surprisingly, the West German press
made much of this "invasion of the private sphere" as the "realization of
Orwell's sinister vision of the dictatorial state," with overtones of Nazi terror.[62] Even so, such measures were introduced to help monitor what civil
society existed and to inspire citizen confidence in the state as the guardian
of public order.

Likewise, new "housing communities," or *Hausgemeinschaften,* were
set up in the early 1950s to help "rationalize" residential life and instill it
with a new developed sense of community. Historical precedents could be
found in the Kaiserreich's *Ehrenämte,* which were late nineteenth-century
agencies of neighborhood-based urban administration, as well as in
Lenin's ideal of small cells of local self-government to help train citizens in
the tasks of democratic political life. But the creation of the housing communities was more the result of Ulbricht's 1951 call for "a stronger education of the people toward the sphere of state concerns, especially in cities
and residential communities." For him, such an initiative was to remedy
creeping "bureaucratism," individual apathy, and the distancing between
citizen and state. Housing communities would then help raise "national
consciousness" and mobilize the masses in the collective construction of
genuinely socialist residential culture.[63] In close cooperation with the
National Front, these housing communities helped build common rooms,
create interhousing sports leagues, and organize parades in connection
with May 1 festivities. Housing community leaders were elected to administer communal life and often had close ties with auxiliary police forces
(ABV); and they too drafted innumerable reports on communal housing
life, material problems, and "uncooperative citizens."

These housing communities also set their sights on penetrating the
private sphere in the name of order and social stability. By early 1953 there
was already much talk within the National Front about using these housing communities to extent patriotism "into every house" and to root out
the influence of Western "warmongers and their agents."[64] While this was
already evident in the early 1950s,[65] this campaign was accelerated in the
wake of the June 17 uprising. Now the housing communities were used to
make sure that everyone knew that the "provocation" engineered by "foreign powers" in Berlin and elsewhere had been successfully suppressed and

to help ensure "loyalty to our government" by keeping a "watchful eye on our residences and families."⁶⁶ Such housing communities were seen as vital in "restoring confidence in the government," as certain supposedly recalcitrant social groups—such as non-SED members, artisans, *Mittelständler,* and farmers—were now targeted for special scrutiny.⁶⁷ One July 1961 Berlin National Front report registered the cold war rhetoric: "we must strengthen our persuasion tactics, since the enemy is trying to beat us in a war of nerves. They want to confuse our people and to precipitate a mass exodus from our republic. Every house must be a defense. . . . If we don't succeed in bringing such progress to every home and to pull together all residences in this common fight, we will be lost."⁶⁸

Such tactics were intensified after the construction of the Berlin Wall a few months later. In one December 1961 report, for example, it was reported that "many negative habits of small segments of the population, such as shiftlessness, listening to RIAS [Radio in the American Sector], watching West German television and black marketeering, are being practiced by families in the home. In these residences such issues must be confronted and discussed, since the formation of politically functioning housing communities is of uppermost significance. The educative role of the housing community is to complement the citizen's broader socialist education received at work and in the factory."⁶⁹ Even if the early 1950s dream of "having a housing community representative on every single East German street" never came to pass, some 30–40 percent of GDR communities were involved in the program by the mid-1960s. Its success of course is difficult to gauge with any confidence; yet it did represent a powerful state intervention into the private lives of GDR citizens in the Ulbricht era.

By the end of the 1960s, the state's growing preoccupation with the private sphere also found expression in a new guise: market research. Whereas the SED concern with private life in the fifties usually centered on issues of housing safety and hygiene, social welfare, and family stability, it took on a decidedly new twist in the sixties. The GDR's Institute of Market Research now routinely sent market researchers into people's homes, asking them for example about furniture preferences, design ideas, and aesthetic predilections. Officially, market research was to encompass "the full scope of conditions under which the realization of use value and the satisfaction of national economic concerns" could best be met.⁷⁰ A surprising amount of painstaking analyses on East German domestic interiors, decorative styles, and consumer habits was drafted and sent to various government committees. Included among them were elaborate consumer questionnaires detailing deep-seated gender, generational, and even class differences in East German taste and consumer spending.[71] Frank and quite unfavorable comparisons to West German consumer trends were common in these papers. These reports on generational and class distinctions became even more detailed in the 1970s, as modern furniture styles were increasingly associated with the young, educated, urban, and upwardly mobile; disproportionate dissatisfaction with available decorative items and housewares was also recorded among students.[72] Recently several historians have rightly remarked that these marketeers served as veritable foot soldiers in the wider crusade to modernize East German material culture and to bring the country along the path of "consumer socialism."[73] But it was also true that these marketing scouts were valued for their role in gauging private dissatisfaction and identifying the "psychological barriers" obstructing the full development of socialist domestic culture. Seemingly trivial issues about domestic lifestyle often attracted considerable attention from these officials. One 1963 Institute of Market Research report on upholstered furniture, for instance, conceded that many GDR families were forced to use the living room as a makeshift bedroom and the sofa as a bed. Poorly designed sofas, so the report concluded, are thus leading to a dangerous "physical and moral wear and tear on our workers," since the "gap between the supply and demand" of modern, well-made furniture is deepening resentment and criticism toward the state.[74] From this perspective, the interior design crusade took on a decidedly more political dimension.

Particularly revealing in this regard are the shifts in the 1970s. By now we are generally familiar with the standard line about the relative liberalization and normalization during the Honecker years. Many observers have noted the ways in which the ascent of Erich Honecker in 1971 marked a significant relaxation in GDR social engineering, as the SED moved from intense cold war antagonism and internal political transformation toward more accommodating ideas of diplomatic cohabitation and domestic stabilization. In so doing the state supposedly eased its demands on and scrutiny of everyday citizens. The East German sociologist Thomas Gensicke summarized this view when he said that "[t]he result was the slow decline of the idealized image of a fully formed, ideologically driven new socialist citizen. The withdrawal of the regime from the private sphere created a new free space for the development of materialism, pleasure-seeking and individuality. The one-time identification with the system, official public life and ideological commitment eventually gave way to a decline in the legitimacy of the system, to a turning away from publicness and ideal-ism altogether. . . . The 1970s was then a period of retreating to new private and individual free spaces wherein one could take refuge from the large events outside, which went hand in hand with the draining of all ideal-ism."[75] Many GDR memoirs from the period recount the degree to which great energy and interest were now invested in the private sphere, as people increasingly abandoned public life and political activity altogether. This was certainly noticeable in recollections of East Germans after 1989, as well as in the GDR home advice literature. Everywhere cropped up the term *diversity,* as the Ulbricht-era campaign to standardize East German domestic culture gave way to a new celebration of relative difference. The 1970s saw a new emphasis on imaginative varieties of interior design styles, even if the furniture models themselves remained virtually unchanged from the 1960s (fig. 5). The trend toward more "individual forms" and per-sonalized expression was noted in market research data as well.[76] Arts and crafts objects now made a comeback and were integrated in easy cohabi-tation with East German industrial modernism.[77] All of this was inter-preted as part of the Honecker era's benign neglect of the domestic sphere, as citizens increasingly used their homes (or rooms, in the case of children) as theaters of pent-up individuality and subcultural pursuits.[78] The histo-rian Adelheid von Saldern put it succinctly when she argued that "the older the GDR got, the more important the private sphere—and especially the home—became for everyday people. This implied a new appreciation of and respect for the private sphere. The dwelling served as a symbol for a private sphere *de facto* protected from the state and Party."[79]

But did the state ever really back off from the private sphere? My research thus far has shown that the 1970s détente in no way spelled a relaxation in the measures used to monitor private lives. On the contrary, they were intensified considerably in scope and ambition. The more inva-sive and anxious tone is unmistakable in the seventies market research reports. In the name of creating new "socialist living ensembles," increas-ing stress was placed upon the need to conjoin "personal interests" with those of society. One 1971 market research report made this very clear in stating that "the dwelling is no counterworld to the sphere of labor, no so-called 'private ivory tower,' but rather is more and more an integrated ele-ment of a comprehensive socialist everyday life."[80] The same went for the "housing community" literature. Admittedly, the more ham-fisted lan-guage of the communities as a vital means of "raising national conscious-ness" and theoretically doing away with the private sphere in the name of

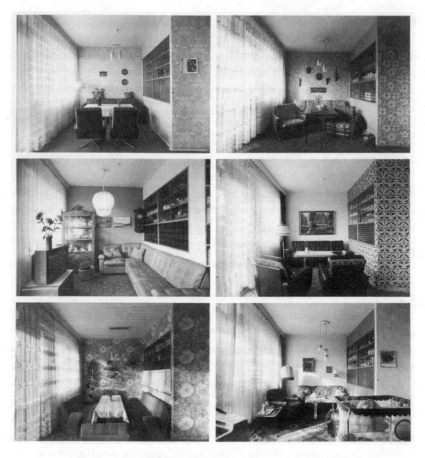

Fig. 5.   P2 living rooms. (From the exhibition catalog *Tempolinsen und P2: Alltagskultur der DDR* [Berlin, 1996], 91.)

"national community" had clearly fallen off under Honecker. In the 1970s there was also a discernible shift toward the defense of the nuclear family as the "true cell" of socialist community and personality.[81] Yet what looked like a state retreat from the private sphere was often simply a new strategy, in this case extending the state's reach into home life in the name of a broader definition of social welfare. Such developments need not be read as necessarily negative, though. After all, they went hand in hand with a 1970s idea of the "therapeutic state," one that strove to devote more time and energy to the care of at-risk citizens, such as children and the elderly. Efforts to strengthen the bonds between individual and community found other expressions as well. The organization of competitions, festivals, and social events within the housing communities—much of which was closely associated with the National Front–sponsored "Mach Mit!" (Join In!) program to refurbish and beautify East German neighborhoods—appreciably intensified under Honecker.[82] It was also during this time that the Hausbuch program was significantly enlarged and more vigorously enforced. Moreover, it was increasingly tied to security agencies, considered as it was "an important part of the public work of the People's Police."[83] By 1972 the Hausbuch program was reported to be in operation in half of East German residential communities and 75 percent of East Berlin housing estates.[84] That its remit had been expanded along the way was evident in a 1973 letter from a People's Police (*Volkspolizei*) official to the editor of the journal *Die Volkspolizei,* in which he praised citizens for enforcing the Hausbuch initiative and supplying useful information to the police about "shiftless residents and asocial behavior."[85] Such evidence is by no means conclusive, given that enforcement and information gathering varied dramatically place to place, year to year. Yet it gives some indication of how the Hausbuch program was being remade and politicized at the time. Not least, the stepped-up activities of the Stasi in the seventies and eighties (much of which, it should be remembered, focused on activities within the home) further illustrate this abiding state preoccupation with the private sphere.[86]

Why did this happen in the 1970s? The potential threats from West Germany and the West more generally had been clearly mitigated by the construction of the Wall and the advent of *Ostpolitik.* National security, international recognition, and domestic stability had all been achieved, while the economy was posting quite satisfactory results overall. A growing sense of normalization apparently pervaded the country, as a freer home life—along with a more accepted devotional life and youth culture—became oft-cited expressions of the early Honecker reform attitude. However, it seems that it was precisely this new distancing of state and citizen that fueled renewed state apprehension about conduct in the home. For in the state's eyes, the home still remained an uncontrolled arena of individual freedom, private detachment, and potential political dissent. The fifties campaign to construct new homes as symbols of domestic security and the good life eventually gave way to growing government fears that these same "homes for heroes" had become dens of domestic misery and political menace. This seems to me a key, if neglected, effect of the famed Ostpolitik, in that the relaxation of East-West tensions—coupled with the widespread perception that the GDR would continue to fall further and further behind West German economic development—gave cause for state concern that the home warranted renewed political attention.

The 1977 publication of Maxie Wander's oral history of GDR women—*Guten Morgen, Du Schöne!*—loudly bespoke this deep reservoir of dissatisfaction at the core of GDR domestic life. The book was extremely novel at the time, not least because it featured frank confessions by female citizens about "real existing socialism." In particular nineteen unidentified women provided unguarded accounts of their personal lives, complete with detailed reminiscences about their work and sex life.[87] While this book became a kind of cult book in the GDR, it was hardly an isolated case. A sizable number of seventies and eighties novels and paintings made the same point, as alienation and domestic despair became notable new cultural themes.[88] Not that all the news was bad, however. One 1977 questionnaire, for instance, recorded that a majority of people polled were quite content with their home life and went on to place "good living conditions" next to "good family life" and "interesting work" as the most important indices of a "satisfactory life."[89] Even so, the SED could not fail to see what was happening. The increased contraction of social life to the home, or put differently, the appreciable value of the home as the cherished locus of relative freedom and pleasure, meant that private life now took on new political gravity, one that the state felt it needed to watch very carefully.

Such changes also marked a significant shift in the relationship between public and private. This is especially the case in terms of GDR social policy. For all of its interest in the private sphere, the state in certain respects left families relatively alone in the 1950s and 1960s. While it is certainly true that the Party tirelessly championed the nuclear family as the bedrock of social stability and political peace, and did much to socialize youth into the virtues of socialist ideology, the emergence of the family— and with it private life—as an object of state intervention was very much a product of the mid- to late 1960s and grew dramatically in the 1970s.[90] In part this was simply because the regime was preoccupied with the pressing issues of reconstruction, provisioning, and public order in the 1950s. The 1961 construction of the Berlin Wall and de facto "normalization" meant that the state was in a better position to look beyond crude productionism and infrastructure concerns toward more nagging social and domestic problems. Much of this initiative was spearheaded by the actions of engaged women's groups, who successfully made the case to the government that domestic issues deserved more state assistance. No less significant is that the state was beginning to see these problems differently. Over the course of the 1960s and 1970s the GDR had adapted a range of Western social science models in developing their new fields of behavioral psychology, pedagogy, criminology, and urban sociology. East German selfhood and "socialist personality" now became fresh objects of study and policymaking (see Greg Eghigian's contribution to this volume).[91] To be sure, these trends were not perforce bad in themselves. While the new marriage of social science and the state often included expanded notions of "asocial" behavior and social deviance, it also brought great benefit to suffering citizens. The cumulative effect, however, was that home life and private comportment became more and more the object of state scrutiny. In this sense, the preoccupation with the private sphere was a blend of old ideology and new science, one in which the dwelling acted as a testing ground for socialist education and normative citizenship.

If nothing else, such tensions reveal the fact that private life was never all that private. Günter Gaus's famous formulation that GDR life had become a veritable "niche society" of small circles of trusted family and friends is misleading in this respect. After all, the state's growing concern with home life also pointed up the dangerous dialectic of privacy and politics at the heart of GDR domestic life. There are telling parallels here to the well-known phenomenon of *Eingaben,* wherein GDR citizens wrote to the state mostly as private *Bürger* with specific individual complaints. This elaborate institutionalized "culture of complaint," whose number of Eingaben reached over one million per year by 1989, neatly pointed up the strange politicization of private life.[92] That local, regional, and national-level representatives were routinely chastened by the central government for not answering citizen complaints promptly enough was not only to guarantee their rights to petition as socialist citizens; it was also to help overcome rampant "bureaucratism" and the growing gap between state and citizen, a gap that the state knew very well existed and was in danger of opening up beyond repair. What is so interesting, though, is that increasing control of private life also went hand in hand with the citizens' usage of these complaints (the majority of which focused on domestic concerns such as poor heating, leaky roofs, shoddy construction, and overdue repairs) to preserve and assure a decent private life, usually in the form of a safe, clean, and quiet domicile free of undue state interference. Not to say that these grievances were redressed; many—if not most—were not. Still, the fact that so many citizens wrote to their local state representatives pleading their case suggested at least a certain citizen engagement with the state over individual concerns. In this regard these complaints were both "system-sustaining" and potentially subversive.[93] And yet in its capacity as provider of security and prosperity, the state had a vested stake in its image as the paternalist guarantor of a certain notion of domestic order and private happiness. As a consequence, the state paradoxically served as both the foe and guardian of the private sphere.

It was in this context that the home assumed such unusual political proportions in the GDR. The changing ideals of GDR domestic life—as noted in the two exhibitions under discussion—marked the shift in ideology toward a more industrially oriented "socialist modern." But looking at things from a purely aesthetic standpoint is ultimately too limiting. For even if the decorative elements of the home may not have changed all that much from the mid-1960s, the sociological role of the home (as outpost of surveillance and locus of alternative identity formation) did change dramatically. A 1977 editorial in the home decoration magazine *Kultur im Heim* neatly captured the heightened significance of private life: "if the living space [*Wohnraum*] were only a repository of individual accents, subjective fantasies and 'tastemaking,' there would be no need to treat it as a social issue—it would be a purely private affair. But its primary significance in the education of the human being, in the richer formation of socialist conditions of reality, as well as in its chief function within social psychology makes its form a paramount public [*res publica*] affair."[94] That GDR social life had become increasingly privatized over the decades—often focusing on the activities, stylization, and memories of the home—clearly colored much of the post-1989 musings about the East German past. This post-Wall nostalgia for old GDR furnishings and memorabilia as symbols of a lost world (see Daphne Berdahl's contribution to this volume) made plain just how powerful these identities were for countless people.[95] In the end, the home may not have been all that private or free, but it did serve as a kind of refuge and alternative world for many East Germans.

NOTES

Research for this essay was kindly supported by the Graham Foundation and the British Academy, for which I am grateful. Thanks too go to Greg Castillo for his constructive criticism.

1. Recent titles include Gavriel Rosenfeld, *Munich and Memory: Architecture, Monuments and the Legacy of the Third Reich* (Berkeley: University of California Press, 2000); Brian Ladd, *The Ghosts of Berlin: Confronting German History in the Urban Landscape* (Chicago: University of Chicago Press, 1997); H. Glenn Penny, *Objects of Culture: Ethnology and Ethnographic Museums in Imperial Germany* (Chapel Hill: University of North Carolina Press, 2002); Elizabeth Ten Dyke, *Dresden: A Paradox of Memory and History* (London: Routledge, 2002); and Janet Ward, *Weimar Surfaces: Urban Visual Culture in the 1920s* (Berkeley: University of California Press, 2001).

2. See, for example, *Geschichte des Wohnens*, vol. 4: *Reform Reaktion Zerstörung*, ed. Gert Kähler (Stuttgart: Deutsche Verlags-Anstalt, 1996), and *Geschichte des Wohnens*, vol. 5: *Von 1945 bis Heute*, ed. Ingeborg Flagge (Stuttgart: Deutsche Verlags-Anstalt, 1999). See also Joachim Petsch, *Eigenheim und Gute Stube: Zur Geschichte des bürgerlichen Wohnens* (Cologne: DuMont, 1989).

3. Tilman Harlander, *Zwischen Heimstätte und Wohnmaschine: Wohnungsbau und Wohnungspolitik in der Zeit des Nationalsozialismus* (Basel and Boston: Birkhäuser, 1995); Axel Schildt and Arnold Sywottek, eds., *Massenwohnung und Eigenheim: Wohnungsbau und Wohnen in der Grossstadt seit dem Ersten Weltkrieg* (Frankfurt/Main: Campus, 1988); Tilman Harlander and Gerhard Fehl, eds., *Hitlers Sozialer Wohnungsbau 1940–1945* (Hamburg: Christians, 1986); Gerhard Fehl, *Kleinstadt, Steildach, Volksgemeinschaft: Zum "reaktionären Modernismus" in Bau- und Stadtbaukunst* (Braunschweig: Vieweg, 1995); Marie L. Recker, *Die Grossstadt als Wohn- und Lebensbereich im Nationalsozialismus* (Frankfurt/Main: Campus, 1981); Manfred Walz, *Wohnungsbau- und Industrieansiedlungspolitik in Deutschland, 1933–1939* (Frankfurt/Main: Campus, 1979); and Barbara Miller Lane, *Architecture and Politics in Germany, 1918–1945* (Cambridge, MA: Harvard University Press, 1968).

4. Ralf Dahrendorf, *Society and Democracy in Germany* (New York: W. W. Norton, 1967), 285–96. More recent titles include Robert Moeller, *Protecting Motherhood: Women and the Family in the Politics of Postwar West Germany* (Berkeley: University of California Press, 1993); and Erica Carter, *How German Is She? Postwar West German Reconstruction and the Consuming Woman* (Ann Arbor: University of Michigan Press, 1997).

5. Robert Moeller, *War Stories: The Search for a Usable Past in the Federal Republic of Germany* (Berkeley: University of California Press, 2000), esp. 1–21, 88–122. See also Michael Krause, *Flucht vor dem Bombenkrieg: "Umquartierung" im zweiten Weltkrieg und die Wiedereingliederung der Evakuierten in Deutschland, 1943–1963* (Düsseldorf: Droste, 1997).

6. Hannah Arendt, *The Human Condition* (Chicago: University of Chicago

Press, 1958), esp. 22–78; and Jürgen Habermas, *The Structural Transformation of the Public Sphere* (Cambridge, MA: MIT Press, [1962] 1989).

7. Joy Parr, *Domestic Goods: The Material, the Moral and the Economic in the Postwar Years* (Toronto: University of Toronto Press, 1999), 21–39; John Morton Blum, *V Is for Victory: Politics and American Culture during World War II* (New York: Harcourt Brace & Jovanovich, 1976), 101–4; D. Albrecht, *World War II and the American Dream: How Wartime Building Changed a Nation* (Washington, DC: National Building Museum and Cambridge, MA: MIT Press, 1995); and Detlev Peukert, *Inside Nazi Germany* (New Haven: Yale University Press, 1987), 247.

8. Paul Betts, *The Authority of Everyday Objects: A Cultural History of West German Industrial Design* (Berkeley: University of California Press, 2004), esp. 23–72.

9. *Parteiauftrag: Ein neues Deutschland,* ed. Dieter Vorsteher (Berlin: DHM, 1997); and Paul Betts, "The Politics of Post-Fascist Aesthetics: 1950s West and East German Industrial Design," in *Life after Death: Violence, Normality and the Reconstruction of Postwar Europe,* ed. Richard Bessel and Dirk Schumann (Cambridge: Cambridge University Press, 2003), 291–321.

10. The famed Nixon-Khrushchev "kitchen debate," in which the then U.S. vice president and the Soviet premier sparred over the meaning of modern kitchen appliances at the American Pavilion of the 1959 Moscow Fair, is perhaps the most dramatic instance of the more general politicization of material culture. Elaine Tyler May, *Homeward Bound: American Families in the Cold War Era* (New York: Basic Books, 1988), 17–18; Karal Ann Marling, *As Seen on TV: The Visual Culture of Everyday Life in the 1950s* (Cambridge, MA: Harvard University Press, 1994), 278; and, more generally, Mary Nolan, "Consuming America, Producing Gender," in *The American Century in Europe,* ed. R. Laurence Moore and Maurizio Vaudagna (Ithaca: Cornell University Press, 2003), 243–61.

11. W. L. Guttmann, *Workers' Culture in Weimar Germany: Between Tradition and Commitment* (New York: Berg, 1990), 54–106, 287–313.

12. Quoted in Werner Kirchoff, "Schlusswort auf der gemeinsamen Tagung des Sekretariats des Nationalrats und des Ministerium für Bauwesen am 24. Oktober 1973," Bundesarchiv Berlin (hereafter BAB), DY 6/2349. Engels's *Zur Wohnungsfrage* was republished as a pamphlet by East Berlin's Dietz Verlag in 1948 and was widely quoted in reports and Party journalism.

13. Richard Stites, *Revolutionary Dreams: Utopian Vision and Experimental Life in the Russian Revolution* (New York: Oxford University Press, 1989), esp. 190–222; Milka Bliznakov, "Soviet Housing during the Experimental Years, 1918 to 1933," in *Russian Housing in the Modern Age: Design and Social History,* ed. William Craft Brumfield and Blair A. Ruble (Cambridge: Cambridge University Press, 1993), 85–149.

14. Herbert Riecke, *Mietskasernen im Kapitalismus, Wohnpaläste im Sozialismus: Die Entwicklung der Städte im modernen Kapitalismus und die Grundsätze des sozialistischen Städtebaus* (Berlin: Verlag Kultur und Fortschritt, 1954), 7.

15. Riecke, *Mietskasernen im Kapitalismus,* 36–37. See too *Wie komme ich zur einer Wohnung?* (Berlin: Tribüne, 1954); and Gisela Karau, *Sozialistischer Alltag in*

der DDR (East Berlin: Staatssekretariat für westdeutsche Fragen, 1970), esp. 24–26.

16. Susan Reid and David Crowley, eds., *Style and Socialism: Modernity and Material Culture in Post-War Eastern Europe* (Oxford: Berg, 2000), esp. introduction.

17. Walter Ulbricht, "Die grosse Aufgaben der Innenarchitektur beim Kampf um eine neue deutsche Kultur," in "Fragen der deutschen Innenarchitektur und des Möbelbaues: Bericht über die Arbeitstagung des Instituts für Innenarchitektur der Deutschen Bauakademie über die Fragen der Innenarchitektur und des Möbelbaues am 14. März 1952," quoted in Greg Castillo, "Domesticating the Cold War: Cultural Infiltration through American Model Home Exhibitions," paper delivered at the "The Postwar European Home" conference, Victoria & Albert Museum, London, 2003, 9.

18. Christoph Klessmann, *Zwei Staaten, Eine Nation: Deutsche Geschichte, 1955–1970* (Bonn: Bundeszentrale für politische Bildung, 1997), 406–7.

19. Thomas Hoscislawski, *Bauen zwischen Macht und Ohnmacht: Architektur und Städtebau in der DDR* (Berlin: Verlag für Bauwesen, 1991), esp. 38–43, 101–11, 297–310.

20. Peter Marcuse and Fred Staufenbiel, eds., *Wohnen und Stadtpolitik im Umbruch: Perspektiven der Stadterneuerung nach 40 Jahre DDR* (Berlin: Akademie Verlag, 1991); and Klaus von Beyme, *Der Wiederaufbau: Architektur und Städtebau in beiden deutschen Staaten* (Munich: Piper, 1987).

21. Herbert Nicolaus and Alexander Obeth, *Die Stalinallee: Geschichte einer deutschen Strasse* (Berlin: Verlag für Bauwesen, 1997), 233–50.

22. "Sixteen Principles for the Restructuring of Cities in the German Democratic Republic," in *Architecture Culture, 1943–1968: A Documentary Anthology,* ed. Joan Ockman (New York: Rizzoli, 1993), 127–28.

23. "Der Kampf gegen den Formalismus und Literatur, für eine fortschrittliche deutsche Kultur: Erschliessung des Zentralkomitees der Sozialistischen Einheitspartei Deutschlands auf der Tagung am 15, 16, 17 März 1951," *Tägliche Rundschau,* 18 April 1951, quoted in Castillo, "Domesticating the Cold War," 15.

24. Simone Barck, "Das Dekadenz-Verdikt: Zur Konjunktur eines kulturpolitischen 'Kampfkonzepts' Ende der 1950er bis Mitte der 1960er Jahre," in *Historische DDR-Forschung,* ed. Jürgen Kocka (Berlin: Akademie-Verlag, 1993), 327–44.

25. Walter Ulbricht, "Sozialistischer Wohnungsbau im Siebenjahrplan," in *Deutsche Architektur* 8, no. 12 (1959): 645, quoted in Thomas Topstedt, "Wohnen und Städtebau in der DDR," in *Geschichte des Wohnens,* vol. 5, ed. Flagge, 442.

26. Greg Castillo, "Domesticating the Cold War: Household Consumption as Propaganda in Marshall Plan Germany," *Journal of Contemporary History* 40, no. 2 (April 2005): 261–88; quotation is from 269–70.

27. Quoted in *Besser Leben—Schöner Wohnen: Raum und Möbel,* exhibition catalog, ed. Deutsche Bauakademie und dem Minister für Leichtindustrie (East Berlin, 1954), 8.

28. *Besser Leben,* 3.

29. Jakob Jordan, "Über einige Aufgaben des Instituts für Innenarchitektur der Deutschen Bauakademie," *Deutsche Architektur* 3 (1954): 9.

30. Jordan, "Über einige Aufgaben," 10.

31. Jordan, "Über einige Aufgaben," 14.

32. *Besser Leben*, 3.

33. *Besser Leben*, 74.

34. Claudia Freytag, "Neue Städte—Neues Wohnen: 'Vorbildliche Wohnkultur' in Wolfsburg und Stalinstadt," in *Aufbau West Aufbau Ost: Die Planstädte Wolfsburg und Eisenhüttenstadt in der Nachkriegszeit,* ed. Rosemarie Beier (Berlin: DHM, 1997), 318.

35. With the result that the periphery—the GDR, Poland, and Czechoslovakia—was at the forefront of East Bloc design.

36. Nikita Khrushchev, *Besser, billiger und schneller bauen* (East Berlin, 1955), cited in Topstedt, "Wohnen und Städtebau," 486.

37. Topstedt, 485.

38. Hein Köster, "Schmerzliche Ankunft in die Moderne," in *Wunderwirtschaft: DDR-Konsumkultur in den 60er Jahren,* ed. NGBK (Cologne: Böhlau, 1996), 99.

39. Adelheid von Saldern, *Häuserleben: Zur Geschichte städtischen Arbeiterswohnens vom Kaiserreich bis heute* (Berlin: Dietz, 1995), 315.

40. Dominique Krössin, "Kultur im Heim: Geschmackserziehung versus Eigensinn," in *Fortschritt, Norm und Eigensinn: Erkundungen im Alltag der DDR,* ed. Dokumentationszentrum Alltagskultur der DDR e.V (Berlin: Ch. Links, 1999), 151–64.

41. "P2 macht das Rennen: Wohnungsbau als sozio-kulturelles Programm," in *Tempolinsen und P2: Alltagskultur der DDR* (Berlin: Be-Bra, 1996), 98.

42. In the early 1960s the architect emerged as a new cultural hero in the GDR, as perhaps best seen in the following novels: Karl-Heinz Jacobs's *Beschreibung eines Sommers* (1963); Erik Neutsch's *Spur der Steine* (1964); Brigitte Reimann's *Franziska Linkerhand* (1974); as well as Stefan Heym's posthumously published *Die Architekten* (2000).

43. Waltraud Nieke, "Hauptsächliche Entwicklungstendenzen des Bevölker-ungsbedarfs nach Wohnraumtextilien und Probleme ihrer Forschung," PhD diss., Hochschule für Ökonomie, Berlin, 1967, 41. The original passage comes from Marx and Engels, "Deutsche Ideologie," in *Werke,* vol. 3 (Berlin, 1959), 28.

44. Petra Gruner, "'Neues Leben, neues Wohnen,'" in *Wunderwirtschaft,* ed. NGBK, 95.

45. Nicolaus and Obeth, *Die Stalinallee,* 233–50.

46. Winifried Stallknecht, Herbert Kuschy, and Achim Fetz, "Architekten Wohnen im Versuchsbau P2," *Kultur im Heim,* January 1964, 3–7.

47. Karin Zachmann, "A Socialist Consumption Junction: Debating the Mechanization of Housework in East Germany, 1956–1957," *Technology and Culture* 43, no. 1 (January 2002): 73–99.

48. Donna Harsch, "Squaring the Circle: The Dilemmas and Evolution of

Women's Policy," in *The Workers' and Peasants' State: Communism and Society in East Germany under Ulbricht,* ed. Patrick Major and Jonathan Osmond (Manchester: Manchester University Press, 2002), 151–70.

49. Topstedt, "Wohnen und Städtebau," 523.

50. Ina Merkel, "Der aufhaltsame Aufbruch," in *Wunderwirtschaft,* ed. NGBK, 11–15; and Jochen Fetzer, "Gut verpackt . . . ," in *Wunderwirtschaft,* ed. NGBK, 104–11.

51. Martin Kelm, *Produktgestaltung im Sozialismus* (Berlin: Dietz, 1971), 81.

52. Merkel, "Consumer Culture in the GDR; or How the Struggle for Antimodernity was Lost on the Battlefield of Consumer Culture," in *Getting and Spending: European and American Consumer Societies in the 20th Century,* ed. Susan Strasser, Charles McGovern, and Matthias Judt (Cambridge: Cambridge University Press, 1998), 290.

53. Quoted in Horst Redeker, *Chemie gibt Schönheit* (Berlin: Institut für angewandte Kunst, 1959), 14. For background, see Raymond Stokes, *Constructing Socialism: Technology and Change in East Germany, 1945–1990* (Baltimore: Johns Hopkins University Press, 2000); and, most recently, Eli Rubin, "The Order of Substitutes: Plastic Consumer Goods in the *Volkswirtschaft* and Everyday Domestic Life in the GDR," in *Consuming Germany in the Cold War,* ed. David Crew (Oxford: Berg, 2003), 87–120.

54. Jörg Petruschat, "Take Me Plastics," in *Von Bauhaus bis Bitterfeld: 41 Jahre DDR Design,* ed. Regine Halter (Giessen: Anabas, 1991), 111–12.

55. Ina Merkel, . . . *Und Du, Frau auf der Werkbank: Die DDR in den 50er Jahren* (Berlin: Elefanten Press, 1990), esp. 43–105.

56. This can be noted in the remarkable success of Karl Smolka's best-seller, *Gutes Benehmen von A–Z* (East Berlin: Verlag Neues Leben, 1957). See too Anna-Sabine Ernst, "The Politics of Culture and the Culture of Everyday Life," in *Between Reform and Revolution: German Socialism and Communism from 1840–1990,* ed. David Barclay and Eric Weitz (Providence and Oxford: Berghahn, 2002), 489–506.

57. Nicole Andries and Majken Rehder, *Zaunwelten: Zäune und Zeitzeugen— Geschichten zur Alltagsgeschichte der DDR* (Marburg: Jonas, 2005); and Isolde Deutsch, *Hammer, Zirkel, Gartenzaun: Die Politik der SED gegenüber den Kleingärtnern* (Berlin: Books on Demand GmbH, 2003).

58. These sources are discussed in my ongoing book project, *Tyranny of Intimacy: A History of East Berlin Private Life* (Oxford: Oxford University Press, forthcoming).

59. Hanns Hopp, "Ansprüche zur Eröffnung der Arbeitstagung für Innenarchitektur am 14.3.1952," 19, Stiftung Archiv der Parteien und Massenorganisationen der DDR (hereafter, SAPMO) DH2/DBA/A41.

60. Joachim Staadt, *Eingaben: Die institutionalisierte Meckerkultur in der DDR* (Berlin: Freie Universität Berlin, 1996), 9–13.

61. See, for example, "Spionage des 'Sozialen Helferrings,'" *Berliner Zeitung,* 26 January 1950; "Die Spionage- und Terrorzentralen in Westberlin," *Tägliche Rundschau,* 22 May 1952; "Amerikanisches Spionzentrum in der DDR zerschla-

gen," *Neues Deutschland,* 23 September 1953; and "Schluss mit USA-Wühlarbeit," *Neues Deutschland,* 26 February 1957.

62. "Hausbuch für die Deutsche Demokratische Republik," *Der Tag,* 20 December 1952.

63. Karl Bönninger, *Die Einrichtung der Haus- und Strassenvertrauensleute als Form der Teilnahme der Massen an der Leitung des Staates in der DDR* (Berlin: VEB Deutscher Zentralverlag, 1954), 15–86.

64. "Büro des Praesidiums des Nationalrats der Nationalen Front des demokratischen Deutschland," Berlin, 15 May 1953, BAB DY6/0189.

65. According to one report, members of one Berlin Hausgemeinschaft along with several "Aufklärer" from the National Front helped "motivate" the local residents by means of music and chanting the following refrain:

Alles aus den Betten raus, wir kommen jetzt in Euer Haus!
Auf jeden von Euch kommt es an, den Besten als Vertrauensmann!

"Informationsbericht, Berlin, 30 March 1953," BAB, DY 6/ 4626.

66. "Vertrauliches Schreiben!" memo from the Ausschuss der Nationalen Front des demokratischen Deutschlands der Hauptstadt Berlin zur 1. Sekretäre der Stadtbezirke des demokratischen Sektors, 19 June 1953, BAB, DY6 / 4626.

67. "Aufklärungsplan für die Weiterführung der Wahlen der Leitungen der Haus- und Hofgemeinschaften," 17 July 1953, BAB, DY6/0189.

68. "Protokoll der Tagung der Berliner Ausschusses der Nationalen Front am Montag, den 24.Juli 1961," Ausschuss der Nationalen Front des demokratischen Deutschlands der Hauptstadt Berlin, 3–4, BAB, DY 6/2529.

69. "Direktiv für die Tätigkeit einer Brigade des Nationalrats in Karl-Marx-Stadt Berlin," Büro des Präsidium, 2 December1961, BAB, DY 6/ 0189.

70. Dr. Moedel, "Marktforschung—eine Führungsaufgabe in der Industrie," *Die Wirtschaft* 3/1966, Beilage.

71. See, for example, Harald Lorenz, "Grundlagen für die Gestaltung des Möbelsortiments," Institut für Marktforschung, 1969, Bundesarchiv Dahlwitz/ Hoppegarten (hereafter, BADH) DL102/393.

72. Werner Bischoff and Waltraud Niecke, "Grundlagen für die Gestaltung des Möbelsortiments im Perspektiv—und Prognosezeitraum," Institut für Marktforschung, 1971, BADH, DL 102/554.

73. Annette Kaminsky, *Wohlstand, Schönheit, Glück: Kleine Konsumgeschichte der DDR* (Munich: C. H. Beck, 2001), 71–115. See too Ina Merkel's contribution in this volume.

74. Erhard Krause, "Die Angebots- und Nachfragesituation bei Pölstermöbeln bis 1965," Leipzig, 1963, BADH, DL 102/243.

75. Thomas Gensicke, "Sind die Ostdeutschen konservativer als die Westdeutschen?" in *Das Ende eines Experiments: Umbruch in der DDR und deutsche Einheit,* ed. Rolf Reissig and Gert-Joachim Glaessner (Berlin: Dietz, 1991), 285.

76. Waltraud Niecke, "Die Entwicklung des Bevölkerungsbedarf nach Wohnraummöbeln in Zeitraum bis 1985," Institut für Marktforschung, 1979, BADH, DL 102/1339.

77. Stefan Wolle, *Die heile Welt der Diktatur: Alltag und Herrschaft in der DDR, 1971–1989* (Munich: Ullstein, 2001), 362–66.

78. Ina Merkel, "Leitbilder und Lebensweise von Frauen," in *Sozialgeschichte der DDR,* ed. Hartmut Kaelble, Jürgen Kocka, and Hartmut Zwahr (Stuttgart: Klett-Cotta, 1994), 366.

79. Saldern, *Häuserleben,* 313, 329.

80. Waltraud Nieke and Werner Bischoff, "Tendenzen der Entwicklung der Wohnbedürfnisse und der Nachfrage nach Wohnraummöbeln," Institut für Marktforschung, 1971, 4, BADH, DL 102/591.

81. *Sozialistische Beziehungen in Familien und Hausgemeinschaften bewusster gestalten* (Berlin: Abt. Presse und Information, 1971).

82. Simone Tippach-Schneider, "'Blumen für die Hausgemeinschaft': Kollektivformen in der DDR—ein Überblick," in *Fortschritt, Norm und Eigensinn,* ed. Dokumentationszentrum Alltagskultur der DDR e.V, 243–55.

83. Werner Symmangk and Edwin Plenikowski, "Formen, Methoden und Organisation der Arbeit mit den Hausbuchbeauftragten in einem Meldestellenbereich," 1971, BAB, DO1/46632. For background, see Richard Bessel, "The People's Police and the People in Ulbricht's Germany," in *Workers' and Peasants' State,* ed. Major and Osmond, 59–77.

84. "Vermerk: Information des Leiter der Abt. PM/BDVP Neubrandenburg," 12 December 1972, BAB, DO1/46357.

85. Oberst der VP Fischer to the Editor of *Die Volkspolizei,* 3 May 1973, BAB DO1/46357.

86. Jens Gieseke, *Mielke-Konzern: Die Geschichte der Stasi, 1945–1990* (Stuttgart: Deutsche Verlags-Anstalt, 2001); and David Childs and Richard Popplewell, *The Stasi: The East German Intelligence and Security Service* (Basingstoke: Macmillan, 1996).

87. Maxie Wander, *Guten Morgen, Du Schöne!* (Berlin: Buchverlag Der Morgen, 1977).

88. Katharina Belwe, "Zwischenmenschliche Entfremdung in der DDR: Wachsender materieller Wohlstand versus Verlust an sozialen Kontakten," in *Die DDR in der Ära Honecker: Politik, Kultur, Gesellschaft,* ed. Gert-Joachim Glaessner, (Opladen: Westdeutscher Verlag, 1988), 499–513.

89. Alice Kahl, "Zum Verhältnis von Wohnzufriedenheit und Wohnortverbundenheit an neuen Wohnungsbaustandorten in der DDR," *Wissenschaftliche Zeitschrift der Humboldt-Universität zu Berlin: Gesellschafts- und sprachwissenschaftliche Reihe* 28, no. 4 (1979): 532.

90. Harsch, "Squaring the Circle," 166–67.

91. See too Angela Brock, "The Making of the Socialist Personality: Education and Socialisation in the GDR, 1958–1978," PhD diss., University College London, 2005.

92. Staadt, *Eingaben,* 1–9.

93. Mary Fulbrook, *The People's State: East German Society from Hitler to Honecker* (New Haven: Yale University Press, 2005), 269–88.

94. Friedrich Moebius, "Der Wohnraum als 'Abbild' und 'Aktion,'" in *Kultur*

im Heim, April 1977, 34, quoted in Marion Godau, "Die Innengestaltung in der DDR," in *Wohnkultur und Plattenbau: Beispiele aus Berlin und Budapest,* ed. Kerstin Dörhöfer (Berlin: Dietrich Reimer, 1994), 109.

95. Daphne Berdahl, "(N)ostalgia for the Present: Memory, Longing and East German Things," *Ethnos* 64, no. 2 (1999): 192–211; and Paul Betts, "The Twilight of the Idols: East German Memory and Material Culture," *Journal of Modern History* 72, no. 3 (September 2000): 731–65.

The Travels of Bettina Humpel

One Stasi File and Narratives of State and Self in East Germany

Alon Confino

The legitimacy of modern ideological regimes, that is, all regimes, is partly based on their ability to provide the perception and the reality of good life, improvement, and material well-being. Thomas Jefferson articulated this idea in one of the most audacious ideological promises ever made when he pledged a society committed to the "pursuit of happiness." Stalin acknowledged the suffering of the collectivization as well as its ideological raison d'être when he noted in 1935 that "life has become better, life has become more cheerful."[1] And Goebbels declared over the burning books in Berlin's Opernplatz on March 10, 1933, "Oh, century, it is a joy to live!" as the Nazis set out to build a racial civilization.[2] Liberalism, communism, Nazism; happiness, cheerfulness, joy: the legitimacy of political regimes depends in large measure on maintaining the right balance between ideological promises for a better future and the actual everyday experience.

Also the East German dictatorship made promises, of course: "The socialist state serves as both the embodiment of the people's interests and the executor of its will. . . . [It serves as a] comprehensive form of democracy as well as the continually improving fulfillment of the material and spiritual needs of all working people."[3] But the self-image of the East German dictatorship was undermined by the contradiction of a state that repressed and terrorized for the alleged benefit of human freedom. East German society was in fact characterized by a high degree of dissatisfaction that corroded the regime from within. Understanding East Germany means, among others, to capture the relations between the well-intentioned official rhetoric of real-existing socialism and its dreary, depressing everyday existence. Indeed, emancipatory rhetoric did not simply clash with repressive reality; often it turned into it. And ultimately the inability of the state to provide happiness, cheerfulness, and joy engendered individual strategies to cope with this predicament.

I would like to explore how a specific promise for a better future transformed in the course of the years into an instrument of repression, which in turn resulted in multitude individual strategies of collaboration and opposition with an oppressive regime. I focus on a topic that became an obsession in East Germany, for rulers and ruled alike, as a, perhaps *the,* symbol both of unattained possibilities of personal fulfillment and of ultimate repression and ideological rigidity: the practice of traveling. Traveling and tourism, which I use interchangeably, have become in the modern world a vehicle for personal freedom and self-expression and, for political regimes, a measure of their ability to fulfill material promises. What were, then, the travel narratives made by the East German state to represent itself and by the East German citizens to represent their sense of self?

I

This question is closely linked to the relations in East Germany between state and society and between self and collectivity. It is tempting to view the East German society as wholly determined by an omnipotent state. Sigrid Meuschel argued that the claim of the state (and therefore the Party) for total control resulted in a "shut-down" (*Stillegung*) of social institutions and activities as the state expanded its powers to all spheres of society, be it the economy, family, or leisure: "It was not the state that withered away during the decades of Party rule, but instead it was much more a process of withering away of society."[4] Jürgen Kocka presented a somewhat similar idea when he argued for the primacy of political decisions over social processes in East Germany, given that East Germany was first and foremost a political creation maintained by the international order of the cold war. Political power molded society in an unparallel way, although, added Kocka, not in a total way.[5] Both arguments, which include elements of the modernization as well as the totalitarian approaches, seem too clear-cut to capture the intricate relations between state and society, between the claim to control and its actuality, between political intention and actual experience. Society is never shut down and cannot wither away; when this happens, this is also the end of human history.

It is also tempting to follow a current dominant approach in historical methodology, especially in cultural history, namely, to explore an object of investigation within its larger context. In our case, it means to explore the self (that is, the individual's actions, practices, and values) within the context of its surrounding culture and society. On one level this is a fruitful approach, as we move back and forth between the motivations and actions of the individual (the text) and the cultural and political context that gave them meanings. But on another level, this approach is now used more as a methodological reflex and less as a vehicle for thoughtful consideration of the relation between self and society. For one result of this mode of proceeding—which often does take into account contradictions, negotiations, and mediations—is that it nonetheless assumes a hierarchy: the cultural (as well as social and political) surrounding acts as a context within which the self can be intelligibly understood, but it is not clear how the self made by cultural context has any impact on this cultural surrounding within which it operates. The cultural surrounding defines and gives meaning to the self, but what were the limits of these definitions, how did the idea of the self and the actions of the individual influence the surrounding culture in return? These relations are often left unexplored.

When we attempt to interpret how human beings act in the world, the separation between self and culture, text and context, and state and society is not successful. We should interpret these relations neither as dichotomous nor as having implicit, built-in hierarchies of explanation. Instead, we should see these relations as commingling and overlapping. But how, exactly, are we to do it? And how does this problem of method translate into a history of traveling?

II

I suggest approaching these questions by reading a Stasi (State Security Service) file that tells a story that, I argue, is central to the relations of state, society, and self in East Germany as well as to the modern history of travel. In 1988, Bettina Humpel—a citizen of East Germany, a Stasi informer for sixteen years, and a longtime employee of the Travel Office of the German Democratic Republic (GDR) at home and abroad—fabricated an excuse to visit a long-forgotten aunt in West Berlin and crossed over to the West.[6] The file includes some two hundred pages of mostly dry reports by Humpel's case officers. There are almost no reports about actual traveling, tourist resorts, or East German tourists. It may seem peculiar to explore the meaning of travel in East Germany through this

Stasi file. It may be part of the history of surveillance and denunciation, of political control, or of betrayal. But why is this case illuminating for the history of traveling?

The reason is precisely because it does not quite fit within current approaches to and interpretations of travel, although they all make some sense of it. We usually use the practice and representation of travel to reconstruct historical identities by exploring the values, beliefs, and imagination that travel enables, while the meanings of this story lie in the limitation imposed on travel. We often use an approach that views the actual travel as a symbolic practice to interpret and represent reality, while in this case it is the inability to travel that is significant. We usually use sources such as guidebooks, documents of tourist associations and journals, diaries, posters and postcards, and exhibitions and displays, while the Stasi file, as a historical record, is obviously different. Moreover, much of the existing literature on tourism has until recently assumed as its model an autonomous individual operating in a liberal regime.[7] This normative model cannot possibly be revealing about travel experiences in the socialist, oppressive regime of East Germany. Humpel's Stasi file thus illuminates better than most sources, and at times with shocking frankness, how notions of travel linked the intention of the socialist state and the actual experience of one of its citizens.

The revelatory potential of the Stasi file as an interpretative key is significant. It enables us to explore the cultural and political meanings of travel in a state that radically controlled it. It situates travel in this gray area, often more abstractly theorized than historically explored, between the making of the self and the disciplinary techniques of the state. I would like to use the story of Bettina Humpel as an indicator of meanings that can potentially assume general dimensions. Specifically, I use it to illuminate the relations between two topics: the travel narratives made by the East German state and the ways Humpel made herself under the aegis of the state—first by collaborating and then by leaving.

Humpel's story does not fit within an interpretation that separates self and culture, text and context, state and society. Humpel simultaneously suffered from the regime (she could not travel freely) and was part of its oppressive apparatus. As a traveler she took part in social activities of leisure, while as a Stasi informer she was part of the political structure that attempted to control leisure as an autonomous social activity. She tried, quite creatively as we shall see, to make the best of her life, while being limited by the control mechanisms of state and ideology. Her story illuminates not only how state socialism molded the individual, but also how the individual used the system and ultimately, by choosing West Germany, discarded it altogether. The file provides us with a window to the ways the disciplinary techniques of the state shaped, and were shaped by, the life and actions of its citizens.[8] Let us turn, then, to discuss first state narratives of travel in East Germany.

III

Bettina Humpel, code name "Constanze," was recruited by the Stasi in 1972 after her husband, Hartmut Humpel, himself a Stasi informer at the time with the code name "Manfred Wagner," recommended her to the organization. They supplied information to the Stasi under the common category of *Inoffizielle Mitarbeiter* (*IM*), or "unofficial collaborators." She joined on April 26, 1972, by writing a letter and choosing her code name, a customary initiation rite that linked the individual to the Stasi. "Wagner" had been a representative of the Travel Office of the GDR in Bulgaria and was promoted in 1972 to be chief representative in Bäderdreieck in Czechoslovakia. His wife got a job for the tourist seasons in the Travel Office of the GDR in Karlovy Vary.

The first document about her is dated March 28, 1972; the last one is from the summer of 1989. The file includes reports from Stasi case officers who briefed her regularly and periodical evaluations of her performance and reliability. Every once and a while, an officer responsible for Humpel produced an "analysis of hitherto existing co-operation," which included an assessment of her ideological and political attitudes, as well as personal characteristics such as "honesty and trustworthiness." The file contains no documents by Humpel. It expresses the voice of the Stasi and crafts a narrative made by the East German state for itself about itself.

The narrative is dominated by the wish to be everywhere and to watch everyone in German society. This was perceived and outwardly projected as a sign of strength and omnipotence. The recruitment of Humpel fit well within the inner development of the Stasi and its relation to East German society. In the late 1960s Erich Mielke, the head of the Stasi from 1958 to 1989, wanted to reach beyond the (relatively) limited and professional group of informers by broadening the range and composition of the service into the four corners of society. This change was reflected in the 1968 transformation of the terms *Geheime Informatoren* (secret informants) and

Geheime Mitarbeiter (secret collaborators) into *Inoffizielle Mitarbeiter* (unofficial collaborators). Mielke recognized that people would not like to identify themselves as informants but would see a virtue, however self-serving it may be, in contributing to protecting the state.[9] The change showed a keen psychological insight. It aimed at associating collaboration with an individual choice, stressing the personal and material relations and interests between the collaborator and the Stasi, in contradistinction to associating collaboration with a professional career.[10] The new vision of the Stasi substantially expanded the number of unofficial collaborators. This grew from about 20,000 to 30,000 in the 1950s to around 100,000 in 1968, and then it jumped to around 180,000 in 1975.[11] Recruiting Humpel must have been seen to the Stasi as another small step toward total control of society. She was not a member of the ruling Socialist Unity Party (SED) at the time of her recruitment and thus added to the Stasi's aim of drawing all citizens into a network of denunciation and collaboration, making East Germany a nation in the service of its State Security Service.[12]

But the wish for total control contained its own seed of destruction: it could never be achieved and ultimately betrayed paranoia.[13] A closer reading of the Stasi file reveals sentiments very different from control and composure. The 1976 report of Humpel's yearly cooperation was explicit about the duties of the GDR tourist representative in Karlovy Vary. Humpel's task was the "protection of individual and private [East German] tourists [in Czechoslovakia]. She is employed to provide information about appearances relating to the politics of contact and the activity of contact, especially the meeting activity between citizens of the GDR and citizens of the non-socialist world. Furthermore, she is employed to detect negative political-operational as well as unstable ways of thought and behavior by citizens of the GDR. Her aim is to detect activities that point at intent of unlawful leaving of the GDR."[14]

It is easy to forget that this passage is about the meaning of travel, which is usually associated with liberty, frivolity, and the breaking of boundaries, but it was produced by state authorities responsible for travel, namely, Department VI, which was in charge of controlling cross-frontier traffic, and the Division of Foreign Tourism. Angst and distrust are the dominant sensibilities that pervaded the East German state representation of itself to itself through travel: angst from the potential leisure displacement of its own citizens, from illicit contact, Western spies, ways of thinking, and ways of behavior.[15] The rhetoric is built on euphemisms and on reversing the usual meaning of essential features of leisure displacement.

The prohibition to travel is presented as "protecting" East Germans. Contact among travelers is presented as political and therefore dangerous. Colonel Müller, director of Department VI, and Captain Daberkow took this way of thinking in their 1988 report to its logical conclusion by reversing basic notions of human character and behavior. Humpel is portrayed as "honest and trustworthy" when she informs on her fellow citizens, while she is judged not "open and honest" when she leaves the Stasi and the country.[16] It is a paradox of modern dictatorships that, while they inflict so much suffering and inhumanities, they simultaneously have at their core a fundamental insecurity, whereby they see threats everywhere and want to be loved by everyone.

How did this perception of angst and control relate to earlier representations of travel by the East German state? By the time Humpel began to collaborate with the Stasi in 1972, the East German state narratives of travel had gone through both dramatic changes and fundamental continuities. The angst from travel is evident from the beginning of East Germany, but it was mixed in the postwar era with some optimism and lightness that are the hallmarks of travel sensibilities. The traditional characteristics of travel such as relaxation, vacation, and recreation were emphasized. Most important, after 1945 in both East and West Germany travel was viewed as an entitlement for all working people, not anymore as a privilege. In East Germany this was a heritage of the struggle for equality of the working-class movement in the nineteenth and twentieth centuries.

East Germany thus stressed the importance of travel. Those who believe today in the triumphalist teleology of democratic capitalism may forget that communism was built on the principle that "the new [postwar] life must become more beautiful," as the *Junge Welt,* the magazine of the communist youth movement Free German Youth (Freie Deutsche Jugend, or FDJ), put it in 1947 to its young readers and future citizens and tourists.[17] The rise in production and the new distribution of wealth were aimed at ameliorating the conditions of Germans of all classes, making it possible to overcome the capitalist alienation from work and to enjoy leisure time. The communist project was based on the prospect that sooner rather than later it would overtake the West. As the *Junge Welt* stated confidently in 1961: "The United States will be [economically] surpassed by 1970."[18] After the war, even before the foundation of East and West Germany in 1949, the German authorities in the occupied zones organized travel programs and propagated them widely. Precisely *because*

Germany turned in 1945 into piles of rubble, vacations became a measure of the system's ability to create a better life. In 1946 the Free German Trade Union Association (FDGB) sent seven thousand people to vacation homes. In 1947 the Vacation Service of the FDGB was established; its aim was to send on vacation all members of the organization and their families.[19]

The state representation of postwar travel was a mixture of ideology and fun, indoctrination and traditional gushing travel descriptions. "Vacation Pleasure" was the title of a photograph showing young people at a beach.[20] But tourism was not only a matter of fun: every Young Pioneer and student should be a tourist, according to the Free German Youth, because it promoted a sense of collectivity and love of the socialist Heimat.[21] This combination of ideology and pleasure was well articulated in a report of June 1947 about eight thousand Berliner youths who were sent out to vacation camps. It was another success, so the story went, of the German communist authorities in the Soviet Occupation Zone and the Soviet Military Administration. The camp director, Herbert Fölster, twenty-three years old, was a member of the resistance group Saefkow and spent "a long time" in National Socialist prison. But he did not lose his humor or his love for playing the guitar—in short, a good sport, with socialist ideals and commitment for the collectivity. At the same time, the camp was described as a "highly romantic event" of camp fires, adventures, and stories of faraway lands.[22]

This representation continued throughout the existence of East Germany. But if the idea of vacation was promoted, the idea of free travel caused by the end of the 1950s enormous concern among authorities. In 1960–61 the exodus from East Germany reached proportions not seen since 1953. From January to August 1961, 155,000 East Germans had gone over to the West. Since 1945, three million people had fled communist rule (one out of six persons).[23] The prohibition to travel and its ideological justification were in place before the building of the Wall on August 13, 1961. The existential angst over travel thus made it a topic in East German society in general and in the SED in particular that reveals values and beliefs about history, communism, and East German identity.

Just how the notion of travel became a topos on which the East German state was built can be seen in a meeting that took place in July 1961, two weeks before the erection of the Berlin Wall, between young East Germans and the Free German Youth's Central Committee and local leadership of the Rostock district.[24] Entitled "Vacation from Ourselves?"

(*Urlaub vom Wir?*), the meeting on the island of Rügen was dedicated to issues of vacation and travel. The format of the meeting was not a dialogue between the people and the Party but was characterized by questions, mostly about the prohibition to travel, and answers, given in a form of a catechism. And this, as it is well known, is never open for discussion. It is worthwhile to quote it extensively.

I would like to know whether it is really necessary to limit us [members of the FDJ] from traveling to West Germany and West Berlin?

Heinz Keßler [secretary of the Central Committee of the FDJ] answered him:[25]

One imagines what will happen if we send tomorrow 6000 FDJ members to Munich. We know exactly how they would be treated as representatives of the workers and peasants' state. . . . They will have to reckon with corresponding chicaneries.

Horst Krenz, the First Secretary of the Rostock District, added:[26]

As long as there are no democratic conditions in all of Germany, we should see it as a matter of honor not to spend our vacations in the states of the militarists.

But there seemed to be someone who disagreed.

I can indeed see that members of the FDJ cannot travel, but why is it the case for other young people. I cannot understand this. Not everyone is a criminal over there [in West Germany]. All I want is simply to visit someone. And when one has a strong character, one can certainly see what the conditions are over there [and choose to live here].

I believe when you say that you don't understand certain things, *answered promptly comrade Horst Sindermann [candidate of the Central Committee].* But even if you don't understand everything, then ask the elders who know about the difficult class struggles in Germany, and listen to their advice. . . . There are people that hold the finger high to check which direction the wind blows. They want, so to speak, to stand between the fronts . . . but this is impossible. These people also did not want to believe us in 1933. They claimed that we exaggerate everything and that fascism is not so bad. These people should finally take care of their families that experience so much suffering, and at long last become intelligent. I say it as a communist. And communism has been so far in Germany always right.

The high-spirited words excited all. Roaring applause followed. A young person with character humbly intervened.

I did not experience this [the Nazi period]. I am nineteen years old and would only like to visit my relatives. Over there after all one speaks German just like us.

Heinz Keßler seized the microphone.

Why do we say with such clarity that no one should travel thoughtlessly to West Germany? Certainly not because we want to separate someone from his relatives. Did we divide Germany? We made proposals in order to arrive quicker to reunification and normal relations. . . . You have to understand, we have hundreds of examples as proof of what they do over there with young people from our republic. First they squeeze them and then send them back with spying missions.

If one's basic idea of travel is to "get away from it all," then the slogan of the meeting "Vacation from Ourselves?" put this idea in question. A responsible East German citizen could not simply enjoy traveling thoughtlessly; he or she should instead have given preference to ideological and historical considerations. The limits imposed on traveling were represented as protective measures justified by morality (no vacations among the militarists), the past (communism has always been right), and experience (the elders know best). Sindermann is representative of a whole generation of East German communists whose experience under Nazism set the tone for elevating the primacy of ideology and of drawing the "correct" lessons from historical experience over immature consideration. Born in 1915, he became a member of the Communist Youth Association of Germany (Kommunistischer Jugendverband Deutschlands) at the young age of fourteen. Arrested in 1933 for political activity, he spent eight months in prison. In 1934 he became the secretary of the Dresden branch of the Communist Youth Association. A year later he was arrested again, tortured in prison, and sentenced to six years. At the end of his prison term in 1941 he was kept incarcerated in Sachsenhausen, Mauthausen, and finally Ebensee. After 1945 he emerged as one of the leadership group of the SED and was a member of the Central Committee between 1963 and 1989.[27] Sindermann translated this life experience into the idea that "even if you don't understand everything, then ask the elders who know about the difficult class struggles in Germany." The tone of the answers of the FDJ functionaries was patronizing, one of distrust of the people they led. They were treated as immature children who cannot be trusted to travel to West Germany because their weak character would lead them to become spies. And the way Keßler, Krenz, and Sindermann looked down at their fellow citizens reminds one of Captain Daberkow and Colonel Müller, who judged Humpel's independent behavior in 1988 as not open and honest.

The East German state combined the pretension of full control and an unsettling angst from the practice of popular travel. The narrative strategy of the East German state put itself at the center, communicating and representing its actions and achievements. The state made traveling a public and political action, thus blurring the lines between public and private sphere, between apolitical fun and political intent. The West German state, to add a point of comparison, hid itself and gave center stage to the individual, the consumer, and the travel industry; the state sought to limit public regulation and explicit politicization by shifting the travel responsibilities onto the citizen.[28] This is one of the secrets of the historical success of liberal democracy: while the rhetoric of liberty, freedom, and free choice creates true opportunities as well as new types of discrimination, it also shifts much of the onus for personal happiness and self-fulfillment from the regime onto the individual. The leadership of the SED thus did itself in by its own contradictory thinking: if the Party is in total control, then it is also responsible for everything. In one sense, in this kind of regime personal responsibility and self-fulfillment are easier to negotiate than in a liberal regime that puts the pressure of being happy and successful on the individual—as citizens of East Germany learned only too well after 1990—for it is easier to blame the regime than oneself.

The East German state saw traveling as ideologically essential for the structuring of national and cultural life—first as an entitlement, then as a threat. The two went together—simultaneously and contradictorily—for a long time, too long, but could not last forever. The contradiction between the promise of a good life and the dreariness of everyday life corroded the SED legitimacy. From 1961, when traveling was hermetically sealed, East Germany underwent stabilization; its citizens could not leave or travel freely, and they attempted to make the best under the given conditions. At the same time, a gap between ideological promises, on the one hand, and popular mentalities and material conditions, on the other, remained. It is in this gap that the story of Bettina Humpel fit.

IV

Humpel's file does not include documents written by her, but there is plenty of information about her life, actions, even motivations. The Stasi agents, like those of every security service and intelligence agency, attempted to combine sharp political analysis with psychological insights into people's driving forces. Without these qualities, the organization would amount to little more than a collector of facts.[29] The Stasi exhibited both sides: it collected in a paranoid way useless facts about the everyday life activities of millions of people, but it also had its moments of keen psychological insight. As a historical document that poses problems of interpretation, the Humpel file shares some similarities with documents of the Inquisition, where the voice of the authorities is the only one that is openly expressed. The key word is *openly,* for the voice of the accused and of Humpel is present surreptitiously.

Bettina Humpel joined the Stasi in 1972 at the age of thirty-four. This seemed to have been related to her second marriage in December 1971 to Hartmut Humpel, a representative of the Travel Office of the GDR in Bulgaria, who had been a Stasi unofficial collaborator for some time. A report from March 1972 states that it was Hartmut Humpel who made the link between her and the organization.[30] Originally a ladies' tailor, Bettina Humpel had been working at the time at the general administration of the Travel Office of the GDR, where she must have met her husband. When he became the chief representative in Bäderdreieck in Czechoslovakia, she followed him and began working in the office as well.

Why did Bettina Humpel join the Stasi? A definite answer cannot be established from the file, but by listening to what is and is not said, by using conjecture, imagination, as well as the present historical literature on East Germany, a strong hypothesis can be advanced. Reconstructing the case and motivation of Humpel must begin with the fact that there were very few women in the Stasi organization and in its network of collaborators. In an organization that possessed gender prejudices and stereotypes, often of the most pronounced *kleinbürgerlich* (petty bourgeois) kind, and a patriarchal state of mind, 85 to 90 percent of the unofficial collaborators were men.[31] In one Stasi memorandum on the work of women as unofficial collaborators their activity is linked, among others, to the social spheres of theater, leisure and vacation, hotels, restaurants, and pubs.[32] To men who associated the activity of espionage, defense, and power politics with masculine qualities, these social spheres may have been linked to the alleged soft sensitivities of women. In addition, the work of women collaborators was often connected to that of their spouse. In general, a special loyalty to the regime and a wish to safeguard the system were important among middle-rank employees in the state and economy sectors. These collaborated in order (among others) to gain advantages from the system such as the privilege to travel abroad or to compensate for not being SED members.[33] This overall depiction is congruent with Humpel's case. She joined the Stasi thanks to her husband after he had already been a collaborator for some time, and she worked in the area of leisure and vacation. Her collaboration no doubt helped her husband's position, and, as middle-ranked employees, both could continue a profession that was quite attractive in the GDR.

Was she ideologically committed? Humpel was not an SED member when she joined the Stasi. Throughout her Stasi collaboration she seemed rather uninterested in ideology or in developing any initiative concerning her work as an informer. Her case officers repeatedly noted that she was cooperative but in an unhelpful way. She was constantly reproached for having "to undertake absolutely stronger efforts to improve the operational results."[34] She took this critique seriously and without resistance: "'Constanze' is willing to take to heart the critique directed at her and to improve her operational work."[35] But she did not really change her behavior or become more "operationally" helpful.

Most collaborators had commingling, overlapping, and at times contradictory motives. The ideological component was the main motivation, or, to put it in a different language, the subjective recognition in the basic justice of socialism and the ensuing willingness to help the state against its enemies. But other, more personal and practical motivations were significant as well. A 1967 questionnaire of unofficial collaborators in the district of Potsdam produced the following main motives: 60 percent collaborated because they recognized the social-political necessity; 49 percent because of an ethical sense of duty; 40 percent because of practical reasons; 27 percent because of reasons of personal advantage; and 12 percent collaborated for self-interest (*selbstzweck*) motivations.[36] When Humpel joined the Stasi she most probably commingled a very basic support in the regime with a great dose of reasons of personal advantage.

Her relation with the Stasi seemed more like a marriage of convenience than one of love. Following the sealing of East Germany by the Wall, an unspoken, pragmatic arrangement took shape between state and society. Like other East Germans, she may have agreed to be an informer in order to be able to improve her life within a system that in 1972 seemed destined to remain in place for decades. Significantly, there is no mention in the file of blackmail or of Stasi intimidation as a motivation to collaborate. In these dual relations, she lent support to the regime by the very act of joining the Stasi, and she may have gotten something in return. Was it permission to remain with her husband abroad when he was assigned in 1972 to a new position in Czechoslovakia? Was it the temptation to secure her new job abroad as a representative of the Travel Office of the GDR? Probably, although the file is silent on these questions. Regardless, in her own little, unhelpful way she became part of the repressive system. Whether and in what ways her reports actually helped the Stasi in any crucial way, we don't know, though we may doubt it. We also don't know whether she destroyed any lives in the process.

By 1976, Humpel had joined the SED. She moved to work as a representative of the Travel Office of the GDR in Karlovy Vary, Czechoslovakia. A 1976 comprehensive report on her collaboration pointed out that the "cooperation takes place on the basis of political-ideological conviction. For the unofficial collaborator the unofficial cooperation is self-evident and necessary."[37] But it seems that Captain Anders, her case officer, and Major Rückheim, director of the Division of Foreign Tourism, collapsed two very different ideas. Although Humpel joined the Party, the historian must wonder how much this was an act that represented communist convictions and how much it was a way to get along by using the system. On the same page, Anders and Rückheim analyze her work as satisfactory on "concrete," small-scale tasks, whereas she remains unsuccessful in the context of more complex projects that demanded initiative and motivation.[38] This had been the pattern of collaboration from the beginning. She seemed to view her collaboration as necessary, but the reports do not support an interpretation that put ideology at the center.

Still, she obviously knew how to talk the talk and walk the walk of state socialism since in 1978 she was rewarded by becoming the organizer of sightseeing tours (*Stadtrundfahrt*) in East Berlin and was a member of the Party leadership of the Travel Office of the GDR in the Berlin district. This was, in many respects, a lucrative job because the sightseeing tours provided an opportunity to meet people from the West, who often rewarded the tour guide with Western consumer goods. Many of the reports describe the problems created in the workplace by the appearance of consumer goods in a society defined by shortage. The sensitivity of the topic is demonstrated by Humpel's reticence to talk about anything connected to consumption with people who were not SED members. At the same time, rumors were rife that Humpel colluded with certain tour guides to whom she assigned Western tour groups; in return she received regularly presents, namely, "bribery."[39] During the workday, according to the reports, she was busy taking care of private matters. By the mid-1980s, she was portrayed as taking care of herself.

What emerges from her story, to return to the discussion at the beginning of this essay, is not separateness between text and context, state and society, self and collectivity, and public and private, but rather their overlap. A wide gap developed in East Germany between the intentions and expectations of the regime and the motivations and experience of most of its citizens. Contrary to the expectations of Keßler, Krenz, and Sindermann in 1961, East Germans did not become obedient subjects waiting for the demise of capitalism in order to start traveling and enjoying consumer goods. In their minds, East Germans anguished about the impossibility to travel and to consume. Many found ways around it. Humpel secured an attractive job in Karlovy Vary, in what seemed to have been her give-and-take compromise with the regime, and she later found her ways of enjoying Western consumer goods.

But the gap between rulers and ruled should not be interpreted as a dichotomy between regime and society. Humpel's case may indeed indicate how power got diffused in East German society in part *because* of the growing proliferation of the Stasi. The post-Wall arrangement in East Germany broke any conventional separateness between regime and society and created areas of overlap where values and interests had to be negotiated. For the Keßlers, Krenzes, and Sindermanns, 1970 came and went, and the communist bloc did not surpass the West. One result of recognizing this was the enormous proliferation of the Stasi operations in German society in the 1970s and 1980s. If a high standard of living could not make people quiet, then being part of the system would, by distributing punishments and rewards. The recruitment of Humpel was a symbol of the power and control of the state, but it also meant that this power was now distributed, negotiated, and articulated in more complex ways. Her story should be interpreted not so much in terms of the power or limits of dictatorship, an investigation that methodologically takes the intentions of the regime as its point of departure, but in terms of the growing overlap between authority and society.[40] The state, as one scholar put it, "did not so much rule *over* society as *through* it."[41] Bettina Humpel seemed an ordinary citizen: her case shows that the regime needed a degree of popular cooperation in order to carry out its policies from above. Coercion and indoctrination could not by themselves sustain the regime. Her joining the system strengthened the regime by giving it a small measure of popular collaboration, even though she joined for reasons that did not seem wholly ideological.

The regime saw in travel both a historic-ideological entitlement of the working class and a source of angst. It attempted to mold its subjects by keeping their travel desires in check for unlimited time until the victory of socialism. This, among others, created a society where a certain level of unhappiness was constant; and because the SED pretended to control everything, it was blamed for this state of affair. But for the historian it seems opportune to pose a hypothetical question: Was the SED leadership's travel angst justified? Had the travel ban been lifted in 1988, would East Germans have left en masse? After all, forty years of socialism did create a particular society, with its colors, smells, sense of Heimat, and social security. This is a speculative question, but in thinking about it, Bettina Humpel's story has in store for us one last surprise.

V

The story did not really end when Humpel crossed over to West Berlin on March 24, 1988. Humpel ended her collaboration with the Stasi on January 1987 and returned to her old job as a ladies' tailor. The report of May 3, 1988, noted her change of attitude in the previous years. She had hardly informed or provided information anymore. This development was not inevitable, but it does fit into a recognizable pattern of Humpel's years-long collaboration as well as of general trends in East German society. What began in 1972 as collaboration characterized by some ideological and mostly practical motives turned by the mid-1980s into a total disillusion with the regime. By breaking her relations with the Stasi Humpel denied the state the semblance of conformity. Breaking up an unofficial collaboration relation was not difficult: one had to tell of the relations to a third person in order for the Stasi to terminate the collaboration; it was not interested in keeping contacts with people who were unwilling or unreliable. In 1986 there were more East Germans who declined to inform as unofficial collaborators than new recruits; the rate of rejections rose to between 30 and 40 percent of all terminated activities of unofficial collaborators.[42] The 1972 coexistence of conformity, ideological belief, and dissatisfaction broke down by the mid-1980s into a multitude of acts that wore the legitimacy of the regime away: when we consider that Humpel severed her ties with the Stasi after sixteen years and that the Stasi had difficulties recruiting new unofficial collaborators, then the disintegration of the regime seems slightly less surprising.

In the meantime, Humpel had been planning her move to West Germany. Luckily for the historian, the Stasi officers, who wanted to know why she had left, provide us with details about the case. The secret file reveals a hidden story. For many years Humpel had an affair with an Austrian man who used to come to Karlovy Vary. We can now understand better the importance for Humpel of her position at the Travel Office of the GDR and why it was worthwhile to collaborate with the Stasi in order to keep it. Citizens of East Germany could travel without a visa to Poland and Czechoslovakia from 1970; Humpel did not need to work for the Stasi from 1972 if she merely wanted to visit Karlovy Vary. But she did have to maintain her collaboration over the years if she wanted to be able to keep her job, which allowed her to live in Karlovy Vary for extended periods and to spend time with her Austrian. She now planned on living with him in Austria. Through a West Berlin friend who worked in West Germany's Deutsches Reisebüro (German Traveling Office) Humpel located in the city a long-forgotten aunt who invited her for her birthday. From West Berlin she flew to Munich and met the Austrian man, and they drove together south to Austria. But after two days she changed her mind about her Austrian. She returned to Munich and, according to the report of December 1, 1988, wanted to get to West Berlin in order to return to the GDR before her visa would expire. The East German authorities would thus never know of the whole affair. But she had no money to fly back to West Berlin.

Fearful of the legal proceeding that would await her in the GDR, she decided to stay in West Germany. From August 1988 she was in touch with her husband. Living in Speyer and working in a women's clothing shop, she experienced difficulties adjusting to West German life. She earned little, felt lonely, and apparently was accepted only by immigrant workers from Yugoslavia. On November 22, 1988, Hartmut Humpel showed up in the office of the local police in Berlin-Mitte to inquire about the possible return of his wife to the GDR. The Stasi pondered and investigated the matter: Why on earth did she want to return? The idea of a GDR citizen who wanted to return to East Germany was as problematic for the Stasi as the idea of a citizen who wanted to travel abroad. By the summer of 1989, when the last report in the file was written, the matter was still being debated. I can understand Humpel's desire to travel freely, as I can understand her wish to live where she felt at home. That is what the SED leadership, it seems, failed to comprehend: for most citizens of the GDR freedom to travel (*Reisefreiheit*) was not equal to freedom to emigrate

(*Ausreisefreiheit*). I don't know if the history of East Germany would have been different had the SED allowed free traveling in, say, 1988; probably not. But it is a speculation worthwhile pondering, and it attests to the importance of travel in our life.

On November 9, 1989, history made irrelevant the matter that stood between the Humpels and the Stasi. On that night, the GDR became the first, and perhaps the only, state in history whose demise was announced in terms and metaphors of travel, when member of the Politburo Günter Schabowski declared that "private travel abroad can be applied for without conditions." One wonders what Bettina Humpel felt on that night, whether it was a sense of historical irony or a tragic sense of missed opportunities. Perhaps both.

VI

It may be asked how typical the story of Bettina Humpel really was. The issue of representativeness is a fundamental one in historical studies, but the question is *mal posé*. It assumes implicitly that the significance of a given historical case grows in proportional amount to its representativeness. In fact, a representative historical case is at times just marginally revealing since it demonstrates what had already been learned. It is worthwhile remembering the notion of "the exceptional normal," to use the words of the late Italian microhistorian Edoardo Grendi, when "the smallest dissonances prove to be indictors of meaning which can potentially assume general dimensions."[43] The value of the Humpel case lies not in enumerating what was and was not typical. Humpel's life story, like all life stories, commingled the typical and the exceptional. Most East Germans who fled to the West had not actively tried to go back: in this sense, Humpel's story seems exceptional. At the same time, the Stasi career and motivations of Humpel, as we have seen, did characterize larger trends in East German society. Rather, the value of Humpel's case lies in understanding how both the typical and atypical can illuminate our understanding of East German society. And in this respect, Humpel's case is revealing on the theme of socialist modern, which brings us to where this essay began.

The East German regime, like all modern regimes, had to confront what I call "the problem of happiness," namely, the modern idea that happiness and self-fulfillment are entitlements of all citizens. Neither *happiness* nor *self-fulfillment* are fixed terms; they are dynamic and controversial concepts. They can be psychologically unsettling; they cannot be ignored or done away with. The issue of traveling encapsulated these traits. On the one hand, affordable leisure was an aspect of the social contract between regime and citizen that characterized the post-1945 arrangement in Europe on both sides of the Iron Curtain. The GDR provided leisure as part of a social welfare regime that also provided day care, social insurance, and the right to work. But the collectivized, politicized, and spatially and psychologically limited form of leisure offered by the GDR only exacerbated the problem of happiness. It was too much of a scripted promise of happiness, and while the promise of happiness in liberal democracy is also scripted in (different kinds of) bounded ways, this is a script also based on the rhetoric and geographical mobility of imagination, unpredictability, excess, and freedom (in people's mind, even if not in the reality of vacation). The typical and atypical elements in Bettina Humpel's life story—joining and leaving the Stasi, leaving and wishing to return to the GDR—symbolize the possibilities and missed opportunities of socialist modern.

As a Marxist-Leninist state, the East German dictatorship believed that history has a script. Bettina Humpel, in her own little way—partly collaborating with the regime, partly opposing it—undermined this script, thus showing the profundity of the words of Alexander Herzen, Marx's great intellectual rival, written some 150 years before the demise of East Germany: "If humanity marched straight toward some result, there would be no history, only logic. . . . If history followed a set libretto it would lose all interest, become unnecessary, boring, ludicrous. . . . history is all improvisation, all will, all extempore—there are no frontiers, no itineraries." This, of course, is a lesson that is always pertinent. And only time will tell whether the present-day proponents of the capitalist, free-market, American-based historical script will learn it as well.

NOTES

I am indebted to the thoughtful comments of Paul Betts, Molly Nolan, and Katherine Pence.

1. Sheila Fitzpatrick, *Everyday Stalinism: Ordinary Life in Extraordinary Times: Soviet Russia in the 1930s* (New York, 1999), 6.

2. Helmut Heiber, ed., *Goebbels-Reden*, vol. 1: *1932–1939* (Düsseldorf, 1971), III.

3. Autorenkollektiv, *Kleines Politisches Wörterbuch* (Berlin, 1967), 471, cited in Corey Ross, *The East German Dictatorship: Problems and Perspectives in the Interpretation of the GDR* (London, 2002), 99.

4. Sigrid Meuschel, *Legitimation und Parteiherrschaft. Zum Paradox von Stabilität und Revolution in der DDR* (Frankfurt a/M, 1992), 10.

5. Jürgen Kocka, "Eine durchherrschte Gesellschaft," in *Sozialgeschichte der DDR*, ed. Hartmut Kaelble, Jürgen Kocka, and Hartmut Zwahr (Stuttgart, 1994), 547–43. See also the discussions of Richard Bessel, "Real-Existing Socialism through the Looking-Glass," *Bulletin of the German Historical Institute London* 19, no. 2 (November 1997): 15–29; and Ross, *East German Dictatorship,* 47–50.

6. I changed the names of Humpel and her husband. While the file is available for consultation (following the regular proceeding of working in the Stasi archive), it seems unnecessary for the purpose of this essay to use the Humpels' real names. Those who have a special reason to seek this information can consult the file. I did not change the names of the regular Stasi personnel.

7. For some exceptions see the special issue of *Slavic Review* 62, no. 4 (winter 2003), entitled "Tourism and Travel in Russia and the Soviet Union"; and Shelly Baranowski, *Strength through Joy: Consumerism and Mass Tourism in the Third Reich* (Cambridge, 2004).

8. Viewed in this way, travel seems an exemplary topic from the atelier of Michel Foucault.

9. David Childs and Richard Popplewell, *The Stasi: The East German Intelligence and Security Service* (London, 1996), 83. See also Mike Dennis, *The Stasi: Myth and Reality* (London, 2003).

10. Jens Gieseke, *Mielke-Konzern. Die Geschichte der Stasi 1945–1990* (Stuttgart, 2001), 111.

11. Ibid., 112–13.

12. On denunciation and collaboration in the GDR and the Third Reich, see Gisela Diewald-Kerkmann, "Vertrauensleute, Denunzianten, Geheime und Inoffizielle Mitarbeiter in diktatorischen Regimen," in *Doppelte Zeitgeschichte: Deutsch-deutsche Beziehungen 1945–1990,* ed. Arnd Bauerkämper, Martin Sabrow, and Bernd Stöver (Bonn, 1998), 282–93.

13. On the language of control and subversion in East Germany, see Alf Lüdtke, "Sprache und Herrschaft in der DDR. Einleitende Überlegungen," in *Akten. Eingaben. Schaufenster. Die DDR und ihre Texte. Erkundungen zu Herrschaft und Alltag,* ed. Alf Lüdtke and Peter Becker (Berlin, 1997), 11–26.

14. Bundesbeauftragte für die Unterlagen des Staatssicherheitsdienstes der ehemaligen DDR (Federal Authority for the Records of the State Security Serivce of the Former GDR; hereafter BStU), 641/87, 16.6.1976, 93. Page numbers refer to the record made by the archive.

15. The fear of the East German authorities of setting their citizens free reminds me of the fear of nineteenth-century Russian authorities of emancipating the serfs. In both cases, the rulers were concerned about spatial displacement of perceived unruly and untrustful subjects. In Russia, when the serfs were finally emancipated in 1861 there was no seismic movement of peasants across the land. The East German case cannot be verified, because East Germany never gave its citizens the possibility of free traveling; when it did, on November 9, 1989, this already coincided with the dissolution of the regime. But one wonders whether East Germans would have left their native land en masse had the regime lifted the

ban on traveling in, say, 1980. We shall return later to this interesting hypothetical question.

16. BStU, 641/87, 3.5.1988, 173.

17. *Junge Welt,* October 29, 1947.

18. *Junge Welt,* November 25–26, 1961.

19. Hasso Spode, "Tourismus in der Gesellschaft der DDR. Eine vergleichende Einführung," in *Goldstrand und Teutonengrill. Kultur- und Sozialgeschichte des Tourismus in Deutschland 1945 bis 1989,* ed. Hasso Spode (Berlin, 1996), 16.

20. *Junge Welt,* July 16, 1947.

21. Rudy Koshar, *German Travel Cultures* (Oxford, 2000), 177.

22. *Junge Welt,* July 25, 1947.

23. Henry Ashby Turner, *Germany from Partition to Reunification,* rev. ed. (New Haven, 1992), 87–88.

24. *Junge Welt,* July 28, 1961.

25. The FDJ was an important locus of power in East Germany. Heinz Keßler, born in 1920, was a cofounder of the FDJ in 1946 and ended his career in the GDR as the last serving minister for national defense (from 1985). He became a member of the Central Committee of the SED in 1946 and from 1950 was secretary of the Central Committee of the FDJ. See Helmut Müller-Enbergs, Jan Wielgohs, and Dieter Hoffmann, eds., *Wer war wer in der DDR. Ein biographisches Lexikon* (Berlin, 2000), 421.

26. The paper meant Egon Krenz, first secretary of the FDJ in the Rostock district in 1960–61, who for a brief moment in 1989 replaced Erich Honecker as leader of East Germany. Also Honecker started his SED career in the Free German Youth. Müller-Enbergs, Wielgohs, and Hoffmann, *Wer war wer in der DDR,* 475.

27. Müller-Enbergs, Wielgohs, and Hoffmann, *Wer war wer in der DDR,* 801.

28. See Cord Pagenstecher, *Der bundesdeutsche Tourismus: Ansätze zu einer Visual History: Urlaubsprospekte, Reiseführer, Fotoalben 1950–1990* (Hamburg, 2003).

29. I am indebted to the work of Michael Confino on the Russian secret police's keen observation of the relations between Necaev and Bakunin. See Michael Confino, *Violence dans la violence: Le débat Bakounine-Necaev* (Paris, 1973).

30. BStU, 641/87, 28.3.1972, 49.

31. Gieseke, *Mielke-Konzern,* 112–13. Barbara Miller, *Narratives of Guilt and Compliance in Unified Germany: Stasi Informers and Their Impact on Society* (London, 1999), 20–21.

32. Annette Maennel, *Auf sie war Verlaß. Frauen und Stasi* (Berlin, 1999), 127–28.

33. Gieseke, *Mielke-Konzern,* 126.

34. BStU, 641/87, 21.3.1974, 81.

35. BStU, 641/87, 26.2.1975, 82.

36. Gieseke, *Mielke-Konzern,* 125–26. See also Anna Funder, *Stasiland: True Stories from behind the Berlin Wall* (London, 2003).

37. BStU, 641/87, 16.6.1976, 90.

38. BStU, 641/87, 16.6.1976, 90.

39. BStU, 641/87, 9.11.1981, 126.

40. See the important work of Thomas Lindenberger, "Die Diktatur der Grenzen. Zur Einleitung," in *Herrschaft und Eigen-Sinn in der Diktatur. Studien zur Gesellschaftsgeschichte der DDR,* ed. Thomas Lindenberger (Cologne, 1999), 13–44.

41. Ross, *East German Dictatorship,* 63.

42. Gieseke, *Mielke-Konzern,* 131.

43. Edoardo Grendi, "Microanalisi e storia sociale," *Quaderni Storici* 7 (1972): 506–20. The citation is from Giovanni Levi, "On Microhistory," in *New Perspectives on Historical Writing,* ed. Peter Burk (University Park, PA, 1992), 109. On this problem in relation to traveling during and after the Third Reich see my essay, "Dissonance, Normality and the Historical Method: Why Did Some Germans Think of Tourism after May 8, 1945?" in *Germany as a Culture of Remembrance: Promises and Limits of Writing History* (Chapel Hill, 2006), 214–34.

Belonging

Youth as Internal Enemy
Conflicts in the Education Dictatorship of the 1960s

Dorothee Wierling

The following essay evolved in conjunction with my research project about biographical and historical experiences of those born in 1949 in the German Democratic Republic (GDR).[1] It became clear to me that the GDR leadership and its representatives in the institutions of youth education had high hopes that the generation of postwar children, who seemed untouched by the direct influence of National Socialism and who grew up under the influence of antifascist and socialist educators, would augur a new society composed of radically new citizens (*Neue Menschen*). The sixties in the GDR were a phase of partial modernization.[2] "Modernity" was a project both of technological and of social and political progress, very similar to the often quoted Lenin definition of socialism as "electrification plus Soviet power." After closing the borders, in particular, there was a growing belief that socialist development was possible and convincing—in the long run—for those who were still skeptical or even hostile. At the same time, therefore, the sixties marked the high point of pedagogical optimism directed particularly toward those born after the war. By the middle of the decade, however, this optimism turned into disappointment and aggression against those who proved resistant toward this educational mission.

I would like to sketch three shifts in the educational conflict with GDR youth in the 1960s. At the beginning of the decade, the building of the Berlin Wall in 1961 put youth for the time being superficially in the hands of educators. In the mid-1960s, conflict arose over Western-oriented youth subcultures. At the end of the decade, "1968" in Europe stood for reform and revolutionary hopes of youth above all. In all three phases male youth stood in the center of public protest in the GDR. Their social backgrounds and the symbols that they used were not always the same, however. The fact that the educational functionaries commonly inter-preted these diffuse protests according to cold war ideological models transformed youth subcultures into highly charged confrontations with power. Since the regime set such narrow boundaries on behavior, these restrictions could easily lead to violations of these boundaries. This essay examines such boundary violations and their consequences. I address these developments as an expression of generational conflict, the existence or possibility of which was always officially denied in the GDR. This study is based on biographical interviews and especially descriptions of conflict from the files of the Socialist Unity Party (SED), the mass youth organi-zation Free German Youth (FDJ), the National People's Army (NVA), and the state educational administration. Students and universities will not be examined here.[3] I am most interested in those who were between fourteen and eighteen years old, who in this time period were at the center of political interest. However, the promise to these youths in the relatively liberal 1963 Youth Communiqué declaring "Youth of today, Masters of tomorrow—Give youth trust and responsibility"[4] was not put into prac-tice. By the end of the GDR, the most prominent functionary of the 1949 generation had only achieved a position as the head of the "Young Pio-neers" children's organization.[5]

I

On September 26, 1961, the Department of People's Education in the Cen-tral Committee of the SED received the following information about the behavior of the twelfth grade in a secondary school in Anklam: a group of students applied voluntarily for the NVA "only after a long discussion." In an evening political event on September 20 the class decided "not to sing along with the closing song." On September 21, the day after the sign-ing of the "Defense Law"[6] in the Volkskammer the class decided to appear in school in black clothing. "We are carrying our future to the grave" was their explanation. The students put a funeral wreath with red candy on the teacher's lectern for the Party secretary of the school, who taught the class for its final hour of the day. The whole faculty basically ignored this provocation, and only the regional and district leadership of the Party opened an investigation of the incident. References were made to two "ringleaders" from the school, who were arrested. Other students were to be transferred to other schools as long as they helped to explain what happened. Some were kicked out of the FDJ. On September 24, the following Sunday, the superintendent of the area pled for the students. On September 25 the following text was found on the blackboard in the school's chemistry room: "Freedom, freedom, we want to be free! Down with your Führer! Up with revolution! Free yourself and flee over there [to the West]! Get your own weapons and beat the National People's Army! Long live all former students! Hang the teachers!" The alleged author was immediately arrested. Otherwise the report contained the statement that three teachers already belonged to the faculty before 1945 (which implied, but didn't state, that they were former Nazis) and other teachers had supposedly been their students—this also only implied a possible connection between them. The Party and the FDJ supposedly could not have played a positive role in the school. In order to change this, Anklam's "Production Brigades" would look after the students in the future, and the students would more frequently take part in weekend harvesting work. "The decree against listening to NATO broadcasts and Western television (must) be implemented."

On October 4 the SED Politburo saw the minutes of a meeting with twenty-two students from Anklam, who had indeed been expelled, and their parents. The latter were for the most part employed in the farmers' cooperative (LPG) or in rural handicraft, and four fathers had been killed in the war. Two fathers were SED members; one was a member of the German Farmer's Party. Almost all the parents agreed with the decided measure with justifications like "No state would like such a thing." Only a few mothers expressed that they found the punishment of their children to be too harsh, because they were incited to do this deed by people like theology students who had in the meantime fled to the West. One mother, however, said about her brother-in-law, who served in the NVA, that under Hitler such students would rightfully be shot. Some parents promised to make amends for their children by performing future "quality work" in their respective professions. These students were in the meantime employed in various apprenticeships and hoped after repentance and showing proof of their willingness to be of service that they would be allowed to take the Abitur test that would allow them to attend university.[7]

In the internal Party publications, the Anklam case became a synonym for the dangerous opposition of youth against the policies of the GDR leadership and the Party after the shutting of the borders and before the introduction of universal military service. The severe punishments showed how the leaders panicked in the face of the collective action of the students and the supposed compliance of the teachers. The building of the Berlin Wall a month beforehand seemed justified again considering such hostile elements. The particular danger of this action lay on the one hand in their refusal to defend the GDR against the West or even to see West Germany as an enemy. On the other hand the danger was also linked to the "closed nature" of the class, which apparently survived until the end since the expulsion of so many students implied that the SED's offer to protect cooperative students was rarely taken up. The report's references to the caretaking superintendents, the older teachers, and the theologians, who had befriended some students, aimed to suggest general political links to the church, the West, and the Nazi past. In this sense, the irritated SED comrades offered a multifaceted explanation for the threatening conflict with the Anklam students.

Between January and September 1960 alone, 43,658 persons between fifteen and twenty-five years old fled the GDR; of these the majority were male youths. The number of the so-called *Rückkehrer* (those who returned to the GDR) was 10,546 in the same time period, but this hardly changes the general tendency, especially since the returnees were seen as obstinate and untrustworthy.[8] The building of the Berlin Wall and the closing of the borders along the whole western border of the GDR was supposed to end not only the real but also the virtual, so-called mental border crossing. The closed border was also meant to proscribe the educational arena, in which friends and foes would be clearly defined and every "enemy contact" would be even more rigidly thwarted. To counteract the perception that by building the Wall the GDR leaders exerted an act of force against its own population, the leadership enacted campaigns that connected heightened "vigilance" and more severe punishments against alleged opposition with displays of agreement and enthusiasm for the "anti-fascist protective wall." Such campaigns were especially directed at youth. For example, this support was "proven" in the form of FDJ contingents in production, the creation of FDJ order groups, and the organization of so-called voluntary applications to the NVA. All these measures had moderate success. Numerous young workers expressed the suspicion toward the economic campaigns that the GDR was close to bankruptcy and that the Wall served to propel the economy.[9] FDJ youth were purposefully enlisted for the so-called Blitz Action against NATO-Broadcasters, in which in September 1961 twenty-five thousand youths positioned thousands of television antennas "in the direction of socialism." This meant that roof antennas pointed toward the West were destroyed. The FDJ newspaper *Junge*

Welt from September 20, 1961, reported the successful destruction of 1,588 antennas in the districts around Karl-Marx-Stadt alone.[10] In the same time period, students and apprentices from across the GDR were encouraged to pledge in a written declaration to give up "eavesdropping" on Western radio and TV broadcasts. Since there was no law against Western media consumption and none was planned, it was hoped that such personal pledges would achieve the necessary moral sense of wrongdoing in violations of these self-determined rules.

Despite such displays of agreement after the building of the Wall the political leadership anticipated stronger unrest and protests especially from youth. Unrest was already common in the time before 1961, and protests filled the file reports of the FDJ and the SED: extreme right and National Socialist statements or rituals; defamation of Party leader Walter Ulbricht; attacks on police; vandalism; public playing of Western music on portable radios; memorials of the June 17, 1953, uprising; the founding of Teddy Boy clubs; or correspondence with the foreign legion.[11] Gangs and "rowdies" were the names given to every alarming youth group that consciously broke from the control of the FDJ or were established in opposition to the FDJ. The reports mentioned such primarily proletariat youth subcultures without subjecting them to serious political analysis. Alongside these reports attention was also paid to the connection between bourgeois and church influences on schoolchildren. The high school student (*Oberschüler*) was seen as a key figure in the fight between old and new educational influences. The reputation of bourgeois elites was linked to him in terms of social background and political attitude. The case of Anklam gained its meaning through this connection. At the same time, it shows in detail how forced and misguided this interpretation was. On the one hand these incidents concerned the GDR's rising generation of children of the war years, who in the face of the threat of military duty were motivated more likely by thoughts of peace and concern for their personal future than in aggressive opposition. Some actions, such as defacing the blackboard in the chemistry room, demonstrate more an undirected and uncontainable gesture of adolescent student protest through childish or ironic use of rebellious slogans. The SED was incapable of such a differentiated analysis; neither its own fear of popular opposition nor the need for simple explanations that confirmed its fears allowed for more complex explanations.

This case also exemplifies how solidarity among the students and within the families was, or was supposed to have been, broken, as parents became pupils of the state themselves and people were humiliated by self-incriminating confessions. This was a common pattern of "managing conflict" by state institutions that was all the more ineffective the less those concerned had to lose—that is, among those least interested in taking part in dynamics of GDR social transformation. With the closing of the border to the west, the bourgeoisie and the church remained weakened internal enemies. Their influence on youth was to be systematically eliminated. Further school reforms served to secularize and eliminate bourgeois elements, particularly in the high schools. The peak of the fight against the churches and the campaign against the young congregations was over, but the latter were still closely monitored, and their influence, particularly in the rural and bourgeois milieus, alarmed observers.[12]

The building of the Berlin Wall had an ambivalent effect both on state and party politics and on society in the GDR. While it was clearly an open act of repression, which narrowed each individual's biographical options and range of choices, it at the same time gave politics more freedom to open up and come to terms with a population now fixed in place. This also applied to a rigid youth policy, which, determined by fear and panic immediately after 1961, went through a different, more liberal shift in 1963. Encouraged by Ulbricht, the chief editor of the student newspaper *Forum* and the later chair of the Youth Commission of the SED Central Committee, Kurt Turba, pursued a policy that was supposed to take into account the facts in the Youth Communiqué mentioned previously. That is, the closing of the border should bring about an internal opening so as to align the post-1945 generation through offers of engagement without interrupting the all-important modernization process. After August 13, 1961, the state now admitted that its dialogue with youth had been severed, that their questions had not been taken seriously, and that youth were too quickly called agents of the enemy. Instead, all youth who were evaluated as "still standing apart" were to be integrated into the GDR's state-building project as conversation partners.[13] The promise of socialism would then convince the postwar children that alternative experiences and possibilities were no longer available or necessary.

2

In the autumn of 1965 a forbidden demonstration took place in Leipzig's inner city. Demonstrations like these had not occurred since June 17, 1953.

"On October 31 around 2,500 persons collected on the Leuschnerplatz and adjoining streets. In this group were numerous Comrades and FDJ functionaries, security forces in civilian clothing, etc. Around 500–800 young members of Beat groups were there," said the Party information. The Beat fans came from the whole district in order to protest against a decision made by a commission of the District Council a few days before to rescind the licenses of over fifty amateur Beat bands, which effectually forbade them from playing. They gathered in a rather disorganized manner without banners or loudspeakers in the inner city and were split up by units of the People's Police, whereby 267 demonstrators were loaded into the truck parked nearby and brought first to the police station and then for several weeks to forced labor in a lignite factory south of Leipzig. Some so-called ringleaders were subsequently put on trial. The police presence remained strong in Leipzig on the day after the demonstration, especially in the afternoon when a local soccer game against Austria was taking place. However, they could not prevent large messages such as "We just want the Beatles" from appearing on walls and streets the following night and even days later. The regime hardly won the day on October 31.

The Leipzig Beat demonstration was only the most spectacular expression of a conflict that had taken place in all corners of the GDR for years and that after the summer of 1965 became the actual core of youth conflict. From the beginning the Anglo-Saxon Beat groups, especially the Beatles and Rolling Stones, were just as popular among GDR youth as among youth in the West. The music was heard on West German radio broadcasts, recorded on cassettes, and played on homemade equipment. The way that the Youth Communiqué was formulated, it seemed that youth could dance to their own beat as long as they remained discreet about it.[14] In any case participants in discussions of this programmatic text drew the conclusion from it that "Now we can admit that the Party also tolerates the Twist."[15] The GDR's youth broadcaster DT 64 (named after the German Meeting [*Deutschlandtreffen*] of Youth, a national festival that took place in the streets of East Berlin in 1964) aimed to connect the nation's youth interest in pop music with political information that conformed to the system. Broadcasters were bound to regulations that stipulated that at least 60 percent of music played, as in all media and dance clubs, must be from the GDR or other socialist countries.

In the hope of binding the "amateur guitar groups" more strongly to the German language[16] and the FDJ, the Central Council of the FDJ called for a national "guitar group contest" in May 1965. However, the

Party canceled this event that summer. Research had shown that participating groups were still oriented toward Western models. The loss of control over youthful, border-crossing attitudes, together with the critical situation in literary and film production, led to a shift in GDR cultural and
youth policy. That autumn district officials were advised to register all
Beat groups. Their licenses were to be rescinded if they violated the 60 percent rule; if there were any "excesses" on stage; if they had English band
names or unkempt appearance (meaning long hair in particular); didn't
know the notes; were under suspicion of "shirking work" (i.e., if a musi-
cian was unable to maintain steady employment beyond his music gigs);
demanded too high a fee; or didn't pay enough taxes. In the district of
Leipzig these rules affected fifty-four out of fifty-eight registered bands,
including those who had been highly praised by the official organs of the
SED earlier that year and who had played in the Leipzig city festival earlier that summer. The youth reacted to the news of the ban with a determined, if ill-prepared, protest. Consciously or not, the educational functionaries helped spread the news about the demonstration by constantly
warning schools and factories about the upcoming event.[17]

In the end, the attempt to prevent or limit Western music consumption through personal pledges, bans, controls, pronunciations, and sanctions completely failed. Young East Germans increasingly listened to,
viewed, and recorded the West German "Deutschlandfunk," Radio Luxemburg, and the West German TV show *Beat-Club.* Representative youth
questionnaires also revealed a growing openness in admitting to this
leisure practice. The number of those who declared that they didn't listen
to Western broadcasts or were even against listening to them sank drastically during the course of the sixties. This was true for students at the poly-
technic schools, those at the advanced high schools, university students,
apprentices, young workers, boys and girls, and urban and rural youth.[18]

In the eyes of the education functionaries, the "NATO-Enemy Broadcasts" were a gate through which the "opposition" could invade and take
over GDR youth and turn them into internal agents. Although this view-
point brought an entire generation under suspicion, the threat in the sixties
seemed particularly to come from male working-class youth. This reflected
the widespread belief that the FDJ had very little influence among apprentices and especially young workers and that the "outsiders" (*Gammler*)
and "Beatles Fans" came overwhelmingly from the proletariat.
Researchers at the Leipzig Central Institute for Youth Research (ZIJ),
founded in the mid-sixties, worked to prove this impression by systematic

investigations with ever greater claims to represent all youth. These researchers measured youth's ideological outlook on a scale ranging from extreme agreement to rejection of the positions of the GDR, socialism, the Soviet Union, the SED, and imperialism. They determined that the "progressive" opinions came most often from girls, high school students, and rural youth, whereas the "backward" ones came from boys, workers, and urban youth. The seventeen-year-old high school girl from a Mecklenburg village became the ideal GDR youth, and the eighteen-year-old male worker from Berlin was the negative example of a refusenik and passive skeptic. This conclusion clearly and embarrassingly contradicted the socialist ideal type.[19]

Beat fans were alarming not only for their musical tastes but also for their outward lifestyle that demonstrably set them apart from the state's idealized image of youth. Long hair, known as the mushroom head (*Pilzkopf*), and particular fashions were markers of this "negative appearance."[20] This style was fueled by images that came into the country via foreign mass media. Mothers, sisters, girlfriends, and professional tailors sewed the desired shirts, blazers, and especially flared pants. Shoemakers remade women's boots in various sizes with new heels to match those found in the pictures. These prized getups were meticulously cared for and maintained. In speeches and publications by educators, the disgust that suffuses the derogatory descriptions of Beat fans often stemmed less from the filth and external appearance of the observed youth than from the provocative crossing of gender boundaries, the weakening of a form of masculinity that was connected to practical clothing, soldierly haircuts, rigidly controlled body language, and the proletarian masculine ideal. Youth were called "outsiders, loiterers or beatniks," and their way of "dancing apart" (to rock and roll) or playing guitar was denounced as the expression of undisciplined, effeminate, out-of-control bodies. Those among the Beat generation who had been taken into custody had their hair cut by force and were brought to the dirty coal factory in their beloved fan clothing. Some who were identified as "ringleaders" had "Western decadence" and "American anti-culture" written on their bodies: their tattoos were shown in small photos as evidence in the Leipzig newspaper when it reported on the demonstration and its presumed leaders.[21]

Youth subcultures also developed distinctive forms of sociability. These came from youth clubs, where young people went regularly to dance on weekends, or from Beat bands, which youth often followed to their concerts in neighboring towns. During the week and outside such concerts, or during times when the FDJ clubs were closed, youth met at set places, often in front of movie theaters. Solid groups emerged from this experience, such as the Leipziger Capitol Gang (named for the Capitol Cinema). In these groups one would make an appearance, listen to transistor radios together, and look to incite conflicts with passersby or police. All of this was closely connected with common "eavesdropping" on Western broadcasts, as well as swapping recordings, photos, and addresses of Western fan clubs. Clublike unions were also founded, often creating features parallel to those of the state youth unions, such as statutes, identification cards, and other rituals. All of this resembled the leisure behavior of Western youth, just as the disgust of the older generation found like expression in the West. In the GDR this phenomenon carried a particular charge from the fact that originally apolitical cultural symbols acquired heightened meaning from the politicization given to them by GDR educators. These symbols thereby became the very stuff of alternative youth style in the GDR. Therefore, a decorative pin in the form of two crossed surgical needles gained additional symbolic significance above and beyond that used among youth themselves when functionaries interpreted them as antagonistic emblems of those who supposedly declared themselves vaccinated against socialism. Such official interpretations were designed to scare youth away from this symbol, but it had the opposite effect in frightening the educators and giving the subcultures new power.[22]

Apart from overt conflicts, youth continued to fight for autonomous spaces in the sixties. From the perspective of the FDJ and the SED, such spaces acted as vacuums that would be filled by the "enemy" if state forces were negligent. In their eyes, consumption of Western music was inseparable from a dangerous vulnerability to Western imperialism in general and West German expansion in particular. Young men went to the NVA as draftees with these perceived threats in mind, as surveys often showed.[23] In this sense, the control and planning of leisure had both real and symbolic meaning for securing the borders.

The FDJ and the educational powers set their sights on infiltrating schools through regular checks and through FDJ meetings. This presence was, however, much more difficult to maintain in the factories. The reality shock that often accompanied first-time socialist employment, as shown in several surveys, rudely challenged the trumpeted certainties of socialism's economic superiority.[24] Thus on a daily basis, the FDJ secretaries on-site in the schools, factories, and residential youth clubs confronted the dilemma of trying to strengthen educational and controlling functions of youth on the one hand, while experiencing strong resistance and attempts at autonomy on the other. Many of these secretaries, particularly if they were young themselves and part of this milieu, did their best to comply with the wishes of the youth to the extent that maintaining contact with them was reported to their superiors as a measure of success. The guitar band contest in the summer of 1965 represented a similar attempt at a centralized level. When the Central Committee expressed dissatisfaction toward this youth policy in December 1965 at their Eleventh Plenary Session, consequences followed: From top to bottom there were shakeups in personnel, forced "self-criticism," and a new wave of controls and sanctions that drove youth further into silent conformity, without making their social spaces accessible to educators. The disciplining effort and political influence of the FDJ remained limited in the case of working-class youth. In the schools, by contrast, attitudes of conformity and hypocrisy reigned, which were acknowledged as such and regretfully reported to superiors.[25] The basis for a true, political conviction was most manifest at the technical schools and universities, although this depended on academic discipline and was closely connected to achieving an elevated social position.

The West, especially among proletarian youth, conversely remained a dream, a fantasy world cultivated through symbols and stories. Among GDR youth there was always the effort to make this dream a reality. Thousands of youth defiantly became "border assailants" (*Grenzverletzer*), seized in trains, in restricted areas near the border, or even in the no-man's-land along the border. The overwhelming number of these attempted flights from the GDR failed and ended with incarceration and house arrests. Police reports were not shy in mentioning the influence of Western television or Beat music or the external appearance of the "mushroom head" haircut. The physical border crossing symbolized the final, clearest expression of youth's antagonism toward the GDR. Here, too, the educational and control authorities proved remarkably blind to the conflicts plaguing their own society. Their interpretations of these incidents stood in stark contrast to the statements of the captured youth reported in police dossiers. Typically, youth explained their motives as primarily due to familial, work, or school conflicts; desire for adventure and travel; or longing for parents living in the West.[26] Reports about flight attempts, groups listening to music, correspondence about Beat groups, reading the West German teen magazine *Bravo,* the appearance of long-haired youth, the formation of bands, and conflicts with the police appeared within the FDJ and Party leadership under the rubric of "Information," "Special Incidents," or "Enemy Activity," along with other common signs of youthful misbehavior such as defacing an Ulbricht portrait or using Nazi symbols or slogans. These reports were witness to not only the obsession of functionaries with a youth population that stood under general suspicion, but also to the dynamic and symbolic quality of this conflict.

Despite the mistrust by Minister of People's Education Margot Honecker, and indeed after the repressive shift in youth policy after the December 1965 Eleventh Plenary Session, rational and scientifically minded youth research emerged that had its roots in the liberal early sixties. This was spearheaded above all by the ZIJ and its head, Walter Friedrich. The two "Mushroom Haircut Studies" ("Pilzkopf I and II" or PKI and PKII) of 1968 came from this institute.[27] The survey of about 320 vocational students, among whom about one-sixth were so-called mushroom heads, showed almost no distinction between this group and less noticeable groups of youths. This was especially the case in research topics such as leisure, in which the togetherness of informal friendship groups played the largest role; in good personal contacts with colleagues; and in reference to the limited value placed on the FDJ. Differences between general youth and the mushroom heads existed, however, in the longhairs' more limited job satisfaction, greater political skepticism, and limited identification with the GDR. The researchers could not prove, however, that the mushroom heads differed from their short-haired colleagues more than girls differed from boys or high school students differed from apprentices. The conclusions drawn from a picture test were also ambiguous. Those tested were told to evaluate three pictures of male youth according to productivity, political engagement, and modernity and to grade them according to "likeability." The pictures showed the prototype of a well-groomed young man in "civilian" dress, the prototype of a young FDJ functionary, and one of a mushroom head. A Leipzig actor portrayed the latter in a wig, by miming defensive body language and unfavorable demeanor. The same actor also played the civilian. The middle picture of the young man was recognizable through an indicated FDJ shirt and by his determined body language. The reactions to these three pictures showed the desired results to the extent that the mushroom head did get the lowest points for achievement, political engagement, and likeable appearance. However, the FDJ functionary also came out at the bottom in terms of likeability and modernity. The young civilian was at the top especially with highly "modern values." Seventy percent of those surveyed described him with the adjective *modern,* while only 39 percent considered the FDJ member or the mushroom head to be modern. The commentators tried to salvage this result by suggesting that the long-haired one was hardly recognized by those in his age group. But there was little denying the result that the desired model was by no means successful among working-class youth. What had they hoped for, when they asked the respondents to apply the characteristics of modernity to each of the three young men on the pictures? Obviously, three possible ways of defining *modernity* were offered: the outspoken nonconformist, the political activist, and the well dressed but unpolitical young man, whom the sociologists gave the label of a civilian, although none of the other photographs showed a man in military uniform. While the researchers clearly had wished the FDJ activist to represent modernity most convincingly, it is clear that the handsome civilian, placed in front of what seemed like a park, was offered as the second best representation of a modernity that the SED was willing to accept as positive in the late sixties: oriented toward a good life without the political vision of the future.

3

"On October 4, 1968 at 11:30 pm 'R.,' a railroad track technician from the track workshop in Plagwitz born on February 6, 1949 . . . reported that he had found homemade inflammatory pamphlets in several mailboxes in his apartment building. The provocations were written by hand on a page from an arithmetic book and were directed toward state council chiefs. The analysis of the handwriting showed that R. had produced these inflammatory pamphlets himself. R. was a FH [voluntary helper] of the VP [People's Police]. EV [judicial inquiry] introduced, arrest order applied for, since suspicion exists of further crimes committed by him."[28]

In February 1969, a report came from the Eighth High School of Leipzig to the Department of People's Education. Two students in the ninth grade had been observed as they "wore pins with the Czech national colors at a UTP [Educational Day in Production], took them off of their jackets and put them on their sweaters. When asked by Comrade H. why they wore these symbols, whether they wanted to express sympathy with the Czech Communist Party or with counter-revolutionary forces, they declared that 'they didn't know yet.'" Comrade H. reported further that other students at this school had also taken up "protest positions . . . and indeed in such a form that while Colleague I. drew a blackboard picture, they stood up and put both arms up with balled fists. Under the leadership of Student C. (Kl. 12a, Border Assailant 1968) who is under judicial proceedings, further students are building a so-called protest party." The parents of the first two mentioned students, who were members of the SED, had to justify their continued upbringing of their children to their Party group. Other measures against the perpetrators are not known.[29]

At the beginning of September 1969 police investigations into a matter in the district of Leipzig uncovered that two fountain constructors, ages twenty-three and nineteen, "since spring 1968 have collected, exchanged and disseminated inflammatory writings dropped as insertions into balloons. On August 24, 1968 in the village restaurant Roda, in the district of Grimma, both gathered youth around them at a dance event and organized speaking choirs whose content was directed in a slanderous way against the measures of our brother armies in the Czechoslovakian People's Republic. Since 1967 F. has had written connections to a 'Star Club' in Munich. He has obtained information from there about possibilities for an illegal departure from the GDR. Upon searching his apartment inflammatory writings and letters to and from Munich were found. EV introduced, arrest orders proclaimed. Delivery to the UHA [institution for investigative custody pending trial]."[30]

These three reports were typical for the years 1968–69. It seems clear that they are related to the Prague Spring and the resulting invasion of the Warsaw Pact states into Czechoslovakia on August 21, 1968, which represented a peak in the expression of political opposition.[31] However, it is worthwhile to investigate the meaning of such reports beyond this occasion. "Inflammatory leaflets" with slogans against the invasion of Czechoslovakia and against the GDR leadership were found not only in many locations in the city and district of Leipzig but throughout the whole GDR.[32] In most cases the producers and distributors were either caught in the act, denounced by neighbors, or captured later. The report cited first is remarkable, however, for the question of whether the young man wanted to divert suspicion by reporting his own crime himself or whether he did it out of vanity as a former police helper. Did his "inflammatory leaflets" have any relation to the invasion that had occurred two weeks beforehand? One possible way of reading this incident is that it has less to do with political protest in a narrow sense than with a diffuse action against the state and its supervisory organs that was meant to challenge and scare them in this phase of heightened alarm and "watchfulness."

Many of these protests around August 21 took place in the streets, public transportation, restaurants, and factory cafeterias. Openness instead of secrecy, provocation instead of conspiracy, seemed to prevail. Those arrested in the district of Leipzig, as far as their professions are known, were without exception young workers, who apparently acted spontaneously and alone in half the cases. In the police reports from July to December 1968, the invasion of Czechoslovakia played a prominent role in the content of protests only between the end of August and mid-September. Afterward the cases of "provocation," "rowdiness," "opposition," or "desecration of state symbols" returned to the usual level and were seen mostly in terms of fights with police, alcohol-induced riots, and youthful gang activity. The social structure of arrests stayed the same: mostly twenty-year-old, male workers from various economic areas. It seems obvious that public protest in the summer of 1968 should be understood less as an expression of directed political opposition than as the usage of an appropriate symbol for broad resistance of proletarian youth against a paranoid controlling power. This interpretation is supported by the final cited report, in which the perspective of the SED state toward collecting and distributing inflammatory writings and the rowdy group protest against the invasion of Czechoslovakia was associated with the everyday milieus of youth subcultures noted in certain locations (restaurants), events (dances), associations (West German fan clubs), and other dangers (flight from the republic). The fluctuating politicization of the youthful protest milieus can be attributed to a mixture of foreign and internal factors that fueled this power game. This gamelike character was shown in the second example. Here too a sign of protest, the Czech flag, could mean political opposition in February 1969. This is exactly where the allure, danger, and ambiguity lie. When the students claimed that they did not know (!) what the flag meant, not only is there a clear threat here, but also it is precisely the multiple meanings of the symbol that renders the educator helpless. In such a context everything that happens behind the backs of the teachers becomes dangerous. A "ringleader" and an "offense" associated with him serve to transform a simple "protest gesture" into a "protest party." The symbol "1968" proved itself as a successful instrument of struggle.

In June 1968 the new draftees came into the NVA. Many of them spent August and September in the Thuringian Forest on the border of Czechoslovakia without news or holidays. Instead, they were exposed to directed political campaigns and close care by superiors, who tried to counteract soldiers' uncertainty, boredom, and impatience through especially good provisions and stepped-up activity. Morale reports expressed little evidence of open "enemy arguments." The clearest expression of fear from a draftee were the words "I don't want to go to war. I'm only 18."[33] Nevertheless, the political department of the army had every reason for concern, if not about resistance to orders then for an inclination among almost all draftees toward the regular reception of Western radio and TV broadcasts. In the barracks, orders explicitly forbade this and disobedience was severely punished. Accounts by former draftees spanning the entire duration of the GDR show that this regulation was routinely disregarded. According to the filed reports, the shortage of supervision meant that the draftees "on vacation and when going out fall under the same influences as before their military service and thus serve as carriers and disseminators of enemy arguments within the barracks." This led above all to political indifference ("All armies are the same"); to criticism of the GDR; to denial of the antagonistic relationship to West Germany; or to a refusal to shoot at another German, who was seen as just another ordinary soldier.[34] Such beliefs appeared "among not inconsiderable numbers of soldiers and lower officers" and led "in final consequence to doubt about the aggressive character of the West German state." Apparently they existed independently from current political or military conflicts and could just as easily be stirred up at the numerous routine training courses in 1968 about questions concerning the new constitution. Those recently called to service tended toward more openness in such questions than the older draftees, and officer trainees or young officers seldom admitted that they ignored orders outside the barracks. The "friend-foe problem" remained unsolved, and even in the NVA "ideological border crossing" could not be completely thwarted. Those in power became painfully conscious of this fact especially in August 1968, when the GDR came so close to military emergency.[35]

4

GDR educators expressed their confidence less in pedagogical optimism as such than in a firm if abstract conviction in their ability to plan educational results through the complete control of every educational situation and relationship. The important pedagogical teaching master was Anton Makarenko, who was widely popularized in the GDR and constantly quoted: "I have an endless . . . and unbounded trust in the unlimited power of educational work. . . . If a person is badly educated, then the educator is exclusively at fault. If a child is good, then one can also thank his upbringing . . . and no pedagogy can be so powerful as our Soviet pedagogy, because here there are no conditions that stand in the path of a person's development."[36]

According to a mechanistic input-output model, it was expected that in the framework of the socialist educational dictatorship optimal conditions were also present in the GDR for the full formation of the human character. Failure to achieve this goal was due either to the influence of the opposition, which served to thwart it, or to one's own failure. In any case, the fate of the educator was intimately linked to the development of the pupil, and therefore hostility between both was inherent from the outset. Behind this conviction stood the vulgar Marxist view that was rooted in a simple ideology of progress. The educational energy emanating from this optimism concentrated on the perceived bulwarks of socialist society: the working class and youth. Members of these social groups were attributed with class instincts along with a quasi-natural quality and readiness for developing a socialist personality. The development of pedagogical goals was also served by eliminating unwanted bourgeois elements from society and by educating a new generation that had no ties to the past. The youth conflicts in the fifties and early sixties were seen as hangovers from this past. Those involved in these conflicts were indeed still of the age to have lived through the last war years and the immediate postwar years or ostensibly stood under the influence of bourgeois or church influence. Commentary about youth criminality before 1960 moved in this direction.[37] The behavior of those born into the GDR then seemed to confirm this interpretation and its underlying educational optimism. Hanna Voss, born in 1950, explained:

> I became a Pioneer, like everyone. There was no question of this, and I must say, that through this muddled origin with all the moving about of my parents, I also didn't have any grandparents, so before 1945 there was no anchor for me, and it was simply a horrible time and as a child it was already clear to me that I had to go and do something against this fear. In a totally unconscious way, I didn't become German, but a GDR-citizen. . . . I didn't want to have anything to do with fascism, it would be best if it had never happened and we could start all over. I believe that is our childhood experience. . . . From this conglomeration, which for me had a strong social imprint, I find

myself in retrospect to be partly fanatic and dogmatic, you see? So I was a fanatical Pioneer, and the best was carrying the pennant in front of the group, and campfires and camping and singing and drilling and discipline and reporting and always getting to be leader, you see? This went on a rather long time, and it also played a role that mom was alone in a village with three kids—and she never married my father—she had three illegitimate children, so she was branded. We were poor, we were illegitimate, and through this zeal for participation and through achievement in school, I tried to forget my social origins. I was mostly successful; I was really accepted in school. . . . And I still know, that I—when was that? 1961?—could go to the Pioneer meeting, because we did a lot as a Pioneer group and they had to collect for me, because my mom alone without education with three children couldn't do it. She had 360 Marks per month and fed four people on that and furnished an apartment. To this day I don't know how she did it. She must have really sacrificed for us. Oh well.[38]

Hanna Voss describes her radical break with the past, in which she grew up seemingly open and ready for participating in the new age. At the same time, her description also illustrates that, in other cases in which parents and grandparents had something to say about the past, official antifascism was relativized or at least could be commented on through experience. Above all this citation shows that it was not just a totalizing influence of education but also a biographical and psychological disposition with suitable needs that could not be guided that made the offer of education acceptable or even desirable. This offer of acceptance, power, and a bright future was attractive to many children of this period. Familial roots, mobility, declassing, as well as frequent parental silence about the past created a vacuum in parts of this generation that the Pioneer organization, for example, could fill. It was different in the rural, proletarian, religious, or bourgeois milieus, for whom the end of the war meant less of a break than it did for Hanna Voss, the daughter of a refugee who was lower middle class.[39] In this case, as in other life stories of the first postwar generation, the start of political connections was linked to the familial fate, especially that of the mother and her difficult sacrifices. The emotional attractiveness of this life path held well until puberty, when the need for autonomy and the increasingly differentiated view of reality were mutually strengthened and usually led to efforts to retreat or free oneself from the grip of the collectivity.

This break, which appeared for most in the seventh grade, when students were being prepared to be taken into the FDJ, could only be explained by the official caste of educators as the still effective "enemy influences" from the older generation and/or Western media, influences that were still to be confronted with increasingly perfect and uniform surveillance. That the attempts at autonomy by youth were only strengthened and at most driven underground, as in forbidden groups, was only comprehended by a few, and they had no decisive influence over political or pedagogical affairs. Among the few "modernizers," who were moved above all by an empirically grounded and differentiated image of youth, belonged Kurt Turba, the author of the Youth Communiqué of 1963, and Walter Friedrich, the director of the ZIJ. Friedrich had criticized the automatic trust in the class instinct of proletariat youth and demanded that social background no longer be viewed as the sole basis for personality development since empirical results of youth research did not prove a connection between (proletariat) class background and (progressive) consciousness. SED circles sharply criticized him for this thesis, since he concluded that limitations in access to higher education for nonproletariat children were not justified and education on the basis of a "class standpoint" should be dismissed as senseless. Above all his thesis questioned the basic hypothesis of GDR education: that the proletariat and its corresponding class consciousness were the determinants for a successful educational policy.[40] The discussion of how much educational process could be determined and guided remained a central theme of pedagogy during the sixties and intensified the desperation of educators who didn't want to take responsibility for the "failure" of youth education.[41]

Disappointment about the limits of the educational dictatorship led in 1965 not only to a higher degree of surveillance and mistrust compared to 1963 and 1964. At the same time, the educational institutions created even more perfect displays of an idealized "youth life" that had little to do with reality. A telling example of this is the attempt after 1965 to call a socialist "singing movement" into being, which aimed to defeat the Beatles with revolutionary workers' songs. Mostly this was limited to group sing-a-longs at meetings of functionaries, and even there it often failed when the "Friends of Youth" didn't know the lyrics.[42] The more youth silently watched these events, and the less information about deviant youth managed to get to union and Party leaders, the more the significance of the GDR political youth organization declined. At the beginning of the seventies this process could still have been compensated for by the great international revolutionary movement, whereby the 1973 World Festival for Youth in Berlin provided a notable highpoint for GDR youth. At the beginning of the eighties, however, youth and the youth organizations had resigned to accept their differences. The silent tolerance of youth subcultures and the production of their own rock music effectively defused the once-intense symbolic conflict over the West.[43]

However, as analyses of the end of the sixties suggest, there was success in only connecting a small minority of postwar youth with socialist goals. The political structures of the GDR were certainly built on passion and pathos, but even more so on order and discipline. Where conflict arose, the goal of obedience always trumped personal initiative. The politically reliable portion of youth was therefore hardly in a position to woo the great majority into engagement and action. Rather, they became an instrument in the educational dictatorship, while an increasingly greater number of the young generation behaved passively and silently, a significant minority of which even rebelled and resisted in various ways. With this the socialist project lost hold of all of the youth.

5

In opposition to youth stood a generation that was young in the 1930s and 1940s and strongly influenced by the crisis periods of the Weimar Republic and National Socialism. One cannot speak of a unified "reconstruction generation" in the GDR—but one may attempt to characterize the generation of educators in the postwar German East. One must differentiate between familial educators and those pedagogues in the GDR who were commissioned and controlled by the state and Party. Differences must also be noted between those born before World War I and the so-called Hitler Youth generation. The majority of the former lost power in the Soviet Zone (SBZ) and its successor state, the GDR, as former Nazis and therefore experienced a rapid social decline. On the other hand, the younger among them—the so-called Hitler Youth generation, born in the second half of the 1920s—were much more strongly politicized under National Socialism and were thus harder hit psychologically by its defeat. Yet it was exactly these people who formed the educator generation for youth born in the GDR. Given the significant flight of bourgeois segments among them, those who remained in the fifties and sixties rose socially often through local political roles and quick training in those professions in which personnel exchange was most fluid in the postwar period due to both denazification and the Stalinist "purges."[44] Chief among them were the pedagogical professions. By contrast, in influential positions on the education front, as in the Central Committee of the SED, the generation that had the say gained their political socialization in the political struggles of the Weimar Republic, often in the communist youth union. They survived Nazism in the resistance or in exile. The generation of antifascists as well as the Hitler Youth generation thus saw the needs and attitudes of postwar youth as alien and incomprehensible in light of their own experiences as youth. The older antifascists tried sometimes to transfer their own romantic, lofty memories of the proletarian youth movement of the Weimar period to postwar youth. The Hitler Youth generation also recalled their youthful communal experiences as a model, even as they placed their own reeducation at the center of their reconstructed autobiographies. The deep personal crisis they experienced at that time, which they only appeared to overcome through the shift of identification to the old antifascists, together with their experience of advancement in socialism, made them into loyal and authoritarian figures who reacted to the apathy of the young generation with hatred and resentment. Konrad Naumann, born in 1929, remembered during the Eleventh Plenary Session in December 1965, "It was 1945, the comrades who came back from the concentration camps at Buchenwald, Dachau, Majdanek, held us rather tightly by the collar, so we could hardly breathe, and even if we weren't in agreement, they pushed us where they wanted to and turned us into respectable, useful people."[45] He apparently wanted to pass this experience of force on to the new generation.

The state-party educational system stood in an ambivalent relationship to the familial one. On the one hand, teachers and parents belonged to the same generation and shared similar historical experiences and values. They were united in their rejection of the style of the "longhairs" and their music, much as did the parents' generation in the Federal Republic. On the other hand, most of the parents rejected the political goals of state education. From this tension emerged a contradictory attitude toward public education, which one might appreciate in principle for its authoritarian structure, while at the same time one would avoid open conflict with it. In only the most rare situations, such as in the religious milieus, could GDR children and youth rely upon clear parental support against a teacher. Instead of strengthening their children, parents had to fear being infantilized themselves and subjected to educational measures. The effects of these difficult relationships between youth, parents, and the state on the development of selfhood among youth are not easy to measure. Much suggests that generational conflict within families in East Germany—differently than in West Germany—was silenced and repressed by the larger conflict between the private and the public spheres.

The state's fear of youth was justified. But the hysteria with which it reacted to this internal enemy in the sixties hid the true danger that emanated from this postwar generation: those who finally grew up did stay quiet—and with it the society as a whole stagnated.

Translated by Katherine Pence and Paul Betts

NOTES

This essay is an updated version of an essay that first appeared in 1994 in Hartmut Kaelble, Jürgen Kocka, and Hartmut Zwahr, eds., *Sozialgeschichte der DDR* (Stuttgart, 1994), 404–25.

1. Dorothee Wierling, *Geboren im Jahr Eins. Der Geburtsjahrgang 1949 in der DDR. Versuch einer Kollektivbiographie* (Berlin, 2002).

2. On the topic of the modernity of the GDR and cases of modernization that were inherent to the system, see Sigrid Meuschel, "Überlegungen zu einer Herrschafts- und Gesellschaftsgeschichte der DDR," *Geschichte und Gesellschaft* 19 (1993): 5–14, 9. For a critique of this article, see Detlef Pollack, "Modernization and Modernization Blockades in GDR Society," in *Dictatorship as Experience: Towards a Socio-Cultural History of the GDR,* ed. Konrad Jarausch (New York and Oxford, 1999), 27–45.

3. For more on this topic, see Armin Mitter and Stefan Wolle, *Untergang auf Raten. Unbekannte Kapitel der DDR-Geschichte* (Munich, 1993), 400ff. See also Marc-Dietrich Ohse, *Jugend nach dem Mauerbau. Anpassung, Protest und Eigensinn (DDR 1961–1974)* (Berlin, 2003), 25–42.

4. Kommuniqué des Politbüros des ZK der SED zu Problemen der Jugend in der DDR, Schriftenreihe des Staatsrats der DDR 5/1963. The text deals less with the problem of youth and more with problems of the GDR and the youthful potential to help solve these problems. Wierling, *Geboren im Jahr Eins,* 189–215.

5. Wilfried Poßner, *Immer bereit. Kämpfen, spielen, fröhlich sein* (Berlin, 1995). Poßner gained this function at age thirty-six, and in 1989, a few weeks after the fall of the Wall, he stepped back from it after he was pressured to do so.

6. "The Law for Defense of the German Democratic Republic" contains various "Measures for Strengthening Defensive Readiness," such as the possibility for limiting civil rights, confiscating private property, and mobilizing citizens for personal service; see www.documentarchiv.de/ddr/1961/verteidigungsgesetz. A general draft was first introduced in 1962 in the GDR, but before that there was considerable pressure on high school students, who had to bribe their way into higher studies with a "voluntary" commitment to the army.

7. Bundesarchiv Stiftung Archiv der Parteien und Massenorganisationen der DDR (BA-SAPMO) DY-30 IV 2/905/27, Blatt 29–31, 63–74.

8. Jugendarchiv des Instituts für Zeitgeschichtliche Jugendforschung (JA-IZJ) A 3727, unpaginated. The FDJ archive has since been integrated into the Bundesarchiv Berlin.

9. For example, see the opinions of youth in Karl-Marx-Stadt and in Berlin that were reported to the FDJ leadership. JA-IZJ A 5852, unpaginated.

10. Helmut Müller, "Die Bedeutung des Kampfauftrags des Zentralrates der Freien Deutschen Jugend vom 18. August 1961 für die Mobilisierung der Jugend zur Stärkung und Verteidigung der Deutschen Demokratischen Republik," unpublished Diplomarbeit, Leipzig 1962, 92ff.

11. Examples are from Wierling, *Geboren im Jahr Eins,* 171f.

12. Among the most important school reforms before the building of the Berlin Wall were the introduction of polytechnical education in the seventh through twelfth grades on October 1, 1958; the "Regulation for Protecting a Solid Order in the General Schools" from November 12, 1959; and the "Law for Socialist Development of the School System in the GDR" from February 25, 1965. The reports about the activities of the Young Congregation (JG) to the responsible Central Committee Department give the explanation that the influence of the church among youth continued to exist the most where youth ministers were engaged and worked in a "modern way." Numerous youths not only were members of the JG and the FDJ but also held important functions. The JG was mostly successful among rural youth, girls, and high schoolers (including those in the new "Extended High School" [Erweiterten Oberschulen, or EOS]). For 1962–63, for example, see BA-SAPMO DY-30 IV 2/14/173, Blatt 3–8, 13–22, 25–35. For the bourgeois and religious milieu, see Christoph Kleßmann, "Relikte des Bildungsbürgertums in der DDR," in *Sozialgeschichte der DDR,* ed. Hartmut Kaelble, 254–70.

13. Stenographisches Protokoll der gemeinsamen Sitzung der Jugendkommission beim Politbüro des ZK und der Regierungskommission für die Ausarbeitung des Jugendgesetzes, March 29, 1963, BA-SAPMO IV 2/2.111/8, explizit bei Horst Grenz, 87.

14. The respective German phrase was that "die Jugend soll nach ihrem eigenen Takt tanzen, solange sie taktvoll bleibt," Jugendkommuniqué, 33.

15. BA-SAPMO, DY 30 IV A 2/16, Bd. 17, Informationen über die bisherigen Erfahrungen . . . October 30, 1963, unpaginated, 5.

16. In the imitation of their idols most groups sang English songs, which in the eyes of the Party was the language of imperialism. Therefore, Ulbricht viewed the national honor of the GDR to be in danger in his speech delivered at the Eleventh Plenary Session of the Central Committee of the SED in December 1965. For the connection between defense against Anglo-Saxon popular culture and a positive redefinition of German culture after 1945 in both German states, see Uta Poiger, *Jazz, Rock and Rebels. Cold War Politics and American Culture in a Divided Germany* (Berkeley, 1999).

17. For the history of demonstrations and experiences of some participants, see Dorothee Wierling, "Beat heißt schlagen. Die Leipziger Beatdemonstration im Oktober 1965 und die Jugendpolitik der SED," in *Unsere Medien, unsere Republik*

2: 1965: Warten auf den Frühling, vol. 4, ed. Adolf-Grimme-Institut (Marl, 1993), 41–43; and Dorothee Wierling, "Der Staat, die Jugend und der Westen. Texte zu Konflikten der 60er Jahre," in *Akten. Eingaben. Schaufenster. Die DDR und ihre Texte,* ed. Alf Lüdtke and Peter Becker (Berlin, 1997), 223–40. For the connection between Beat music and SED cultural policy, see Michael Rauhut, "DDR-Beatmusik zwischen Engagement und Repression," in *Kahlschlag. Das 11. Plenum des ZK der SED 1965,* ed. Günter Agde (Berlin, 1991), 52–63. A literary treatment is Erich Loest, *Es geht seinen Gang, oder Mühen in unserer Ebene* (Stuttgart, 1978). See the latest treatment of the topic by Marc-Dietrich Ohse, *Jugend nach dem Mauerbau,* 83ff. The fact that the news of the coming demonstration spread so easily has nurtured the legend that the Stasi itself provoked the gathering in order to get rid of the obstinate Beat fans once and for all. But there is no evidence of such a scheme in the files.

18. In the "Survey [19]69" of the Central Institute for Youth Research (ZIJ), 67 percent of youth named Radio Luxemburg and Deutschlandfunk as their favorite stations. Only 7 percent were against "eavesdropping" on Western broadcasts, while the larger rest admitted at least to the consumption of music broadcasts. The publicness of this admission, according to the researchers, grew continually since the beginning of the sixties. JA-IZJ B 6273,U 69 Teil I, 39f.

19. Ibid. This study included comparative dates from 1962, 1964, and 1966. These studies only commented ashamedly on marked differences according to age, sex, region, and status. Such differences were drawn based on generally high agreement when asked appropriate ideological questions or statements. These results show the limited source value of the ZIJ studies as a source. The answers and percentages derived in the anonymous surveys don't say much in themselves but offer interesting insights through the named differences between the various groups as well as changes over time.

20. Dorothee Wierling, "'Negative Erscheinungen'—zu einigen Sprach- und Argumentationsmustern in der Auseinandersetzung mit der Jugendsubkultur in der DDR der sechziger Jahre," *WerkstattGeschichte* 5 (1993): 29–37.

21. Interviews and letters that were sent to me after an article in the *Leipziger Volkszeitung* give us information about subcultural self-display and the cost connected with this, as well as the networks created by this practice. They could not be included here individually due to space constraints. For the description of the demonstration, its participants, and the arrested in the print media of the GDR, see, for example, the *Leipziger Volkszeitung,* November 5, 1965, 4, under the title "Beatles, Ledernacken, Aggression": "These tattoos are a program. They are the expression of an anti-spirit, that absolutely must be kept far from our youth." This was the caption under the pictures of men's arms with inscriptions like "Money rules the world / Trust the US Army / Honorable trust in the Fatherland."

22. This information about the meaning of the pins comes from an interview with W. Koschek, who got it from VP members during an instruction after he was led away from a Leipzig Kino for the purpose of "personal surveillance." Another popular symbol was the Eiffel Tower as a pin that came into the country from the vacationing delegation of the French Youth Union; presumably this pin gained a

diffuse symbolism for a long time due to its rarity and its nod toward Paris as a location of youthful desire.

23. For example, in information from early summer 1968: "Among the newly called up draftees doubts about the aggression of West German imperialism are linked to the most widely spread misunderstandings." Bundesarchiv, Militärisches Zwischenarchiv Potsdam (BA-MZP) VA-P-01/5922, 157. These files too are now integrated into the Bundesarchiv Berlin.

24. Indicative was, for example, the answer to the question whether one would recommend one's own child for entrance into their current profession. Among apprentices who had passed the Abitur exam, 45.2 percent said yes; among other apprentices 26.1 percent agreed; and among young skilled workers only 15.9 percent agreed. ISA 68, Schnellinformation, 50ff, JA-IZJ B 6288.

25. Youth clubs remained spaces of relative autonomy. They emerged in the sixties in residential areas; despite formal leadership and regular disciplinary measures, the FDJ and the Party could never completely control them. See the treatment of this problem, for example, in the reports of the FDJ district leadership to the Central Committee Youth Department in summer 1965, BA-SAPMO IV A/2/16/109.

26. Staatsarchiv Leipzig, Bezirksbehörde der Deutschen Volkspolizei (BDVP) 24.1/348 with numerous case descriptions. In the first half of 1965 the number of youth who tried to break through the border from the district of Leipzig rose in comparison to the previous year by 70 percent to seventy-nine cases. The successful border crossings sank, however, by 40 percent to sixteen. Staatsarchiv Leipzig, BDVP 24.1/435, 41. In the same time period the portion of youth amounted to 62 percent of the border breakthroughs, and those from fourteen to eighteen years old alone were 17 percent. Staatsarchiv Leipzig, SED IV A 2/16/464.

27. Staatsarchiv Leipzig, SED IV B-2/16/707.

28. Staatsarchiv Leipzig, BDVP 24.1/360, Blatt 97 reverse side.

29. Stadtarchiv Leipzig, Stadtverordnetenversammlung und Rat der Stadt, Abt. Kultur, March 10, 1955, unpaginated.

30. Staatsarchiv Leipzig, BDVP 24.1/360, Blatt 63.

31. Stefan Wolle, "Die DDR-Bevölkerung und der Prager Frühling," *Aus Politik und Zeitgeschichte* B (36/92): 35–45.

32. Ohse, *Jugend nach dem Mauerbau*, 194–210.

33. BA-MZP VA-P-03/7460, Blatt 73.

34. BA-MZP, for example: VA-P-1502, Blatt 4; VA-P-04/1531, Blatt 29, 40, 50.

35. Rüdiger Wenzke, *Die NVA und der Prager Frühling 1968. Die Rolle Ulbrichts und der DDR-Streitkräfte bei der Niederschlagung der tschechoslowakischen Reformbewegung* (Berlin, 1995).

36. Quoted by Günther Schmidt, "Die determinierende Rolle des Zieles im pädagogischen Prozeß," in *Makarenko heute, Beiträge zur Kollektivierung,* ed. Alexander Bolz and Edgar Günther (Berlin [Ost], 1973), 81–104, 88.

37. It was stated in a speech from 1963 about youth criminality and property offenses in both German states that whether one would become a thief "is always a question of his own decision, a question of if and how much he had emancipated

himself from un-socialist, old thinking and living habits and therefore was free to act." JA-IZJ B 6262, 17ff.

38. Interview with Hanna Voss (peudonym), transcript, 6ff.

39. See Wierling, *Geboren im Jahr Eins,* 24–59.

40. This postdoctoral thesis (*Habilschrift*) was finally published in a softened version. Walter Friedrich, *Jugend heute* (Berlin, 1966).

41. See those controversies written in the journal *Forum,* vols. 8, 15, 22, and 23 (1963).

42. A report by the FDJ district leadership of Zwickau from 1967 said: "At this event choir leaders, musical pedagogues, singing leaders and joyfully singing FDJ kids from various areas participated. It was demonstrated there, how one can create excitement with our songs. All those present got to know youth songs through rehearsing. On March 18, 700 Pioneers and FDJ kids took part in a meeting for struggle in Zwickau. Singing was central to this event." JA-IZJ 6.361, unpaginated.

43. Michael Rauhut, *Schalmei und Lederjacke. Rock und Politik in der DDR der achtziger Jahre* (Erfurt, 2002).

44. On the typical life stories of this generation, see Lutz Niethammer, Alexander von Plato, and Dorothee Wierling, *Die volkseigene Erfahrung. Eine Archäologie des Lebens in der Industrieprovinz der DDR* (Berlin, 1991). See also Dorothee Wierling, "The Hitler Youth Generation in the GDR: Insecurities, Ambitions and Dilemmas," in *Dictatorship as Experience: Towards a Socio-Cultural History of the GDR,* ed. Konrad Jarausch (Oxford and New York, 1999), 307–24.

45. BA-SAPMO DY-30 IV/2/1/336, Blatt 198.

"The Benefits of Health Must Spread Among All"

International Solidarity, Health, and Race in the East German Encounter with the Third World

Young-Sun Hong

I

The 1950s and 1960s were both the zenith of the cold war and the heyday of decolonization. During these decades, the battle lines between the first and second worlds ran squarely down the middle of the third world. However, the countries of the third world were both the object of and audience for this contest between the capitalist and communist blocs, and the existence of this audience affected the policies of the main cold war protagonists in two distinct ways.

On the one hand, domestic policies were often influenced by the anticipated reaction of other countries. The desire to gain the support of the newly independent countries of Africa and Asia in the international arena provided leverage for those seeking to implement certain types of reform at home and put pressure on governments to comply with the wishes of this international public. For example, in the United States, both civil rights activists and the communist left pointed to the gap between the rhetoric of equality and realities of persistent segregation, and they actively sought support from the United Nations and the countries of the third world in their fight against continuing racial injustice at home.[1] On the other hand, the countries of the capitalist and communist blocs were pressured to put their money where their mouths were, so to speak, in the form of development and assistance policies, which would demonstrate their commitment to helping the countries of the third world advance toward their respective visions of modernity.

The cold war was symbolized more than anything else by the division of Germany and the ensuing ideological rivalry between the two successor states. However, the cold war was more than a power struggle between the two Germanys or between the two blocs. With the progress of decolonization, the cold war was increasingly fought by the two German states within a global arena. In this essay, I will examine one important but neglected front in this cold war between the two German states: the foreign cultural policies of the East German government during the 1950s and 1960s, especially the medical exchange programs established to train health-care workers from the socialist and nonaligned countries of Asia and Africa.

The East German government hoped to make these training programs into the centerpiece of its campaign to secure the loyalty of these newly independent countries and influence their development in accordance with their respective ideologies. The East German decision to place such emphasis on these medical exchange programs was undoubtedly influenced by the regime's own understanding of the central role of democratic health care in the construction of socialism, and East German health officials involved in these programs worked diligently to convince their international audience that the benefits of modern medicine and public health could only be fully realized within a socialist system and that political freedom, economic development, and social progress depended on the solidarity between the third world and the international socialist movement in their common struggle against imperialism, racism, and all forms of exploitation and oppression.[2] However, although the countries of Africa and Asia hoped to draw on Western expertise and resources to improve the quality of their own health-care systems, the success of these medical exchange programs was, I will argue, limited by a number of factors intimately bound up with the East German understanding and practice of socialism. Together, the lukewarm reception of these programs by their intended audience and the flagging ideological energies of the Ulbricht regime led to the gradual abandonment of these programs by 1970 and their transformation into programs for recruiting cheap immigrant labor for the health-care sector.

These medical exchange programs came to play an important role in the East German government's efforts to win the hearts and minds of the peoples of the newly independent countries of Africa and Asia for several reasons. First, health care and hygiene lay close to the heart of their own vision of socialist modernity and their project for constructing socialism at home. The right to work was the foundation of the East German conception of citizenship, and this principle was reinforced by the linkage of the entire spectrum of socialist social programs to the workplace (if not to productivity itself).[3] However, a healthy body was both the precondition for the productive labor that ultimately financed these social programs and a good in itself. As Walter Friedeberger, a future deputy minister of health, wrote in an article entitled "Health, Productivity, and Happiness," which he published on the occasion of the tenth anniversary of the founding of East Germany, the socialist state had "the obligation to do everything we can to ensure that people live lives that are as long and healthy as possible and that their productive work is not diminished by sickness and infirmity. Without exploitation and oppression, without the threatening scourge of war, socialism provides the best conditions for a life of health, happiness and prosperity for the laboring masses."[4]

In the same way that the East German regime made health and hygiene into a central element of its positive conception of socialist citizenship at home,[5] medical and hygiene programs were central to the construction of East Germany's relations to the third world. This vision of improved health and longevity as one element of a broader program of social transformation resonated strongly with many third world countries, and this allowed East Germany to present itself as the patron and protector of these countries. However, there were limits on the extent to which the East German approach to health care and hygiene could be generalized to the countries of Africa and Asia. Since the last third of the nineteenth century, improvements in public health in Germany and elsewhere in Europe had been based on the sanitary movement, the application of bacteriology to the struggle against epidemic disease, the expansion of hospitals and health insurance, and the creation of a spectrum of preventive social hygiene programs to combat the health problems associated with urban living in an industrializing society. However, although Germany had been a leader in the development of clinical and social medicine in Europe, the conditions in many parts of Africa and Asia precluded the direct application of those strategies that had so successfully reduced mortality rates over the past half century. Moreover, the East Germans did not have experience and expertise in the field of tropical medicine that was in any way comparable to that of France, England, or other countries with longer histories of colonial rule. Nor did East Germany have much experience in treating the health problems unique to developing countries under the social and economic constraints prevailing there. Ironically, then, the relatively brief colonial interlude of the German empire limited

the ability of the East German regime to meet the needs of the decolonizing countries whose support the government was attempting to cultivate,
though the full scope of these problems would only gradually become
apparent.

The East German government also relied on medical exchanges to
cement ties with the countries of Africa and Asia because this was one of
the few avenues left open to it by the aggressive diplomacy of West Germany. The cornerstone of West German foreign policy during these years
was the Hallstein Doctrine. West Germany maintained that it, and not
East Germany, was the sole legitimate representative of the German
nation in the international community and the legal successor to the German Reich, and the Hallstein doctrine stated that West Germany would
not grant diplomatic recognition or maintain official contacts with any
country that recognized East Germany. In fact, West Germany cut diplomatic relations with Yugoslavia (1957) and Cuba (1963) when these countries recognized East Germany.

The Hallstein Doctrine severely constricted the diplomatic freedom
of the growing number of newly independent countries. The Hallstein
Doctrine was proclaimed in 1955, the same year that the Bandung Conference was held, and the West German insistence that these countries choose
sides in the cold war was a direct challenge to the basic principles of nonaligned movement. Because of Bonn's aggressive nonrecognition policy, in
the 1950s East German diplomatic relationships and cultural exchanges
outside of Europe were limited to China, North Korea, Mongolia, Vietnam, and a few prominent nonaligned countries such as Egypt, Indonesia,
and India.

In 1960, seventeen African countries gained their independence from
France and Britain, and many other countries in Africa and Asia won
their independence through both peaceful and violent means in the following years. Although the Western powers may have been alarmed at the
spread of communism (both real and imagined) in the third world, the
newly independent countries of Africa and Asia could not easily be won
over to either side. Many of these countries were convinced that they
shared common interests that were not identical with those of either bloc,
and they toyed with a policy of third worldism, which they hoped would
enable them to collectively pursue policies suited to their own needs without succumbing to pressures from either the capitalist or communist
blocs.[6] While the United States and its allies opposed anticolonial and liberation movements in Indochina, Algeria, Cuba, and the Congo during

this period, both China and the Soviet bloc supported these movements in their struggle against "racialized systems of oppression."[7]

American anticommunist paranoia notwithstanding, in the early 1960s China and the Soviet Union did have reason to be optimistic about their future prospects in Africa. Ghana was the first sub-Saharan country to achieve independence (1957), and as early as 1960 the Nkrumah government began to adopt socialist policies at home and to pursue a policy of nonalignment in its relation to the two blocs. Kwame Nkrumah, a staunch opponent of colonialism and racism and an advocate of Pan-Africanism, visited Soviet bloc countries in 1961 and officially adopted a one-party political system and a planned economy in 1962. According to Nkrumah, the damage inflicted on the country by a century of colonial rule precluded the 'traditional path of capitalist development' and, instead, necessitated the reliance on socialist economic policies to achieve rapid economic development, national autonomy, and social equality.[8] However, some third world countries did not have the luxury of choosing their allies. When Guinean president Sékou Touré chose independence over membership in the French Union, the departing French cut off all economic and technical contacts and also engaged in such petty acts of retribution as ripping out phones, smashing lightbulbs, and stripping the police of their uniforms and weapons.[9] The French hoped that, since the country had been so completely dependent on France economically and commercially, these measures would bring Guinea to the brink of chaos—and back into the community. While the Western powers, including the United States, did not want to do anything to undermine de Gaulle's policy and ignored Guinea's plea for international aid, East Germany immediately recognized the country and was the first country to sign international trade and cultural treaties with Guinea.[10] Other communist countries soon followed East Germany's lead, and by 1961 there were about fifteen hundred technicians and other aid workers from China and the Soviet bloc working in the country.[11]

The changing international constellation spurred the efforts of both Germanys to curry favor with the new African states. Understandably, the East German government specifically targeted Africa in its efforts to gain broader diplomatic recognition around the world. However, only a few of the newly independent African states dared to defy the Hallstein Doctrine. Guinea signed cultural exchange agreements with East Germany in 1958, and Ghana, Mali, and Zanzibar followed in 1961, 1962, and 1964, respectively.[12] The refusal to officially recognize East Germany made it even

more important to find other ways of building ties to the newly independent countries of the third world, and the government believed that whatever legitimacy the East German regime could acquire abroad would
undoubtedly reinforce its legitimacy at home. While denouncing the Hallstein Doctrine as a gross infringement upon the sovereign rights of other
countries, the East German government emphasized that its foreign policy
was based on the principle of anti-imperialist solidarity, a principle that
was enshrined in its 1968 constitution. As one leading health politician put
it, these diplomatic factors forced the German Democratic Republic
(GDR) to make a virtue out of necessity and to rely on a broad spectrum
of humanitarian aid and cultural exchange programs to build diplomatic
bridges to these newly independent countries without running afoul of the
Hallstein Doctrine.[13] The East German regime took seriously international cultural exchange activities because of their potential value as step-
ping stones for diplomatic relations with the new independent countries.[14]
In the words of one East German expert on Africa, the "breadth and variety of quasi-state and non-governmental relations constituted a solid
foundation in Africa for the ambitious political plans of later years."[15]

Ironically, the last major reason why the East German government
relied on medical exchange programs to establish good relations with the
countries of Africa and Asia was the shortage of qualified medical personnel at home. Although the East Germans also constructed hospitals and
medical schools in these countries, they were reluctant to send physicians
to these countries because East Germany itself suffered from an acute
shortage of doctors. This was due in part to their exodus to the West.
From 1954 to the construction of the Berlin Wall in 1961, 3,371 physicians
fled the GDR.[16] During this period, the largest medical team sent by East
Germany to the third world included only eight doctors and ten nurses,
who were dispatched to Congo during the "Congo crisis" of 1960–61.[17]
Instead, the government focused on inviting young men and women from
third world countries to East Germany for training in health work. Due to
the high cost of educating physicians, the East German medical exchange
programs focused on training midlevel health workers, such as nurses,
doctor's assistants, and lab technicians.[18] For example, in 1963 twenty-
nine physicians came to East Germany from around the developing world,
while sixty midlevel health-care workers came from Africa alone to study
in the country.[19]

This East German strategy of training midlevel health workers also
nicely meshed with the needs of the newly independent countries. During

the colonial period, medical services had been concentrated in the urban areas and restricted to Europeans. In addition, although missionaries and social reformers had attempted to spread the gospel of hygiene among the indigenous peoples, they were both engaged in an unceasing struggle against indigenous medical practices, which they dismissed as witchcraft. This often deprived Africans of the only source of health services available to them. During the interwar period and the years immediately following World War II, British and French colonial authorities began to systematically expand medical services for workers in agriculture and mining. However, these programs were primarily designed to increase the production of food and raw materials and to ensure the existence of an adequate supply of native labor rather than to enhance the health and welfare of the populace.[20] As R. R. Scott, the medical director of Tanganyika, pointed out in his 1942 public health program, increased production of raw materials, better infrastructure, and better management of African labor force were all "indissolubly bound up with the raising of the standard of living and hygiene. I have dealt rather with the single medical link than with the whole chain of betterment—but this link must be well and truly forged if it is to take its proper share of the strain which the whole chain is called upon to bear."[21]

When the colonial powers left at independence, sub-Saharan African countries had neither a health-care infrastructure suited to their specific needs nor a system for training health-care workers at any level to fill the vacuum created by the departing Europeans, and one of the top priorities for the leaders of these newly independent states was to promote the training of physicians and health workers and to expand public health facilities in rural areas.[22] Since most of the population of Africa and Asia lived in rural areas far from the few existing hospitals, health-care officials in these countries felt that their most pressing need was for workers to manage and staff rural health-care centers. These workers had different responsibilities and needed a different set of skills than those that the European medical schools provided to either doctors or nurses, and the inability of the East German medical bureaucracy to recognize this and/or to adapt their existing curricula to meet the needs of these foreign trainees was to be a persistent source of friction and frustration for both sides. In the absence of a clear program for meeting the needs of these trainees, they were generally assigned menial work, which quickly and deeply alienated those visitors who often had substantial education and experience in their native lands and who had high hopes for what they might learn in East Germany. This further aggravated the problems caused by the paucity of East German expertise in the area of tropical medicine.

The enthusiasm of these trainees—and the governments that sponsored them—for the East German model of socialist health care was also dampened by other factors as well. These trainees from Africa and Asia were no less sensitive than the Germans themselves to the hardships caused by the pervasive shortages of material goods, despite the initial expectations on the part of the East Germans that these visitors from presumably primitive cultures and underdeveloped lands would see the socialist country as a land of plenty. While the sponsoring governments obviously hoped that these trainees would eventually move into positions of leadership and authority in their native countries and that they would share the nationalist values of the postindependence governments, the East Germans took a more rigid view of political education, and many of the trainees were alienated by the combination of political indoctrination and the instrumentalization of these development and exchange programs for overtly political aims. But there was also a deeper and more systematic contradiction in this attempt by the East Germans to present their own health and hygiene programs as a model of socialist modernity to be adopted by the countries of Africa and Asia. The East German sense of the superiority of its own vision of socialist modernity was itself made visible or imaginable through the construction of difference from those very colored peoples of the third world whom the East German regime was trying to convince to emulate its socioeconomic system and cultural values. Despite the compressed experience of both Nazism and denazification, many German health-care officials retained a core of essentially racist attitudes toward both the colored peoples of Africa and Asia and their cultures. These beliefs regularly colored their attitude toward the aims of these exchange programs and their judgments of the trainees themselves, thus further limiting the appeal of the socialist project to these peoples.

II

The encounters between the East Germans and African trainees in the first half of the 1960s soon revealed the limits—as well as aspirations—of East German international cultural politics in the area of medical aid. Long before the influx of contract workers from Algeria, Cuba, Mozambique, Vietnam, North Korea, and Angola in the late 1970s and 1980s, East Germany had encountered people of color from the developing world, albeit in much smaller numbers.[23] However, in contrast to the vast amount of research on foreign immigrant workers in West Germany, the question of foreigners and racism in East Germany has attracted scholarly interest only in the last decade. Even here, though, the focus has been primarily on contract workers during the last years of the East German state. But the third world was present in both East and West Germany in the 1950s and 1960s. During these years, several hundred foreign students, mostly those from Africa, the Middle East, and Latin America, crossed the German-German border in both directions. Those who moved to the West frequently complained about the politicization and indoctrination to which they had been subjected in the East, while those moving to the East complained about racism and indifference in the West. They thus voted with their feet but then soon realized that the one state did not fare much better than the other. A writer in the West German daily *Frankfurter Rundschau* called this phenomenon "development aid psychosis."[24]

The first group of Africans to receive health-care training in East Germany were eighteen men from Mali, who arrived in East Berlin in September 1961. They were primarily high school or college graduates who had many years of health-care experience in their home country. These men were largely children of elite families whose fathers had worked under the French colonial administration and retained their positions after independence.[25] In East Germany, however, these trainees encountered a training system that was ill-suited to their needs and a bureaucracy that was unresponsive to their concerns. When the terms of this exchange program were first being worked out, Malinese health minister Sominé Dolo had specifically requested that the program focus on tropical medicine. Also, in view of the wide range of responsibilities that these trainees would have in the rural health-care centers where they would be working, Dolo asked that they also be given training in anesthesia, dentistry, sanitary inspection, and medical laboratory techniques. And German language instruction was to be kept at a minimum in order to maximize the time available for practical training. Dolo believed—mistakenly, as it turned out—that this last request could be easily met because there were enough East German doctors who spoke fluent French.[26]

Whatever hopes Malinese health officials originally placed in the East German training system were soon disappointed. The foreign language textbook that the students were supposed to use was unavailable, and the medical faculty had failed to design a course of study that would provide the students with the training that had been specified in the exchange agreement. Even though these trainees had years of health-care experience in Mali, they were required to clean rooms and make beds for several months as an ostensible part of their basic training. While the East German educational system was primarily designed to produce general nurses working in hospitals, the Africans needed medical officers, midwives, physician's assistants, and sanitary inspectors who possessed a much broader body of knowledge and skills than those required for nurses. East German health officials either were unable to understand the actual conditions of the health system in sub-Saharan Africa and the corresponding educational and training needs of health workers or were unwilling to adapt their curriculum to meet these needs.

The gap between what these trainees had been promised and the training they actually received was so broad that the Malinese government began to have doubts about the East German training program.[27] In a note to the East German trade mission in Bamako, the Malinese Ministry of Foreign Affairs expressed its concern that East German authorities were having "serious difficulties" providing appropriate training to these students, and the ministry even questioned whether East Germany was capable of offering the training that had originally been agreed upon.[28] The Malinese students themselves gave vent to their dissatisfaction in an interview with Radio Berlin International. They questioned why they were placed in a class below their level and kept apart from the German students. As the host reported to the Ministry of Foreign Affairs after the program, "the students had gradually come to the belief that it would be better to return to Mali."[29]

The initial experience of the Malinese hardly served to enhance the prestige of East Germany and its socialist medical system. However, the experience of foreign trainees in West Germany was hardly more favorable. In the 1960s, the West German government and the German Hospital Association organized a large-scale program to recruit nurses from the developing world, in particular from South Korea, India, and the Philippines, in an attempt to alleviate their own shortage of health-care workers. In 1966, one out of every five nurses working in South Korea went to work in West Germany.[30] As with the trainees going to East Germany, these women had been promised that they would receive advanced training in nursing, but instead they had to spend much of their time doing housekeeping work in hospitals and taking care of the basic physical needs of the patients, thus freeing German nurses from such menial tasks. Although these women frequently complained about this discriminatory division of labor, German health administrators and officials continued to character-ize this work as development aid, and they argued that such work would teach these women the value of discipline and hard work, which they could then disseminate to their fellow citizens when they returned home. The West Germans seldom asked how such unskilled physical labor would help Asian nurses contribute to the development of their countries. Some even believed that such housekeeping labor was the surest way to help these women get used to the way Europeans do things and to gradually learn the German language. These problems did not go unnoticed. The World Health Organization likened the West German recruitment policies to the white slave trade and criticized the country for undermining its own efforts to improve the health-care systems of developing countries.[31] Why should the organization spend so much time and money training nurses in Korea if so many of them would quickly leave to work in Germany?[32] Bundestag president Eugen Gerstenmaier responded in a pretty tactless way to these criticisms, arguing that, since West Germany contributed so much money to the United Nations and its organizations, the country had the right to profit from its contributions.[33]

Development aid was hardly altruistic. It was often used by both blocs to cement alliances with third world countries, and political leaders often discussed such aid in militarized terms.[34] For example, John F. Kennedy once wrote to Secretary of State Dean Rusk suggesting that the Peace Corps might be used to roll back the influence of technical assistance provided to African countries by the communist bloc in a sort of reverse domino theory: "Ghana has accepted 50 to 70 Peace Corps volunteers," he wrote. "Guinea is asking for 40 to 60 road builders and engineers from the Peace Corps. If we can successfully crack Ghana and Guinea, Mali may even turn to the West. If so, these would be the first communist-oriented countries to turn from Moscow to us."[35]

East Germany was no exception in this regard. The first East German education and training programs for children from third world countries were created during the Korean War (1950–53) to demonstrate the soli-darity of the East German people with the victims of imperialist aggres-sion. In 1952 East Germany created the Committee for Korean Aid (Koreahilfsausschuß), and in 1953 the government invited 600 North Korean children to come to East Germany for basic education and occu-pational training. When Korean hostilities came to an end, East Germany broadened its solidarity policy. The Committee for Korean Aid was reorganized as the Solidarity Committee for Korea and Vietnam, and in 1955 and 1956 the government invited 348 Vietnamese children to study in East Germany.[36] By 1960, the politicization of development discourse and international cultural politics was well under way. East German officials portrayed the training of health-care workers from Africa and Asia as an important contribution to the "political and economic consolidation of national liberation movements" and to the "peaceful competition between socialism and capitalism around the world."[37]

The endless circulation of these state-socialist buzzwords was something third world trainees could not avoid. When four men from Niger arrived in Dessau in 1962, for example, representatives of the Health Ministry and the Solidarity Committee, as well as the local Party, trade unions, and medical facilities, all welcomed them with open arms, proclaiming that "imperialism is our common enemy and that this recognition will sustain them in their struggle at home."[38] These lofty ideals, however, were not easily translated into practice. Proclamations of international solidarity could not ensure smooth relations between African trainees and individual East Germans. Two Nigeriens who were housed with a German widow soon had to move out after quarreling with the landlady, undoubtedly over the strict house rules. Nor could they gloss over the failure of the East Germans to provide a meaningful course of study. These trainees, including their group leader, Ide Mamoudou, who had worked as a nurse for eight years in Niger, were required to complete a six-month period of housekeeping work. They found this work demeaning, and they protested by showing up late for work, leaving early, or simply refusing to do the work. Even after this initial period, their schedule was disproportionately geared to work (four and a half days a week) and allotted only one day for classroom instruction (plus a half day of "self-study"). All of these problems led to a series of conflicts with the hospital administration and faculty. The chief physician, for example, refused to work with the most defiant trainee and asked the Health Ministry to deport him.[39] It is hardly surprising that all the Nigeriens wanted to return home much earlier than originally scheduled. When they left the country, however, State Secretary of Health Gehring sent a letter to the Dessau hospital praising the administration and staff for "contributing through your untiring labor to strengthening international solidarity and friendship with the peoples of Africa."[40]

However, political commitments cannot survive on rhetoric alone. The effectiveness of these programs in training African and Asian health-care workers for the tasks they faced at home and in promoting international socialist solidarity was often undermined by the same assumptions—especially, the superiority of socialist modernity—on the German side that made these programs appear so important in the first place. Some of these problems can be seen in the fortunes of a group of students who came from Zanzibar to study in the mid-1960s.

III

In 1964 Annemarie Stenger, an East German physician who was teaching at a hospital constructed by the East Germans in Zanzibar, addressed a letter to the medical school in Quedlinburg, where twenty young Zanzibaris were about to begin their training to be public health workers and medical specialists. The people of Zanzibar, Stenger wrote, believe that "the Germans can do everything better than they can" and are filled with confidence in the people of the GDR.[41] Stenger also assured the Quedlinburg faculty that they would have much more promising material to work with than had been the case with earlier students from Guinea, Ghana, and Mali. After Zanzibar gained independence from Britain, a socialist government had been established there, and most British and Arabian physicians and medical officers soon left the country. As part of a plan to fill the gap created by their departure, the government carefully selected a group of health-care workers to be sent to East Germany for additional training. These fifteen men and five women were all comparatively well educated and experienced. Most of them had graduated from Lumumba College or Nasser Technical School; they had already passed their nursing exams; and they generally had five to ten years of health-care work behind them. In addition, Stenger reported that they also had one other important credential: to the best of her knowledge, they were all of working-class origin.[42]

The experiences of these Zanzibaris proved to be typical of those of students from all African countries. To begin with, the living conditions and political atmosphere affected foreigners and ordinary East Germans in similar ways. The African students also had to bear the shortages that were constantly weighing down upon the socialist project, though the Germans seemed to have expected that people from the developing world would view the East German standard of living as an improvement over what they were used to at home. The shortage of housing and the poor quality of the living quarters assigned to these students were such chronic problems that one health official feared that it would damage the "reputation of the GDR in the developing countries."[43] A couple of these women were housed in a room right next to the hospital mortuary. One of these trainees, twenty-nine-year-old Gladys N. from South Africa, worked as a midwife in Erfurt and wanted to remain in East Germany because of the apartheid system in her homeland. Gladys was pregnant and pointed out to the administrators that her current room was too small for both a room-mate and a baby, and she pled in vain for a new apartment.[44] With her due date approaching soon and her boyfriend about to begin his university studies in Berlin, she repeatedly petitioned the Health Ministry to find her work and a place to live together with the father of her baby in Berlin. The officials, however, replied only rarely and always in the negative.

The government also went to substantial lengths to isolate African trainees from other East Germans and to limit their opportunity for social, and sexual, relations with them. Most health-care trainees from Africa and Asia spent most of their training period in Germany in Quedlinburg, an idyllic, medieval town. The location was undoubtedly chosen in part because of its relative isolation.[45] From 1961 on, the number of third world trainees in health care grew rapidly, and in 1965 the Quedlinburg medical school—which trained about 450 students from developing countries from 1965 to 1973—was renamed the Training Institute for Foreign Citizens (Ausbildungsstätte für ausländische Bürger).[46] Despite this virtual ghet-toization of African students in Quedlinburg, ordinary East Germans were occasionally exposed to these Africans by official media coverage of the cultural exchange program, and the accompanying pictures showed exotic images of young African women dressed in colorful African outfits leisurely strolling together down a street lined with medieval timber-framed houses.[47] This news coverage was intended as propaganda for ordinary East Germans, and the people who were actually involved in administering these training programs spent a great deal of time trying to prevent these Africans from developing close personal relationships with their German hosts.

These efforts, though, were only partly successful. Within a few months of their arrival in Quedlinburg, the school reported to the Health Ministry that the African students had entered into a few "undesirable" relationships with German students that had led to pregnancies.[48] School officials in Quedlinburg and elsewhere were extremely sensitive about such sexual relationships between East German citizens and African students. The director of the medical school in Potsdam, for example, panicked when he realized that four men from Zanzibar, who had just completed their training, had some free time before they were scheduled to return home. He was worried that these Africans had "an increasingly strong need for a variety of female acquaintances." Although he blamed the German women involved with these African men, he nevertheless asked the Health Ministry to transfer the men from Potsdam to Quedlinburg, where they would have fewer opportunities to socialize with German women.[49]

Africans reacted against their daily difficulties in the GDR in a variety of ways, ranging from absenteeism to direct confrontation with the authorities. Some of them even left a trail of petitions documenting their efforts to work things out. What is most interesting though is that the Zanzibaris often resorted to *collective* petitions to improve their living and learning conditions. Their petitions were always cordial and grateful, but, at the same time, they were full of confidence and hope that things would change for the better. Perhaps they really did believe in East German socialism, as Stenger had claimed.

The pervasive material shortages affected Africans differently than they affected Germans. While ordinary Germans were more than happy with whatever pork products the regime was able to provide, African Muslims found that their diet was somewhat restricted, especially since other kinds of meat were in short supply.[50] The Zanzibari men complained to the Health Ministry that "we are of the firm conviction that a decline of our health and a decrease in the ability to concentrate—both of which are dependent on nutrition—will be the unavoidable consequences" of the poor quality and low nutritional value of their food in East Germany. While many East German teachers and health officials blamed the poor performance of African students on poor discipline, language problems, and laziness, these Zanzibaris turned the tables on the East Germans by arguing that the poor living conditions were hindering their learning. They offered to let the Health Ministry deduct extra money from their monthly stipends to procure better-quality food, a request to which the ministry acceded.[51]

These foreign trainees were also burdened by language problems. Most of the African students came from former French or British colonies, and, given their difficulties with separable prefixes and armies of umlauts, it is not surprising that they felt that their studies would proceed more smoothly if they could get their hands on medical dictionaries and medical books written in French or English, and they were willing to use their own money to buy English texts on anatomy, anesthesia, and tropical dietetics. Although this may have been an eminently reasonable request, politics intervened, and the Health Ministry rejected their requests, arguing that this ran counter to the government's desire to escape from the influence of British colonialism, and reminded the students that the Zanzibari government "would certainly not look kindly upon it if, in questions of training and continuing education, the citizens of its country were to rely on English-language literature."[52]

Curricular problems continued to hinder later cohorts of African trainees. In 1967, two Zanzibari students were allowed to study anesthesia at the Robert-Koch Hospital in Dessau. According to the head nurse, they were both "very clever, open-minded, eager to learn and extremely disciplined."[53] The problem was that the faculty in Dessau did not appear to have the slightest idea of what to teach these men.[54] Knowledge of anesthesia was important for African health-care workers because they often had to administer anesthesia to patients until they could be brought from remote rural areas to a clinic. But in East Germany anesthesiology was a specialty for physicians, and the hospital staff in Dessau was unprepared to appropriate instruction to these men. Nor were the East Germans particularly adept at building upon the traditional medical and healing practices of these peoples. The two students eventually wrote to the East German government complaining—politely—that in Dessau they hadn't learned "anything useful" and asking to be transferred to another place "where we could learn something." "We would like to inform you," they wrote a little later, "that it would be like a punishment for us if we have to remain in Dessau." In the end, though, their request was rejected.[55]

East German medical instructors stuck rigidly to their traditional curriculum, and only a few German medical educators realized that the East German education offered to the African students was primitive.[56] As one teacher in Quedlinburg pointed out,

> It will not be easy for us to provide the training desired by the Africans in a way that our friends will be able to meet all of the challenges they will face when they return home. . . . We hardly have even a theoretical knowledge of many of the most prevalent diseases there, and our friends already know more about these than we do. . . . Only now do we really see how different our ideas are from the realities there.[57]

Both trainees and administrators were left adrift by the gap separating what the Africans wanted to learn from what the East Germans were able to provide. As a result, for lack of any better ideas, the training provided to these students often consisted primarily of menial tasks and basic nursing practice, and, as a result, these students often had difficulties in getting their credentials recognized by their home countries.[58]

IV

In the end, East German medical training programs failed to become the fulcrum for an ambitious program of international cultural relations not simply because they were burdened by the problems of socialism at home in East Germany. More important, in the sphere of medical training and hygiene, they were unable to present to the Africans a program for socialist modernity that was relevant to their health-care needs. But the goals of these programs were also compromised by prejudice and essentially racist views of the Africans. Although most of these trainees were well-educated individuals who had grown up in urban centers, in the eyes of many East Germans they were bushmen who embodied the entire spectrum of stereotypical views of Africans that had been forged since the colonial era. Even in the 1980s, when an unprecedented number of people of color were living in East Germany, many East Germans still felt that contract workers from Mozambique and Angola had just stepped out of the jungle, and they were assigned the most demeaning, filthy jobs that no German workers were willing to accept.[59] In the 1960s, the same racial bias often led many German doctors and nurses to believe, as many of their written evaluations indicated, that the most important asset African trainees could take home from Germany was a respect for order, discipline, and punctuality.

These problems were compounded by the fact that racism in East Germany could not be publicly discussed because it could not exist in a socialist country. However, the issue could not be avoided completely, as can be seen in the story of Antoinette D., a sixteen-year-old Malinese girl who came to East Germany in 1960 for medical training.[60] When she arrived in Berlin, Antoinette, together with two other Malinese girls, was assigned to a hospital in Berlin-Buch. For several months, however, they were asked to do only unskilled manual work, since the hospital staff had no idea about "what to do" with these African girls and did not bother to organize a program specifically designed for them.[61] Obviously, this was not an auspicious beginning, but, ironically, the celebration of International Women's Day led to an improvement in their situation. On March

8, 1961, three women from the Health Ministry decided to visit these African trainees in order to demonstrate the spirit of international solidarity. However, when they saw how unhappy these women were, they persuaded state officials to take steps to improve their training.[62] Eventually, Antoinette completed the basic training in Quedlinburg and was allowed to study midwifery in Leipzig. In Leipzig, however, Dr. Haferkorn, the director of the midwifery program, wrote a damning evaluation of Antoinette, claiming that she "does not show either energy or willpower. She cannot think logically. In addition, she is extremely unreliable and dishonest." Antoinette, in turn, wrote to the ministry to challenge Haferkorn's motives:

> You [Health Ministry officials] can judge for yourselves whether someone could make it all the way from Africa to East Germany without doing anything. That is very curious. If I wanted to play around, I could stay at home. But I have come here to learn a profession and then return home. What the director says is pure silliness, and the people back in Mali will never believe it. Since I've been here, the director has not given me any money. . . . If the people in Mali knew that, they would be very unhappy. . . . The director is not very honest. If the director does not want to have me in her school, she should say the truth rather than insisting that I do not want to work. The director has really taken away my spirit. If she were a student in Mali, no one would treat her the same way that I have been treated here in East Germany.[63]

There was one aspect of state-socialist modernity from which these non-Western trainees could not escape: surveillance by the authorities and indoctrination in the principles of socialist citizenship. As comrades of the East German "welfare dictatorship," these students, like all citizens, were enmeshed in a tight network of surveillance and political education, which Konrad Jarausch has characterized as "coercive care."[64] Volumes of correspondence between the Health Ministry and medical schools, instructions from the top, and inspection visits from the Health Ministry to local teaching hospitals testify to both the extent of the regime's desire to keep foreigners under tight control and their paranoia that neglected students might become saboteurs.[65] The chair of the trade union (FDGB) required local union officials to "precisely" and "continuously" monitor these foreign students and file regular reports evaluating the potential of these students to become "highly qualified and class-conscious medical cadres and friends of the German Democratic Republic."[66]

Just like East German citizens, these foreign trainees were constantly evaluated by all of the officials with whom they came into contact: school directors, department chairs, doctors, advisors, and nurses. They were evaluated according to the traditional German values of work discipline, order, diligence, punctuality, and personal hygiene and appearance, as well as character and personal behavior.[67] Character and comportment were especially important, and even excellent academic and job performance would not prevent a student from receiving a bad evaluation if their personal behavior did not comply with certain political and ideological standards.[68]

Over the years, the practice of writing evaluations became increasingly ritualized, and it functioned in two important ways intended to promote stability. On the one hand, this enforced record keeping made local agencies increasingly complicit in the coercive structure of the regime. On the other hand, it was through this practice that authors of evaluation articulated and enacted the basic principles of socialist citizenship, which were applied to both East Germans and foreign students. The standardized evaluation form focused primarily on the development of the socialist self over the course of the training period. Evaluators took seriously the category of the self, and they were particularly sensitive to the failure to develop confidence and a sense of self-awareness. Especially among foreign students, traits such as shyness, passivity, and sensitivity were regarded as childish, backward, and even something innate to nonwhite races. However, the desired, ideal self was not private or egoistic but rather worked in harmony with the overlapping network of social collectivities in which it was embedded, and the theorists of socialist society believed that participation in these collectivities was essential to transforming individuals into socialist citizens.[69] Written evaluations usually followed a standard structure, beginning with the description of character of the individual followed by academic and work performance and ending with the description of his or her interaction—or lack thereof—with the collective. This last element often counted most.

For these foreign health-care trainees, the nursing or hospital station collective, which the regime regarded as the primary connection to "progressive families," was the basic social collectivity into which they were to be integrated and with which they had to interact successfully.[70] However, although this collectivity was supposed to have a strong socializing influence on the individual, these African and Asian health-care work-ers—like many East Germans—found it to be a dreadful experience, and they preferred to spend their time with the African Student Union or other students from their home country who were also studying in East Ger-many. In addition, cultural differences, language barriers, and traditional German attitudes toward foreigners made it even more difficult for these students to perform the desired self-fashioning of the socialist citizen in a German context, and many of these students were marked down because of their insufficiently enthusiastic participation in these rituals.

Many of these problems can be seen in the case of Cora N., a seven-teen-year-old South African girl who began her nursing training at the Quedlinburg medical school in September 1969. There would probably have been nothing distinctive about her experiences in East Germany had her pregnancy not attracted the interest of high-ranking state officials. This "pressing and complicated" problem became even more pressing and complicated when Cora sought an abortion against the wishes of both her doctor and school authorities. Cora was not able to procure the abortion after all. But her case went all the way to the Socialist Unity Party (SED) Central Committee, which sought to make Cora into an example of the power of the social institutions of the socialist state to remold the charac-ter of this obstinate young woman and thus bring her around to the proper understanding of her obligations. In the words of the state secretary of the Health Ministry, "The best help for her would be, in my opinion, if we helped her to arrive at a socialist understanding of the problem. . . . I will see to it that careful medical and social support is provided."[71]

First, the government granted Cora all available medical and welfare benefits: Cora was admitted to a maternity home where she delivered a girl named Rita; she received a paid postnatal vacation; and Rita was admit-ted to a nursery where her mother was expected to visit her regularly. In September 1970, Cora was able to resume her training in a German-only class in Quedlinburg, and, after three years, she received her state nursing certificate. Since she had originally wanted to become a nurse educator, she was then permitted to continue her studies at the Technical College for Health and Social Welfare Administration in Potsdam.[72]

In Potsdam, Cora had to work as a nurse at a district hospital for a semester, and her future enrollment in the teaching program depended on her evaluations. She received high marks in every area—academic, work, and relations with the collective—except for her supposed neglect of her duties toward her three-year-old daughter. Not only did she fail to visit

Rita every weekend, as her collective had suggested. Her response to repeated questions about Rita's well-being ranged "from exaggerated foolishness to defiance." Her supervisor concluded that, based on "her total self-development," Cora should not be allowed to continue with her studies in medical pedagogy.[73] Perhaps because of the symbolic significance of her case, this evaluation was overruled, and in September 1973 Cora was allowed to begin her studies in nursing education.

Two years later, however, the school asked the Health Ministry for permission to expel her. Although Cora was very smart and spoke fluent German, she had, as the director of the college put it, an "attitude problem," meaning that she was unwilling to participate in collective activities and other politico-ideological group projects. Cora made trips to West Berlin, slept during indoctrination, participated only passively in student activities, and invited outsiders to the dorm in the evening.[74] Finally, Cora failed to demonstrate a "sufficient sense of obligation" toward her daughter—despite urgings from teachers, colleagues, and all of the other mass organizations to which she belonged.[75] In the end, they were unable to bring about a "decisive reorientation in Cora's behavior."[76] The youth organization (FDJ) at the Potsdam college also wrote its own evaluation of Cora's development. Under the category of "Position and Comportment in the Collective," the evaluation cited all the important political and ideological meetings and mass ceremonies in which she did not participate or in which she played only a passive role. The evaluation also emphasized that Cora did not respond to many initiatives from the collective and the study group intended to help her. For example, hoping to correct Cora's alleged neglect of motherly duty, one German student of the study group took it upon herself to act as sort of a godmother for Cora and Rita, and she invited them to her house "in order to create [for Cora] a familial atmosphere and a place that she can call home."[77] As the FDJ secretary at the Potsdam college put it, despite numerous "tough confrontations and discussions," Cora did not show "tact, courtesy, comradeship and responsibility" for the collective and its members. He concluded that Cora lacked the character required to become a teacher.[78]

Although Cora came close to being expelled from both the school and the country, she was given one last chance to prove herself by agreeing to work closely with the nurse collective and an assigned mentor while working for a year as a nurse in a district hospital in Dresden-Friedrichstadt.[79] Now it was the staff and colleagues there who had a chance to evaluate Cora, and Cora seemed to pull it off this time. After all those years, she finally received positive marks on her interaction with both the hospital collective and the FDJ at the Technical University Dresden. Although Cora's attitudes toward the collective had wavered a bit at the beginning, the evaluator wrote, "we assumed the obligation of molding her into a proper member, and for this reason her behavior was discussed at almost every meeting of the membership."[80] As a result, things turned out well, and, during a three-day political indoctrination, Cora even kept the minutes and cooked for the collective.[81] Unfortunately, this was not good enough. Cora's mentor was unhappy because she refused to break up with her politically questionable African boyfriend, and he was determined to expel her despite her support from the African student association.

Again, Cora's case went all the way to the Central Committee, which in July 1976 ordered her to leave the country within six weeks. The last documentation of Cora's misadventures in the land of actually existing socialism is a letter from July 1977. At that point, Cora was living in Zambia, where Rita would soon enroll in a school. In the letter, Cora was asking for copies of her transcripts so that she could resume her studies there. She concluded her letter with a comment on how much she had learned in Zambia, where, in contrast to East Germany, she had been entrusted with many important responsibilities.[82]

All of the various medical exchange programs of the East German government were designed to demonstrate to the world that the socialist regime was solidly based on the accomplishments of modern medicine and technology and that this knowledge was used to advance the progress of mankind. Although the East German government insisted that this combination of modernity and international socialist solidarity would help the newly independent states of Africa and Asia chart a path toward a better future, a variety of factors—many of which were intrinsic features of the East German socialist system—prevented the programs from coming anywhere near realizing the hopes that the government had originally placed in them.

During the 1960s, the Asian nurses working in West Germany experienced many of the same problems as the African and Asian trainees in East Germany. To a certain extent, this reflects the continuity and commonalities of the nursing training systems in both states after 1945. However, from the beginning the West Germans regarded these nurses as foreign workers rather than as students, and these recruitment programs benefited the West Germans more than the countries from which these women came. In West Germany, the exploitation of and discrimination against health trainees, who were recruited for three-to-five-year terms to study and work in hospitals and nursing homes, frequently led to international scandals and accusations of human trafficking, and the East German regime never tired of attacking the West Germans for their treatment of these trainees and other migrant workers. However, as we have seen, the East Germans were entangled in their own contradictory policies toward peoples of the third world, both at home and abroad.

By the mid-1970s, the failure of the socialist economic and social planning to resolve the contradictions of industrial modernity, especially between the state planning and the market, led to an increasingly pragmatic, economistic approach to state legitimation.[83] This new approach tended to blur the boundaries between, on the one hand, the education and training of third world peoples as part of genuine development aid and, on the other hand, the exploitation of these foreigners as cheap labor. Thus, beginning in the early 1970s the medical exchange programs that had been the cornerstone of East German foreign (cultural) policy in the 1950s and 1960s diminished in importance, and the people from Africa and Asia who came to East Germany increasingly came not as students who would someday help build their own nation but—beginning with the Algerians in 1974—as contract workers helping to prop up a tottering socialist industrial economy.

NOTES

1. Martha Biondi, *To Stand and Fight: The Struggle for Civil Rights in Postwar New York City* (Cambridge, MA: Harvard University Press, 2002); Carol Anderson, *Eyes Off the Prize: The United Nations and the African American Struggle for Human Rights, 1944–1955* (Cambridge: Cambridge University Press, 2003); Thomas Borstelmann, *The Cold War and the Color Line: American Race Relations in the Global Arena* (Cambridge, MA: Harvard University Press, 2002).

2. In fact, the concepts of (under)development and the third world were products of cold war ideological rivalries.

3. Peter Hübner, *Konsens, Konflikt und Kompromiß. Soziale Arbeiterintressen und Sozialpolitik in der SBZ/DDR 1945–1970* (Berlin: Akademie-Verlag 1995). See also Peter Hübner, "Der Betriebe als Ort der Sozialpolitik in der DDR," in *Repression und Wohlstandsversprechen,* ed. Christoph Boyer and Peter Skyba (Dresden: Hannah-Arendt-Institut für Totalitarismusforschung, 1999), 63–74.

4. Walter Friedeberger, "Gesundheit, Leistungsfähigkeit, Lebensfreude," *Alles für Deine Gesundheit* (March 1959): 1.

5. Young-Sun Hong, "Cigarette Butts and the Building of Socialism in East Germany," *Central European History* 35, no. 3 (October 2002): 327–44. See also

Wolfgang Woelk and Jörg Vögele, eds., *Geschichte der Gesundheitspolitik in Deutschland. Von der Weimarer Republik bis in die Frühgeschichte der "doppelten Staatsgründung"* (Berlin: Duncker & Humblot, 2002).

6. Mark Duffield, *Global Governance and the New Wars: The Merging of Development and Security* (London: Zed Books, 2001), 22–23.

7. Gerald Horne, "Race from Power: U.S. Foreign Policy and the General Crisis of 'White Supremacy,'" *Diplomatic History* 23, no. 3 (summer 1999): 437–61. On China, see Alaba Ogunsanwo, *China's Policy in Africa, 1958–1971* (Cambridge: Cambridge University Press, 1974). See also Young-Sun Hong, "Kalter Krieg in der Ferne: Dekolonisierung, Hygienediskurse und der Kampf der DDR und der USA um die Dritte Welt," in *Umworbener Klassenfeind*, ed. Uta Balbier and Christiane Rösch (Berlin: Ch. Links, 2006), 77–94.

8. Stephen Michael Kirby, "The Two Germanys in Subsaharan Africa, 1957–1972: Ideological Universalism versus Traditional Statecraft," PhD diss., University of Virginia, 1993, 145f. Nkrumah organized the first meeting among the independent African states in Accra in April 1958. See Olajide Aluko, "Ghana's Foreign Policy," in *The Foreign Policies of African States*, ed. Aluko (London: Hodder and Stoughton, 1977), 72–97.

9. William Attwood, *The Reds and the Blacks: A Personal Adventure* (New York: Harper & Row, 1967), 21.

10. John H. Morrow, *First American Ambassador to Guinea* (New Brunswick: Rutgers University Press, 1968), 249.

11. Attwood, *The Reds and the Blacks*, 21; Ladipo Adamolekun, "The Foreign Policy of Guinea," in *Foreign Policies of African States*, ed. Aluko, 100. Touré, however, advocated the idea of positive neutrality and repeatedly emphasized that he was concerned "with the problems of developed and developing nations rather than with a struggle between the West and the East." Morrow, *First American Ambassador*, 103.

12. Bundesarchiv Berlin (hereafter BAB), DQ1/4217, Bericht über die Ergebnisse der Reise einer Regierungsdelegation der DDR in die afrikanischen Republiken Ghana, Guinea und Mali (May 12–June 5, 1964).

13. BAB, DQ1/3073, Friedeberger to Daub (July 18, 1963).

14. BAB, DQ1/3073, Friedeberger to Daub (July 18, 1963).

15. Hans-Georg Schleicher, "Afrika in der Außenpolitik der DDR," in *Die DDR und Afrika*, ed. Ulrich van der Heyden, et al. (Münster: Lit., 1993), 15.

16. BAB, DQ1/2491, *Der Arzt als Diener des Sozialismus* 30 (August 26, 1961). To alleviate this acute shortage, the government planned to train eleven thousand new physicians by 1965. BAB, DQ1/3073.

17. According to 1963 statistics compiled by the Health Ministry, through July 1962 only seventeen doctors, twenty-one nurses, and one technician had been sent abroad as part of these exchange programs. BAB, DQ1/3073.

18. BAB, DQ1/3073, Ministry of Health (hereafter MfG), Bericht über bisher durchgeführte und geplante Maßnahmen im Gesundheitswesen gegenüber ökonomisch-schwachentwickelten Ländern.

19. BAB, DQ1/3073, MfG, Übersicht über die Anzahl . . .

20. Meredeth Turshen, *The Political Ecology of Disease in Tanzania* (New Brunswick: Rutgers University Press, 1984), 149–53.

21. Cited in Ann Beck, *A History of the British Medical Administration of East Africa, 1900–1950* (Cambridge, MA: Harvard University Press, 1970), 159.

22. John Iliffe, *East African Doctors: A History of the Modern Profession* (Cambridge: Cambridge University Press, 1998), 118ff.

23. For more on these contract workers, see Annegret Schüle, "Vertragsarbeiterinnen und—arbeiter in der DDR: "Gewährleistung des Prinzips der Gleichstellung und Nichtdiskriminierung?" *1999* 17 (2002): 80–100; Andreas Müggenburg, *Die ausländischen Vertragsarbeiter in der ehemaligen DDR. Darstellung und Dokumentation* (Bonn: Mitteilungen der Beauftragten der Bundesregierung für Belange der Ausländer, 1996); Eva-Maria Elsner and Lothar Elsner, *Zwischen Nationalismus und Internationalismus. Über Ausländer und Ausländerpolitik in der DDR 1949–1990* (Rostock: Norddeutscher Hochschulschriften Verlag, 1994); Almut Rieder, *Erfahrungen algerischer Arbeitsmigranten in der DDR* (Opladen, 1994); Marianne Krüger-Potratz, *Anderssein gab es nicht. Ausländer und Minderheiten in der DDR* (Münster and New York: Waxmann, 1991); Sandra Gruner-Domic, "Die Migration kubanischer Arbeitskräfte in die DDR 1978–1989," PhD diss., Humboldt-Universität, Berlin, 1992; and Gruner-Domic, "Zur Geschichte der Arbeitskräftemigration in die DDR. Die bilateralen Verträge zur Beschäftigung ausländischer Arbeiter, 1961–1989," *Internationale wissenschaftliche Korrespondenz zur Geschichte der deutschen Arbeiterbewegung* 32 (1996): 204–30.

24. Archiv des Vorstandes der SPD (hereafter ASPD), DW8/7G, *Frankfurter Rundschau* (May 30, 1962), "Eine große Chance—nützen wir sie? Was vom Osten enttäuschte ausländische Studenten von Westdeutschland erwarten"; ". . . ob schwarz, ob weiß. Ausländerstudium in zwei deutschen Staaten," *Berliner Zeitung,* June 1, 1960. The citation is from *Berliner Zeitung.* There were many foreign students who hoped to escape racial discrimination in West Germany by moving to East Germany, where, they hoped, "die fremden Studenten nicht wie im Zirkus bestaunt, nicht als exotische Neuheit herumgereicht."

25. BAB, DQ1/1767, Bericht vor dem pädagogischen Rat (November 9, 1961). Mali's president, Modibo Keita, who was a longtime supporter of Marxist social policies, allowed East Germany to establish economic and trade missions in Bamako in May 1961.

26. BAB, DQ1/1767, Somine Dolo to Sefrin (September 8, 1961).

27. BAB, DQ1/1767, Note No. 220 from Mali's Foreign Ministry to the GDR trade commission (April 19, 1962); Archiv des Auswärtigen Amtes (AAA), MfAA/A14429, Gross to MfAA (December 8, 1961)

28. BAB, DQ1/1767, Note No. 220 from Mali's Foreign Ministry to the GDR trade commission (April 19, 1962).

29. Archive of the Foreign Office (hereafter AAA), MfAA/A14429, Memo on a meeting with Granzow at the Radio Berlin International (July 19, 1962).

30. "Urgent Steps Asked to Halt Nurse-Drain," *Korea Times,* September 14, 1966.

31. Bundesarchiv Koblenz (hereafter BAK), B149/22429; German embassy in Manila (August 11, 1967).

32. BAK, B149/22429. Citing from a report sent by German embassy in Seoul (February 15, 1968), BMA (Fittges) to Gerstenmaier (April 2, 1968).

33. BAK, B213/11962. Gerstenmaier to labor minister (April 12, 1967).

34. Duffield, *Global Governance and the New Wars,* 35.

35. Cited in Elizabeth Cobbs Hoffman, "Diplomatic History and the Meaning of Life: Toward a Global American History," *Diplomatic History* 21, no. 4 (fall 1997): 510. This militarized view of development assistance can also be found in a promotional brochure put out by the U.S. Public Health Service, which emphasized how overseas health missions were making "exceptional strategic contributions to the carrying out of the foreign policy of the United States and its allies," *U.S. Public Health Service, Health Abroad: A Challenge to Americans. Iran: One of Many* (n.p., n.d., presumably 1954), 1–2, 8.

36. On North Korea, see Elsner and Elsner, *Zwischen Nationalismus und Internationalismus,* 18. On Vietnam, see Mirjam Freytag, *Die "Moritzburger" in Vietnam. Lebenswege nach einem Schul- und Ausbildungsaufenthalt in der DDR* (Frankfurt am Main: IKO, 1998), 46f.

37. BAB, DQ1/3073. Präsidiumsvorlage über die Aufgaben der Vorstände und Leistungen der Gewerkschaft Gesundheitswesen zur Arbeit mit den in Gesundheitseinrichtungen arbeitenden und studierenden ausländischen Bürgern (May 22, 1962).

38. BAB, DQ1/6481, Nimtz, Report on trip to Dessau (August 22, 1962).

39. BAB, DQ1/6481, Nimtz, Aktennotiz (January 21, 1963).

40. BAB, DQ1/6481, Letter from Gehring (January 25, 1965).

41. BAB, DQ1/6480, Stenger to Sandau (September 12, 1964).

42. BAB, DQ1/6480, list of students from Zanzibar; Stenger to Sandau (September 12, 1964); Annemarie Stenger, "Als Fachlehrer in Sansibar," *Humanitas* (November 1966).

43. BAB, DQ1/10467, Konzeption zur weiteren Entwicklung der Aus- und Weiterbildung von Bürgern aus Entwicklungsländern im Gesund- und Sozialwesen (November 1973).

44. BAB, DQ1/6481 (January 6, 1969).

45. BAB, DQ1/10467, Stellungnahme zur Umwandlung der medizinische Schule Quedlinburg in eine zentrale Schule für ausländische Bürger im Gesundheitswesen (November 17, 1968).

46. BAB, DQ1/10467, Stellungnahme zur Umwandlung der medizinische Schule Quedlinburg in eine zentrale Schule für ausländische Bürger im Gesundheitswesen (November 17, 1968).

47. For example, see BAB, DQ1/6481, *Freie Presse Karl-Marx-Stadt,* February 20, 1965.

48. BAB, DQ1/1767, "Bericht vor dem pädagogischen Rat" (November 9, 1961), Nimtz's memo (October 3, 1962), and letter from Sohr to Kranhold (October 23, 1962).

49. BAB, DQ1/6480, Director of the Medical School in Mühlhausen, Thuringen to MfG (September 29, 1966).

50. This issue was often mentioned in official correspondence. For example, BAB, DQ1/1767, Nimtz's memo (October 12, 1961) and report to the pedagogical council of the Quedlinburg school (November 9, 1961).

51. BAB, DQ1/6480, (November 4, 1965).

52. BAB, DQ1/6480, Frenz (director of the Quedlinburg Institute) to Nimtz (April 29, 1965) and Sohr to Frenz (May 24, 1965).

53. BAB, DQ1/5981, Head nurse Seiler to Sohr (July 14, 1967).

54. BAB, DQ1/5981, Sohr to Shaame (May 17, 1967).

55. BAB, DQ1/5981, Muhamed Shamme to Sohr (June 21, 1967), Muhamed to Sohr (July 3, 1967), and letter from September 7, 1967.

56. BAB, DQ1/1767, Report to the pedagogical Rat (November 9, 1961).

57. BAB, DQ1/1767, Habedank to MfG (January 22, 1962).

58. BAB, DQ1/10467, Kolbe (director of the Quedlinburg school) to MfG (April 27, 1972).

59. The statement comes from an interview by Annegret Schüle with an East German textile worker presented at the conference "Fremde und Fremd-Sein in der DDR" at the Zentrum für Zeithistorische Forschung Potsdam (ZZF) on December 6–8, 2000. See also Jan Behrends, Dennis Kuck, and Patrice Poutrus, "Historische Ursachen der Fremdenfeindlichkeit in den Neuen Bundesländern," *Aus Politik und Zeitgeschichte,* B39/2000 (September 22, 2000): 15–21.

60. For more on her experience in Berlin and Quedlinburg, see BAB, DQ1/1767, Nimtz's Memo (May 5, 1961) and Nimtz's Memo (n.d.).

61. BAB, DQ1/1767, Aktennotiz by Nimtz (May 5, 1961).

62. BAB, DQ1/1767, Aktennotiz by Nimtz (n.d.).

63. BAB, DQ1/1767, Antoinette D. to MfG (October 12, 1963).

64. Konrad Jarausch, "Care and Coercion: The GDR as Welfare Dictatorship," in *Dictatorship as Experience: Towards a Socio-Cultural History of the GDR,* ed. Jarausch (New York: Berghahn Books, 1999), 47–69.

65. BAB, DQ1/3073, MfG, Aktenvermerk betr. Zusammenarbeit mit der Liga für Völkerfreundschaft (July 1, 1963).

66. BAB, DQ1/3073, Präsidiumsvorlage . . . (May 22, 1962).

67. Many of the initial evaluations contained language with clearly racist overtones. However, the Ministry of Foreign Affairs soon urged the responsible officials to be more careful in their choice of words for fear of offending officials from these African nations. AAA, MfAA/A14429, Fritsch to Kroll (February 15, 1963).

68. BAB, DQ1/6480, Seeländer to MfG (September 29, 1966).

69. Oleg Kharkhordin, *The Collective and the Individual in Russia* (Berkeley: University of California Press, 1999), is a sophisticated study of this phenomenon in the Soviet context.

70. BAB, DQ1/3073, Präsidiumsvorlage . . . (May 22, 1962).

71. BAB, DQ1/10470, Werner Hering (director of the Abt. Gesundheitspolitik at the SED Central Committee) to Mecklinger (October 24, 1969) and Mecklinger to Werner Hering (November 1969).

72. BAB, DQ1/10470, Haas to MfG (October 18, 1971).

73. BAB, DQ1/10470, College for Health and Welfare Studies in Potsdam, "Beurteilung zum Abschluss des Praktikum . . . " (July 1973).

74. BAB, DQ1/10470, Mehwald to MfG (October 14, 1974) and "Antrag auf Exmatrikulation" submitted to the Central Committee of SED, Department International Relations (June 17, 1975).

75. BAB, DQ1/10470, FDJ-Leitung and FDJ-Sekretär Rosenthal, "Stellungnahme zur Lehrerpersönlichkeit von Cora N."

76. BAB, DQ1/10470, Mehwald to MfG (October 14, 1974).

77. BAB, DQ1/10470. FDJ-Leitung (seven members) and FDJ-Sekretär Rosenthal, "Stellungnahme zur Lehrerpersönlichkeit von Cora N."

78. BAB, DQ1/10470, FDJ, "Stellungnahme zur . . ."

79. BAB, DQ1/10470, Mehwalt to MfG (November 24, 1975).

80. BAB, DQ1/10470, Beurteilung der Studentin Corah B. N. (May 27, 1976).

81. BAB, DQ1/10470, Beurteilung der Studentin Corah B. N. (May 27, 1976).

82. BAB, DQ1/10470, Cora to the school in July 1977.

83. Beatrix Bouvier, *Die DDR—ein Sozialstaat? Sozialpolitik in der Ära Honecker* (Bonn: Dietz, 2002). For further reading on the comparison with West Germany, see Young-Sun Hong, "Migrantischer Transnationalismus: Geteilte Geschichten zwischen West-Deutschland und Südkorea im Spannungsfeld von Rassifizierung und Gender," in *rel/visionen. Postkoloniale Perspektiven von People of Color auf Rassismus, Kulturpolitik und Widerstand in Deutschland,* ed. Kien Nghi Ha, Nicola Laure al-Samari, and Sheila Mysorekar (Münster: Unrast-Verlag, 2007), 74–85.

"Asociality" and Modernity

The GDR as a Welfare Dictatorship

Thomas Lindenberger

Communities are always built on relationships of inclusion and exclusion. The socialist community envisioned by Socialist Unity Party (SED) ideologists was no exception. They too defined the boundaries between those who belonged and those who were alien (*das Eigene und das Fremde*); yet the alien was not defined ethnically but socially, as belonging to a different class. This binary logic of class was, however, drained of specific historical content by the social "liquidation" of the nonworking classes in the German Democratic Republic (GDR). In the following essay, I will sketch out how the SED state and its jurisprudence reacted to this problem and how it developed "solutions" for it by developing a new juridical discourse about "asocial behavior." Furthermore, I will compare these findings with the so-called underclass syndrome in modern liberal capitalist societies in order to address the extent to which one can describe the GDR as a specifically "modern" society characterized by social disciplining and the welfare state.[1]

The legal identification of the "asocial" as "alien" within socialism began after the construction of the Berlin Wall in 1961 and led in 1968 to the following paragraph of the new GDR Strafgesetzbuch (StGB), or penal code:

> Whoever endangers the collective social life of citizens or the public order by withdrawing himself from a regular occupation, even though he is capable of working, or whoever pursues prostitution or whoever engages in other unseemly ways of earning income, is punishable by probation, imprisonment, rehabilitative labor or house arrest of up to two years.[2]

Recent research into the history of jurisprudence during the late GDR by Johannes Raschka explicitly documents that this statutory offense was in no way a legal trifle or historical triviality.[3] In the 1970s, the same penal norms were once again enforced,[4] and in the 1980s, GDR courts sentenced approximately seven thousand people per year[5] on the basis of this paragraph to "measures of penal responsibility" according to GDR legal jargon.[6] Annual statistics largely maintained this average; shortly after its introduction, the numbers were about four thousand sentences per year. Its high point was the year of the world youth festivals, during which the SED state used this legal paragraph to prevent some thirteen thousand people from damaging the image of an idealized GDR in front of an international audience. The early 1980s served as another watershed in the development and enforcement of asociality.[7] One year before the collapse of the GDR, six thousand or so people who received a prison sentence for asociality accounted for one-fourth of all newly sentenced prisoners.[8] Moreover, these figures were even higher if one adds in the high number of those apprehended for asociality who were given lesser punishments or subjected to socially pedagogical education measures on the grounds that their behavior was categorized as less dangerous.

The relatively poor state of research at this time, however, unfortunately does not yet make it possible to give a precise or quantitatively accurate social profile of individuals who were charged with asociality by GDR authorities. The lawyers Manecke and Bischof cited statistics from 1967 in master's theses on administration of justice in the district of Leipzig, saying that four-fifths of those individuals who were subjected to sanctions under the regulation limiting residences (Verordnung über Aufenthaltsbeschränkung [VOAB] from 1961) were men, and 55 percent of them were between the ages of eighteen and twenty-five. Moreover, they noted among the majority of these persons a lack of education and vocational training, few familial connections, and above-average alcohol consumption.[9]

In severe cases, which could already be specified as such after a second offense, the law designated sentences of up to five years. According to Inga Markovits's recent analysis of the penal practice in Rostock district courts, those who were accused of asocial behavior were more often taken into investigative custody (U-Haft) and were "harshly" dealt with, compared to treatment of those who attempted to flee the state. The accused could hardly count on the support of lay people involved in their cases, who were often quite biased in their judgments. The "work collective" usually presented itself as "society's plaintiff" in these court cases, in stark contrast to its common role as "society's defender" for those accused of attempted flight from the republic. In those cases involving "asocial behavior," the work collective normally handed down harsh punishments.[10]

The use of the word *asocial* was not born with the new penal code in the 1960s, nor was it novel in the political or juridical lexicon of the GDR. On the contrary, it was an "old friend" from the linguistic arsenal of social exclusionary discourse, on which more or less all twentieth-century political ideologies drew. In the Third Reich, the stigma of "asocial" became a central element of its murderous politics of annihilation.[11] In the Soviet Union's period of high Stalinism—which for part of the SED elite represented a concrete model of a viable worker state—a similar notion of "societal aliens" and "parasites" was used to stigmatize, arrest, and destroy tens of thousands during the so-called purges of the late 1930s.[12]

In the 1950s, too, GDR prosecutors as well as other party and state functionaries continued to use the attributive word *asocial* (just as its corresponding experts did in the FRG), but they did so in an unusual mixture of traditional social discipline and modern class struggle. In order to justify maintaining the possibility of sending an accused to a "Home for Social Care" (*Arbeitshaus,* or workhouse, as defined in Paragraph 42 of the penal code) as a legal security measure, the GDR's first penal textbook from 1957 contained the following:

> In the German Democratic Republic there are still a number—albeit a decreasing one—of people formed into work-shy and asocial elements by the capitalist and especially the fascist past as well as the "occidentalist" missionary activity of West German, West Berlin and foreign defamation and propaganda centers. These people prefer an effortless parasitic existence (especially in the form of prostitution) instead of the productive work of building society. They reject and oppose the cultural-reformatory activities of the "worker and peasant state" and its social organizations, and even foster recruiting sites for class enemies, foreign agents, provocateurs, terrorists and spies.[13]

The authors recommended a moderate usage of the workhouse as a security measure, for it was assumed that such an idea would be stricken from the new GDR penal code. As a result, they commented on a part of the still valid bourgeois penal law that by 1957 was considered anachronistic and excessive. To be sure, the Arbeitshaus represented one of the clas-

sic symbols of early capitalistic social discipline, which had long been criticized sharply by the left and the workers' movement.[14] In light of the then
still prevalent application of "bourgeois law" against the bourgeois classes
and the elements attributed to them, Stalinist prosecutors did not refrain
from defining antiquated legal sanctions according to the cause of class
struggle. Arguments based the danger of the asocial on its potential to
broaden the social footing of the class enemy. The asocials were not
directly class enemies themselves, but they were seen as especially unstable,
shifty elements standing between the majority of "normal" petty law-
breakers on the one hand and political criminals on the other. Precisely
this middle position between the extremes of punishable modes of behavior emerges again under completely different political and social conditions in later criminological definitions of asociality.

In any event, the authors of this 1957 penal textbook, Hans Gerats,
John Lekschas, and Joachim Renneberg, avoided the term *asocial* altogether. They did so even when they described the practitioners of the presocialist modes of production that the GDR tried to do away with
(namely, private farmers, craftsmen, small industrialists, private business-
men, and especially traders), using words that could be seen as synonyms
for *asocial*, such as *parasitic, enemies of the people, exploiters, speculators,*
and so forth.[15] At the same time, it must be noted that in the everyday language of the state police and other "upholders of the law," *asocial* was
used in the 1950s more in passing than as established jargon to designate
odd and unfitting behavior and lifestyles.[16]

With the conclusion of the collectivization of agriculture, the SED
leadership believed that they had substantially eradicated presocialist
modes of production. Class antagonism supposedly no longer existed
within the country. This had decisive consequences for the politics of criminal law. Deviant behavior could no longer be fought as a result of a continuing domestic presence of the class enemy. Now the majority of offenders came from the social status of the "good," that is, the new workers.
From 1961 on, the SED leaders developed a new politics of law enforcement (*neue Rechtspflegepolitik*) for them, which attempted to dispense with
and decriminalize simple, minor crimes of the mass of workers as much as
possible. Through the broad incorporation of employed laypeople into the
legal process, crimes were to be punished didactically, while avoiding stig-
matizing sentences such as imprisonment. At the same time, however,
penal law was used to define the new boundaries of the community; after
the community lost the "class enemy" as the concrete symbol of its quin-

tessential outsider or antithesis, a new negative definition of communality had to be constructed. Along with so-called rowdiness, which I cannot elaborate upon further here,[17] *asocial behavior* stepped into the breach.

In the beginning of this new definition a special regulation was created due to especially acute contemporary conditions. On August 24, 1961, ten days after the erection of the Wall, the Council of Ministers passed a regulation for limiting residencies (the VOAB), which was only replaced in 1968 by the already cited paragraph on asocial behavior in the penal code.[18] It gave the courts the possibility of imposing residency restrictions on people who had been sentenced to imprisonment or to probation. The "organs of state power" could change the judges' orders through orders for and prohibitions from staying in specific areas as well as through injunctions to "take up a specific form of work." In the name of defense against general dangers, a circuit court could impose such restrictions following an application to the same "organs," even if the person in question hadn't been convicted beforehand. The crucial passage that served as the precursor to the codification of the asociality paragraph in 1968 states: "Work education [*Arbeitserziehung*] can be meted out by the judgment of the county court to those shirking work upon demand of the local organs of state power."[19]

Thus, in the months after the erection of the Wall, a formal legal basis was established to force former border crossers, border traffickers, and farmers who had been against collectivization—in short, those who were obstinate—to adopt the positions assigned to them in the now closed GDR society. Against especially "stubborn" resisters, the courts ordered sentences of prison labor camps if it was deemed necessary.[20] This decree, conceptualized first as an instrument to force instant good behavior of all GDR citizens, had a career that extended beyond the immediate needs of the day. Increasing stabilization within the GDR did not lead to the decree's repeal by any means; on the contrary, it was later stylized as the core of what was "new." In 1962 none other than John Lekshas and Joachim Renneberg, who (together with Hans Gerats) five years earlier had foretold the dismantling of the workhouse as it had appeared in the old penal code, published an article in the academic journal *Neue Justiz* (New Justice) arguing for a renewed campaign against asociality using all possible punitive and didactic resources. This had to do with the revised version of a speech they had given in December 1961 at a convention of the penal code commission of the Ministry of Justice and of the penal law section of the "Walter Ulbricht" German Academy for National Jurisprudence, which had worked with experts already for some years on the new version of GDR criminal law. Under the lovely title "Lessons of the Twenty-Second Party Plenum of the USSR Communist Party," they took up the problem of criminality, which "still" existed in socialist society thanks to the remnants of the old exploitative order, which—if one took Khrushchev's promises for communism seriously—would soon die out. From there they came to another dimension of the socialist administration of justice:

> The more the socialist society develops and becomes established, the more it became clear that emerging alongside criminality there is another behavior inimical to society, which must be forever banned if communism is to succeed fully. But it can only be liquidated with the assistance of state force until communism is fully established. The danger is the asocial parasitic lifestyle of a number of individuals. What is the danger to society emanating from this lifestyle, and why does it grow along with the continuing progress of communism?

To this question Lekschas and Renneberg gave a two-part answer. First, they stated that asociality undermines the main rules of life and the legality of socialism and communism. The asocial being "lives off of the society without making his work capacity available to it." Second, asocial behavior is the "breeding ground for a plethora of criminal acts," including "counterrevolutionary activities in the GDR" and is therefore the "root source of criminality." In the GDR, the campaign against asocial elements is "inseparable from our larger fight against the counterrevolutionary activities of the class enemy" and thus is of "burning contemporary relevance." As they put it, the state "must not shy away from the full application of the decree of August 24, 1961, which is to be understood also as a weapon in the fight against asociality."

To the objection that this would revive a criminal law within socialism that was like that in exploitative capitalist society, Lekschas and Renneberg responded axiomatically, "Every comparison to capitalist-imperialist criminal law is misguided at the outset." Similarly, measures against asocials could not be compared with one another for the simple reason that "they are not based on the same historical conditions." Socialist society should fight against asociality first and foremost without force by guaranteeing "normal social conditions for existence," just like in the fight against criminal acts. During the "socialist revolution" the fight against asocial elements, so they continued, was limited largely to the fight against criminal acts that these elements committed against the socialist community, so state force was not yet directed toward the higher goal of the "removal of asociality" altogether. Socialism was not able to create the "objective requirements" necessary for this next step in one fell swoop. That is why, so they reasoned,

> at the beginning of socialist construction . . . [asociality] had not yet truly become one's own "personal fault," that is, the responsibility of an individual. Asociality must, however, become the "personal fault" of an individual, if the use of force is to have any real, particularly educational effect. At the current level of social development achieved in the Soviet Union as well as in the GDR, asociality has already become the "personal fault" of those individuals who have succumbed to such lifestyles.

This statement had less to do with the punishability of a "perpetrator type" than with a concretely identifiable mode of behavior. The overwhelming majority of citizens complied "consciously and with discipline, willingly recognizing its necessity" with the labor law code's determination of a "political and moral duty" to work. Still "a number of demoralized parasitic elements still disregard this law of life." Due to the deep conflict between these aspects of society, Lekschas and Renneberg declared that "the working masses demand from the state strict measures for the liquidation of asociality."

Lekschas and Renneberg then offered their first concrete suggestion: "Measures of force in the form of work education—that is, a new form of curtailment of freedom—should be used if other measures have proven or prove fruitless." As far as the authors were concerned, this had to do with a long-term goal and clearly not short-term shock therapy for those who did not want to adjust quickly enough to the closing off of the GDR. Ideally, local authorities, mass organizations, and factories would be demanded "to work consciously and systematically to eliminate all visible forms of asociality by fully exploiting resources available through labor laws and branches of the law, to eradicate the roots of asociality once and for all. This goes in particular for the education of youth." In addition, such measures of rehabilitative "improvement work" were to be used as the "first step of exerting state force against those individuals" who "are on their way toward slipping totally into an asocial lifestyle." This work duty in a socialist factory, which would be "limited, but not too short (maximally three or five years)," could then be "fortified with the threat of future *Arbeitserziehung* or even imprisonment in cases of shiftlessness or shirking work."

Lekschas and Renneberg, together with other GDR legal experts at the time, linked the asocial lifestyle with a lexicon of unflattering terms describing what was supposedly alien to socialist society. Stigmatic terms like *parasitic, demoralized, degenerate, shiftless, obstinate, work shirking, work-shy, prostitution, alcoholism, idleness,* and *illegal accumulation of wealth* were all used repeatedly. Those accused of possessing such toxic characteristics and their social environment were all classified in a "very special category of degraded and asocial elements," a veritable "special kind of lumpen proletariat." In one instance, they even spoke of them as a distinct "class" unto itself.

The legal battle against prostitution showed the way in which the "measures against asociality" were to be played out legally. The courts preferred to give prostitutes "sentences of a special kind"; they aimed at reeducating them into the virtues of "honorable" work through short-term transfers to "homes for social care," as GDR jargon called the venerable institution of the Arbeitshaus. According to Lekschas and Renneberg, this kind of punishment was "in keeping with the spirit behind the decree of August 24, 1961." As far as they were concerned, this example shows that "criminality [in this case, prostitution] and asociality may not be identical in the forms in which they are committed, but one cannot grant any principle difference in their social essence, and, in fact, they blend into each other." For them, this linkage was especially strong in light of "still relatively common recidivism, which unites criminality and asociality." What was particularly noteworthy was the extent to which they thought the campaign against these closely associated "modes of behavior that were a menace to society" needed to be regulated in a more unified manner in future criminal law.[21]

The campaign against prostitution, then, provided the model for the battle against "work shirkers." This genealogy remained evident in the qualifying clause introducing Paragraph 249 of the StGB that was established later: "Whoever thus endangers the collective life of our citizens or the public order. . . ." There were clear similarities between this terminology and the earlier campaign, since prostitution, unlike other crimes such as pimping and running a bordello, was not always legally punishable "in and of itself" but only insofar as it threatened public order and security.[22]

The other possible line of action—fighting prostitution according to the regulation limiting residence (the VOAB)—is something penal code reformers debated for years, rejecting it in the end with the reasoning that "There are prostitutes who are either unable to work or who are caught in circumstances of labor law that make work education infeasible."[23]

At the same time, it must be stressed that, in the GDR's criminological studies conducted in the 1960s on the asociality and recidivism that was dealt with in conjunction with it, shiftlessness and prostitution were by no means always mentioned in the same breath. With respect to asociality, the central issue was always clearly the fact that the livelihood of those concerned was not earned through regular work. It was quite another matter that, according to the "reigning" opinion, this issue also applied to prostitution, to the extent that it would make sense to use the same means to criminalize and fight it too.[24]

In any case, let us return to Lekschas and Renneberg. A few months later, they had to retract parts of their essay because it relied too heavily on theories of class antagonism as the backbone of GDR legal policy.[25] This by no means altered the fact, however, that their concept of asociality continued to be discussed and used in GDR law practice. At its core the concept of asociality continued to represent lifestyles seen as alien to socialism and punishable in extreme cases throughout the shifting developments of GDR legal policy up through 1989.[26] In their 1967 commentary on the asociality paragraph in the proposed GDR penal code, Manecke and Bischof seamlessly built on Lekschas and Renneberg's interpretations, identifying the central criterion of an asocial lifestyle as a continual, unwarranted, and unreformable disinclination toward work. They too drew sharp boundaries between society and the "asocials": "The asocial way of life, seen as the conjunction of a mode of behavior and its corresponding objective preconditions, has led these people to stereotypical behavior and stubbornly entrenched moral positions, characterized by isolation from socialist society as well as the widespread rejection of socialist morality and lawfulness." As such the authors clearly defined the asocial individual as the very antipode to the socialist lifestyle.[27] This rhetoric dealt less with individual cases than with a collection of people who opposed socialist society by withdrawing themselves from it. The social form of the existence of asociality emerged as a key subject of study in socialist criminology that developed during the 1960s.[28] The formulations of the Babelsberg lawyer Heinz Blüthner represented this new attitude. In 1968 he defined *asociality* in GDR cities in the following way:

The disregard of basic legally established and moral norms over a long period of time by a group of people arises out of a social position that is congruent with this attitude, out of a specific configuration of living conditions, and out of the relationship to other people, to certain collectivities and to society. Indicators of asociality are not just one or the other singular manifestation per se, but rather the concentrated expression of negatively formed societal relationships resulting from a crassly deviant lifestyle that departs from lawful norms and the bases of socialist morality. It is the complex expression of a specific totality of negatively formed societal relationships that manifests itself in asociality. At once alien and inimical to society, this system of asociality ultimately affects more or less all societal relationships.[29]

Thus, the framework of this especially "modern" and comprehensive systems theory of GDR reality defined asociality as its own social subsystem and as a destructive alternative world (*Gegenwelt*) counter to the constructive-optimistic system of socialism. Theoretically, in this subsystem all attitudes and behaviors opposed to socialism collected and strengthened each other. Such systems-theoretical descriptions made it possible to overinflate the essential difference between the overwhelmingly "normal society" and the small minority of "asocials." Those who deviated and visibly did not fit in were thus defined beyond their actual social relationships and made into aliens in their own land.

For the legitimization and social practice of Party domination in the GDR, this formulation was useful in several ways. First, the definitive *externalization* of the class enemy, according to the penal theories at the beginning of the 1960s, removed a burden from the punitive policies of the SED regime toward the vast majority of its own population. It allowed for a differentiated way of viewing the now remaining criminality that was definitely rooted within the GDR. "Asociality" (and "rowdiness") thereby functioned as the midpoint on a continuum of social danger between the two extreme poles of petty offenses to be punished most mildly—as the overwhelming majority of criminal acts were—and the small minority of serious crimes, including those that were political. These two novel creations of GDR penal law symbolized the publicly recognizable form of deviance still persistent even following the forced physical closing of GDR society and the externalization of class antagonism that was taken for granted. Even though deviance arose internally in the GDR, it still supposedly had to do with behaviors that were classified categorically as "essentially alien" to socialism. The ideological and symbolic function of asociality derived precisely from this divided contradictory position. In order to separate these deviants from the less serious legal infractions of the "normal" majority and thereby to validate their relative "normality," the discourse of lawyers and criminologists constructed "asociality" and "rowdiness" as "the alien among us" (*das Fremde im Eigenen der DDR*).

Discussion of "the system of asociality" defined it not least as a GDR-specific counterworld in clear opposition to the majority of diligent workers. This "negative milieu" apparently functioned according to its own rules or laws alien to the GDR. The socialist state concentrated on identifying and rehabilitating individuals designated as part of this milieu one at a time, by subjecting them to compulsory education measures so as to reintegrate them back into normal society. The desired results of the campaign against asociality had nothing to do with a final selection for exclusion, as the case was under the Nazi dictatorship. Rather, it aimed to eradicate certain social relationships, which by their very existence called into question the SED's claim to monopolize the establishment, control, and direction of *all* social relationships under its dominion.

The discursive logic of exclusion and alienation used a fixed canon of symptoms (such as work shirking, alcoholism, undereducation, criminal recidivism, theft, lack of discipline, and spontaneity) that defined an opposite social polarity to the "ruling" working class. At the same time it constructed the latter's "positive" characteristics, which were the canon of virtues that had been common within workers' culture since the Wilhelmine period and cultivated by the organized worker's movement as part of the discourse about the lumpen proletariat: diligence, honesty, collegiality, solidarity, collective consciousness, a sense of family, a love of order, and so forth.[30] Asociality—and with it rowdiness—defined not only that which was foreign to socialism but also *ex negativo* that which was essential to it. Without "asociality" there were no "socialist workers" and no "socialist way of life."

With the help of this short excursion into the history of GDR civil law and crime policy, this case study suggests the ways in which the SED state attempted to develop and legitimize its own concept of a "socialist human community" independent of a fixation on the class enemy. This was by no means straightforward. After 1960–61 the SED vowed repeatedly that—following the victory of socialist modes of production—the "political-moral unity" of the people and the Party had already become a historical

fact within the GDR. This "political-moral unity" of people, state, and
Party was a central pillar of SED ideology, and the politics of administering justice primarily served to validate it through social practices of inclusion and exclusion. The stigmatization of certain lifestyles and behaviors
as "asocial" and "rowdylike" constituted a central element of this staging
of "moral" unity. Without a doubt, this was one of the few political fields
on which the SED could count for popular support: work brigades and
popular opinion endorsed the harsh punishments against "parasites" and
"idling workers."

This example of the cultural construction of "aliens" in one's own
population is well suited for using a sociohistorical perspective to test out
the pertinence of the paradox of insufficient political legitimacy and stability that characterized the SED regime, as suggested by Sigrid
Meuschel.[31] This paradox was characteristic of the GDR as a whole. Precisely because the state strove to suppress autonomous social processes of
communication, and thereby simultaneously constructed a closed-off
sphere for itself, communication and interaction between the SED and the
population were reduced to a set of unquestioned "unpolitical" understandings that blocked the formation of any collective political will. This
fact had an inclusive, positive side: the regime and the population alike
saw the value in striving toward the just access for everyone to values such
as material security, prosperity, peace, and family. However, it also had its
exclusionary, negative side as well. Concepts such as asociality and rowdiness and their practical application in daily legal practice acted as one of
the few "bridges" in the fragile and often tacit but sometimes explicit
agreement between the SED state and its citizens. For decades this
identification and practical exclusion of what was "alien" to the community existed side by side with the fundamental lack of political legitimization of the SED regime and weakened it considerably.

How can these findings be interpreted in light of the overarching
question of the GDR's specific "modernity" in the context of the twentieth
century? How can the described strategies of exclusion and reinclusion by
state-directed educational measures be situated sociohistorically? Previous
research on GDR society has by and large reproduced an image of a
socially homogeneous society of workers, even if this image has also been
fractured critically. An essential element of this image was plainly the
extensive security of the material and social existence of wage workers.
The SED attempted to guarantee this security by means of a broad redis-
tribution of social achievements, offers of qualification for higher profes-

sions, and "leisure culture," especially on the shop-floor level of society. It is exactly in this social sphere that both the negative and the positive sides of the stigmatization of asocials, their exclusion as well as their educational reintegration, were institutionally anchored. The point where the "bottom" of the "good" society of workers ended and the transition to a "negative milieu" began was addressed and adjudicated individually month after month before conflict commissions and courts; in brigades and parent groups; by the People's Police and social workers, doctors, and psychologists, on a case-by-case basis, through both punishment and social welfare. Since the mid-1980s, for example, the Brandenburg steelworks had their own "brigade against drinkers" with its own social workers.[32] In another example, the former leader of a large collective farm of the Havelandian fruit farming region told me that several persons in charge regularly took care of the work duty of thirty to fifty "asocials" during the harvesting season.

Historians and social scientists have shown little interest in studying this link between egalitarianism and conformity.[33] Much of GDR historiography ignores the mutual pact between the regime and the population that traded social security and consumption for political obedience and external conformity. This exchange also featured a dark side, in that the material and symbolic privileging of the "ruling" working class was also linked to the stigmatization of "parasites" and "idlers." This relates to how the relegation of workers' existence to a substratum was regulated enduringly and solidly integrated in the symbolic arsenal of regime legitimation. Unlike other industrial societies, which create an underclass from immigrants who are willing to conform and strive to move up, GDR society recruited its bottom layer exclusively from its own people.[34] It thus appears relevant to draw upon the term *underclass,* a concept developed within Western postindustrial welfare states, to understand the function that this practice of labeling played in underpinning systems of domination.

To be clear, I am not using this concept simply as a catchword or superficial label to describe the social situation of the estimated segment of the adult population (10 percent) who are uneducated and occupy the bottom layer in the GDR societal hierarchy.[35] In making an analogy to the underclass discourse of Western societies, I am concerned with the effects of an enduring process of affixing such labels to social groups. Saturated by the weight of empirical evidence and underpinned by practices of domination, *underclass* as well as *asociality* became symbolically laden concepts reified as "second degree" facts of social reality. Thus, the concept of asociality in the GDR played a similar function to that of the underclass in Western industrial countries: Both are simultaneously descriptive and value loaded. Plus, such terms also engender both critically intended empirical studies of new forms of urban poverty and controversial interpretations or suggestions for handling these problems through social policy. In postindustrial welfare states, this discourse represents both the process of stigma fixation through the identification of an outer limit of the social community as well as attempts to eliminate such exclusions within the framework of state-sponsored social engineering.[36]

Two aspects of this interpretation can be linked with our line of questioning.

1.   Both the culturally pessimistic conservative statement by Charles Murray advocating a curtailment of social spending as well as the supposedly liberal welfare-state position of William Wilson trace the underclass to a loss of the integrative ability of the traditional workers' milieu.[37] But what is relevant here is not the description of poverty as such but rather the cultural and/or structural factors that allow a part of the poor to appear to exist permanently beneath society or beyond its borders.[38] The underclass became acute among the masses in North America and Great Britain, as the networks of the old class culture increasingly disintegrated. Previously these networks provided social care for marginal groups and had helped integrate these groups into the class milieu. The function of social care was taken over by state welfare.[39] These state achievements combined stigmatization with material dependence on support to the extent that state governments undertook long-term "management" of marginalized ways of life. These life arrangements were then disconnected from the labor market and its associated social networks not only because the social distances within the working community increased but also because its collective political power to integrate those at the very bottom of wage-dependent and impoverished classes eventually fell apart.

2.   The underclass discourse also constructs a quasi-hereditary social position at the margins and within the lower levels of society, with the result that it can be linked to a large extent with racial discourse.[40] Interpretations of how "race" was a causal element in the formation of the underclass vary according to ideological presuppositions. Conservatives exclusively foreground individuals' behavior and their reproductive habits, arguing that their use of state welfare encourages them to lead an existence separate from the "normal" working society. The fact that this behavior is observed by critics overwhelmingly in African American "bro-

ken" families is not further scrutinized by such theorists. Progressives, by contrast, see the construction of an underclass as the process of class differentiation, overlaid with the effects of racial discrimination. The term *underclass* has become more or less synonymous in public parlance with the cliché of the African American, single, "welfare mother." For this reason, the most important representative of this class-based argument, William Wilson, prefers to use the term *new urban poor* instead.[41] In effect, both descriptive and attributive variants still amount to defining the underclass in sociological terms, which with closer inspection is constructed as a set of quasi-hereditary characteristics gained during early socialization among a closed group of individuals.

Points of affinity between the "negative milieu" of the GDR's state socialist system and the underclass of Western industrial countries do exist, despite all of the obvious differences of social conditions and historical context. Among the most notable are labor's lost resources of hegemonic power as a class in the political sense; the hypertrophy of the welfare state; the legal dependency of the individual; the idea that a social position could be passed on and limited to specific families and their offspring; and, finally, the state's shifting focus from pluralistic social care to criminal prosecution and security politics as the main means of addressing the problem of exclusion and reintegration, as witnessed in the state's "management" of new poverty.[42] Granted, comparison does not mean calling two things equal but is rather a heuristic method to approach a more precise understanding of the issue.

As in postindustrial societies of the West, the GDR also featured a working class that was essentially robbed of its social autonomy. The working class—at the very latest after June 17, 1953—could only assert its collective bargaining power in the fragmented publics on the shop-floor level but never again in the macroworlds of large factories, collective combines, and industrywide branches, to say nothing of the larger Enterprise GDR.[43] In state socialism the social integration into work processes became a monopoly of planning and controlled direction by the SED, against which only the informal powers of limited negotiation remained. Meanwhile, it has become typical of class relations in a late industrial bourgeois society that the relatively autonomous power of workers' self-determination in the sphere of united social care and sociopolitical integration has been taken over by the state. What has remained has been resources for social integration at the local level. The SED state purposefully used these resources to reproduce the world of respectable, law-abiding GDR workers through the incessant interplay of stigmatization, "conversion" through punitive forced education, and select inclusion of only the "converted." The main principle that went along with this arrangement of honorary "laypeople" (judges, police officers, social workers, youth officials, and probation officers) prohibited the development of an alternative public sphere composed of engaged experts, whose relative autonomy in Western societies during that time provided a "fermenting agent" for the criticism of socially exclusionary practices and in part compensated for the dissolution of traditional networks of solidarity.[44]

At the same time, actual substantial social advancement for many workers in the GDR in the 1950s and the 1960s created a sediment of "those left behind"; they were ascribed the practical and symbolic function of social outsiders in their own land, stuck in a lowly world while the majority of workers were rising above their modest but honorable beginnings. To what degree did society follow the criminological and educational discourse to perceive these people as part of a circumscribable counterworld of nonsocialist lifestyles? Or contrary to these official viewpoints, were these people actually integrated into localized relationships of socialist everyday life by their helpful fellow citizens? Perhaps GDR citizens saw potential "asocials" as more "inconspicuous" and de facto "more apolitical" than the ideologically laden judgments by the state's educative dictatorship asserted. These remain open questions for want of research.

It is now well known that the dynamic of social advancement characterizing the early GDR gave way to sclerosis. But whatever effects this sclerosis had on the "underside" of the social hierarchy, such issues have found little resonance in sociohistorical research on the GDR to date, despite the undeniable symbolic significance of these phenomena within the realm of social disciplining and the myriad traces that they left behind both in the social structure and in everyday life. Newer sociological research on East Germany's social structure has shown for the late GDR a disproportionately high recruitment of "uneducated and untrained individuals" (*Ausbildungsloser*) from families of unqualified workers, suggesting a long-term settlement of the *juste milieu* of GDR society to the bottom.[45] Some social grievances were widespread across all circles in the GDR even if they were taboo in public discussion (such as alcoholism, child abuse, and domestic violence).[46] It is surely no coincidence either that making asocials the scapegoats for these grievances became even more pronounced in the 1970s when the social system of mobility as a whole began to close off and the self-recruitment of two main social groups—the socialist service class and the qualified working force—began to dominate.

Regardless of the degree to which the reality of the "asocial milieu"— the underclass of state socialism—actually correlated with all of those who were labeled "asocial," the point here is to explore the remarkable ideological and institutional efforts with which GDR authorities sought to define, identify, and correct this "asocial parasitic way of life." And given the recourse to decades-old stereotypes of social exclusion, these concepts should be studied and situated within German social history as a whole.

The described phenomena of an exclusionary discourse of "social racisms" (*Sozialrassismus*) structured into GDR daily life can be seen as a result of inherited patterns of social thought rooted in modern industrial society. "Much about the GDR was explicitly modern"[47]—above all in the sense of that "first" modernity of high industrialization, which determined the planned economies of the Eastern Bloc and the horizon of imagined communities till the bitter end. The basis for conceptualizing the "modern," future-oriented GDR welfare state also originated in this period.[48] Together with these conceptualizations the dilemma of defining the "boundaries of social discipline" also became a central question: What should happen to those who were not integrated into "the initial blueprint of social engineering" inherent in the "totalitarian claim to authority"?[49]

Unlike the National Socialist dictatorship, state socialism responded to this dilemma not with the final physical annihilation of those stigmatized as "asocial." It also did not fall back on the heyday of the socialist eugenics debate in the 1920s, when strategies of negative eugenics developed involving voluntary sterilization. In this welfare power structure (*Machtdispositiv*)[50] imagined for the socialist *future,* doctors and welfare politicians had still dominated. In the power structure developed for the socialist human community of the *present,* the power to define social exclusion and inclusion lay instead clearly with the representatives of criminal prosecution and state security. They were entrusted with the initiation and direction of those procedures, which no longer were directed toward bodies and lives but rather were focused on the consciousness and behavior of individuals. They were to connect their social energies with the mass mobilization of "norm-enforcing" educators.

At no point did the state socialist government wish to refrain from using the morally loaded stigmatization of those who remained "at the bottom" to appeal to the "us" of the orderly workers. Whether they could have avoided these terms appears doubtful, since doing so would have been believable only at the price of acknowledging social differences and cultural diversity. Precisely this acknowledgment was irreconcilable with the historical justification for leadership and the SED monopoly over the truth. In the transition to a postindustrial service-oriented society in the West, permissive ways of dealing with "nonconformist" behavior could develop, as working worlds and living situations became more differentiated. By contrast, what remained unchanged among the SED elite during these very same decades and up until the bitter end of "their" state was the worldview learned in the class struggles of the Kaiserreich and the Weimar Republic, especially the Manichean friend-foe mentality as a guiding force of social politics. In the development of a real state with this worldview, penal, security, and political procedures crowded out the medical and social ones as means to assure its existence. Still, this development left the underlying premise of an antagonistic opposition between "proletariats and Lumpen"[51] unchanged. Fusing the "classical" industrial skilled worker with the ideal image of the "model" GDR citizen, sociohistorical "normality" moved to the core of state security doctrine and produced an especially rigid and sustainable variant of authoritarian social disciplining.[52] This legitimized itself in the sense of "classical-modern" social state utopias, claiming the right and ability to guide all social processes: In order to achieve and fulfill this utopia, no one was allowed to escape the utopian state's benevolent interventions. Those who persistently turned away the "advantages" of socialist work, whether due to ineptitude or willful aversion, stood with half a leg in the camp of the class enemy and with a whole one already in prison.

Translated by Katherine Pence, Paul Betts, and Maria Arroyo

NOTES

This is an expanded version of Thomas Lindenberger, "Das Fremde im Eigenen des Staatssozialismus. Klassendiskurs und Exklusion am Bespiel der Konstruktion des 'asozialen Verhaltens,'" in *Fremde und Fremd-Sein in der DDR, Zu den historischen Ursachen der Fremdenfeindlichkeit in Ostdeutschland.*, ed. Jan C. Behrends, Thomas Lindenberger, and Patrice G. Poutrus (Berlin, 2003), 179–91. See also Thomas Lindenberger, "'Asoziale Lebensweise'. Herrschaftslegitimation, Sozialdisziplinierung und die Konstruktion eines 'negativen Milieu' in der SED-Diktatur," *Geschichte und Gesellschaft* 32, no. 2 (2005): 227–54. The version of the essay that appears in this volume was revised before the publication of Sven

Korzilius's book *"Asoziale" und "Parisiten" im Recht der SBZ/DDR. Randgruppen im Sozialismus zwischen Repression und Ausgrenzung* (Cologne, 2005), and so it has not incorporated this and other most recent literature.

1. Compare Konrad H. Jarausch, "Care and Coercion: The GDR as Welfare Dictatorship," in *Dictatorship as Experience: Towards a Socio-Cultural History of the GDR,* ed. Konrad H. Jarausch (New York, 1999), 47–72.

2. StGB (Penal Code) 1968, 5. Abschnitt, Sonstige Straftaten gegen die allgemeine, staatliche und öffentliche Ordnung, § 249: Gefährdung der öffentlichen Ordnung durch asoziales Verhalten.

3. Johannes Raschka, *Justizpolitik im SED-Staat. Anpassung und Wandel des Strafrechts während der Amtszeit Honeckers,* Schriften des Hannah-Arendt Instituts für Totalitarismusforschung, vol. 13 (Cologne, 2000). See also Falco Werkentin, *Politische Strafjustiz in der Ära Ulbricht* (Berlin, 1995); and Inga Markovits, "Two Truths about Socialist Justice: A Comment on Kommers," *Law & Social Inquiry* 22 (1997): 849–78, here 870–75.

4. See Friedrich-Christian Schroeder, "Verschärfung der 'Parasitenbekämpfung' in der DDR. Vergleich zu den übrigen sozialistischen Staaten," *Deutschland-Archiv* 9 (1976): 834–43.

5. See Raschka, *Justizpolitik,* 326.

6. The statistics are according to the yearly "Informationen über die Entwicklung der Kriminalität," which the general state administration of the GDR prepared for the secretary of the SED Central Committee. Stiftung Archiv der Parteien und Massenorganisationen im Bundesarchiv (hereafter SAPMO-Barch), DY 30 J IV 2/3J-991–2190. In official publications of the GDR, such information never appeared. The euphemism "measures of penal responsibility" is taken from the third chapter of the 1968 GDR Penal Code.

7. See Raschka, *Justizpolitik,* 326.

8. Horst Luther and Christine Weis, "Zur Anwendung des Strafrechts in der Deutschen Demokratischen Republik," *Recht in Ost und West* 34 (1990): 289–92, here 291.

9. Kurt Manecke and Josef Bischof, "Die Asozialität und ihre Bekämpfung," *Neue Justiz* 21 (1967): 374–77, here 375f.

10. Markovits, "Two Truths," 870–75. For a perspective from educational science, see Matthais Zeng, "Transformation und Erziehung. 'Asoziale' im Spiegel einer gebrochenen Gesellschaft," *Dialogische Erziehung. Information der Paulo-Freire-Kooperation* 3, no. 4 (1999): 8–23; Matthias Zeng, "'Asozial'—Arm—Ausgegrenzt. Zur Tradierung eines Begriffes," *Soziale Arbeit* 6 (2000): 214–21.

11. Wolfgang Ayaß, *"Asozial" im Nationalsozialismus* (Stuttgart, 1995); Patrick Wagner, *Volksgemeinschaft ohne Verbrecher? Konzeptionen und Praxis der Kriminalpolizei in der Zeit der Weimarer Republik und des Nationalsozialismus* (Hamburg, 1996).

12. Paul Hagenloh, "'Socially Harmful Elements' and the Great Terror," in *Stalinism: New Directions,* ed. Sheila Fitzpatrick (London and New York, 2000), 286–308; Barry McLoughlin, "'Vernichtung des Fremden': Der 'Großen Terror' in der UdSSR 1937/38. Neue russische Publikationen," *Jahrbuch für historische Kommunismusforschung* 8 (2000–2001): 50–88, here 71.

13. Hans Gerats, John Lekschas, and Joachim Renneberg, *Lehrbuch des Strafrechts der Deutschen Demokratischen Republik. Allgemeiner Teil* (Berlin, 1957), 669.

14. See, for example, Friedrich Engels, *Die Lage der arbeitenden Klasse in England (MEW 2)* (Berlin [East], 1985), 496–500.

15. Gerats, Lekschas, and Renneberg, *Lehrbuch.*

16. A report from 1957 describes *Strichjungen* or "street boys" at the Friedrich-straße train station as "asocial youth." Stellvertreter Operativ (des Polizeipräsidiums der VP Berlin), May 2, 1957, Besonderheiten der Cliquenbildung in den VP-Inspektionen, Landesarchiv Berlin (hereafter LAB), C Rep. 303/26, Nr. 137, Blatt 167.

17. On the construction of youth "rowdiness" as a formal criminal act as well as its meaning during criminal police surveillance and the disciplining of GDR youth, see Thomas Lindenberger, "Öffentliche Polizei im Staatssozialismus. Studien zur Sozialgeschichte der Deutschen Volkspolizei, 1952–1968," postdoctoral thesis (Potsdam, 2001), chap. 9.

18. § 4 Einführungsgesetz zum StGB und zur StPO, Jan. 12, 1968, GBl. I, 97; Hans Hinderer and Wolfgang Peller, "Die Strafbestimmungen zum Schutze der staatlichen Ordnung," *Forum der Kriminalistik* 3, no. 5 (1967): 13–16, here 14f.

19. Verordnung über Aufenthaltsbeschränkung (Decree on Limiting Residency), from August 24, 1961, GBl. II, 343.

20. Falco Werkentin, *Politische Strafjustiz in der Ära Ulbricht* (Berlin, 1995), 264–66.

21. John Lekschas and Joachim Renneberg, "Lehren des XXII. Parteitages der KPdSU für die Entwicklung des sozialistischen Strafrechts der DDR," *Neue Justiz* 16 (1962): 76–91, here 76–78, 81–83, 85–87, 90f.

22. By no means did this limiting formulation play a role in the application of the "asociality" paragraph; see Schroeder, "Verschärfung," 837–39.

23. Bericht über den Stand der Gesetzgebungsarbeiten am StGB und dem Änderungsgesetz zur Strafprozeßordnung vom 16. April 1962, cited in Uta Falck, *VEB Bordell. Geschichte der Prostitution in der DDR* (Berlin, 1998), 86.

24. In contrast, talk of "immoral excesses," "rape," and "precociousness" appeared regularly in police reports and legal documents pertaining to youthful "rowdiness." The sexuality of young people was in a more immediate way relevant to domination than that of adults, for puberty was perceived as a critical phase of integration of the whole young person into the order of adults. Among adults, on the other hand, the state socialist discourse placed work in a socially regulated form in first place, in order to define social belonging. Sexuality was in comparison of secondary significance.

25. John Lekschas and Joachim Renneberg, "Zur Überwindung von Dogmatismus und Sektierertum in der Strafrechtswissenschaft," *Neue Justiz* 16 (1962): 500ff.

26. Compare Zeng, "Transformation."

27. Manecke and Bischof, "Asozialität," 376.

28. See Erich Buchholz et al., *Sozialistische Kriminologie. Versuch einer theoretische Grundlegung* (Berlin, 1966), as well as Gerrit Bratke's judicial perspective,

Die Kriminologie in der DDR und ihre Anwendung im Bereich der Jugenddelinquenz. Eine zeitgeschichtlich-kriminologische Untersuchung, Kriminologie und Rechtspsychologie, vol. 6 (Münster, 1999).

29. Heinz Blüthner, "Zum Problem der Asozialität und ihrer Bekämpfung in Großstädten (1)," *Die Volkspolizei* 4 (1968): 385–87, here 386.

30. See Thomas Lindenberger, *Straßenpolitik. Zur Sozialgeschichte der öffentlichen Ordnung in Berlin 1900–1914* (Bonn, 1995), 398f.

31. See Sigrid Meuschel, *Legitimation und Parteiherrschaft. Zum Paradox von Stabilität und Revolution in der DDR 1945–1989* (Frankfurt am Main, 1992).

32. See *Brand,* a documentary film, book/script: M. Ehlert and L. Pehnert, production: Tele Potsdam, contracted by ORB 1996; I thank Thomas Reichel, Brandenburg/H., for the suggestion.

33. W. Engler, *Die Ostdeutschen. Kunde von einem verlorenen Land* (Berlin, 1999); with respect to the disciplining of youthful workers, see also S. Kott, *Le communisme au quotidien. Les entreprises d'Etat dans la société est-allemande* (Paris, 2001).

34. The noteworthy substratification of foreign workers such as contracted workers from Vietnam, Angola, and other allies can only be talked about within the GDR context first in its very last years and then only for very specific technologically antiquated branches of industry. See the essays by Dennis Kuck and Annegret Schüle in *Fremde und Fremd-Sein in der DDR. Zu den historischen Ursachen der Fremdenfeindlichkeit in Ostdeutschland,* ed. Jan C. Behrends, Thomas Lindenberger, and Patrice G. Poutrus (Berlin, 2003).

35. D. Wittich, ed., *Momente des Umbruchs. Struktur und Lebensqualität in Ostdeutschland* (Berlin, 1994), 26.

36. Armin Nassehi discusses this ambivalence in terms related to the concept of "the underclass," such as the much discussed concept of exclusion in the French context. Armin Nassehi, "Exklusion als soziologischer oder sozialpolitischer Begriff?" *Mittelweg* 36, no. 5 (September 2000): 18–25.

37. C. Murray, *Losing Ground: American Social Policy, 1950–1980* (New York, 1984); W. Wilson, *The Truly Disadvantaged: The Inner City, the Underclass, and Public Policy* (Chicago, 1987); for an overview of the discussion, see M. Kronauer, "Die Innen-Außen Spaltung der Gesellschaft. Zu den Begriffen 'Exklusion' und 'Underclass,'" in *Integration und Ausschliessung. Kriminalpolitik und Kriminalität in Zeiten gesellschaftlicher Transformation,* ed. M. Althoff et al. (Baden-Baden, 2001), 29–41.

38. See the depiction of the international research discussion on exclusions and "underclass" in P. Bremer, *Ausgrenzungsprozesse und die Spaltung der Städte. Zur Lebenssituation von Migranten* (Opladen, 2000), 11–25.

39. See in this sense the long-term studies on help for those on probation and discharged from prison in Jonathan Simon, *Poor Discipline: Parole and the Social Control of the Underclass, 1890–1990* (Chicago, 1993).

40. Whether or not this construction is substantiated enough in underclass literature does not play a role here.

41. William J. Wilson, *When Work Disappears: The World of the New Urban Poor* (New York, 1996); Bremer, *Ausgrenzungsprozesse,* 21.

42. Simon, *Poor Discipline*, 252.

43. Peter Hübner, *Konsens, Konflikt und Kompromiß. Soziale Arbeiterinteressen und Sozialpolitik in der SBZ/DDR 1945–1970* (Berlin 1995).

44. See Wilfried Rudloff, "Die Tradition der deutschen Wohlfahrtspflege und der Weg der DDR," in *Diakonie im geteilten Deutschland. Zur diakonischen Arbeit unter den Bedingungen der DDR und der Teilung Deutschlands,* ed. I. Hübner and J. C. Kaiser (Stuttgart, 1999), 37–61, here 51–54; as well as the example of youth care in the GDR-FRG comparison, Wilfried Rudloff, "Öffentliche Fürsorge," in *Drei Wege deutscher Sozialstaatlichkeit,* ed. Hans Günter Hockerts (Munich, 1998), 199–229, here 219–22. The overwhelming significance of the millions of GDR citizens pressured into "honorary" functions for the socialization and practices of domination in the GDR belongs to the still broadly unworked aspects of their history; on some of these arenas, see Thomas Lindenberger, "Vaters kleine Helfer. Die Volkspolizei und ihre enge Verbindung zur Bevölkerung 1952–1965," in *Nachkriegspolizei. Sicherheit und Ordnung in Ost- und Westdeutschland 1945–1989,* ed. G. Fürmetz et al. (Hamburg, 2001), 229–53; Renate Hürtgen, "Der Vertrauensmann in den siebziger und achtziger Jahren. Funktionsloser Funktionär der Gewerkschaften?" in *Schein der Stabilität: DDR-Betriebsalltag in der Ära Honecker,* ed. Renate Hürtgen and Thomas Reichel (Berlin, 2001), 143–58; and H.-A. Schönfeldt, *Vom Schiedsmann zur Schiedskommission. Normdurchsetzung durch territoriale gesellschaftliche Gerichte in der DDR* (Frankfurt, 2001).

45. Kai Maaz, *Ohne Ausbildungsabschluss in der BRD und DDR: Berufszugang und die erste Phase der Erwerbsbiographie von Ungelernten in den 1980er Jahren,* MPI für Bildungsforschung Berlin, Selbständige Nachwuchsgruppe Working Paper no. 3 (2002), 27; see more comprehensively K. Maaz, "Konsequenzen von Ausbildungslosigkeit in unterschiedlichen Gesellschaftssystemen. Berufszugangschancen von Jugendlichen ohne Berufsausbildung in der DDR und der BRD in den 80er Jahren," manuscript (Berlin, 2001), 104–14.

46. See above all the examples supported by technical literature and dissertations in S. Gries, *Kindesmißhandlung in der DDR. Kinder unter dem Einfluß traditioneller autoritärer und totalitärer Erziehungsleitbilder* (Münster, 2001), 148–200; as well as the impressive study based on interviews with thirty-one experts from science, the police, justice, social work, and women's advisory boards in the GDR by M. Schröttle, *Politik und Gewalt. Eine empirische Untersuchung über Ausmaß, Ursachen und Hintergründe von Gewalt gegen Frauen in ostdeutschen Paarbeziehungen vor und nach der deutsch-deutschen Vereinigung* (Bielefeld, 1999), 285–303.

47. Jürgen Kocka, "Ein deutscher Sonderweg. Überlegungen zur Sozialgeschichte der DDR," *Aus Politik und Zeitgeschichte* 40 (1994): 43–45, here 43.

48. Rudloff, "Tradition," 37–41.

49. Detlev J. Peukert, *Grenzen der Sozialdisziplinierung. Aufstieg und Krise der deutschen Jugendfürsorge 1878 bis 1932* (Cologne, 1986), 307.

50. M. Schwartz, "'Proletarier' und 'Lumpen'. Sozialistische Ursprünge eugenischen Denkens," *Vierteljahresheft für Zeitgeschichte* 42 (1994): 537–70, here 570.

51. Ibid.

52. M. Zeng, *"Asoziale" in der DDR. Transformation einer moralischen Kategorie* (Münster, 2002), 167–74, describes a "dilemma of social work" in the new German states after the *Wende,* which emanates from the passing down of the term *asocial* used in East German society, against which there is little to be done for the time being but which works against the goal of training a new generation of social education workers.

The World of Men's Work, East and West

Alf Lüdtke

Honor and Income in the East

In the weekly "argumentations" that the East German Socialist Unity Party (SED) Politburo gave to the German Democratic Republic (GDR) press, the following was communicated on October 19, 1989, one day after Erich Honecker's resignation as both general secretary of the SED and GDR state council chairman: "Go out and report objectively on what moves the working population who produces our wealth. Egon [Krenz, his successor] spoke yesterday [during his television address] about German quality workmanship. Yes, be sure to appeal to their sense of honor. German workers have always worked well."

As the GDR and its ideology were slowly falling to their knees in 1989, this argumentation remarkably used the appeal of "quality work" as an attempt to maintain the status quo and preserve the GDR state. It used this concept in three revealing ways. First, in the face of political crisis, the cultural pattern of "German quality work" was seen by GDR "superiors" as a source of hope for stabilization; second, "quality workmanship" in this case was not touted as specific to the GDR but rather was attributed more generally to "German workers"; third, "working well" was construed as creating "honor," in other words, respect for oneself and for others, something that long predated the end of World War II in 1945 or even the founding of the GDR in 1949 for that matter. The few demands from the factories that became known in the autumn of 1989 indirectly confirmed that "good work" had assumed great importance for the workers themselves. Workers from Bergmann-Borsig in Berlin, for example, based their demands to the SED to initiate broad reforms primarily in terms of this idea of "good work." For them, reform meant that there

234

should no longer be barriers to "quality work" and that it should be compensated with "real money."

In another example, on September 25, 1956, the deputy chairman of the GDR's State Planning Commission (SPK) wrote a memorandum to his boss, Bruno Leuschner, about the emigration of workers from the GDR, what was commonly described as "flight from the republic" (*Republikflucht*). In it he made plain that he was aware that there was a concerted West German effort to entice away East German skilled laborers. But he also conceded that such headhunting "was aided extraordinarily" by the "many deficiencies in the organization of work in our factories and their erratic rhythm of production." For him, the consequences were clear: "In many cases, workers are leaving precisely because they 'would like to work in an orderly fashion.'" The numbers involved underscored the gravity of the problem; just one year before (1955), 102,000 of those leaving the GDR—almost 40 percent of the 270,000 "emigrants from the Republic"—were workers. The struggle to "finally be able to work correctly," or more specifically, deep dissatisfaction about irregular delivery schedules as well as shortages in economic organization, materials, and tools, dominated the monthly reports from countless factories across the GDR during the 1950s and 1960s. Local SED organizations agreed with the factory union administrators (BGL) on this issue. At the Bergmann-Borsig factory for power-plant generators, for example, it was recognized by all concerned that "non-rhythmic" work flows were impeding output targets, to the extent that it was hindering both the quantity and quality of production. These problems endangered the goal of raising productivity, even though this was the central goal animating countless proclamations and planning documents at the time. The classic Marxist authors provided an inexhaustible source for these texts. Invariably Lenin himself was invoked as justification, since he had always claimed that the increase in work productivity was "the most important thing for the victory of the new social order."

Perhaps the "international class struggle" as well as the late 1950s "Overtaking without Catching Up" (*Überholen ohne Einzuholen*) campaign moved the Party functionaries. But like most citizens, the large majority of workers wanted to know what this meant in terms of everyday life and where the "overtaking" of capitalist West Germany would become tangible. Occasional leaps forward, such as the definitive end of rationing in May 1958, did nurse dreams of a comparable East German "economic miracle," but these were short lived. For their part, the "immediate producers" (Karl Marx) saw little reason to mess around; as the supposed "ruling class," the workers shrewdly used this new ideological latitude to their own advantage. In many branches of industry, particularly in mechanical engineering, both the internal and public criticism of "false" working norms made clear that the celebrated "producers of social wealth" were actually using their individual opportunities for selfish personal income generation. Economists as well as SED and state functionaries complained year in and year out that it was too easy to fulfill and even exceed production targets. Attempts to counter this with "technically" or "scientifically" based work norms (TAN) were ultimately unsuccessful, however. Instead, the effort to optimize one's own work life, that is, minimizing labor intensity while at the same time maximizing good wages, remained central for many workers. In this sense, the "cash nexus" was by no means overcome for GDR workers and became particularly pronounced during times of prolonged hardship in the GDR at least until the late 1960s.

Discussion transcripts and reports from the factories showed just how much efforts to secure "good" remuneration dovetailed with the concern for worker appreciation. Colleagues and superiors alike—to say nothing of both society and the state more generally—were supposed to appreciate the individual's own activity and production. However, even among colleagues "orderly work" no longer appeared to be a matter of course. Only the interest in wages and the preoccupation with individual success—as opposed to concern for "achievements of high quality"—shaped the general attitude of production workers. This at least was the main thrust of a December 1962 speech transcript by the Factory Party Administration of the "May 8th" machine-tool engineering factory in Berlin. According to this report, the connection between low-quality work, sub par products, and diminished wages was "not yet recognized" by employees. Especially the older ones had supposedly "partially forgotten" (the original draft stated "completely forgotten!") the attention "they had once paid to the achievement of a higher quality of work in the former capitalist factories." In those days, "high quality" had been necessary; the struggle for existence and the need to keep one's job made it clear to everyone that they would lose their position by producing poor-quality work. Today, the report went on, things were different. Under socialist social relations, every person's existence is guaranteed, and now "a few believe" (in the first draft, it was "they") that "the law of quality work" can be simply disregarded.

According to the report, two solutions were necessary. First, "the character of our state" and the resulting responsibility of its workers must be made plain to all. Second, the "new character of work in socialism needs to be clarified with greater emphasis than before." That is to say, in earlier times before socialism "it would not have occurred to anyone to read the newspaper during the running time while the machines were in the middle of a long automated process or to sit by the machine and (just) keep an eye on it." Back then "workers kept an eye on their machines but at the same time created order in the workplace." In the future, the report concluded, "we must restore" this worker ethos. But this went well beyond avoiding breakdowns and minimizing additional work. "Did not these given examples also reveal a disregard for the work of other workstations?" asked the report. Apparently, only a few cared about how the next colleagues working on the same machine would deal with deficiencies or worn-out tools. Emphasis instead must now be placed on "the redevelopment of work pride among colleagues and with it, the honor of one's own profession." Everyone must "from now on stake his whole sense of honor on performing high quality work." In other words, "up to now the honor in one's profession has been insufficient!"

Three years later, the vocational honor of skilled laborers and its supposed decline emerged as a film theme. The 1965–66 film *Berlin Around the Corner* (*Berlin um die Ecke*) centers on Paul, an old turner who provides a youth brigade, the "Children of the GDR," with real live examples of the daily requirements for quality work. The film, however, furnishes no happy ending. Paul, played by Erwin Geschonneck, one of the GDR's favorite actors, dies, while the "wild" youth brigade dissolves. Its brigadier, Olaf, portrayed by another GDR star, Dieter Mann, disappears at the end into the unknown. To be clear, this film by no means celebrated that kind of worker's "own way of doing things" (*Eigensinn*) of the kind of worker who concentrated only on himself and a few buddies, while keeping the "rest of the world" at arm's length. That kind of rebelliousness was played out in another film from 1965, *The Trace of Stones* (*Spur der Steine*), in which the actor "Manne" Krug played the construction brigadier "Balla." However different in style and message, both films failed inspection at the Cultural Ministry and remained forbidden until right before the collapse of the GDR. The self-image of many male workers evidently corresponded to a mixture of both Olaf and Balla; and the criticism that real workers heaped on other artistic representations of work and workers indicated that such fictional figures could hardly have been "realistic" enough.

For a year beginning in the fall of 1972, Werner Heiduczek recorded his observations as a worker at Bitterfeld's chemical combine. In February 1973 the author noted a typical practice. One section of the factory had received the quality mark of Q, "the only chemical product from this combine affixed with this label." A merit of distinction was on the way. And yet in a conversation with Heiduczek, one insider whispered that "everything is not running there as it should." The capacity of a new machine there was only being pushed to 80 percent. This informant had analyzed suggestions for improving the factory over the last few years. Apparently, the factory section recognized for its excellence had always been awarded large bonuses by continuously rationalizing production. For the informant this meant that "If one wanted to, one could produce even more right away." But that was what the workers expressly wanted to avoid. The decisive thing was to control production and be rewarded for it, making sure "that one only gradually let the cat out of the bag. This way, one always stayed in good stead." Everyone knew this, and everyone played along. This took place not only at the point of production but also among the "technical intelligentsia," division managers, and factory administrators, who all took part in overseeing the steady but closely controlled increase in "quality" work and products. The assertion of worker autonomy, or Eigensinn—whether seen in the individual distance from those above, from one's peers, or from those "below"—had solidified into a collective practice of asset preservation *(kollektive Besitzstandswahrung)*.

Wolfgang Engler has attempted to interpret this social definition of work in the GDR according to a term borrowed from Norbert Elias—the "society of the working man," or *arbeiterliche Gesellschaft*—on the ground that most workers saw themselves as "owners of work." In this formulation, the "working class" did not rule politically but they did reign at a social level. Engler points out that the notion of work as the property of everyone, an idea that was promoted and supported socially in the GDR, caused a backlash among male workers. Because they had been increasingly undermined in their roles as paternal protectors, so argues Engler, "they clung to the body and namely, to the bodies of those men who either did not work at all or did not work physically. Precisely because the man was no longer a man, he attached great importance to at least appearing like one." Masculine body language and ways of life marked by subordination thus became a habitus in their own right for what sociologist Dietrich Mühlberg has called the "common people" *(kleine Leute)*. "Uninhibitedly" men displayed "their beer bellies as much as their sexual potency."

What is often overlooked, however, is the flip side of this phenomenon. After all, Engler ignored the work that was actually performed by individuals under difficult and often crisis conditions, be it for one's own brigade, the workshop, or factory. Indeed, it was possible "to make lemonade from lemons." That applied not only—in one famous example—to the much-celebrated construction of elevators in East Berlin's television tower that were built on time despite canceled deliveries of badly needed Western electronic components. But apart from such spectacular cases the common "sporadic work conditions" forced workers to search for makeshift solutions almost on a daily and nightly basis to meet even the most basic production requirements, at the very least just to secure their wages. After so many years most workers made no fuss over resorting to "organizing" goods through personal connections or semilegal channels in the constant quest for needed production elements, as, say, undelivered special screws were sought in the workshop right next door, at another factory, or elsewhere in the country. Such strategies were necessary for production to run at all. Among those involved, this "keep going despite everything" work style cultivated a sense of individual willfulness and ingenuity (Eigensinn) such that in moments of uncertainty, workers proved to be stubborn and arrogant or, as Engler describes them, "rough and intractable." This common assertion of selfhood was based on countless similar experiences over the decades across the country that proved to these workers time and again that they would get the job done. Neither guidelines nor planning from above was ever going to change these conditions; rather, the "troubles at our level" (Erich Loest) were only ever to be overcome—if at all—by one's own imaginative solutions and individual willingness to help out.

In her memoir, *Die Geliebte, die Verfluchte Hoffnung* (The Beloved, Cursed Hope), the author Brigitte Reimann called attention to what she sensed was "a kind of consciousness of obligation" among the people who worked in production. As she saw it, desk work and writing did not produce the same sense of duty toward society, at least from her perspective in the early 1960s. Only those who delivered tangible, visible, and immediately measurable work, she contended, behaved "correctly" and "acceptably." After the 1960s the spectrum of cultural images of GDR work and workers broadened markedly. Weekly newsreels, magazines, and television increasingly showed images of office work, planning activities, development, technical construction, as well as corrective welfare, educational, and/or scientific undertakings. That did not mean, however, that the central privileges given to manual production work were revised. Quite the contrary, all the way until 1990 employees who were categorized according to their places of work as "production" workers and "basic production workers" were remunerated by only having to pay 5 percent income tax; all others, as so-called salaried employees, by contrast were forced to pay 20 percent income tax.

Out of this situation emerged a host of conflicts that became the subject of regular and open debate. One key issue in particular was the payment and position of foremen within industry. Foremen often earned less gross income than workers in the 1950s, although their salaries were elevated to 10–20 percent higher than production workers by the late 1960s. Even then because foremen were viewed as salaried employees, their income after taxes was actually less than that of the employees they supervised and managed. Frequent resignations of foremen from their posts, often accompanied by stinging letters of complaints to Party superiors, revealed that this state pay scheme was widely perceived as unjust. From mid-November 1989 through the end of 1990, over three hundred letters a day arrived at the Free German Trade Union Association (Freier Deutscher Gewerkschaftsbund [FDGB]) central newspaper *Tribüne*. Revealingly, the written complaints about this tax scheme were then categorized and filed by the editors under the heading of "justice." It was no coincidence that the overwhelming majority of letters came from working women. One typical note read: "When do we low-level salaried employees get to pay only 5 percent income tax as the workers do? . . . A third of our income is deducted, and we don't work any worse than our colleagues in 'production.'" Or as another put it: "We work just as conscientiously as production workers"; in this case, fifty signatures were appended, most of whom signed as "long-standing FDGB members."

"Quality Work": Definition and Self-Image

German industrial workers who went to the Soviet Union in the early 1930s—whether to seek work or for political reasons—often experienced a strong distrust of foreigners. Over and over again they described the attitude of Russian administrators and colleagues as evidence of a deep cultural rift between Germans and Russians. As noted in their letters, the "Russian comrades" were seen as incapable of building a one-axle handcart in such a way that it could sustain a heavy counterweight; others wrote that "the Russians" apparently lacked a basic understanding of mechanics. German returnees from the United States during the same period furnished comparable examples. U.S. colleagues required everything to be "foolproof," so they said, whereas the German workers were usually able to solve technical problems themselves. Such proud sentiments of German problem solving and technical mastery were not limited to the workers' own testimony. Indeed, the importance of "manual skill" as an economic resource was embraced by industrialists and engineers alike as a key dimension of "German quality work." Moreover, practical skill was part of a positive self-image that countless soldiers also held dear. After all, was not the notion of the German army as a "steel mill on wheels" (Curzio Malaparte, 1941) equally dependent on one's own on-the-spot initiative as the work of those back home in factories in Essen or Dortmund?

Skepticism toward Soviet work and production methods remained strong after 1945 and continued long after the founding of the GDR in 1949. If anything, it was even intensified by the experiences and stories from former soldiers who had fought on the eastern front. The attitude of the Soviet victors, especially during the dismantling of what was left of Germany's industrial infrastructure, did nothing to mitigate the strong disdain and even contempt toward "the Russians." When "contract workers" were brought to the GDR in the 1970s from other socialist republics in Eastern Europe, or even from so far afield as sub-Saharan Africa, Vietnam, or Cuba, the racist component of "German quality work" remained present and was quickly and openly activated at various times. While these racist attitudes toward foreign workers developed in Germany, among German workers a community was promoted for rebuilding after World War II. In 1945 and 1946 placards that were produced by the municipal government in Hanover called upon "everyone to help" the bombed-out local populations, refugees, and even concentration camp survivors. In these woodcuts, male workers—notably with proletarian caps, not military ones—were shown clearing away ruins and assisting in reconstruction efforts. Across all of the occupational zones, experiences in the factories were remarkably similar. It was the employees, and especially the union-organized men, who took the lead in rubble clearing, reconstruction, as well as the resistance against the Soviet expropriation of the country's remaining infrastructure. The importance of rebuilding and "working" as both national community initiative (*volksgemeinschaftliches Ziel*) and collective experience was invoked in the May Day slogans of the major trade unions (i.e., the West German Deutscher Gewerkschaftsbund [DGB] and the East German FDGB). By the same token, these slogans were also accompanied by warnings that only hard work would bring about self-purification, self-healing, and a better future.

The postwar German community forged through work made the later discrimination toward guest workers that much more striking. In West Germany, the Italian working immigrants who arrived in the late 1950s "fit" into the racially colored clichés of foreign workers as much as the Turkish immigrants did a few years later. Apart from all of the officious gestures of solidarity with these new "colleagues," countless German workers and factory administrators harbored great mistrust toward these new arrivals and their alleged "aversion to work." In the name of expediency, the "bloody foreigners" from Turkey ("Kanaken") were assigned most often to jobs that were particularly laborious, dangerous, and dirty: in transport and stopgap unskilled labor crews.

Achievement Consciousness in the West

How did standards among German workers in West Germany look compared to those of their East German counterparts? In 1957, Heinrich Popitz published his study *Gesellschaftsbild der Arbeiter* (Societal Image of Workers). It was based on questionnaires and statistical surveys conducted in 1953 and 1954 in a West German iron and steel factory in Dortmund and revealed sharp distinctions between various worker groups in relation to their "social images." While it was acknowledged that "the bosses [had become] nicer" and the administrators for their part "more congenial," the authors contended that there was an essential similarity, in that "All workers . . . see society as a dichotomy—one that is at once rigid and mobile, inaccessible and 'partnerly.'" Typically they tended to see themselves more on the side of those whose power was limited; when in doubt, society would most likely fail to grant these persons either recognition or justice. Against this workers set forth a distinct consciousness of their own performance, whether they were skilled or semiskilled workers, specialized or unskilled laborers. Each group saw itself as embodying true "human labor" (*menschliche Arbeit*) of at least equal value to that of "dead capital" (*toten Kapital*). For them, the main distinguishing criterion of human labor was "physical work" (*körperliche Arbeit*), that is, "human activity that is most obviously 'labor' whose achievement creates immediate value." As one of the interviewees put it: "For in the end, they [the others who don't perform physical labor] do live off the productivity of workers."

Particularly for a group of iron rolling mill workers (*Umwalzer*), the authors revealed to what degree confidence of experience as well as the mastery of both work method and machinery—which often meant simply a good understanding of the particular dynamics of each apparatus—determined the successful production of a good product and in turn the avoidance of risky work accidents. No less significant is that it helped cultivate a feeling of self-worth, as well as providing more latitude in terms of the space and time for individual autonomy (*Eigensinn*).

Even so, two caveats need mentioning in terms of Popitz's study. First, it included only younger and middle-aged workers in the first blush of that hallowed economic boom period famously known as the "economic miracle." It was only a few years later when this development really began to take effect, slowly eradicating as it did the still palpable privations of the industrial "proletariat." Second, the research centered exclusively on a large factory in a concentrated industrial area. What was missing was the overwhelmingly large number of workers in small and medium-sized factories across the region, as well as those working outside this and other industrial belts in small cities and in villages.

The perceived linkage between the valued physicality of work and the claim that manual workers were the true embodiments of "productive work" was based on everyday networks of work such as those in domestic or neighborhood agricultural and garden economies. While the economic and structural crises in heavy industry caused a mental and emotional shock in the early 1970s, such "blows of fate" in this setting actually strengthened collegial and neighborly cooperation among those who experienced (and remembered) the can-do resolve and economic upswing of the late 1950s and 1960s. Worker pride was closely connected to pride in work. In the face of economic crisis the collective Eigensinn of workers motivated them to seek out their own solutions together to overcome pressing structural hardships and what they saw as unfair treatment; in the end, this attitude helped ensure the livelihood of working men for many years to come. Fitting with this pride in work that surged in the first postwar decades, an icon of the manual worker was even erected in front of a high-rise building in Frankfurt am Main in 1954 as part of the federal "Kunst am Bau" public art and sculpture program. This figurative statue, several meters tall, featured a relaxing miner. Never again was the cultural significance of (male) manual industrial labor culturally represented in such a direct, positive way to the West German public.

Working Outside the Factory: Refuge during Crises

In both East and West Germany, work has functioned for decades as a goal-oriented activity for men in industrial production. Their products were defined by and valued for their practical utility; their exchange value was of course also important, and it was in this context that product aesthetics came into play. But to a great extent, this work is defined in concrete terms (*gegenständlich*): working materials (*Werkstoff*) and working components (*Werkstück*) are worked on with working tools (*Werkzeug*), as the workers make use of their bodily strength and "manual skill." Such labor is then organized and run according to factory logic. The "immediate producers" stand in a relatively horizontal "working relationship" with one another, which in West Germany also eventually led to a certain "solidarity among employees" (*Arbeitnehmerverhältnis*). Employers or consumers are as a rule almost like outsiders, including anonymous customers or directors with whom workers related only in the abstract. Such relationships have been well studied, but wage-earning work outside of that organized within the factory is rarely addressed by scholars or politicians. It is, however, very present in the experiential world of the workers, their colleagues, family members, and their neighbors. An Oldenburg study of dock workers, pipe fitters, and welders in the northern part of West Germany in the mid-1980s showed that the "overwhelming majority" was involved in countless productive activities outside the factory. This included "repair, installation, and renovation work in the home, on the car and on household consumer appliances." Half of the ninety-eight studied cases showed that for these workers a certain phase of their life was devoted to work on a greater goal, such as their own house, boat, or workshop. For them, all resources were marshaled to this goal and undertaken "without breaks." Others concentrated for long stretches of time on specific projects ranging from repairs to gardening, devoting one to one and a half days a week to these activities over many years. Nearly a third of those polled said that they were regularly busy with an array of skilled manual-work activities of all kinds.

Strikingly, two-thirds of the study participants experienced, or at least described, such work outside of the factory as "completely different" than that done in the workplace. For the majority, the appeal of work outside the factory was multifaceted. Around half of them felt that it was only under such conditions that they could develop their own abilities, make their own decisions, and enjoy complete sovereignty over the work process. No less significant was the cooperation and exchange with others outside the factory as well. Notably, the amount of energy involved was usually taken in stride. Only about a fourth judged this exertion to be at times burdensome. As one such worker put it: "If I'm forced to do work [that is, for a livelihood], then I would like to be able to arrange it myself here [in the garden]." Yet for about two-thirds of those polled, such activity was less "work" than a "hobby." For many of them, the payoff of work outside of the factory was not simply compensation; rather, what was prized was the fact that it was their "own work" (*das Eigentliche*). As many explained, it was only after work that things really began. If nothing else, this study made plain that for many work outside the factory was necessary not only for economic success but seemingly also for raising their social status. Above all, it seemed necessary for ensuring the recognition of the male worker as "an upstanding man" within his household, family, neighborhood, and residential community.

It is also worth bearing in mind that this study was conducted during a period of gradually increasing mass unemployment. In fact 2.2 million people, or 9 percent of those able to work in West Germany, were registered as unemployed in 1987. The situation was particularly grave in the local shipyards where the industrial workers in this study were employed. What seems to have happened, however, is that the decline in men's salaried work was compensated for by a new premium placed on "leisure time work" (*Freizeit-Arbeit*). While this may not have brought them much money, it provided great psychological support in giving them the chance on a daily basis to prove to their wives, children, relatives, and neighbors that as men they were not washed up. Such sentiment found similar expression in a piece of documentary fiction about a large industrial city in East Germany—Leipzig—that appeared in the late 1970s. In it the hero is repairing a spin dryer on a Sunday morning when he remarks: "And I messed with the thing much longer than necessary, since as an old toolmaker I was so happy to have proper work [*richtige Arbeit*] between my fingers again. I toyed with the fantasy of how it would be for me to do this kind of thing all the time—repairing dryers and washing machines, driving around house to house in my van, having a quick chat, a cup of coffee, removing and installing pieces, could that be a life for me?" The parallel between this episode from Leipzig and the experiences of those in West Germany discussed previously fits up to this point. After that one can see a big difference between East and West, especially in the ability of workers to make ends meet through work outside the factory. In the East German story, the hero from Leipzig continues: "A little tip money in my pocket, the removed parts taken home, repaired, and sold off cheaply on the side—it easily adds up to the same dough I'm making now."

Alternate Modernity?

The editors of this volume propose to reconsider East German socialism as "modern." This emphasis challenges the focus on repression as pivotal for East Germany, a focus that regained momentum after the *Wende* of 1989–90 and, in its wake, the opening of the archives of the "organs" of repression. Still, explorations of modern facets of social relationships or imaginations, especially in people's practices, do not contradict the valence of scrutinizing the settings and activities of control from above.

In addition, inquiries into characteristics of the modern might redirect scholars away from evaluating German societies through comparative levels of "modernity" and toward attention to their very processes of striving for and working toward "becoming modern." By this token, what is at stake is not a comparison of states or systems. On the contrary the analysis has to trace and map clues of different or "alternate" practices of working toward "modernity" and the specific configurations in which they operate.

Notions, symbols, and practices of work are particularly intriguing issues in this regard. Working people, whether they held blue- or white-collar jobs, employed notions and images that they derived from "former times" to describe their own everyday activities or those of others. Until the late 1960s this reference point in the past meant the capitalist era, and people in East Germany invoked it explicitly. In one of the cases from late 1962 that I quoted earlier, the particular author of an internal memorandum of the Berlin "May 8th" tool company's SED group referred to what he understood as standard practices of good German workmanship. The author rendered the latter as constitutive of an "honor of labor" that he thought the new state and, in particular, the ruling working class desperately needed. He stressed the point that prior to 1945—that is, during the

evil age par excellence that was the background for the GDR's foundational focus and myth of "antifascism"—workers' conduct had allowed
for more efficiency and productivity than in socialist times. Thus, when
working for the new Germany one should actually orient oneself toward
that older model of "German quality work"; to most people it stood for a
"better Germany" they saw as part and parcel not only of both the Imperial Reich and the Weimar Republic but even more of Germany under
Nazism. At the same time, many East Germans likewise perceived socialist "friends" and neighbors, such as the Soviet Union or Poland, within
this very matrix measuring levels of more or less "proper" work habits and
products. On this score the GDR figured as the most "advanced" case,
representing the "West" within the socialist bloc.

The irony is that perceptions of and claims for "things modern" if not
"modernity" during the decades under consideration here simultaneously
operated in two contradictory arenas. For one, the GDR's comparison of
its own settings and accomplishments to those of other regimes, whether
socialist or Western, employed modern criteria like efficiency and calcula-
bility. In this respect, it was an either/or of "more" or "less" that mattered.
Second, and at the same time, one's own practices differed in important
ways from the binary of "more" and "less" just as they did from the polarity of "traditional" versus "modern." In other words, people didn't just
simply "carry on" established ways of doing or perceiving things (or
people). On the contrary, they developed *specific amalgams* combining
what they had operated in or perceived from former times to be "good
practice" with ways of dealing with the specific demands and opportunities they encountered in their actually existing current "given" settings.
Such amalgams emerged in everyday practice as workers developed multiple ways of innovatively overcoming, for instance, the chronic short supply of screws, switches, semifinished items, or even raw materials that
reigned in most working people's days (and nights). The result was openness to and reliance on self-help and any kind of creative way of finding
solutions to the most pressing shortages or systemic shortcomings. Thus,
people could and increasingly did demonstrate to themselves and to others
the agility and productivity of ordinary workers. By the same token, these
ways of creatively bypassing customary work standards shifted the focus
of "German quality work." The notion had previously revolved around
the products themselves as well as the best standards of tools and work
practices. However, in the East German context "German quality work"

meant the personal ability to solve a task "in spite of" recurrent disruptions of the steady process of daily work and of overall production.

When irregular gaps yawned time and again between official promises and actual delays of production, the feeling of being able to master the regularity of these irregular circumstances fueled many East Germans to stem the tide of a collapse, at least for themselves. Certainly these workers were a minority, but they were the people keeping things going. Only by the very "modern" energy of individuals to act creatively and independently did East Germany overcome repeated chances of breakdown, until its implosion in the late 1980s.

By this token working people actually practiced an "alternate" mode of German quality work. Its particular modernity emerged, even more ironically, much more clearly and forcefully after the fact; only in the 1990s, when they had to compete directly with Western counterparts, did it become visible how GDR working peoples' potential for innovatively mastering tasks on the spot during production matched the most modern styles of industrial production and management that the West had to offer. Thus, to operate on one's own blend of manual and mental dexterity and creativity, which had served both management and workers in the difficult conditions of the GDR economy, proved to embody not backwardness but the most productive mode of coping with changing work tasks in the new market. Still, only in a few cases could East German workers actually take advantage of these resources; the successful relaunch of the East German Filmfabrik Wolfen ("Orwo" films) by the Bayer Leverkusen concern in the 1990s is a rare case in point.[1]

Translated by Katherine Pence, Paul Betts, and Maria Arroyo

NOTES

This essay is a revised and expanded version of the article "Bei der Ehre packen: Männer und 'ihre' Arbeit in Ost- und Westdeuschland," *Frankfurter Allgemeine Zeitung,* May 20, 2000, 3, reprinted as "Männerarbeit Ost—Männerarbeit West," in *Archäologie der Arbeit,* ed. Werner Baecker (Berlin, 2002), 35–47.

For reports from the SED Politburo see Ulrich Bürger, *Das sagen wir natürlich so nicht* (Berlin, 1990), 228ff. See Alf Lüdtke, "'Helden der Arbeit': Mühen beim Arbeiten: Zur mißmutigen Loyalität von Industriearbeitern in der DDR," in *Sozialgeschichte der DDR,* ed. Hartmut Kaelble, Jürgen Kocka, and Hartmut Zwahr (Stuttgart, 1994), 188–213. The files of the SED were cited out of the collection in the Stiftung Archiv der Parteien und Massenorganisationen der DDR im

Bundesarchiv (SAPMO). See the quote from Lenin in W. I. Lenin, "Die Grosse Initiative," in *Werke,* vol. 29, 399–424, here 416, for example, quoted in *Kleines Politisches Wörterbuch* as authoritative proof of "worker productivity," here 7th ed. (Berlin, 1988), 85. For the critique of the workers toward artistic production of the GDR see Arnulf Siebeneicker, "Kulturarbeit in der Industrieprovinz: Entstehung und Rezeption bildender Kunst im VEB Petrolchemisches Kombinat Schwedt 1960–1990," *Historische Anthropologie* 5 (1997): 435–53. The quoted protocols from Werner Heiduczek are found in *Im gewöhnlichen Stalinismus—meine unerlaubten Texte* (Leipzig, 1991), 20, 29. For the concept of the "society of the working man" (*arbeiterliche Gesellschaft*) see Wolfgang Engler, *Die Ostdeutschen: Kunde von einem verlorenen Land* (Berlin, 1999), 198ff, 200ff. On the topos and symbolism of "German quality work" see Alf Lüdtke, *Eigen-Sinn* (Hamburg, 1993), 249ff, 283–350, 406ff, also for army letters of drafted and willingly enlisted Leipzig workers with opinions of Russian and American workers. On "clearing the rubble" (*Aufräumen*) and "reconstruction" see Lutz Niethammer et al., eds., *Arbeiterinitiative 1945* (Wuppertal, 1976); on reactions to guest workers see Jan Motte et al., eds., *50 Jahre Bundesrepublik—50 Jahre Einwanderung: Nachkriegsgeschichte als Migrationsgeschichte* (Frankfurt am Main, 1999); see also Günter Wallraff, "*Wir brauchen Dich": Als Arbeiter in deutschen Industriebetrieben* (Munich, 1966). On a reprint of the 1957 study of worker consciousness in the FRG see Heinrich Popitz, Hans Paul Bahrdt, Ernst August Jüres, and Hanno Kesting, *Das Gesellschaftsbild des Arbeiters: Soziologische Untersuchungen in der Hüttenindustrie,* 5th ed. (Tübingen, 1977), 272ff. For a propaganda brochure on cowork (*Mitarbeit*) see Dirk Cattepoel, *Sozialreise durch Deutschland: Vom Arbeiter zum Mitarbeiter* (Düsseldorf, 1953). On the mentality of the "economic miracle" see Michael Wildt, *Vom kleinen Wohlstand: Eine Kosumgeschichte der fünfziger Jahre* (Frankfurt am Main, 1996). See the Oldenburg study by Johann Jessen, Walter Siebel, Christa Siebel-Rebell, Uwe-Jens Walther, and Irmgard Weyrather, *Arbeit nach der Arbeit: Schattenwirtschaft, Wertewandel und Industriearbeit* (Opladen, 1988), 221, 252. The documentary novel of a Leipzig worker can be found in Erich Loest, *Es geht seinen Gang oder Mühen in unserer Ebene* (Stuttgart and Leipzig, 1978), 86; empirically differentiated, and at the same time analytically provocative, is Michael Vester et al., *Soziale Milieus in Ostdeutschland: Gesellschaftliche Strukturen zwischen Zerfall und Neubildung* (Cologne, 1995).

    1. Regina Bittner, *Kolonien des Eigensinns: Ethnographie einer ostdeutschen Industrieregion* (Frankfurt am Main, 1998).

Desires

Shopping, Sewing, Networking, Complaining

Consumer Culture and the Relationship between State and Society in the GDR

Judd Stitziel

Between the end of World War II and the end of the 1950s, consumers in the Soviet Occupation Zone/German Democratic Republic (GDR) went from coping with existential crises to rummaging through stores filled with goods in search of particular items. During this period, the initial outlines of an East German consumer culture evolved from a mixture of changes and continuities in ideological premises, political promises, popular expectations, social practices, and the workings of the GDR's economy. Included in this mixture were negotiations among various actors—within the Party, state, industry, trade, media, and general population—who proposed diverse ideals for "socialist" consumption and pursued their goals using a variety of practices.

This essay focuses on everyday techniques that consumers used to fulfill their sartorial needs and desires. Given the regime's attempts to influence every aspect of life in East Germany, an analysis of consumers' everyday practices is also a study in the relationship between state and society in the GDR. Contemporaries knew that East Germans' actual consumption patterns differed drastically from the officially promoted "socialist consumer habits" that were supposed to mark the new "socialist personality." Quotidian practices of consumption and expressions of dissatisfaction formed constitutive elements of the GDR's consumer culture, demonstrated consumers' agency, and created highly political meanings within the pseudo "public sphere" of consumption. Both the social construction of demand and the everyday techniques that East Germans used to fulfill their demands for clothing demonstrate ways in which state and society, domination and agency, overlapped, intersected, and shaped each other.

The leadership of East Germany's ruling party, the Socialist Unity Party (SED), based a crucial part of its legitimacy on the claim to "satisfy the needs of the population" and strove to cultivate and regulate these objectively defined needs and wishes, which according to Party ideologues would naturally increase quantitatively and qualitatively in a dialectical relationship with production. The nexus of these promises and the regime's legitimacy eventually found prominent political and economic expression in the "unity of social and economic policies" announced at the SED's Eighth Party Congress in 1971.[1] Although this essay focuses on the first two decades of the GDR, the practices of consumption and dynamics between state and society that it describes have relevance and implications throughout the GDR's history. The regime's efforts to fulfill its citizens' needs achieved mixed results, not only due to the GDR's own economic shortcomings but also because the Party was unable to control and regulate needs, desires, and perceptions of scarcity and affluence even within official institutions, let alone among the population at large. The SED's view of consumption as a manipulable process of "need fulfillment" failed to grasp the creation of demand and value through social practices. By the same token, individuals' agency had its own boundaries. Consumers could use numerous means to ameliorate their material circumstances and to voice discontent, but their actions were limited to the level of tactics and proved incapable of overcoming fundamental constraints of the system.[2] While the SED's domination and consumers' agency influenced and mutually limited each other, consumers clearly did not have the upper hand. The limitations of this agency, along with the regime's ability to diffuse popular criticism, help to explain the regime's remarkable stability over the course of four decades. But ultimately, consumers' dissatisfaction and disillusion and the regime's loss of legitimacy even within its own ranks can help to explain the nature and rapidity of the GDR's collapse and unification with West Germany in 1989–1990, although that topic is beyond the scope of this essay.

"In this year we wear everything that fits and suits us and—has survived the chaos of war. When someone inquisitively looks at the new summer dress made from old curtains, then we just laugh coyly over our shoulder . . . and lightly say: 'That's now the latest.'"[3] When these words appeared in the magazine *Die Frau von heute* (Today's Woman), the organ of the socialist women's committees (*Frauenausschüsse*) in the Soviet Occupation Zone, in March 1946, Germans had been experiencing hunger, physical hardships, and devastating shortages for several years and would continue to do so for several more. The ubiquitous slogans entreating con-sumers to "make new out of old," which German officials had propagated during both world wars, encapsulated these common popular attitudes and practices born out of necessity. Both the SED and consumers under-stood such practices as temporary inconveniences that would gradually be superseded by the opportunity to buy an increasing number and wider variety of inexpensive apparel in stores. The 1950s and 1960s witnessed the birth of both high hopes and bitter disillusion as initial promises of a socialist consumer utopia continued to recede into the future.

In a landscape of images of individualistic opulence and stores full of drab, mass-produced garments, consumers used a wide variety of tech-niques to fulfill their needs and desires, whether they were for purely utili-tarian goods to cover so-called basic needs or for apparel that fulfilled desires for social distinction, individual expression, or nonconformity to official or social norms. These consumer techniques can be grouped roughly into the categories of shopping, sewing, networking, and com-plaining, although many techniques fit none or several of these categories.[4] While some of these practices conformed at least superficially to officially accepted norms, others transgressed official boundaries. Although men increasingly participated in the labors of consumption, women remained the primary actors in this sphere.[5]

Shopping

Starting already in the late 1940s and early 1950s, East Germans embarked on shopping trips with very specific desires and went from store to store and even from city to city in efforts to satisfy them.[6] During the first major stage in the elimination of rationing for clothing and shoes in February 1951, a state trade official remarked that "the streets offered an almost peacetime-like picture, that is, women are beginning to select very care-fully and to look around in several stores and no longer is every available ware bought immediately."[7] Officials noted that consumers made only "supplementary purchases" (*Ergänzungskäufe*): they bought "not simply clothing" but rather very specific assortments, styles, and materials.[8]

Even if a consumer found a sought-after garment that was made of the desired material and matched her or his individual tastes, it was often in the wrong size. Until the end of the 1950s, only about one-third of women and girls and 60 percent of boys could find ready-to-wear apparel that fit them.[9] After measuring over seventeen thousand women of various ages throughout the GDR, officials claimed in 1959 that thirty-three new sizes would replace twenty-seven old ones, which would increase the proportion of women who could wear mass-produced apparel to two-thirds. Their goal was 88 percent by 1965.[10]

The specificity of consumers' demands and the limitations of stores' offerings combined to make shopping an extensive "running around" (*Herumlauferei*) that all too often met with the proverbial response of sales personnel: "*Hamwanich*" (don't have it).[11] The author of a Berlin newspaper article in 1956 provided an account of typical shopping frustrations:

> In Treptow a young girl recently bought a nylon blouse. It was as if she had found a needle in a haystack; for during the last quarter there were only 2 (two) nylon blouses in stock in the HO [Handelsorganisation] stores in the Treptow district.
>
> An expectant mother who wanted to buy herself a tasteful maternity dress had to run through all of Berlin. She was offered a bilious green silk dress and some still more tasteless models.
>
> The young women . . . who in the HO voice the wish to become owners of shoes with the newly popular stiletto heel (9 cm high), get only a sympathetic look from the shoe saleswomen.
>
> For the tea-dance, for the theater one prefers the little evening dress. To inquire about that in the HO borders on frivolity. Certainly, there are silk dresses available—but, oh, only little innocent dresses [*Kleidchen*]. And the Berlin woman was once known for dressing in smart and chic ways.
>
> Despite the progress over the previous year, one can say of Berlin: There is certainly clothing available, but no dresses.[12]

To increase their chances, many shoppers visited stores every week or two or tried to find out when shipments arrived in order to be among the first to peruse the new goods.[13]

Many consumers considered the time, effort, and frustration spent in searching for specific items far more costly than the goods' price in marks. A cartoon in the satirical magazine *Eulenspiegel* captured these sentiments: a woman asks a man, presumably her husband or boyfriend, "what did the seamless stockings cost, Peter?" to which he replies, "above all else perseverance."[14] Prices, however, did influence consumers' purchasing decisions. Shoppers searched not only for desired articles but also for a fair price, in which perceived value and price stood in proper relation to each other. Market researchers and other state and Party officials were well aware of the fact that price was one of the prime reasons for consumers' dissatisfaction with and reluctance to buying most of the apparel in East German stores.[15]

Consumers' abstinence from purchases, combined with the dysfunction of the GDR's economy, caused the growth of enormous stockpiles of unsold consumer goods in stores as early as 1949. Called *Überplanbestände* (stock in excess of the plan) in SED jargon, these unsold wares formed a highly visible and palpable manifestation of the regime's failure to fulfill the needs and desires of its citizens. Surpluses also represented an expression of consumers' limited agency—of their tactic to not buy products that failed to match their wishes, expectations, and perceptions of value and a fair price.[16]

Shopping was significantly more difficult in small towns and the countryside. Since goods generally were concentrated in stores in larger cities, rural inhabitants had to travel to the nearest district capital or even to Berlin to improve the chances of finding the objects of their desires. Trade officials experienced only limited success in their efforts to improve this situation by occasionally traveling through the countryside selling wares out of trailers or holding special sales at market places.[17] The media often joined consumers in demanding that rural areas receive their fair share of the goods, both in terms of quantity and quality.[18]

The regime tried to address this problem through the introduction of a mail-order catalog in 1956. Despite claims that this more efficient and rational retailing technique would lead to improved provisioning, it suffered from the same problems that beset the rest of the GDR's economy. In addition to chronic problems of supply, the mail-order service failed to limit and specialize itself for its target audience. In 1961 the consumer cooperatives established their own mail-order catalog, *konsument,* which was intended for the rural population, while the *centrum* catalog of the state-owned Handelsorganisation (HO) featured more modern and chic models targeted to urban customers. But this differentiation existed only in the pages of the catalogs. Both rural and urban consumers placed orders for the same or similar items with both mail-order services in the hope of increasing their chances of receiving anything at all.[19]

The satisfaction of consumer demand was "mostly a matter of pure chance," as top Party officials noted in 1960.[20] An author in *Frau von heute* exclaimed in 1953, "if one could for once buy in the HO with a set shopping plan! Mostly one gets the long-sought-after sweater precisely when one went out to buy dress material or something similar."[21] Despite the tendency for grassroots reports on consumption to become rosier as they percolated up from the bottom, even Central Committee officials knew that "the population is indignant about the fact that it is obliged [*genötigt*] to 'scour' ['*Abgrasen*'] stores in order to satisfy their wishes to some degree. Many or even most sales occur only because customers give up [*resigniert*], they buy because they do not believe that they will come upon the ware that they actually would like to have."[22]

The centrality of serendipity to shopping encouraged impulse buying, which ran counter to the SED's ideal of rational, planned consumption.[23] Claiming to share shopping frustrations of normal consumers, Bruno Leuschner, chairman of the State Planning Commission, joked at the Textile Conference in 1960 that "one wants to get underwear in a store and must leave with a tie because the right size is not there. I experience the same thing: I'm a size five, and only sizes four and six are there. What should I do there? I buy myself a tie!"[24] Sporadic and random deliveries of seasonal items also contributed to consumers' impulsiveness.[25] Market researchers estimated that at least 40 percent of East German consumers were "impulse buyers" when confronted with "interesting articles" and worried that they might miss the opportunity to obtain a certain article "if they don't immediately grab it and buy."[26] Most prone to buy impulsively, according to market researchers, were consumers with higher incomes who had more disposable income and certain groups—such as women who worked full-time, youth, and white-collar workers—who had "higher standards" and were dissatisfied with normal offerings.[27]

Many of the motivations to buy impulsively also underlay the tendencies of hoarding and panic buying, which flared up particularly during times of political uncertainty—most notably after the construction of the Berlin Wall on 13 August 1961.[28] But also under normal circumstances even false rumors of a shipment of particularly desirable or imported goods could create huge crowds at stores in a matter of hours.[29] So-called irrational consumption could take the less dramatic form of buying two or three pairs of nylon stockings, for instance, just because one happened to find several of a certain style or color, even though one planned to wear them one at a time until they wore out.[30] Another reason to hoard was the fear of "creeping inflation" or rumors of a price increase.[31] A different form of hoarding consisted of keeping an article of clothing for years after it was no longer worn: one never knew whether one might need it again or could use the fabric to make another piece of clothing.

Consumers' searches for apparel were not limited to the territory of the GDR before the construction of the Berlin Wall. West Berlin offered East Germans additional and generally more fertile hunting grounds. Surveys of GDR citizens caught illegally bringing Western goods into East Berlin revealed a mixture of motivations, including price, fashion, quality, and variety of available goods.[32] Despite an exchange rate of at least four East German marks to one West German mark, West German shoes and clothing still cost on average only about 40 to 60 percent as much as similar articles in East Germany. East German officials were also well aware of the fact that consumers' desires to keep up with the latest fashions were as important as price considerations.[33] But East German customs agents could hope to catch only a fraction of the illegally "imported" goods, and there are indications that enforcement was sometimes lax.[34] Alongside those who shopped in West Berlin for themselves were many others, both East and West Germans, who smuggled large quantities of goods into the GDR and sold them on the black market. Everything from fashionable zippers to cheap West German copies of Italian designs flowed into East Germany in significant quantities.[35] Smuggling of everything from nylon jackets to fashion magazines continued, although greatly diminished, even after the construction of the Berlin Wall.[36]

A purchase, however, did not necessarily mean the complete satisfaction of a wish or need. This fact found expression in the large percentage of women who modified their store-bought clothing in some way, whether adjusting length or width, dyeing, or bleaching. Market researchers estimated in 1971 that approximately two-thirds of women's industrially manufactured garments were altered in width or length before being worn.[37] Consumers altered clothes both to make them fit and to conform to fashions.[38]

Sewing

Given stores' unsatisfactory and poorly fitting offerings, it is not surprising that store-bought clothing accounted for a relatively modest proportion of East Germans' wardrobes. Although market researchers lacked data for the 1950s and early 1960s, they noted in 1963 that the GDR lagged behind other countries in the relation between production of ready-to-wear versus cloth sold by the meter: the GDR's ratio of 80 to 20 compared unfavorably with the FRG's ratio of 90 to 10 and the United States' ratio of 93 to 7.[39] Not until 1966, however, did market researchers abandon "the generally prevailing opinion" that 60 to 70 percent of the demand for outerwear was

satisfied by industrially produced garments.[40] The percentage was in fact
much lower. In 1967 researchers conservatively estimated that the 40 million pieces of industrially manufactured ready-to-wear that stores sold each
year were complemented by at least 30 million pieces of outerwear that
stemmed from "other sources."[41] In some assortments, particularly of
women's outerwear, East German store-bought clothing accounted for as
little as one-third of total consumption.[42] The relatively modest proportion
of store-bought apparel in East Germans' wardrobes reflected the preva-
lence of alternatives, including having garments made by tailors, acquaintances, or friends; sewing or knitting oneself; buying or receiving used
clothes; and receiving apparel in packages from the West.[43]

In the 1950s and into the 1960s, a still common and relatively affordable alternative to buying ready-to-wear clothing in a store was to hire a
tailor to personally fit and make one's apparel by hand. Using cloth either
sold by the tailor or obtained by some other means, this option offered the
most individual and best-fitting solutions to sartorial desires.[44] By 1956 the
regime reconsidered its initial encouragement of this practice after realizing that the relatively insignificant price difference between ready-to-wear
and hand-tailored apparel shifted demand in favor of the latter.[45] While
still common, hiring a tailor became increasingly difficult during the 1960s
as the regime raised the prices of custom-made clothing and forced tailors,
along with many other craftsmen, out of business.[46]

Much more common than going to a tailor was sewing or knitting
clothes oneself or having relatives, friends, or acquaintances make them.[47]
Home dressmaking illustrates well how the borders between acts of production and consumption blurred in everyday life in the GDR.[48] Throughout the history of the GDR, consumers continued the practices, common
in times of emergency or scarcity, of "making new out of old" and of using
a variety of ingenious techniques to improvise solutions to their sartorial
problems, needs, and wishes. These practices included repeatedly refash-
ioning a dress to give it a "new" appearance; designing "changeable
dresses" that transformed shapes and functions by the subtraction, addition, or moving of parts; and lengthening or shortening the hem of an old
dress to fit new fashions.[49] Just as women had fashioned dresses out of military uniforms, linens, or curtains during the immediate postwar period, at
the end of the 1960s women improvised solutions appropriate to that time,
for instance, making outerwear out of otherwise scarce and expensive
Silastic, which was sometimes used to cover cheap pillows and cushions.[50]

At least one-third of women's and girls' outerwear articles were individually made. The share could reach as high as three-fourths for assort-ments that were easy to make or that were particularly scarce in stores.[51] A study in 1971 found that 56 percent of East German women owned at least one individually made dress; the percentages were 49 for skirts and 33 for blouses.[52] Individually made clothing generally constituted a very large proportion of the wardrobes of women who owned at least one such arti-cle.[53] Self-made items were less common in men's and boys' wardrobes, market researchers claimed, due to the higher degree of skill required to make such articles (like suits), the greater expense to have them made by a tailor, the relative ease with which men and boys found clothing that fit them, and men's and boys' lesser concern with dressing fashionably.[54]

Although reliable data were scarce and difficult to compare, market researchers estimated in 1973 that the absolute volume of individually made clothing had remained constant or increased since 1959. Despite a slight decline in their relative share of all clothes worn due to the increased volume of industrially made clothing, one-fifth of all outerwear and one-third of all knitted outerwear still were made individually. The figure was almost 60 percent for women's outerwear and children's knitted outer-wear.[55] Contrary to the SED's promises and hopes, both the absolute vol-ume and the relative share of individually made clothing only increased during the 1970s and 1980s, right up to the end of the GDR.[56]

Since virtually all homemade garments, regardless of the wearer's gender, were made by women, home sewing was an important issue in the regime's policies regarding women. From the beginning, official propa-ganda promised to help lighten women's task of producing clothes for themselves and others in the home. Numerous consumer magazines pub-lished paper patterns for everything from aprons to evening gowns.[57] Although many officials admitted in the late 1940s and 1950s that home sewing generally represented an involuntary practice that was necessary to compensate for the supposedly temporary shortcomings of the GDR's textile and garment industries, much of the official discourse either claimed that the practice was totally voluntary or tried to make a virtue out of this necessity. Texts that accompanied paper patterns in consumer magazines often boasted that they were enabling women to realize their "dreams" or were providing those who preferred to give their clothing "a personal touch" with "inspirations" for unique and fashionable models.[58] Official discourses also alluded to stereotypically Protestant values by praising home sewing and knitting as a "meaningful free-time occupation" (*sinnvolle Freizeitbeschäftigung*). But implicit in such statements was the admission that women had to compensate for the shortcomings of East German industry.

By the end of the 1960s, market researchers and others increasingly attacked myths about homemade clothing and argued that it caused economic waste and directly contradicted many of the SED's ideological and social welfare goals.[59] The regional chair of the SED's mass organization for women, the DFD (Demokratischer Frauenbund Deutschlands), in Berlin asserted in 1968 that the reason for the increasing number of women enrolled in tailoring courses was "not because they view it as their hobby! We also don't see it as the solution for trade and economic functionaries' absent feelings of responsibility."[60] A survey of the readers of the women's magazine *Für Dich* in 1968 revealed that although 64 percent of all women sewed "a large portion of their wardrobes" themselves, only 4 percent listed tailoring as a "hobby."[61]

Far from being a "useful free-time activity," home sewing and knitting robbed women of much of their precious free time and represented an economically inefficient use of their labor. Market researchers estimated that the GDR's households spent 210 to 300 million hours per year on hand-knitting outerwear alone, which was equivalent to either 80,000 to 125,000 laborers working forty-eight hours per week or almost one hour per week for every household.[62] Market researchers also demonstrated that, contrary to common assumptions before the late 1960s, home sewing was actually more prevalent among working women and those with higher incomes than among housewives and those with lower incomes.[63] Researchers asserted that these unexpected and undesirable findings demonstrated that the GDR's industrially produced apparel was not meeting the "higher standards" and "demands" of women who worked and had higher incomes.[64] Unless stores' offerings improved, market researchers warned, the situation would worsen as incomes continued to rise. At the beginning of the 1970s, the regime seemed to be as distant as ever from the fulfillment of its implicit and explicit promises to eliminate the need for home sewing for all women by providing plentiful, inexpensive, and attractive industrially produced apparel.

Since stores' offerings did not significantly improve, consumers often complemented the active techniques of shopping and sewing with more passive practices, including abstaining from purchasing apparel in stores, waiting for something better, or substituting something else for the article that they originally desired. These practices also required a significant amount of work. In the early 1960s, market researchers concluded that many if not most consumers repeatedly patched or refashioned articles of clothing and wore them to the point of almost complete physical deterioration.[65] Even after they were no longer worn, garments were seldom discarded but instead kept for years either untouched at the back of wardrobes or transformed into cleaning or polishing rags.[66] Despite claims that variables like the weather significantly affected sales, researchers concluded that consumers had little freedom and that a purchase often represented less a positive choice for an article of clothing than the result of a "no longer postponable utilitarian necessity."[67]

Networking

Informal networks complemented the techniques of obtaining or making desired goods.[68] Most of the evidence on the social practices associated with these networks is indirect: recorded discussions of "connections" or "relationships" (*Beziehungen*) came primarily from those without them who resented those with them.[69] While almost everyone probably used some kind of informal relationship to procure scarce goods, any single individual might have more or fewer connections—for example, access to spare auto parts but no immediate channel for fashionable dresses. Frustration or resentment over a lack of connections nevertheless was a common theme in consumers' complaints:

In the Konsum store no aunt	*Beim Konsum keine Tante*
In the H.O. store no relatives	*Beim H.O. keine Verwandte*
From the West no package	*Aus dem Westen kein Paket*
And you still ask me how	*Und da fragen Sie mir noch*
I'm doing.	*wie es mir geht.*[70]

The type of "relationship" that seems to appear most frequently in official documents, published articles, and citizens' petitions is the one between salesperson and customer. In what appeared to be its most common form, salespeople would hold desired products "under the table" for certain customers when a shipment arrived and allow them to try on apparel in the back room. These connections could stem from family relations, repeated encounters and friendly conversations, small tips or bribes, or past quid pro quo.[71] Officials and the media periodically criticized these practices. The newspaper *Neue Zeit* complained that one could obtain the

Institute for Clothing Culture's chic models only through "relative-like relationships with the corresponding HO-managers," while Paul Fröhlich, first secretary of the district of Leipzig and a member of the Politburo, joked that "like the old Germanic tribes," there also was barter under the store counters of the GDR.[72]

The black and "gray" markets of the immediate postwar years made up another type of informal network, one that continued in a modified form after the establishment of the HO and the lifting of formal rationing.[73] The unofficial economy consisted primarily of goods smuggled from the West or hoarded East German goods, and participants could either use money or barter. Women with tailoring skills often worked on the side, either as favors or for pay. The packages from West Germany that already had flowed eastward in the 1950s became even more important after the building of the Wall and represented a significant method of obtaining scarce wares.[74] Western apparel could enter circulation in the GDR through a number of other channels: retirees who had traveled to the West often returned with goods, relatives and friends brought gifts during visits, and other Westerners sold items on the GDR's unofficial used clothing market.[75] Market researchers estimated that in the mid-1960s as much as 20 to 30 percent of all clothing in circulation in the GDR came from the West; for some assortments the proportion was even higher.[76]

Western clothing served as both a valuable source of sometimes desperately needed goods and a highly prized means of social distinction, although evidence of this seldom appears in written sources. In fact, the role of Western clothing in the provisioning of the East German population was so sensitive that only a very limited number of functionaries in the Institute for Market Research had access to top-secret analyses of gift packages from West Germany that began to be conducted in 1966. The researchers themselves had to indirectly estimate the extent of the presence of Western clothes by comparing their data on the size of consumers' wardrobes with stores' sales and estimates of individually made apparel.[77] The importance of West German apparel in dressing East Germans remained high during the 1970s and dramatically increased during the 1980s. The estimated value of the clothing that arrived in packages alone represented at least 20 percent of the GDR's retail sales and increased from 2.2 billion marks in 1978 to 3.9 billion marks in 1988.[78]

Informal networks and relationships—whether with sales personnel or relatives in the West—did not necessarily correspond to income, social group, profession, place of residence, or party membership. These networks thus added a certain element of randomness to privilege and access to scarce commodities.[79] A woman with a higher income was able to afford a greater quantity and quality of clothing made in the GDR, but she still may have been envious of someone with less income who wore Western apparel received from relations in the FRG. The dress bought in the Exquisit boutique for hundreds of marks did not necessarily bring more social distinction than the jeans received in a package from the West. Party functionaries were privileged in many ways, but they lacked one of the most distinctive and prestigious sources of consumer goods because they were expected to sever all personal connections with the West.[80]

Complaining

When other methods of acquiring or making apparel proved too ineffective or frustrating, consumers wrote letters of complaint to Party and state institutions, manufacturers, trade organizations, editorial boards of magazines and newspapers, and, starting in the 1960s, the television show *Prisma.* In February 1953 the regime established the first laws governing the treatment of both oral and written petitions (*Eingaben*) to official institutions, including required response times.[81] Often with much humor, sarcasm, and wit, consumers used petitions as a vent for anger and frustration and, more important, as yet another technique of obtaining needed goods. As sources that offer insights into both consumers' quotidian practices of consumption and discourses about the respective responsibilities and rights of consumers and the regime, petitions reveal much about the relationship between state and society in the GDR.[82]

A letter dated 25 April 1967 from Magda G. to *Prisma* offers a good example of how petitions often contained thick descriptions of consumers' practices, frustrations, and expectations. Since January, Magda had been running around in vain in search of three items that she desired for her wedding scheduled for Whitsun: a white nylon petticoat, size 40; a nylon shirt; and a pair of white heels, size 37. "To the first two articles," Magda reported, "for weeks I was told only one word, 'export-obligations'. I understand that and resolved to be more simple in my wishes." She said she even would have been willing to give up her wish for white heels if her dress were not already finished, but no amount of "understanding" could bring her "to wear black, green, or red shoes with a white dress." For weeks she had searched for white heels in her size in every shoe store in her hometown of Fürstenwalde (including the Exquisit store), in the nearby cities of Frankfurt and Erkner, in the "many small towns of her work area," and even in Berlin. As a "working woman," she wrote, "you will understand that I unfortunately lack the time to travel every week to our capital," especially because she had an irregular work schedule and was unwilling to sacrifice her annual vacation time. "Is my wish unusual or has the fashion suddenly changed?" she added sarcastically.[83]

Magda's story featured one of the most common themes of petitions and complaints in the media: futilely "running around" in search of "simple" or "basic" items. Like Magda, many complainants noted that this enormous waste of "valuable time" contradicted the SED's emphasis on economic rationality and its promise to lighten the burdens of working mothers while ensuring that all workers gained more leisure time.[84] "My wife and I have been searching for weeks for a woman's suit in black in size g 94," wrote Ernst S. from the small town of Lohmen in 1967. "I don't want to count the cities of Mecklenburg, let alone the stores, that we visited in vain. If I calculate the travel and the time, I could definitely already pay for a suit with the resulting expenses! Is that economical?"[85] After abandoning their futile searches, many consumers resented having to waste additional time, money, and energy on improvising their own solutions. In a letter to *Prisma,* Margarete L. from Eisenach described having to balance her responsibilities as a mother of four with searching for children's clothing in stores "at least once a week" for several months. Margarete ended up having to sew a pair of boy's pants and refashion girl's ski pants into boy's ski pants herself, "which was really only an emergency solution." Some of the items for which she was searching were available in stores but at prices that Margarete considered too high, especially compared to prices "a few years ago" for the same items.[86]

The regime's own propaganda exacerbated consumers' anger about the gap between official promises and everyday reality. The "object of the misery" of Gertraude L.'s months-long search, she wrote, was "not some exaggerated demands, but rather very simply *plain, dark gray bouclé* that one repeatedly presents to us as exhibition pieces in convention centers, exhibition halls, and store windows."[87] After receiving an unsatisfactory form letter from the manufacturer of the women's dress "Anchor and Steering Wheels" featured in *Für Dich* in 1965, Ilse G. asked *Prisma,* "why doesn't one forbid the magazines to publish such fashionable dresses?"[88] Consumers also complained to official institutions that fashion propaganda and stores' offerings did not reflect socialism's claims to fulfill the needs of individuals of all different ages and body types. The infamous uniformity of East German clothing was a favorite subject of sardonic articles and cartoons in the media (fig. 1). Heinz M. from Wilthen, who said he was forced to wear women's sweaters due to stores' poor offerings of men's knitted garments, lamented in 1971: "I still haven't seen a fashion show where one shows . . . something for those of us who are older. Fashion for young people dominates (which certainly is also correct), but we are also still around (for your information: I am 46)."[89] Even paper patterns caused tensions. In addition to errors in the patterns themselves that rendered them useless, women often lacked the appropriate material: "what use to us are the wonderful models when we lack the material for the most beautiful ones?"[90] The effect of such displays was—to quote a local Party leader—"that our working people are being led by the nose" (*an der Nase herumgeführt werden*)[91] (fig. 2).

If consumers finally found a desired article, they often were dissatisfied with its quality or price. The poor quality of goods and the occasional necessity of exchanging items several times contributed to many consumers' sense of moral outrage over a situation that they felt powerless to influence. "You can't at all imagine what one feels like when one gets bad wares each time," Evelin L. wrote to *Prisma* in 1966.[92] Petitioners echoed complaints and parodic cartoons in the press about substandard goods, including socks that developed holes after the first wearing, sweaters that shrank three sizes after the first washing, or shirts with one sleeve longer than the other.[93]

Petitioners often reproduced official rhetoric on the responsibilities and rights of worker-consumers in order to lend weight to their demands for a steady supply of reasonably priced, quality goods. In a petition addressed to Walter Ulbricht in December 1961, the widow E. Falk alluded to her status as a worker and the current official campaign to improve the quality of production before describing several shoddy products that she had bought for her three children. She continued, "after all, one earns one's money not so easily that one can throw it out the window. The prices are high enough already as it is, so that one can demand proper quality for one's money." By invoking official propaganda, Falk, like many other worker-consumers, claimed a right to the fulfillment of the regime's promises: "Now Mr. State Councilor, do I have reason to be angry or not?"[94]

Similarly, consumers invoked socialism's egalitarian principles in protesting the everyday realities of unequal distribution and access to goods. Many complainants claimed that stores were full of items that were

„Hattest du das so in unserem Vertrag verstan-
den: in Farben sortiert?"

Fig. 1. **"Did you understand it like that in our contract: sorted in colors?"**
(From Katja Keppke, "(UN)VERTRÄGLICHES," *Handelswoche,* 20
October 1964, 5. Courtesy Konsumverband e.G.)

appropriate for and would fit all kinds of people except themselves. In
1969, shortly after the launching of the GDR's Youth Fashion Program,
Elsa F. complained in a petition that most of the garments in department
stores were in "mini-style" and suited only youth. The few other models
were appropriate only for particularly "chubby" women or "older grand-
mothers." Faced with these extremes, Elsa asked, "Where does one find
offerings for the working woman between 40 and 60 who is absolutely not
fat and old-fashioned but is rather often slender and would also like to
dress modernly?"[95] At the same time, however, most complaints about the
sizes of clothing in stores appear to have come from women looking for
the larger ones.

The highly publicized but unsuccessful campaign to produce special
models for "stronger women" made larger women feel all the more
justified in complaining about the regime's inability to fulfill their sartorial
needs and desires.[96] Women complained that, if they found articles that fit,
they often were not tasteful or appropriate to their ages (fig. 3). "Many
dresses in [size] m 94 were very womanly and therefore did not at all match
my taste," Gerlinde H. explained. "I'm 26 years old and would like to
appear somewhat youthful in [my clothes] and not already look like 35 to

„Gestatten, Deutsches Modeinstitut!" – „Gestatten, Einzelhandel!"

Fig. 2. Cartoon of a fashion show with a man introducing a dress from the German Fashion Institute (*left*) and another from the retail trade (*right*). (From Peter Dittrich, *Eulenspiegel* 6, no. 30 [1959]: 12. Courtesy Peter Dittrich.)

40."[97] Although most women at least superficially accepted officially propagated definitions of "stronger women" and their special status, some larger women refused to be placed in this category and insisted that their bodies were just as "normal" as the ideal, slender one. Unable for years to find a bright summer dress in size 94 large (an "oversize"), Christine S. from Döbeln wrote, "I am employed in the theater, have a normal figure (chest and hips 112 cm, waist 79 cm), am 1.69 m tall, and 32 years old." Her mother was a "normal" size 82 and could find "a large selection during every season." But since the models and colors were generally very youthful, "judging from the clothing one could take me for the mother and my mother for my daughter!"[98]

Other groups of consumers also complained that they were disadvan-

„Gab's gerade in meiner Größe"

Fig. 3. "They happened to have it in my size." (From Rudi Riebe, "Immer wieder Kleidersorgen," *Handelswoche,* 27 February 1962, 5. Courtesy Konsumverband e.G.)

taged when it came to access to scarce, high-quality, and fashionable apparel. Those from the countryside and small towns felt as if they were being treated as second-class citizens because they received both quantitatively and qualitatively inferior apparel compared to urban dwellers. Many agreed with Manfred S. and Erich H., who proclaimed, "We as the rural population don't want to stand behind the city, for we are modern people and also would like to dress modernly and advantageously."[99] Similarly, those without "connections" in retail stores or relatives in the West resented these inequalities and the fact that such methods were necessary to obtain even basic goods. Christine S. wrote that saleswomen told her that the summer dresses in her extra-large size were sold "in a flash" as soon as the shipment arrived. "Unfortunately I don't know these saleswomen so well that I could have one of these dresses put aside under the store counter for me when it arrives." She said that such behavior was "repugnant."[100]

But asking relatives or friends in the West for consumer goods could also be problematic. Although cartoons that appeared in *Eulenspiegel* in 1961 can be interpreted as supporting the regime's attempt to persuade East Germans to voluntarily reject West German gifts, they also conveyed the feelings of shame and inferiority expressed by many petitioners.[101] More than simply reproducing official propaganda that deprecated Western products, petitioners' reluctance to write what many called "begging letters" (*Bettelbriefe*) to Western relatives and friends reflected the reluctance and even shame often associated with having to rely on West Germans' noblesse oblige rather than being able to buy even the most basic consumer goods in the GDR.[102] "I could get myself a bra from West Germany," Sigrun J. wrote the editors of *Sibylle* in 1965, "but that would be the wrong way. For I believe that we don't yet have to resort to that and thereby make fools of ourselves."[103] After describing her futile efforts to find women's Silastic stockings, men's long socks, and warm children's underwear, Gerlinde M. asked the Ministry for Trade and Provisioning, "does one need to wonder if 'begging letters' are sent to the West? I ask you, are such things necessary? Must we expose [*bloßstellen*] ourselves in this way?"[104]

Frustration and Disillusionment between Stability and Delegitimation

The connections that complainants made between their specific problems and the performance of the GDR's entire political and economic system demonstrate the potential of consumers' critiques to undermine the regime's legitimacy. In order to understand this potential, petitions first must be placed within the larger context of the GDR's ersatz public sphere in the realm of consumption.[105] Consumers certainly articulated demands and voiced discontent in public, whether verbally grumbling and griping with sales personnel in stores or commiserating with fellow citizens on the street, in factories, or in meetings of various state-sponsored organizations. But these public sites generally involved no more than a few dozen participants at any one time. The East German media also included a variety of often conflicting and critical voices that central authorities failed to completely control. In keeping with the rhetoric and superficial trappings of democracy that was an element of all the GDR's political and social institutions, the media created the appearance of an open public sphere by not only publishing its authors' and readers' criticisms but also encouraging readers to submit their opinions and suggestions and to "vote" on which models they liked most and least.[106]

That does not mean of course that GDR citizens enjoyed freedom of the press. More common than explicit censorship, the media's quotidian self-censorship drew the boundaries of mass-propagated discourses. Unpublished petitions to official institutions generally followed these boundaries and conventions. Like the media's publication and even solicitation of criticism concerning consumption, petitions allowed the regime to register, address, isolate, control, and thus ultimately enervate consumer dissatisfaction and disillusion under the guise of an apparently open, democratic, and responsive forum.[107] Many petitioners' explicit claims to be speaking on behalf of other consumers indicate both the lack of an open public sphere and the widespread willingness to participate in the forum that the regime offered as an ersatz. Statements like "I am certain that this not only affects me but rather many women would rejoice with me" or "I know I address a problem that has long interested our population" suggest a lack of faith in the East German media's portrayal of real conditions and their representation of consumers' true concerns.[108]

Given the dominant position of official discourse in the GDR's ersatz public sphere, it is not surprising that most complaints used its language and accepted its terms. This could work to the complainants' advantage. By voicing their myriad complaints in officially acceptable terms and language, East Germans could highlight the system's inconsistencies and hypocrisy. Most letter writers simply asked for the realization of the SED's own tirelessly propagated ideological, social, and economic goals. Whether published in the press or limited to an exchange of letters between individual consumers and functionaries, complaints by consumers almost never demanded something that had not already been officially promised either explicitly or implicitly. Most consumers insisted that their demands were reasonable and modest, that they already had made voluntary compromises and sacrifices, but that the situation had exceeded what might reasonably be expected of them.

But complaints also helped to stabilize the GDR's political system. By adopting the regime's language in order to ask the state to fulfill official promises and to respect worker-consumers' "rights," East Germans reproduced and stabilized official discourses while practicing a form of self-regulation. Criticisms that remained within the boundaries of the official discursive framework implied that the GDR's entire political and economic system, despite its highly visible and dramatic flaws, was fundamentally sound and legitimate and could be reformed through relatively localized, cosmetic measures.

Petitions further undergirded the regime by enacting and reinforcing a paternalistic relationship between state and citizen. The individual consumer generally presented very specific, concrete problems or circumstances that officials attempted to alleviate or at least to justify and explain. The press often published both consumers' complaints and officials' responses; some common complaints could even serve as the basis for public relations campaigns to improve the offerings of specific assortments like children's clothes, clothes for "stronger women," or women's work clothes in a specific town or factory.[109] Unpublished exchanges of letters between petitioners and functionaries followed the same pattern but could become much more personalized and concrete. State officials ordered manufacturers or retailers to provide complainants with specific articles, met with consumers in their homes to discuss provisioning problems, and even accompanied individuals to stores in search of specific items.[110] Of course the majority of complainants simply received form letters, especially as the number of petitions began to increase dramatically starting in the 1960s. But even form letters displayed extensive efforts to justify the situation by educating consumers and explaining the causes of problems, often with a plethora of "objective" reasons and technical details.[111]

Paternalism also was reflected in the common trope in complaints that provisioning problems would not exist if Party and state leaders were aware of them. One common explanation for leaders' ignorance of problems at the grass roots was the observation that many reports became increasingly rosy as they moved upward through the bureaucracy.[112] Apart from those who sincerely believed the myth of leaders' unawareness, petitioners had various reasons to reproduce it. Petitioners could have reasonably assumed that thinly disguising their complaint as an attempt to alert central authorities to problems at the grass roots would increase their chances of success, for official propaganda often entreated East German citizens to actively contribute to the improvement of economic conditions and promised them material rewards in return. Another motivation for reproducing the myth was the opportunity to sharply criticize the regime without risking prosecution: by claiming that the GDR's benevolent leaders knew nothing of the country's true problems, petitioners could attack the regime without questioning its viability and legitimacy and without impugning individual leaders, tactics that could lead to sanctions, imprisonment, or expulsion.

Other petitioners used the distance between rulers and ruled to highlight resentments of inequalities and the immunity of Party and state leaders to the provisioning problems faced by normal citizens. Such complainants sarcastically argued that certain problems would not exist if those responsible for them also had to suffer. In a petition that complained about the lack of various assortments of children's clothing in 1964, Rudi G. asked, "Did one forget while planning that children also live in the GDR or do the responsible employees of the Ministry [for Trade and Provisioning] have no children?"[113] Feelings of neglect, frustration, and resentment could lead to cynicism about the gap between the government and industry on the one side and normal consumers on the other.[114] Consumers' alienation and underlying currents of paternalism also found expression in the claims of many petitioners that specific incidences had damaged or destroyed their "trust" in official institutions.[115]

Petitioners could underscore their disillusionment and lack of trust in the regime by suggesting that their needs and wishes could be satisfied only by abandoning the GDR's system altogether and turning to West German sources. Although petitioners insisted that they would use Western sources only as an absolutely last resort, this veiled threat implicitly questioned the regime's legitimacy by suggesting that the East German state had failed to fulfill its citizens' basic needs. Margarete H., who like Gerlinde M. searched in vain for Silastic stockings in late 1970, asked, "should we then now write begging letters to relatives in West Germany because of every little thing. . . . No, I don't want that, it would go decidedly too far to issue our honorable state such a certificate of poverty [*Armutszeugnis*] only because of faulty planning in the stocking industry's production." Margarete could not have been too concerned about the GDR's reputation, for she had her husband ask his sister in West Germany for the stockings. In fact, she might have never written her complaint to *Prisma* if the stockings had not been confiscated because the package was addressed to her husband.[116]

Of even greater concern to the East German regime than its citizens' reliance on Western goods was the fact that most East Germans, regardless of whether they had direct connections to the West, used Western products as yardsticks of quality, price, and modernity and complained that the GDR's offerings did not measure up. As local officials in Berlin noted in 1967, especially members of the intelligentsia and youth measure the conditions in both German states and West Berlin only by certain superficial appearances like the number and prices of cars, the quality and prices of textiles and other consumer goods, and therefore do not understand that we in the GDR possess the better societal system in Germany and that socialism is superior to capitalism.[117]

In their very specific and unfavorable comparisons between East and West German goods, many petitioners expressed the hope that East Germans would someday catch up to their cousins in the West.[118] After listing the merits of a pair of children's knee stockings "that an aunt in a city 300 kilometers west of here sent," M. Fischer wrote, "may our production reach this level as soon as possible (at stable or sinking prices)!"[119] She added, "twenty years after the war we must finally come to the point where our German neighboring country arrived already two years after the war, namely to be in the position to deliver perfect quality!"[120] Here, too, many petitioners held the regime to its own promises and often overly rosy propaganda. In 1968 Renate M. asked,

> why are Silastic sweaters and nylon dresses and aprons here in the GDR very expensive in comparison to West Germany? Certainly a substantial part has to do with the fact that food is more expensive in West Germany and thus creates roughly a balancing out. But somehow this must be reflected in the light industry's production of textiles. After all, we have already advanced far with the development of technology and have suggestions for innovations and constantly increasing productivity. That must somehow have an effect on the final consumer price.[121]

By the end of the 1960s, petitioners increasingly made overtly fundamental criticisms of the regime by noting that official promises of progress still remained largely unrealized after two decades of "actually existing socialism." Günter N., the part owner of a half-state-owned textile retail store, spoke for many when he wrote to Party leader Günter Mittag in 1968:

> I myself am sometimes unsettled [*erschüttert*] when I see how on the one hand gigantic industrial plants are built overnight from scratch and how on the other hand we fail and founder exactly on the small

things of life, which however are the "alpha and omega" for our people. One sometimes gets complexes [*Komplexe*] about how and why this can be possible. And yet it is so! And unfortunately not only in the textile sector.[122]

Ernst S., a self-described proud member of the SED since 1954, considered it "simply ridiculous that a comrade in the year 1967, after the successful completion of our Seventh Party Congress, still must make a proposal for such a simple problem" as producing sufficient quantities of oversized women's apparel. "Or are my ideas and demands regarding this too illusionary and too high?"[123]

In 1968, as the regime struggled with yet another of its chronic textile provisioning crises, Ministry for Trade and Provisioning officials at the central level responsible for analyzing petitions noted that high-quality industrial goods and textiles no longer stood in the foreground but that "citizens are increasingly and more decisively opposing the condition that often the simplest articles of daily need are not sufficient or are available only temporarily or in bad quality."[124] But East Germans' conceptions of "basic needs" also had changed during the previous two decades. Goods like nylon stockings that had been luxury items were now articles for everyday use. The flames of discontent about the scarcity and high prices of these items were fanned by the regime's tireless promotion of synthetic materials, the low prices for the goods in West Germany, and the common knowledge that the overwhelming majority of these items were being exported.[125]

Such disillusionment and impatience with official promises to improve consumption were common not only among ordinary citizens but also among members of the SED and employees of state institutions. Magda G., the woman who searched in vain for white heels for her wedding in 1967, was a member of the SED and as a full-time employee of her county's agricultural council often explained provisioning problems to female farmers. "I explained to the women that only so much can be distributed as we ourselves produce, and the better we cover and use all reserves, the better we will live. That is not always so easily believed, but I flatter myself that I accomplished it." She did not tell her female farmers, however, that she privately thought that "white heels were no problem one to two years ago and that we must have produced" enough by now so that "they are not scarce wares."[126] Local officials in and around Leipzig in

1965 received a blunt response when they asked sales personnel why they rarely attempted to argue with customers who made disparaging remarks about East German textiles:

> What are we supposed to say to that? The people are right. The situation here was supposed to change now for years, but until now one can say that not much has changed regarding offerings and prices. We get wares that are more expensive than before because the quality allegedly has improved. The customers are interested in part less in the quality than the prices. They then conclude that everything is becoming more expensive. What are we supposed to then answer as salespeople?[127]

There was little that salespeople could say, especially since they were more inclined to agree.

Through the everyday improvisations of shopping, sewing, networking, and complaining, consumers compensated for many of the shortcomings of the GDR's economy while simultaneously disrupting and distorting the regime's attempts to achieve complete control over production and consumption. But regardless of their creativity and industriousness, consumers still depended to a large extent on the formal system of the GDR's economy. The SED's leadership not only tolerated but even encouraged consumers' informal, unplanned actions because the regime relied on these individual actions at the grass roots to soften the impact of the official system's worst failures and to maintain the economy's ability to function. But consumers' spontaneous actions, which often seemed irrational to state planners, also contributed to the chaos and unpredictability of the official system. This in turn led to the need for further unplanned compensatory actions. The official and unofficial systems thus overlapped, shaping and limiting each other.

The strong connection between the satisfaction of consumers' needs and the regime's legitimacy combined with the meaninglessness of citizens' votes at the ballot box to make the consumption of East German products a highly politicized act: the decision to buy or not to buy, to sew one's own clothes, to go shopping in West Berlin, or to receive goods from Western relatives through the mail formed an indirect plebiscite on the GDR's political and economic system. The official discourse that linked achievement in the sphere of production with rights in the sphere of consumption further politicized consumption and strengthened the feeling of justified disgust when needs remained unfulfilled or the relationship between price and value seemed unfair.

No one consumer engaged in all the practices of shopping, sewing, networking, and complaining. Nor did any one consumer experience all the frustrations that accompanied these activities. Certainly a significant proportion of the millions of purchases made each year resulted in some degree of satisfaction. These successes could result from luck, concerted campaigns to provide certain goods, or lowered consumer expectations. The structure and inconsistencies of the GDR's economy, however, ensured that these successes occurred randomly and were mixed with disappointment and frustration. A woman could be satisfied with her dresses but dissatisfied with her shoes or could be one of the lucky customers present when a new shipment arrived on one day but would have to run from store to store looking for a particular item on the next.

Unwilling and often unable to rely solely on the state to fulfill their needs and wishes, East Germans shaped at least part of their fate in the realm of consumption. This mixture of fortune and misfortune along with the ability of individuals to muddle through their consumption problems help to explain the GDR's relative stability over four decades: socialist consumer culture provided fertile grounds for discontent but seldom brought individuals to the point of utter despair. In the long term, however, the disillusionment, frustration, and resentment inherent in this precarious balance, along with the GDR's economic losses and the SED's loss of political control, ultimately contributed to the regime's delegitimation and destabilization. In addition to helping to explain both the GDR's precarious long-term stability and its sudden and peaceful collapse, the paradox of the codependent and overlapping relationship between state and society illuminates many of the contradictions, inconsistencies, and moments of conflict and consensus that characterized the politics, practices, and culture of consumption in the GDR.

NOTES

This modified and shortened version of chapter 7 from my book, *Fashioning Socialism: Clothing, Politics, and Consumer Culture in East Germany* (Oxford, 2005), is published here with the kind permission of Berg Publishers. I also would like to thank the Social Science Research Council's Berlin Program for Advanced German and European Studies at the Freie Universität in Berlin for a fellowship that supported research for this essay.

1. For arguments about the regime basing much of its legitimacy on promises to fulfill its citizens' needs, not only in the 1970s and 1980s, as many scholars have argued, but already in the 1950s and 1960s, see Stitziel, *Fashioning Socialism,* especially chap. 1.

2. For theoretical discussions of practices and tactics of consumption, see Michel de Certeau, *The Practice of Everyday Life,* trans. Steve F. Rendall (Berkeley, 1984); David Sabean, "Die Produktion von Sinn beim Konsum der Dinge," in *Fahrrad, Auto, Fernsehschrank. Zur Kulturgeschichte der Alltagsdinge,* ed. Wolfgang Ruppert (Frankfurt am Main, 1993), 37–51.

3. R. Kn, "Anarchie im Reich der Mode," *Frau von heute,* March 1946, no. 3: 21.

4. Relying heavily on oral interviews conducted in the 1990s, Ina Merkel has sketched many of these "individual strategies of acquisition," primarily in order to examine their "cultural consequences for the lifestyles of individuals" in the GDR. Ina Merkel, *Utopie und Bedürfnis. Die Geschichte der Konsumkultur in der DDR* (Cologne, 1999), 277–300.

5. For an examination of gendered discourses and societal structures regarding consumption in postwar Germany through the mid-1950s, see Katherine Pence, "Labours of Consumption: Gendered Consumers in Post-War East and West German Reconstruction," in *Gender Relations in German History: Power, Agency, and Experience from the Sixteenth to the Twentieth Century,* ed. Lynn Abrams and Elizabeth Harvey (Durham, 1997), 221–38.

6. See Landesarchiv Berlin (hereafter LAB), C Rep. 106, Nr. 142, Aktenvermerk, Köhler, Planök. Abt., Berlin, 19 March 1949.

7. Bundesarchiv, Abteilungen Berlin, Berlin-Lichterfelde (hereafter BA-BL), DL1/3764/1, 23.

8. LAB, C Rep. 106–01–01, Vorläufige Signatur Nr. T/175, Nickel, IZL Konfektion Berlin, to FR LI, Abt. Örtl. Ind. u. Handw., Magistrat von Groß-Berlin, 4 February 1956, 2.

9. Stiftung Stadtmuseum Berlin, Modeabteilung—Modearchiv (hereafter SSB-MA), SM5–18, 4; BA-BL, DE1/3710, 118.

10. Inge Kertzscher, "Konfektion mit neuen Maßen," *Neues Deutschland,* 12 December 1959; BA-BL, DE1/30278, Industriezweigökonomik der VVB Konfektion, 3/21/2.

11. "Das Modehaus ohne Kundschaft," *Neue Zeit,* 11 November 1956.

12. Elfriede Philipp, "Bekleidung—aber keine Kleider. Ein geheimnisvolles Gremium bestimmt, was die Berlinerin tragen soll," *Die Wirtschaft,* n.d. [1955–56], unpaginated, found in LAB, C Rep. 106–01–01, Vorläufige Signatur, Nr. T/176.

13. Sächsisches Staatsarchiv Chemnitz (hereafter SäStAC), ZWK TuK, Nr. 157, Frau L. Bieler, Sangerhausen, to *Für Dich,* 8 October 1968; SäStAC, ZWK TuK, Nr. 33, Manfred S. [and Erich H.] to Kanzlei des Staatsrates der DDR, Berlin, Judenbach, 23 July 1965.

14. *Eulenspiegel* 8, no. 7 (1961), back cover.

15. Stiftung Archiv der Parteien und Massenorganisationen der DDR im Bundesarchiv (hereafter SAPMO-BA), DY30/IV2/6.09/56, 23–24; BA-BL,

DE1/7073, 25; Bundesarchiv, Abteilungen Berlin, Außenstelle Coswig/Anhalt (hereafter BA-CA), DL102/294, 44–45.

16. For more on surpluses in the GDR, see Judd Stitziel, "Konsumpolitik zwischen 'Sortimentslücken' und 'Überplanbeständen' in der DDR der 1950er Jahre," in *Vor dem Mauerbau. Politik und Gesellschaft in der DDR der fünfziger Jahre,* ed. Dierk Hoffmann et al. (Munich, 2003), 191–204.

17. "Industriewaren rollen aufs Land," *Der Handel* 6, no. 1 (1956): 6–7; "Konfektion im abulanten Handel," *Konsumgenossenschafter* 48/1960: 1.

18. "Mit Barbara im Kaufhaus," *Bauern-Echo,* 25 October 1958.

19. The two mail-order catalogs finally closed their doors in 1974 and 1976, respectively. Annette Kaminsky, *Kaufrausch. Die Geschichte der ostdeutschen Versandhäuser* (Berlin, 1998).

20. SAMPO-BA, DY30/IV2/6.10/29, 8.

21. Madelon, "Farbenfroh und schön woll'n unsere Frauen gekleidet geh'n," *Frau von heute* 8, no. 28 (1953): 11.

22. SAMPO-BA, DY30/IV2/6.10/29, 8.

23. Karl-Ernst Schubert and Georg Wittek, "Zur Aufgabenstellung des Modeschaffens in der Deutschen Demokratischen Republik," *Mitteilungen des Instituts für Bedarfsforschung* (hereafter *MIfB*) 2, no. 2 (1963): 64; SSB-MA, SM9–2, 20.

24. SAMPO-BA, DY30/IV2/2.029/195, Protokoll der ökonomischen Konferenz der Textil- und Bekleidungsindustrie am 22. und 23. April 1960 in Karl-Marx-Stadt, 33/2.

25. BA-CA, DL102/73, 49.

26. BA-CA, DL102/357, 31–32.

27. Ibid.

28. LAB, C Rep. 900, IV-2/6/861, Bericht über die Lage im Handel im Stadtbezirk Treptow, SED-KL Treptow, 22 August 1961; BA-DH, DL1/3995, Analyse über die Versorgung der Bevölkerung mit Schuhen und Lederwaren im Jahre 1961, ZWK für Schuhe und Lederwaren des MHV, Leipzig, 17 January 1962, 11.

29. LAB, C Rep. 900, Nr. IV B-2/6/597, numerous memos from Ruth Schirmer, Abteilungsleiter, Abt. Handel/ÖVW, to Ernst Stein and Konrad Naumann, [SED-]BL, Berlin, in October 1971.

30. SäStAC, VVB T&S, Nr. 474, Evelin L. to Redaktion Prisma, Gersdorf, 17 January 1966.

31. SAPMO-BA, DL30/IVA2/6.10/195, Aus dem Bericht der BL Dresden vom 21.12.1970, 9.

32. BA-BL, DE1/24191, Liste der wichtigsten von Bewohnern des DM-DN-Währungsbereiches in West-Berlin gekauften Waren, 19 January 1955; BA-BL, DE1/5446, 3–4.

33. BA-BL, DE1/24191, Liste der wichtigsten, 1.

34. One of several "market observation reports" from 1959 noted that, while some East Germans returning from West Berlin hid coffee and chocolates in their pockets, many others did nothing to hide bulging nylon net bags and large shopping bags from the West German department store C & A. BA-BL, DL1/3907, 9–10. Illegal clothing and shoe purchases in West Berlin were even easier to conceal since the articles could simply be worn while crossing back over the border.

35. BA-BL, DE1/5446, 2; SSB-MA, RB 1958, Nr. 24, 2.

36. SAPMO-BA, DY30/IV2/6.10/156, 38–40, 93, 100, 125–34.

37. BA-CA, DL102/509, 44; BA-CA, DL102/471, 21–22, Anlage 2, 2; BA-CA, DL102/516, 48. Market researchers found in 1970 that only 22 percent of store-bought clothing for female youths and 45 percent of store-bought clothing for male youths did not need to be altered before being worn. BA-CA, DL102/475, 24, 69.

38. BA-CA, DL102/471, 21–22.

39. BA-CA, DL102/28, 117.

40. BA-CA, DL102/150, 46.

41. BA-CA, DL102/484, 16.

42. BA-CA, DL102/730, 8. A study in 1964 found that the per capita production of industrially manufactured clothing from 1962 to 1964 accounted for only 20 to 30 percent of women's and 30 to 40 percent of men's average wardrobes. BA-CA, DL102/150, 8; Erhard Scholz, "Einige Probleme der Ausstattung mit Herren- und Damenoberbekleidung," *MIfB* 5, no. 3 (1966): 26.

43. BA-CA, DL102/150, 46; Scholz, "Einige Probleme der Ausstattung," 26.

44. BA-BL, DL1/3764/1, 21; "Eine Modenschau 'FÜR DICH'," *Für Dich* 4, no. 47 (1949): 7; Lothar Starke, "Gute Maßkonfektion bringt treue Kunden," *Der Handel* 6, no. 18 (1956): 10.

45. BA-BL, DC20/I/4–184, 29; SAPMO-BA, DY30/JIV2/2A/866, Bericht über die Durchführung des Beschlusses des Politbüros vom 10.3.1961 über Maßnahmen zur Verbesserung der Leitung, Planung und Organisation auf dem Gebiete der Versorgung der Bevölkerung—Teil Preise und Handelsspannen, 26–27.

46. SAPMO-BA, DY30/IVA2/6.09/56, Programm für die Entwicklung des Industriezweiges Konfektion in den Jahren von 1964 bis 1970, 23.

47. Home sewing has a long but largely unexplored history. See Barbara Burman, ed., *The Culture of Sewing: Gender, Consumption, and Home Dressmaking* (Oxford and New York, 1999); André Steiner, "Überlegungen zur Monetarisierung des Konsums in Deutschland im 19. Jahrhundert am Beispiel der Kleidung," *Vierteljahrschrift für Sozial- und Wirtschaftsgeschichte* 86 (1999): 477–503.

48. Scholarship on home dressmaking has begun to complicate the relationship of these two categories but has focused largely on capitalist contexts in the United States and Great Britain. See Burman, *The Culture of Sewing.*

49. A. L., "Mode—?" *Frau von heute* 1 (February 1946): 23; "Drei Variationen," *Für Dich* 1, no. 8 (1946): 6; "Ein Kleid?—Vier Kleider!" *Für Dich* 3, no. 3 (1948): 5; "Wenig Stoff—trotzdem ein neues Kleid," *Für Dich* 4, no. 4 (1949): 7; numerous articles in *Junge Welt* from the mid- and late 1950s with titles like "Drei Kleider—ein Schnitt" and "Aus eins mach fünf"; "Aus Omas Leinenlaken," *Konsum-Genossenschafter,* 24 August 1963, 6.

50. SäStAC, ZWK TuK, Nr. 157, Herbert H., Freiberg, to Radio DDR, Berlin, z.Hd. Herrn Dr. K.-Heinz Gärstner, Freiberg, 7 October 1968.

51. BA-CA, DL102/294, 38; BA-CA, DL102/357, 6, 8; BA-CA, DL102/438, 39, 54–55; BA-CA, DL102/471, 27; BA-CA, DL102/543, 11; Ruth Weichsel, "Die sportlich-legere und kombinierfähige Bekleidung erwirbt die Gunst der Konsumenten," *Mitteilungen des Instituts für Marktforschung* (hereafter *MIfM*) 10, no.

3 (1971): 24; Georg Wittek and Erhard Scholz, "Probleme der Erarbeitung und Umsetzung von Bedarfseinschätzungen," *MIfM* 10, no. 4 (1971): 15; Jörg Börjesson and Hans-Peter Seliger, "Zur Einzelfertigung von Oberbekleidung," *MIfM* 10, no. 4 (1971): 25–29.

52. Börjesson and Seliger, "Zur Einzelfertigung von Oberbekleidung," 27.

53. Ibid.

54. BA-CA, DL102/198, 40; BA-CA, DL102/302, 31; BA-CA, DL102/512, 8.

55. BA-CA, DL102/754, 10.

56. Ruth Weichsel, "Individuell geschneiderte Oberbekleidung—Luxus, Hobby oder 'Notlösung'?" *MIfM* 15, no. 1 (1976); Andrea Hartmann, "Veränderte Bekleidungsgewohnheiten unserer Jungendlichen," *MIfM* 24, no. 1 (1985); Ruth Weichsel, "Die Einzelanfertigung von Bekleidung—ein Maßstab des Versorgungseffekts," *MIfM* 23, no. 1 (1984).

57. See readers' letters in *Frau von heute* 8, no. 2 (1953): 17; Edith, "Wir schneidern uns eine flotte Bluse," *Konsum-Verkaufsstelle*, 8/1954:5. Among the magazines that published paper patterns were *Frau von heute, Für Dich, Praktische Mode* (later *PRAMO*), *flotte kleidung, Die neue Mode, Modische Modelle, Saison,* and *Modische Maschen*. The Verlag für die Frau (Publisher for Women) offered "a few million cuts from around 2,000 models" in 1958. Inge Kertzscher, "Wir blättern in Modeheften," *Neues Deutschland,* 11 January 1958, Beilage.

58. "Hübsche Kleider sind kein Wunschtraum mehr," 4, no. 22 (1949): 31; Edith, "Festlicher Auftakt zur Theater Saison," *Neues Leben,* 9/1953: 44–45; *Die Handarbeit,* 1/1968 and 4/1968, 34.

59. SäStAC, ZWK TuK, Nr. 5, Abschrift eines Leserbriefes von Frau Karla R., Mitglied der ehrenamtlichen Frauenredaktion [der *Aktuellen Halleschen Umschau*] und stellvertretende Kreisvorsitzende des DFD in Halle.

60. Annelies Glaner, "Das Kleid dort auf der Stange," *BZ am Abend,* 15 May 1968.

61. Susanne Kluge, "Wie modern muss die Mode sein?" *für dich* 23, no. 29 (1968): 13.

62. BA-CA, DL102/578, 45, 47.

63. BA-CA, DL102/171, 7; BA-CA, DL102/190, 71; BA-CA, DL102/357, 9; Börjesson and Seliger, "Zur Einzelfertigung von Oberbekleidung," 27; BA-CA, DL102/471, 29.

64. BA-CA, DL102/357, 9, 13.

65. BA-CA, DL102/419, 44, 46; BA-CA, DL102/471, 61–63.

66. BA-CA, DL102/512, 5, 6, Anlage 9.

67. BA-CA, DL102/196, 140; BA-CA, DL102/45, 25, 27.

68. On networks in general see Martin Diewald, "'Kollektiv', 'Vitamin B' oder 'Nische'? Persönliche Netzwerke in der DDR," in *Kollektiv und Eigensinn. Lebensverläufe in der DDR und danach,* ed. Johannes Huinink et al. (Berlin, 1995), 223–60.

69. For a suggestive but problematic use of oral history as a source on informal networks see Merkel, *Utopie und Bedürfnis,* 293–6.

70. Gertrud Krause, "Oma Krauses Start ins Glück," *Frankfurter Rundschau* 30.6.1990 [letter from 15 July 1962], quoted in Christoph Kleßmann and Georg

Wagner, eds., *Das gespaltene Land. Leben in Deutschland 1945–1990. Texte und Dokumente zur Sozialgeschichte* (Munich, 1993), 37.

71. Merkel, *Utopie und Bedürfnis*, 293–96.

72. "Das Modehaus ohne Kundschaft," *Neue Zeit*, 11 November 1956; Sächsisches Staatsarchiv Leipzig (SäStAL), BL Leipzig, IV/2/2/127, 27, 74.

73. The "gray market" resulted from the practice during the early postwar years of paying workers at least partly in kind from the products of the factory in which they worked.

74. Christian Härtel and Petra Kabus, eds., *Das Westpaket. Geschenksendung, keine Handelsware* (Berlin, 2000).

75. BA-CA, DL102/294, 47.

76. BA-CA, DL102/198, 40–41; BA-CA, DL102/323, 36–37, 49, 69.

77. BA-CA, DL102/294, 47–9; BA-CA, DL102/198, 41.

78. Compiled from reports in BA-CA, DL102/Karton 244/VA247 and VA248.

79. Unfortunately the current underdeveloped state of empirical research does not provide much concrete evidence to support these hypotheses. Market researchers almost never asked direct questions about the acquisition or use of Western clothing because they anticipated incomplete or dishonest answers. BA-CA, DL102/198, 16, 23; BA-CA, DL102/294, 47.

80. Top Party leaders, however, enjoyed access to Western goods through other channels.

81. Jonathan R. Zatlin, "Ausgaben und Eingaben. Das Petitionsrecht und der Untergang der DDR," *Zeitschrift für Geschichtswissenschaft* 45 (1997): 902–17; Ina Merkel, ed., *"Wir sind doch nicht die Meckerecke der Nation." Briefe an das DDR-Fernsehen* (Cologne, 1998).

82. Katherine Pence has examined this relationship by analyzing letters written by women to Elli Schmidt, the only woman Politburo member before the June 1953 uprising. While the petitions examined later evidence many of the same rhetorical strategies found by Pence, gender plays a more explicit role in her analysis, perhaps in part due to her focus on Schmidt's role as both a woman and "a bridge" between state and populace. Katherine Pence, "'You as a Woman Will Understand': Consumption, Gender and the Relationship between State and Citizenry in the GDR's Crisis of 17 June 1953," *German History* 19 (2001): 218–52. See also her essay in this volume. The petitions examined in this essay were written by both women and men either to Karl-Heinz Gerstner, host of the television show *Prisma*, or to state and Party institutions, trade organizations, and factories.

83. SäStAC, ZWK TuK, Nr. 124, Magda G., Fürstenwalde/Spree, to Prisma, Fürstenwalde, 25 April 1967.

84. SAPMO-BA, DY34/24904, Präsidiumsinformation und Schlußfolgerungen zu Fragen der Versorgung der Bevölkerung entsprechend dem Präsidiumsbeschluß vom 22.7.1966, Fritz Rösel, Mitgl. d. Präsidiums, Paul Kupke, Stellv. d. Vors. des ZV Handel/Nahrung/Genuß, Abt. Arbeiterversorgung/Arbeiterkontrolle, Berlin, 1 August 1966, 1; SäStAC, ZWK TuK, Nr. 199, Charlotte P., Strausberg to Bundesvorstand des DFD, Antragskommission des 2. Frauenkongresses, Berlin, Strausberg, 7 May 1969.

85. SäStAC, ZWK TuK, Nr. 124, Ernst S., Lohmen, Kreis Güstrow, to

Redaktion des "Neuen Deutschland," Leserbriefredaktion, Lohmen, 24 April 1967.

86. BA-CA, DE4/29248, Margarete L., Eisenach, to Deutscher Fernsehfunk, Redaktion Prisma, Eisenach, 25 June 1964.

87. SäStAC, ZWK TuK, Nr. 156, Gertraude L., KMSt, to MHV, KMSt, 25 April 1968 (original emphasis). For more on implications of the regime's false advertising, see Judd Stitziel, "Von 'Grundbedürfnissen' zu 'höheren Bedürfnissen'? Konsumpolitik als Sozialpolitik in der DDR," in *Sozialstaatlichkeit in der DDR. Sozialpolitische Entwicklungen im Spannungsfeld von Diktatur und Gesellschaft 1945/49–1989,* ed. Dierk Hoffmann and Michael Schwartz (Munich, 2005), 135–50.

88. SäStAC, ZWK TuK, Nr. 32, Ilse G. to Prisma.

89. SäStAC, ZWK TuK, Nr. 292, Heinz M. to Karl-Keinz Gerstner, Deutscher Fernsehfunk, Wilthen, 30 July 1971.

90. "Modische Stoffe in Sicht," *Sibylle,* 5/1957: 66.

91. SAPMO-BA, DY30/IV2/1.01/245, 92–93.

92. SäStAC, VVB T&S, Nr. 474, Evelin L. to Redaktion Prisma, Gersdorf, 17 January 1966.

93. SäStAC, VVB T&S, Nr. 109, Ilse H. to MfL, VVB Textilindustrie, Berlin-Altglienicke, 12.4.1967; SäStAC, ZWK TuK, Nr. 124, Isolde Barth, Abt.-Leiter, Abt. Leserbriefe, Wochenpost, Berliner Verlag, to GHD TuK, Abt. Staatl. Güteinsprektion, KMSt, 2 June 1967.

94. BA-CA, DE4/3000, E. Falk to Walter Ulbricht, Auerbach Vgtl., 17 December 1961.

95. SäStAC, ZWK TuK, Nr. 199, Elsa F., VEB Wäscherei-Färberei-Chem. Reinigung, Görlitz [Antrag Nr. 352 an den 2. Frauenkongreß der DDR].

96. On the campaign to produce special models for "stronger women," see Judd Stitziel, "On the Seam between Socialism and Capitalism: East German Fashion Shows," in *Consuming Germany in the Cold War,* ed. David Crew (Oxford, 2003), 51–86.

97. SäStAC, ZWK TuK, Nr. 124, Gerlinde Hantke to K.-Heinz Gerstner "Prima," Geithain, 13 June 1967.

98. SäStAC, ZWK TuK, Nr. 32, Christine S., Döbeln, [unaddressed, but received by MHV], Döbeln, 23 June 1965.

99. SäStAC, ZWK TuK, Nr. 33, Manfred S. [and Erich H.] to Kanzlei des Staatsrates der DDR, Berlin, Judenbach, 23 July 1965.

100. SäStAC, ZWK TuK, Nr. 32, Christine S., Döbeln, 23 June 1965.

101. John Stave, "Vorsicht: Liebesgaben!" *Eulenspiegel* 8, no. 51 (1961): 8–9; Ina Dietzsch, "Deutsch-deutscher Gabentausch," in *Wunderwirtschaft. DDR-Konsumkultur in den 60er Jahren,* ed. Neue Gesellschaft für Bildende Kunst e.V. (Cologne, 1996), 204–13.

102. This reluctance also may have resulted in part from the difficulty of finding appropriate reciprocal gifts. Dietzsch, "Deutsch-deutscher Gabentisch," 204–6.

103. SäStAC, ZWK TuK, Nr. 32, Siegrun J., Kamsdorf/Saalfeld, to Redaktion "Sibylle," Saalfeld, 11 May 1965.

104. SäStAC, ZWK TuK, Nr. 250, Gerlinde M. to MHV, Kostebrau, 9 December 1970.

105. Ina Merkel and Felix Mühlberg, "Eingaben und Öffentlichkeit," in *"Wir sind doch nicht die Meckerecke der Nation,"* ed. Merkel, 17.

106. Madelon, "Was trägt die Frau 1954?" *Frau von heute* 8, no. 46 (1953): 19; "Modelle stehen zur Diskussion," *Konsum-Verkaufsstelle* 13/1954: 5; "Sie hatten die Wahl," *Sibylle* 4, no. 5 (1959): 10.

107. My interpretation combines aspects of the perspectives of Ina Merkel, who enthusiastically but often uncritically celebrates East German consumers' agency and ingenuity, and Jonathan Zatlin, who stresses the regime's attempts to use petitions as an instrument of domination and suppression of discontent. Merkel, *"Wir sind doch nicht die Meckerecke der Nation";* Zatlin, "Ausgaben und Eingaben."

108. SäStAC, ZWK TuK, Nr. 124, Gerlinde H. to Dr. K.-Heinz Gerstner "Prima," Geithain, 13 June 1967; SäStAC, VVB T&S, Nr. 2177, Barbara J. to VVB T&S, Limbach-Oberfrohna, Halle, 28 July 1964.

109. "Frau Frieda Uszakiewicz aus Zepernick fragt," *Die Bekleidung* 5, no. 1 (1958): 3; "Sibylle schlägt vor: Arbeitsschutzbekleidung für die Bitterfelder Frauen," *Sibylle* 12, no. 2 (1967): 61–69; "Der erste Erfolg. Arbeitsschutzkleidung Kapitel III," *Sibylle* 12, no. 5 (1967): 67; SäStAC, VVB T&S, Nr. 109, various correspondence.

110. SäStAC, ZWK TuK, Nr. 5, Dressel, Hauptdirektor, to Rudi Gitschel, 23 December 1964; SäStAC, ZWK TuK, Nr. 33, Memo from Polzin, Fachdirektor, FD Meterware/Raumtextilien, to Sekretariat, Hauptdirektor, Betreff: Eingabe der Bürgerin Marie F., KMSt, 22 November 1965.

111. SäStAC, VVB T&S, Nr. 2177, Hochmut, Abt. Absatz, to Zeitschrift "für dich," 10 December 1963; SäStAC, VVB T&S, Nr. 109, numerous letters from Teucher and Emmrich, general directors of the VVB Trikotagen und Strümpfe, in 1964 and 1967.

112. SäStAC, ZWK TuK, Nr. 249, Kurt A. to MHV, Frankfurt/Oder, 15 April 1970, 3.

113. SäStAC, ZWK TuK, Nr. 5, Rudi G., Merseburg-Süd to MHV, Berlin, Merseburg-Süd, 3 December 1964.

114. SäStAC, ZWK TuK, Nr. 250, Fritz M., Liebstadt to Dr. Gerstner, 5 November 1970.

115. SäStAC, RdB KMSt, Abt. HuV, Nr. 19423, Herbert D., KMSt, to Manfred Löffler, Stellvertreter des Vorsitzenden des RdB für HuV, KMSt, 10 April 1963; SäStAC, ZWK TuK, Nr. 156, W. Eggert, Berlin-Oberschöneweide to Hauptdirektor Dressel, GH Direktion TuK, KMSt, 5 February 1968.

116. SäStAC, ZWK TuK, Nr. 250, Margarete H., Cunewalde, to Karl-Heinz Gerstner, Prisma, Cunewalde, 22 November 1970.

117. LAB, C Rep. 900, IV A-2/9.01/490, 1. Entwurf zur Einschätzung des Bewußtseins der Berliner Bevölkerung, Berlin, 11 January 1967, 9–10.

118. SäStAC, VVB T&S, Nr. 109, Ilse H. to MfL, VVB Textilidnustrie, Berlin-Altglienicke, 12 April 1967.

119. SäStAC, ZWK TuK, Nr. 124, Barth to GHD TuK.

120. SäStAC, ZWK TuK, Nr. 124, M. Fischer, Neustadt/Orla, to GDH TuK, Generaldirektor, KMSt, n.d.

121. SäStAC, ZWK TuK, Nr. 157, Renate M., Anklam, to Deutscher Fernsehfunk, "Prisma," Anklam, 16 August 1968.

122. SAPMO-BA, DY30/IVA2/6.09/139, Günter N. OHG, Modehaus Güni-Tuche, Glauchau, to Günther Mittag, Berlin, Gauchau Sa., 21 June 1968, unpaginated.

123. SäStAC, ZWK TuK, Nr. 124, Ernst S. to Redaktion des "Neuen Deutschland."

124. SAPMO-BA, DY30/IVA2/6.10/200, Analyse über die Arbeit mit den Eingaben im Verantwortungsbereich des MHV im 1. Halbjahr 1968, n.d. [9 September 1968], 2.

125. SäStAC, VVB T&S, Nr. 2177, Hensel, Abt. Leserbriefe, "für dich," to VVB T&S, 28 November 1963.

126. SäStAC, ZWK TuK, Nr. 124, Magda G., Fürtstenwalde/Spree, to Prisma, Fürstenwalde, 25 April 1967.

127. SäStAL, SED-BL Leipzig, IVA-2/6/285, Information an das Sekretariat, Betr.: Zusammenfassung der Informationsberichte der KL Döbeln, Borna und Wurzen und einiger Stadtbezirksleitungen Leipzig zur Versorgungslage per 30.7.1965, SED-BL Leipzig, Abt. LLI/Handel, Leipzig, 12 August 1965, 5.

Women on the Verge

Consumers between Private Desires and Public Crisis

Katherine Pence

Stemming from the influence of Clara Zetkin, a German socialist pioneer from the early 1900s, streams within the socialist movement voiced a commitment to grappling with the "modern women's question" by enacting women's emancipation throughout society.[1] When the German Democratic Republic (GDR) established a socialist state, however, the actual implementation of such goals was mixed and contradictory in practice. Still, the GDR state's assumption of responsibility for transforming the role of women was one way that the regime was radically modern, even if there were a myriad of ways that the ideal execution of these goals was only partially or not quite fulfilled. On the uneven path toward ostensible liberation, women stood at the intersection of other major modern programs for transforming socialist society.

First and foremost, women became a key element in the construction of the new planned economy. According to the Socialist Unity Party (SED), the primary path to female emancipation would be the recruitment of women into the labor force, a goal that also served the regime's dire need to raise industrial productivity. In addition, following Marxist theory, the establishment of socialist economic relations would take care of the "woman question" since this was supposedly tied to class rather than gender oppression. However, the continuation of women's double burden of paid work and housework pointed out the problems with this thesis. In fact, gendered notions of work became an impediment to women's liberation through employment. Since women were consistently assumed to be the bearers of housework, the goal of integrating women into productive labor was therefore also linked to the problems of alleviating women's household burdens, though this seldom meant redistributing this labor to men. One of the major elements of this domestic labor was the task of shopping for goods that were often in short supply.[2] Problems in the consumer economy constituted one of the major dilemmas for the regime, since empty store shelves or shoddy goods became some of the most visible symbols of the GDR economy's limitations. Frustration with the standard of living in 1950s East Germany contributed to trends of flight from the republic and, at its worst, the mass protest of 1953. As primary household shoppers women stood at the crux of this dilemma as they coped with feeding and clothing themselves and their families on a daily basis. This essay focuses on the interwoven modern projects to transform women's roles in the GDR and to construct a standard of living that would rival that in the West. In the arena of consumer culture, the discrepancies between aspirations of progressive programs and the contradictory realities for women and consumers in general in East Germany were strikingly evident.

I will look at how these issues crystallized during the watershed moment of the crisis of June 1953. In the early 1950s high West German unemployment made it unclear whether West Germany's "social market economy" or East Germany's socialist planned economy would prove better equipped to bring about economic recovery and fulfill newly emerging promises of greater consumer abundance.[3] By 1952, however, the discrepancy between the two states widened markedly. As the GDR started to suffer from more severe commodity shortages, the Korean War boom and Marshall Plan aid helped to speed up dramatic West German recovery. An intensified program in 1952 to build socialism through collectivization of agriculture worsened the East German consumer's situation considerably. In the wake of these problems, the country teetered on the eve of a political and economic crisis culminating in the June 17, 1953, uprising. In this year of turmoil, the limits of the budding socialist consumer economy were tested and the regime had to respond with a New Course, a professedly more aggressive program to help the consumer. The crisis was a pivotal moment in the complex path of development of this GDR consumer culture and the problems it created for the relationship between state and citizenry. Rather than view this uprising as a sign of the regime's deficits of modernity, however, I contend that the crisis was an outgrowth of the difficulties of enacting an ambitious state-directed plan for the modern transformation of society and economy. The extremity of the SED's program of modernization made it especially disruptive, leading to the radical reaction from the population and the violent counterresponse of the GDR and its Soviet benefactors. This essay will examine how women in particular were stuck having to grapple with the problems of this disruption, since they dealt most directly on an everyday basis with shortages and other quotidian economic problems. An emblematic figure for these struggling consumers was Elli Schmidt, an activist in the communist women's movement who became a high-ranking Politburo member assigned to a special commission to handle consumer issues in 1953. As leader of this commission, Elli Schmidt took on a complicated role as liaison between the state and the consumer. In this role she embodied the archetypal female consumer, not only due to her presumed expertise in consumer matters but also because of her conflicted position in relation to the socialist party and ideology.

Shopping for an Alternative Modern

In the postwar shortage economy, consumption became a paramount concern to both the German population and its occupying regimes.[4] The four victorious Allies, France, Britain, the United States, and the Soviet Union, had to reconstruct an economy broken by the ravages of war waged by the Nazi regime.[5] These occupiers were concerned with avoiding the problems Germany had experienced in World War I, when Germans responded to severe shortages with bread riots that contributed to a collapse of the kaiser's regime. They also were anxious that poor living conditions could form the breeding ground for extremist politics, as the case had been with the rise of fascism in the 1930s.[6] At the end of World War I the public protest by hungry consumers—women in particular—helped to forge a new relationship between state and society in which the citizenry demanded just distribution of goods as a right and state legitimacy was more closely linked to standard of living.[7] This development in Germany meshed with an international development of a citizen-consumer, whose relationship to the state was defined in part through mutual duties and rights related to material needs and desires.[8] Consumers' active demands for state intervention to relieve shortages combined with modern state welfarist and productivist programs to regulate, control, or promote consumption throughout the industrialized world in the twentieth century. In alignment with this development, the Allied occupiers in Germany after 1945 each worked to control goods distribution through rationing systems that were cornerstones of economic reconstruction in their separate administrative zones. The two German states founded in 1949 inherited this preoccupation with improving conditions for consumers, even after the end of rationing, as they aimed to restore prewar standards of living and eventually to exceed those standards with a blossoming modern mass consumer culture.

In the Soviet Zone and the GDR planners hoped first to provide just distribution of goods through state regulation, and eventually to foster a more vital modern planned economy, that would produce a more colorful variety of products for the ever-expanding needs of the population. After initial land reforms and implementation of reparations policies that shifted economic power relations in the first years after the war, the Soviet Zone's plans for economic reconstruction took an increasingly divergent path from the West in 1948 when the two halves of Germany established separate currencies. That year the Soviet Zone also launched its first economic plan, the Two-Year Plan, organized under a newly created central institution, the German Economic Commission (DWK). The plan pushed to increase production, especially in the steel, iron, coal, and transportation sectors.[9] At the same time, the SED also claimed a commitment to raising production in consumer industries, especially for much needed textiles and shoes, even though investments didn't support these goals sufficiently. As part of the directed economy, state planners determined the prices and assortments of goods and subsidized basic commodities. In the first Five-Year Plan, starting in 1950, the regime promised to normalize distribution of commodities further by eliminating rationing on all goods by 1953 at the latest.[10] Theoretically, state planning would devise an alternative model of a modern economy that would eliminate the exploitation and alienation associated with the capitalist market.[11]

Still, the continuation of shortages en route to this better future made consumers resort to shopping strategies that fell outside of state control, namely, by trading on the high-priced, illegal black market. In 1948 in an attempt to stop the flow of money to the black market and to create a form of retailing reflecting socialist ideology, the DWK founded a Soviet-style state-owned retailing chain, the Handelsorganisation, or HO.[12] Prices in the HO were set at a higher level than basic goods, just below black market prices, to soak up excess currency and prevent consumers from straying to the shadow economy. The HO became the cornerstone of the GDR's retailing system, supported by the Konsum cooperative chain in rural areas, to pave the way for eventual elimination of private, capitalist stores.

Since the image of progress was so crucial in the founding years of the

GDR, especially as it competed with its Western counterpart, economic functionaries and retailers worked not only to produce and sell more goods but also to improve the quality of the shopping experience. The HO was meant to embody a new ideal of *Verkaufskultur,* or "culture of selling," a concept drawn from the Soviet model that was central to the distinctive socialist path toward modern consumer culture.[13] Verkaufskultur included everything that made shopping a pleasant experience: courteous service, broad selection, pleasing atmosphere, and even modern advertising techniques, such as fashion shows and impulse-purchase displays next to cash registers.[14] In order to shift from merely distributing goods to selling them with this sort of culture, retail trade was supposed to take on the role of liaison between industry and the consumer to represent the consumers' interests while also monitoring their demands and guiding their taste.[15] However, as Judd Stitziel points out, the constraints of the political economy and trade officials' own concerns prevented them from fulfilling the role of consumer representative adequately.[16] Rather, female consumers both acting individually and organized as part of the mass women's organization, the DFD, worked to represent their needs as shoppers to the state and the SED. They sent suggestions and inquiries to the state and Party concerning causes for shortages and demanded economic reforms to bring about greater satisfaction of their material needs and desires.

These women had much to complain about, since the efforts to restore a basic standard of living and then to exceed prewar levels of consumption through modern state direction were not simple or uniformly successful. Rationing was eliminated by 1952 for a few key commodities, such as vegetables, tobacco, ersatz coffee, soap, shoes, and textiles. However, the GDR economy would not be strong enough to end rationing altogether until 1958. The burden of negotiating the gap between the promise of Verkaufskultur and the still existing problems in the economy usually fell to the consumers themselves, especially women. In search of scarce groceries, women regularly stood in long queues and dragged their shopping bags from store to store. The extra burden of shopping under these conditions complicated the ostensible state goal to integrate women more fully into the workforce. The conflicting demands on women in this context were constitutive of their modern dilemma in the GDR.

Historians have often worked to measure the degree and nature of women's emancipation under socialism as a hallmark of its modernity. Indeed, the SED state itself described its own superiority over the West in terms of its liberation of women. It pointed to pioneering legislation such as the Soviet Zone's codification of equal pay for equal work in 1946. The 1950 Act for the Protection of Mother and Child and the Rights of Women legislated the creation of state child care, maternity leave, and the qualification of women for entrance into typically male professions.[17] However, the fixation on employment as the basis for women's liberation meant that there was little effort to rethink or transform women's or men's domestic roles.[18]

Some historians have evaluated the successes of various programs for integration of women into the workforce or social policies designed to aid them in this goal as evidence for modernity or lack of modernity of the GDR. In Konrad Jarausch's volume *Dictatorship as Experience,* for example, the two chapters devoted to the status of women in the GDR take this approach to some extent. Lenore Ansorg and Renate Hürtgen examine the contradictions within the emancipatory potential of women's participation in the East German workforce and define this as an aspect of "modern industrial society" but ultimately point to "relativization" of this modernization through lack of collective action in the public sphere, which they see as a sign of "blocked modernity."[19] Dagmar Langenhan and Sabine Ross examine the serious limits to women's advancement within the professions in East Germany. On the one hand, they concede that the GDR was essentially modern since one of the "stumbling blocks" to the "socialist dream of women's equality" was the "internal tendencies of modern industrialized societies 'to divide work along gender lines.'"[20] But rather than citing the high degree of gender equality in the GDR as a sign of its relative modernity as some studies have done, they identify persistence of "traditional models of gender roles" and suggest that the Party's understandings of modernization "hearkened back to the early days of industrialization." They acknowledge that the results of this development were contradictory but ultimately suggest that the GDR suffered from "delayed modernization."[21] As these evaluations suggest, trying to measure the modernization of women's roles leads to thorny problems of definition.

Certainly the uneven developments of both overt women's policy and everyday practices in GDR society can be examined for specific successes and failures of particular types of policies in comparison to other societies.[22] However, I suggest that the ongoing active engagement with the "modern women's question" in all its fraught manifestations was itself constitutive of GDR modernity. It was not only the successes of progressive initiatives, such as the broadening of state child care, that constituted the modern place of women in GDR society. It was also the ways that women negotiated the gap between explicit promises articulated by the state and everyday reality that was central to their position as modern subjects.

The complexity of women's position in this historical context was prominent in the arena of consumer culture. Politicization of consumption in the GDR integrated women into the socialist community in important ways. For one thing, state policies established official programs to improve consumption labeled as measures for "easing the life of the working woman." On the other hand, consumption was also a common concern that facilitated female political involvement. The DFD and other SED groups recognized and exploited this consumer role to recruit female participants in the organization and in socialist life more generally.[23] It is no coincidence, then, that when the SED needed a functionary to handle the complaints of consumers, a woman took on this task. This woman, Elli Schmidt, stood at the center of the conflicted development of consumer culture and became a representative of the average socialist consumer. She became a major figure mediating the crisis that emerged in the spring of 1953.

Women on the Verge of a Crisis

At the Second SED Party Congress in 1952, Party chair Walter Ulbricht optimistically declared that the main cultural and economic goal of the GDR would be an increased effort to construct socialism. A primary aspect of the new campaign for socialism was greater pressure on the private sector of the economy in order to strengthen the state-owned industries and collective farms.[24] Private retailers lost their merchandise supplies unless they contractually joined the HO system.[25] Self-employed entrepreneurs lost their right to ration cards.

These measures had a severe impact on entrepreneurs and farmers, many of whom protested collectivization or fled to the West.[26] From January to April 1953 around two thousand farmers left their plots of land per month to flee.[27] The flight of farmers westward intensified an already bad harvest in the fall of 1952.[28] The discrimination against private enterprises, which led to many bankruptcies, lowered production and upset the trend of economic improvement. In 1952 and 1953 shortages in butter, vegetables, meat, sugar, and even bread[29] worsened so that rations were shortened for these key commodities and prices rose for unrationed goods.[30] In addition, the GDR economy was strained with increasing amounts of funds invested in militarization, heavy industry, and ongoing reparations to the Soviet Union.[31] West German newspapers reported that the population reacted to these hardships with spontaneous riots in November 1952.[32] The plunge into socialism had pitched the country into a major crisis.

In late 1952 and early 1953, the SED leadership recognized that measures needed to be taken to improve the food and commodities situation quickly.[33] Unfortunately, most of their solutions did little to increase the supply of goods. One response to the economic problems in the GDR was the SED's political tightening of control in 1952. Following the lead of other countries in the Eastern bloc,[34] the SED undertook Stalinist-type purges of those state functionaries who were not members of the ruling Party or who did not tow the line of SED leadership. Notably, thirty-six people were fired from the Ministry for Trade and Supply, including its head, Dr. Karl Hamann, who was accused of sabotaging the consumer distribution system.[35] The Ministry for Trade and Supply in turn blamed the "provisioning chaos" in the HO on its director, Paul Baender, and fired him for ostensibly making unlawful investments in the HO chain outside the control of the planning apparatus.[36]

The SED also introduced economic and propaganda measures designed to cope with shortages. One of these was an austerity program called the "regime of thrift" (*Sparsamkeitsregime*). It was introduced on February 3, 1953, to fix consumer shortages by eliminating inefficiency and waste.[37] To focus on distributing goods to those who were most needed for productivity campaigns, the regime continued a policy of "priority provisioning," or *Schwerpunktversorgung,* which allotted commodities to workers in priority factories, especially in heavy industry. To deal with excess purchasing power among consumers, planners raised HO prices. Some of these measures could have convinced the population that the government was addressing the problem of shortages, but many consumers found these measures confusing, severe, or detached from their real needs and concerns.

As an attempt to bridge the gap between the increasingly angry populace and the regime, on February 3, 1953, the Council of Ministers replaced the Coordination and Control Center for Domestic Trade, which had been established the previous May, with a new State Commission for Trade and Supply.[38] The purpose of this commission was to coordinate the central state planning and leadership of trade and provisioning, but it also had the important function of investigating consumer problems, in particular by fielding complaint and suggestion letters from consumers and retailers. To head this commission, the Council of Ministers chose the only female member of the Politburo, Elli Schmidt, a longtime communist, loyal SED member, and head of the DFD.[39] Her appointment to this committee made her one of the most powerful women in the Party, giving her nearly the rank of a minister.[40] In this new post, Schmidt took on the role of an ideal responsible expert female consumer to hear from average shoppers and to represent their needs. As such she embodied some of the conflicting roles of women within the GDR state as it worked to modernize women's roles and the consumer economy simultaneously.

Gender roles were central to the construction of Schmidt's position. Schmidt apparently was not chosen by virtue of formal economic expertise, since she had been trained as a seamstress. It is not clear whether Schmidt was chosen for this position explicitly because she was a woman, but in her own assessment she pointed to her so-called feminine duties as part of her qualifications. Since the late 1940s, she had used her position within the DFD to call for an improvement of material provisions for women. For example, in 1947 Schmidt had agitated on behalf of housewives who had been grouped into the lowest rationing category; she protested that the administration should help these women by eliminating the so-called hunger card.[41] In the spring of 1953 a speech she made at a local factory in Hohenfichte noted that her years as chair of the DFD qualified her for the chair of the State Commission for Trade and Supply:

> In close cooperation with our working people, especially with you women, I have most directly discovered existing shortages and grievances. I have listened to those who always lead the fight against the inadequacies in provisions. As a woman and mother, I found out first about the shortage of diapers and baby clothes. When I wanted to buy socks and shoes for my children, I experienced [firsthand] what was the problem. Now I have been obligated to deal with these problems myself and to bring about reforms.[42]

Such an assessment suggests that government functionaries may have assumed, like Schmidt herself, that not only due to her political agitation through the DFD but also by virtue of her daily domestic activity, she, like other women, was a "natural" expert in consumer matters. When Schmidt assumed her position as head of the commission she began receiving letters from disgruntled female shoppers that made it clear that they too saw Schmidt this way and even claimed authority themselves as consumer experts justified in offering advice to the regime.

Schmidt began receiving letters as soon as she attained her position in February and got even more as the commission began to announce new agendas for improving trade in May.[43] The numerous letters that Elli Schmidt received during her tenure as the commission's head laid out in detail the kinds of problems plaguing consumers and shopkeepers in 1953 on the eve of the June 17 uprising. These letters ranged from sketches of chronic shortages and poor-quality goods to critiques of economic ministries. The letters offer insight into not only the nature of these problems but also how average citizens mobilized rhetoric to fashion themselves as valuable participants in socialist life so that their complaints might be heard. The letters, therefore, reveal ways that the citizens of the GDR forged a relationship with the state.

This epistolary relationship between state and citizenry was codified in the GDR as a right of consumers to appeal to the highest authorities. "The Directive about the Examination of Suggestions and Complaints of Workers," issued in the same month as the establishment of the State Commission for Trade and Supply, provides further evidence of this trend. The directive guaranteed the legal right for average citizens to write letters (*Eingaben*) to government officials asking for help with their daily problems.[44] While this law carried on a tradition of appeals to the government already accepted earlier in the century, this new law also supplied citizens' right to receive an answer to their queries in a reasonable amount of time. The right to petition became perhaps the central means of appeal to the government when problems arose. The letters even helped influence policy in some cases.[45] The letters to Elli Schmidt are particularly revealing, because writers appealed to her not only as a high-ranking party official but also as a woman.

The letters illustrate how the often wary population worked through the new conditions of consumption brought by the transition to socialism. Some petitioners' resentment indicated growing popular awareness of one of the central paradoxes of the modernization of socialist consumption: despite a claim that socialism would bring ultimate equality and democracy, the system also featured extremely hierarchical methods of distributing scarce consumer goods. In addition, many women saw the gap between socialism's claim to bring female liberation and the reality of ongoing gender discrimination in their everyday lives. At the same time, the letters displayed an acute consciousness of how the writers were expected to fit into the new socialist community.

Many letters to Elli Schmidt reflected consumers' responses to specific material shortages. They complained that supply was limited for such food as butter, sugar, and vegetables or such clothing as diapers and shoes.[46] One letter expressed a "desperate need" for "cooking pots for single people, as well as enamel scrub-buckets, which are absolutely not to be had!"[47] Often the available goods were of discouragingly bad quality. One woman complained that the only rubber boots on the market were made out of the synthetic material Igelit, which could irritate the skin of children.[48] Another woman complained that in February 1953 she bought a coat that immediately started to tear and lose its lining.[49]

Consumers expressed resentment not only of shortages per se but also of the structural innovations of the socialist planned economy that sometimes worsened shopping conditions, in their view. One of the main principles of the planned economy was the replacement of free market forces of supply and demand with price setting by central administrators. Prices were set according to a two-tier system. Rationed goods were offered at subsidized prices meant to provide distribution of basic needs to the majority of the population.[50] HO goods were sold without ration cards at higher prices. Despite copious propaganda designed to inform the population of reasons for these pricing policies, prices still often seemed unreasonable and arbitrary to the population, especially when prices had to be increased. In some ways protest of high prices in the GDR paralleled similar protests in West Germany from consumers who wanted politicians to exert more economic controls.[51] But in the GDR, shoppers were angry at the way that these state controls were executed seemingly arbitrarily. Shoppers were also annoyed when the HO offered expensive products like whipped cream or pastries and other confections made with butter that most GDR citizens could not afford at a time when plain butter was not even available with rations.[52]

Another centerpiece of the GDR's program for industry was the coupling of productivity campaigns with material rewards. Consumers also protested these policies, which privileged certain workers in key heavy industries (*Schwerpunktbetriebe*). Letters of complaint revealed bitterness when workers in one industry heard they were excluded from special rations of scarce fats given only to more "valued" workers.[53] One letter from a small factory in Waldheim complained that the workers there did not receive the same goods as other workers at Schwerpunktbetriebe, such as a pound of margarine per worker or rare lemons. These disgruntled workers warned that such "sabotage of our work" would lead employees to refuse to pay union dues and that they would "reject work in any other organization, as long as they are still treated as outsiders."[54] This writer apparently recognized that the threat of withdrawing from the Free German Trade Union Association (FDGB) might carry some leverage in demanding better provisions. Such statements made clear how important the fulfillment of consumption expectations had become as a prerequisite for a healthy relationship between state goals and citizen involvement. In this way, a common thread throughout many letters was the writers' mode of self-description aimed at boosting their credibility and eliciting empathy by displaying their ready participation in worthy socialist life. Many authors of complaint letters foregrounded their membership in organizations such as the DFD and the FDGB to emphasize their willingness to be active members of GDR society, although, as this letter indicated, some citizens presented this participation as contingent on fulfilment of material needs.

Consumers also demanded greater clarity about state policies from their government. One of the most confusing features of the planned economy was the lack of information about why such shortages and inequalities were becoming so prevalent. The population constantly had to adjust to new problematic conditions. Many of the letters asked Elli Schmidt to clarify what was going on in the economy. Christel Horn, a housewife from Ballenstadt, responded to Schmidt's speech in May with a demand for more information on the formation of consumer policy:

> I would like to write today about several questions that occupy me time and again. Your demand [made in Schmidt's widely publicized speech] that the Party and government should have more confidence in the population and enlighten it about necessary economic measures seems very important. . . . The way in which the latest measures (price regulation, reduction in food ration cards, etc.) occurred, hardly contributes to a strengthening of the working people's trust. . . . I believe many functionaries easily [pass new measures without properly informing the population]. They say to themselves that the population won't understand this anyway, so why should we explain it first? Sometimes one believes that certain things shouldn't be discussed. However, if they were discussed openly, [these measures]

would be accepted with greater understanding than in this context of secretiveness [*Geheimnistuerei*].[55]

This letter appealed to Schmidt as the Party insider who would take the population seriously so that they would regain trust in the government. While Horn described the state functionaries as condescending and arbitrary, she seemed to believe that Schmidt would be exempt from such faults and as a consumer representative would deal with her fellow shoppers more openly and respectfully.

Many letter writers not only aimed to complain but also claimed to be of service to the regime, crafting their letters to show how they positioned their private selves within the socialist community. The historian Felix Mühlberg notes that generally petitioners not only tried to present themselves as useful, loyal members of society; they even legitimized their own private desires first by tying them in to societal needs.[56] Consumers seemed to recognize that the information gap put not only them but also the regime at a disadvantage in solving economic problems. Many consumers' testimonials were offered as suggestions that Elli Schmidt, as their representative, should carry to the proper authorities. For example, a letter from Elisabeth Barke warned that the withdrawal of ration cards for the self-employed on the one hand and the favoring of state-run factories on the other "must embitter these people" and would entail "a great danger for our young GDR, because embitterment and need does not coincide with the basis for raising living standards and care for people." She suggested that

> In many cases the children will also be harmed by this measure: the parents attain no ration card and, since fat and sugar are not to be had at the moment, they are forced to use the children's rations for themselves. That is by no means in the interest of the government, which desires above all healthy and robust youth. In addition, it is worth bearing in mind that through this new regulation the door will again be opened to the black market.[57]

Barke rhetorically framed her complaint as useful information for the regime and was clearly aware of what the SED regime saw as social dangers, such as unhealthy youth and the black market.

This tendency of the writers to place themselves and their problems in a wider societal context is revealed in the letter from Elly Voigt, who was distressed by the rise in Perlon (nylon) stocking prices.

> I am employed and besides that, I go to correspondence school. For a year I have been wearing Perlon stockings and have experienced it as a great benefit to be relieved from unpleasant darning of stockings, so that I can preserve a lot of time for my studies and always have stockings without holes. This joy and relief is gone, however, because it pleased someone to raise the price for one pair of Perlon stockings from DM 18.—to DM 36.–.[58]

This woman described her own activity as socially useful to persuade the reader that as an active member of socialist construction she deserved the basic necessities of life.

Another strategy of appeal was to speak on behalf of the masses of specifically female consumers, both housewives and employed women. In a letter complaining about shortages of diapers, Hildegard Köppen wrote:

> I believe I speak in the name of many mothers, when I ask you [Elli Schmidt], to discuss this question [of diaper shortage] with the government and to solve it so that the children will keep their infant ration-card [with which they can receive diapers] for up to one year.[59]

Such writers saw themselves privy to specific consumer knowledge, which gave them authority to speak for all shoppers.

This assumption of the role of consumer representative reveals how women developed a constellation of roles that were to fit into the transforming socialist polity. Some letters suggested how the aggressive policy to recruit women into paid labor put women in the position of juggling the roles of worker, mother, and housewife. In addition, the complaints about difficulties for women indicated how the population increasingly held the government responsible for enacting social programs in combination with greater supply of commodities to help them balance their responsibilities. These letters presented a variety of issues that women were coping with as the regime made its modernizing push to bring more women into employment. For one thing, many households still relied on a male breadwinner when wives could not take on paid labor due to the burden of housework and child rearing. A male worker wrote a protest letter indicating how the privileging of certain factory laborers with higher ration allotments affected families in which housewives had to make do with short supplies if the male breadwinner didn't work at a Schwerpunktbetrieb. He complained that housewives had to do extra work of laundry every Sunday for their husbands due to an overall shortage of work clothes. As a reward for this labor,

> the woman also has the right to a respectably buttered slice of bread. But the basic ration card denies this and one can't take it away from the children, because it's not even enough for our kids. Colleague, you as a woman will understand, that women who today are not in the position to go to work because of their children, still have a right to a somewhat better life too.[60]

When Christel Horn called for better availability of stockings to save working women from the work of darning old ones, she expressed an understanding of the regime's goals of transforming women's roles through social programs like kindergartens, and she acknowledged that this was a gradual process.

> I understand completely that in one year we can't build so many kindergartens and daycare centers to relieve all employed women of this concern. But it would really be a colossal relief for them if they could buy enough Perlon stockings to be freed from eternally darning stockings. Why doesn't our industry take seriously this opportunity to help working women? Isn't this more than just the responsibility of planning?[61]

In other cases, the letters came from women who had already been integrated into the workforce but recognized how this socialist goal had not produced relief from the double burden of housework.

> As an employed woman, I welcome that the government has summoned you, Frau Elli Schmidt, into the Ministry for Trade and Supply. As a woman and mother you know our daily worries that we have when one comes home from work.[62]

Such complaints suggest how integral material concerns were to the overall question of how to transform women's roles under socialism.

As part of the social contract between state and citizenry the regime guaranteed that popular petitioners would receive an answer to their queries. Although this didn't always work out perfectly, the archival files preserve many replies from Schmidt and her commission. Whether penned by an office secretary or by Schmidt herself, the letters aimed to explain the root of some of the problems in the economic system and to reassure the consumers that they should have trust in the regime and its commitment to improving trade. A typical answer to a complaint ended with the statement "We assure you that we are doing all we can to implement the decisions of the Council of Ministers [to increase production, etc.] as quickly as possible and ask you further to have trust in the measures of our regime."[63]

A response written to Elly Voigt, who complained about the price of Perlon stockings, offers another typical strategy for dealing with consumer complaints. In this letter Schmidt explained that GDR industry was not yet able to produce as many stockings as the population demanded. Soon, however, it was planning to train workers in stocking plants to make new Perlon stockings and to convert shut-down factories in the Harz Mountains into underwear factories to raise production levels for the desired commodities. With this explanation and promise of a better future, Schmidt's ministry urged this consumer to have patience and to be satisfied with delayed gratification.

> We have a Five-Year Plan and when one creates the basis for socialism, one can't shift from wearing rayon stockings to general wearing of Perlon stockings from one year to the next. That is neither possible in the Soviet Union nor in the countries of the People's Democracies, and in these countries there are considerable differences in the prices of stockings too. I hope that I have answered your question and think that one should have trust in the politics of our government and also trust in such measures that bring price hikes for certain shortage goods. Everyone can buy rayon stockings in good quality at cheap prices, even strengthened with Perlon, which lasts just as long.[64]

In this response to her complaint, Voigt could recognize a fellow consumer familiar with the problems related to stockings. Schmidt's explanation aimed to enlighten the reader about the reasons for the higher prices in order to relieve her frustration. Simultaneously, it tried to revise the reader's views to restore her trust in the regime and to look to other Soviet bloc countries as parallel examples for building the new socialist society.

In this way, the letter described the process of modernization according to an alternative Soviet-type model.

Such responses suggest that Schmidt had limited power to enact changes based on the letters received and that she may have been just as bound as other members of the Party to ideological constraints, which in part committed the regime to the economic planning structure that was causing such difficulties in production, distribution, and consumption. The responses Schmidt offered to her constituents largely tried to reassure them that the state was thinking about them. In this respect, her role could perhaps be seen more as a public relations tool and one of the "apologists for austerity," as one historian has described female consumer advocates,[65] than as a major locus of change.

However, Schmidt was not purely an apologist for the regime; she also levied important critiques against the system of trade in the GDR, against state ministries, and against SED leadership. She used her role as head of the commission as a source of authority since she was privy to knowledge about the population's needs and desires that other functionaries lacked. As a member of the Politburo during the June 1953 crisis, Schmidt used her position as liaison to the consuming population and as archetypal female consumer to critique this leadership's path. However, her ultimate fate in the wake of this crisis betrays the regime's ambivalence toward consumer culture and toward women's role in positions of power in the socialist state.

A New Course for Elli Schmidt

In the midst of the domestic crisis of shortages, the death of Joseph Stalin on March 5, 1953, posed another challenge to Walter Ulbricht's hard-line policies in the GDR.[66] While Ulbricht blamed the flight of GDR citizens on the open Berlin border between East and West, post-Stalin Soviet leadership began to suggest that Ulbricht's program to build socialism was more to blame by worsening the standard of living in the East. Soviet leaders began to articulate that the GDR should stop the aggressive program of collectivization and building socialism and rather focus more on producing consumer goods and ending some of the more egregious forms of state repression.[67] However, Ulbricht was committed to his program and continued to push productivity in heavy industry and socialism in agriculture. In fact, at the Thirteenth Plenum of the SED Central Committee on

May 13 and 14, 1953, Ulbricht made his policies *more* strict by raising work norms by at least 10 percent. This new policy became one of the main rallying points for protesters during the June 17 uprising a month later.

Significantly, it was at this same plenum that Elli Schmidt, after a few months of service on the commission, made a speech outlining an agenda for solving problems of trade. This speech represented Schmidt's attempt to close the gap between communist ideology and the real needs of the citizenry that she had been reviewing since taking the position as head of the commission. Schmidt's speech was a response to a May 12, 1953, decision in the Politburo exhorting state ministries to improve the provision of mass-produced goods for the population.[68] In this decision the Politburo recognized that due to a lack of initiative in industry, a limitation of energy in retailing, and the Ministry for Finance's rigid pricing policy "in the production of mass-produced commodities, the selection has not been broadened to meet the desires of the population. On the contrary, the selection of goods for certain categories of stock has become more limited and the quality has partially worsened."[69]

Schmidt's speech reflected a mixture of an adherence to a dogmatic belief in the establishment and broadening basis of socialism on the one hand and detailed awareness of actual problems in the population on the other. Clinging to the party line, she looked to the Soviet Union as a model for socialist retailing.[70] For example, she promoted the Soviet-type "productivity wage" (*Leistungslohn*) as a reward for ideal socialist *Aktivist* workers, especially in priority factories.[71] Above all she promoted the further development of the HO as a shopping location for Aktivists, suggesting that, as the decisive forum of particularly urban trade, it should broaden its scope with the establishment of more stores for durables.

Schmidt denounced the usual suspects targeted in the Soviet-style system for blocking economic prosperity, such as capitalist saboteurs, speculators, and retrograde private wholesalers. However, she also directed pointed criticism toward the ministries responsible for consumer problems, saying that they did not prioritize consumption as much as she thought they should.

> We must very seriously critique our Industrial Ministries because they manifest criminal negligence in the production of mass commodities. One even has the impression that they perceive their planned tasks in the area of the production of consumer objects as an annoyance.[72]

Such critiques were not necessarily risky considering the recent purges in the Ministry for Trade and Supply. However, Schmidt's critiques were much more concrete than general attacks on antisocialist "saboteurs" levied against figures like Hamann. Later in the speech she indicted the ministries for paying attention neither to the need for more specialized stores nor to the specific complaints of the consumers.

Unfortunately the Ministries view the task of creating stores for industrially produced goods as highly irrelevant. . . . The critique that the population asserts against the bad quality of fashions, undergarments, stockings and shoes, which light industry produces, receives next to no attention, because otherwise the Ministry for Light Industry would have done much more to improve decisively the work of the consumer industry firms.[73]

In her speech, she implied that many of the problems in the availability of sufficient products remained because the responsible ministers, as men and as elites, lacked knowledge and experience with consumption. She remarked, almost teasingly:

Despite repeated requests, the Industrial Ministries handed in only a total of sixteen suggestions for additional production of mass consumer goods and gave as their reason that their assortment was actually plentiful enough. With this one sees that our Ministers don't go shopping themselves [Laughter!] and don't have any perception themselves of what our population lacks in such important commodities for making life easier as good razor blades, pocket knives that cut, bathing caps, screws and nails, drawing pins, various sizes of cooking pots and buckets, curtain rods and accessories, etc. I suggest that our Comrade Minister should be sentenced to shave himself with the razor blades produced in his factories every morning, so that he knows what a punishment that is. [More laugher!][74]

Thus, Schmidt revealed how detached the ministries regulating production were from actual consumers' needs. It seems that her analysis of their disconnection lay in the fact not only that they were elite functionaries (who perhaps had access to better-quality razors) but also that, as men, they were not the ones who performed the daily task of shopping. By cri-

tiquing the ministers in this way, Schmidt may have been working to legitimize and strengthen her position as the only one in the Politburo who
supposedly could truly understand the plight of the consumer, not just by
analyzing data and letters from consumers but by virtue of her own house-
wifely shopping expertise. But it also is significant that the same types of
concerns voiced in these letters made it to the highest levels of the Party.

The speech was also widely published in the press. Press reports portrayed Schmidt as an honest voice speaking on behalf of the people, such
as in the *BZ am Abend* headline "Full Openness about All Difficulties: Elli
Schmidt Spoke about Provisioning Problems."[75] This speech increased her
fame as a consumer spokesperson. Even more letters arrived after such
publicity. Discussing these problems in the press may have been a way to
convince the population that the government was paying attention to their
material needs, as a way of softening the blow of rising work quotas. At
the same time, Schmidt's open discussion of shortages demonstrated the
worsening crisis that was mounting in the GDR. The Soviet leadership
also studied these shortages to figure out a solution to the problem of mass
flight from East Germany.

After evaluating these problems in the GDR, the Soviet leadership
under Molotov, Beria, and Malenkov developed a program to promote
recovery in the GDR that came to be known as the New Course. In a
meeting in Moscow from June 2 to 4, Soviet leaders presented to Ulbricht
and other top SED leaders their program to stop forced collectivization, to
support private enterprise, to return ration cards to all citizens, and to promote production of consumer goods instead of straining the economy with
too rapid expansion of heavy industry.[76] Ulbricht was hesitant to accept
this new direction, but after extensive discussion in the GDR Politburo
during which Ulbricht's leadership was strongly critiqued, the regime
decided to announce a New Course in a communiqué published on June
11. The New Course reversed some of the most austere measures implemented in 1952 and in early 1953, such as the elimination of ration cards
for self-employed citizens, the recent price hikes, restrictions on private
businesses, and higher taxes. The spirit of the GDR New Course was to
improve the standard of living for the population and to make more consumer goods available. However, the published decree didn't lower work
quotas. The implications of the New Course were, therefore, confusing to
workers and did not quell the anger built up by the impact of the 1952
socialization maneuvers. Rather, in reaction, Berlin construction workers
left their job sites on the Stalin-Allee on June 16 and demonstrated in the

streets to demand lowered work quotas and a better standard of living.[77] The following day, demonstrations broke out across the country and over three hundred thousand workers, employees, housewives, and students nationwide voiced much broader political demands, including an end to the SED regime.[78] Anger over the ongoing material shortages and the high prices in the HO was prominent in the demonstrators' protests. Irate protesters chanted a variety of slogans, including "HO makes us k.o. [knocked out]!"[79] Among the demonstrators' demands was a drop in HO prices by 40 percent.[80] The Americans in West Berlin exploited the situation by offering food to any East German who crossed the border in protest.[81] Soviet forces finally crushed the uprising by invading central Berlin with tanks and killing twenty-one demonstrators.[82]

The uprising changed the way the regime approached the population in important ways, because SED leaders feared a reprise of the events of June 17. As the historian Peter Hübner suggests, the SED leadership found it in its own interest to avoid dissatisfaction among the workers.[83] This threat added new impetus to the regime's efforts in the New Course to provide sufficient food and commodities for the population. The Council of Ministers passed immediate measures to improve supplies of food and manufactured goods for workers.[84] The Soviets also offered more support for these goals by agreeing to send more exported food and cotton to the GDR.[85] The regime's greater attention to consumer needs and attempts to fulfill them, then, significantly marked the New Course and ongoing GDR policy. "Seen in this way, the workers in the GDR profited from June 17, 1953 in the long run," according to Hübner.[86]

However, the uprising led to a major crisis within the SED leadership. Ulbricht blamed Western provocateurs for the uprising, which many SED leaders now called a "fascist putsch attempt" to shift blame away from his own policies. However, the crisis also led to the formation of a faction within the Party that was deeply critical of Ulbricht and his Stalinist party line. Minister of State Security Wilhelm Zaisser and Rudolf Herrnstadt, Politburo member and chief editor of the Party organ *Neues Deutschland*, were the most prominent critics of Ulbricht's strict ideological dogmatism and cult of leadership.[87] They called for the reversal of the most severe measures of building socialism, such as forced collectivization of agriculture, and advocated greater responsiveness to the population's concerns. Emboldened by Soviet criticism of Ulbricht, in July they led a movement in the Politburo to reorganize the party structure to take power from the SED secretariat and enlarge the Politburo and ultimately to challenge

Ulbricht's position by replacing him with Herrnstadt as general secretary.

Notably, Elli Schmidt was one of the most vocal critics of Ulbricht's policies at this time, becoming infamous for referring to Ulbricht by "one of the coarsest expressions."[88] She may have been bolstered in her critique by the recognition, gleaned from confronting citizens' complaint letters, that the actual conditions of production and distribution failed to reflect goals for a better standard of living within socialism. In a July 8 meeting of the Politburo, Schmidt joined Zaisser, Herrnstadt, and other Party leaders such as Anton Ackermann in boldly drawing attention to the Party leadership's lack of attention to the needs of the population.

> The whole spirit that has got into our Party, the sloppiness [*Schnellfertige*], the dishonesty, the turning of a blind eye [*Wegspringen*] to the people and their worries, the threatening and boasting—look where it has got us! You, my dear Walter [Ulbricht], are the most guilty and this is something you don't want to concede, even though the 17 of June would never have happened were it not for all these things.[89]

In making this sharp critique, Schmidt did not refer specifically to problems of consumption, but consumer issues were certainly paramount among the "worries" of the people. However much she may have felt authorized by her awareness of consumer complaints in making her critique, she probably felt isolated in this task of attending to the real needs of the population, as her later comments reveal.

Unfortunately, the brief moment of open criticism sparked by the uprising faded quickly as Ulbricht strengthened his position. Significantly, Lavrenti Beria, one of the most strident critics of Ulbricht within the Soviet leadership (he had even called him an idiot),[90] was arrested as part of a power struggle in the USSR Party; Beria was accused of criminal behavior as an agent of bourgeois imperialism. Without the support of Beria's criticism of Ulbricht, the strength of Zaisser and Herrnstadt's movement deflated. By July 26, at the Fifteenth Central Committee Plenum, it was becoming clear that this spirit of reform would not be tolerated and that any criticism of Ulbricht was anathema. Instead of ousting Ulbricht, the SED disciplined Zaisser and Herrnstadt, expelled them from the SED Central Committee, and forced them into "self-criticism," which meant towing the party line and doing penance for their dissent in exile from the chambers of power.[91]

At this Fifteenth Plenum, Schmidt continued in her role as consumer representative to describe the successes as well as the ongoing challenges for trade in the New Course. She recalled the problems she addressed in her speech at the Thirteenth Plenum. Then her remarks critiqued the "mistakes" already acknowledged in the June 8 communiqué announcing the New Course, such as the "one-sided forcing of heavy industry at the cost of the living standard of the population." She also cited the regime's "false opinion" toward contracts with private retailers, which had led to discrimination against the private sector.[92] She sketched the resulting problem of continuing shortages:

> The buying power of the population is concentrated singly on such goods as butter, sugar, and meats, because in the foodstuffs sector we still have neither enough of a selection nor alternative possibilities. Since we had so little fruit and almost no chocolate, a mother would buy a bockwurst for her child, for example. On top of that, we don't have enough beautiful textiles or shoes, the furniture doesn't meet the desires of the population and there is not enough of it.[93]

She called for measures to improve this situation, such as greater flexibility of financing to make state-run retailing more profitable, decentralization of distribution planning to give responsibility to local districts, improvement of Verkaufskultur, and greater orientation toward the consumers' needs.

However, despite her ongoing willingness to voice such critiques, the turning tide against Ulbricht's opponents made Schmidt preface these remarks with a statement overtly denying support for Zaisser and Herrnstadt. While she was interested in reforming trade and critiquing Ulbricht's policies that had worsened provisions in the GDR, she claimed to have known nothing about how Zaisser and Herrnstadt's critiques were linked to plans for restructuring the Party and ousting Ulbricht. Rather, she tried in vain to save her position by reiterating her support of Ulbricht. While apparently opportunistic, her explanation of her earlier criticisms is especially interesting, because it shows that behind her critique lay a personal frustration with being marginalized within the Politburo and with the lack of support for her efforts to improve the conditions of consumption.

> I would like to say that I often had the feeling of unjustified discrimination in the Politburo. I often said so very openly to Comrade Walter Ulbricht, that in the entire time that I have been a member of the

Politburo, he has never once found time to talk to me for only a short time about my work. Especially not when I was assigned the complicated task of trade (*komplizierte Aufgabe im Handel*). On the 6th [of July at the Politburo meeting] I made demands for the Politburo to develop such collective work, that would give help to all comrades who must manage new tasks, especially in economic questions that I really had to familiarize myself with. I must say, that sometimes I stood alone in these issues until recently.[94]

It is worth noting that as she tried to excuse her behavior she alluded to her difficult responsibility for consumer problems as one of the reasons why she may have been initially sympathetic to criticisms of Ulbricht.

You will justifiably ask, how did you stand by these two comrades [Zaisser and Herrnstadt] during this whole conflict? I would like to say, that I had no sort of relationship to these two Comrades, meaning that the Comrades absolutely did not speak to me about these questions [of ousting Ulbricht]. I would like to say that Comrade Herrnstadt did often give me advice and help for my work, especially for the new task in trade.[95]

Schmidt's explanation here aimed to distance herself from the most controversial question associated with Zaisser and Herrnstadt: the critique of Ulbricht's leadership. However, she was willing to concede a connection to Herrnstadt as an advisor in consumer issues. It seems that Herrnstadt took her and her work with consumer problems more seriously than Ulbricht did. This statement seems to suggest that critics of the regime united around the recognition that consumer problems needed greater attention and that Schmidt was perhaps in some ways most aware of how this issue affected consumers in their everyday lives.

Ultimately, Schmidt's deviation from Ulbricht's path proved more important to her fate than her utility as consumer liaison. Immediately after this speech, Schmidt was voted out of the Politburo. Even after this sanction, Schmidt continued her work of speaking out about ways to improve consumption as part of the New Course. In a speech in early August to the Party organization within the commission, she even referred specifically to some of the letters from consumers she had received, which she claimed expressed optimism in the prospects of the New Course.[96] In a radio address on August 11, she explained to the population how she envisioned the New Course would "satisfy the desires of the population," specifically by satisfying demands of women for goods such as better-tasting margarine and "more variety in types of staples, in fish products like Rollmops." She referred to the integral role of individual women in this process of improving trade by citing another letter from a woman dissatisfied with GDR butter and by applauding "the many-sided cooperation of the population, especially women" for fixing the problems in the consumer economy.[97] However, on August 18 the Politburo rejected an additional appeal by Schmidt to explain her position.[98] By September, Schmidt, like Zaisser and Herrnstadt, was condemned as an enemy of the Party and a supporter of the "saboteurs" who had started the June uprising.[99] As a result of her earlier critiques, she was also censured and evicted from her positions in the DFD and the State Commission for Trade and Supply, which was liquidated in October. After her fall from grace and power as a high-ranking member of the Politburo, she was forced to retreat to a much more marginal position reflecting her earlier tailor's training; she became head of the Institute for Clothing Culture. Although given a pardon in 1956 as part of de-Stalinization throughout the Eastern bloc, Schmidt never attained the heights of power that she had for that brief period as consumer representative in the State Commission for Trade and Supply.

Conclusion

The moment of crisis in 1953 was an important turning point for the construction of consumer culture in the GDR. Consumer concerns stood alongside oppressive work quotas at the crux of the population's crisis of faith in the regime. Elli Schmidt's activity on the State Commission for Trade and Supply provides an important window into the complexities of this period of unrest. Since the commission aimed to bridge the gap between state and citizenry, it offers a rare look at the relationship between elite party politics and everyday life in this tumultuous process of building "real existing socialism." Consumers writing to Schmidt enumerated some of the issues plaguing them in the nascent planned economy: rigidity of production and distribution, uneven and inequitable distribution of goods to various sectors of the population, and a paucity of clear information for the regime about demand and needs and for the population about policy changes. The details of this crisis that emerge in these let-

ters show how consumer dissatisfaction was at the forefront of East German concerns and could have played a role in jeopardizing the regime.

Party leaders seemed to recognize this danger. The state's attempt to
manage this turmoil by making Elli Schmidt a consumer liaison showed
that there was some effort to deal with this situation before the uprising
occurred, even if Ulbricht himself didn't immediately heed the warnings
from the Soviets that he should work more to increase consumer supply.
Indeed, the commission's task to listen to consumers suggests that there
was at least a meager attempt to form a more dynamic, dialectical relationship between state and citizenry to alleviate the problems in the economy, even if the weight of repressive power lay in the hands of the state.
The commission's responses to petitioners also combined an effort to pla-
cate them with a seeming interest in genuinely understanding their concerns. The fact that Schmidt was willing to put herself on the line in the
Politburo for the sake of consumers suggests that the Party contained
members working to shape policies in response to real needs of the population. Schmidt's own career was sacrificed after the uprising, but the concerns that she voiced to some extent resonated in the greater attention to
improving trade that became a central tenet of the New Course and other
programs for consumer modernization in later years.

The records from the commission give insight into both sides of this
relationship between state and citizenry at this especially dynamic
moment. The letters written by ordinary consumers showed how, rather
than accepting the state policies passively, they worked to cope with a
steadily transforming consumer landscape and to assert their own
responses to state policy. These consumers combined expressions of personal desire or frustration with broader statements about how as active
participants in the larger socialist community they deserved the right to a
decent material standard of living. Their employment of socialist-based
rhetoric demonstrated many writers' savvy sense of what entailed
respectable socialist citizenship in the eyes of the regime—especially a
commitment to productive labor and to the ideological community. By
asserting their identities as workers and members of the FDGB and DFD,
these letter writers seemed to show a willingness to play by the rules of the
regime, as long as the state held up its end of the bargain by fulfilling its
promises. Ultimately they displayed acute consciousness of the ways that
each citizen was an integral part of a regime that aimed at modern societal
transformation.

However, the possibilities for more open exchange about consumer concerns were cut short when Schmidt and her fellow critics of the regime had to succumb to party discipline and a fall from power. The rapid turn in Schmidt's career from a high-ranking consumer representative to a marginal figure was clearly an expression of Stalinist-type mechanisms of power in the GDR. But in her case, it was also a dramatic embodiment of the contradictory position that the regime held toward consumption and toward women. Consumers were promised a better standard of living only to find that ideological strictures hindered fulfillment of these promises. Likewise women were offered the image of equality and dissolution of gender barriers in socialism, but these promises mixed with new challenges in negotiating ongoing burdens of housework, such as shopping, still ascribed consistently to women. Like the women in factory committees and the DFD who struggled against bureaucracy and indifference to improve the rigid system, and like the average shopper who stood in lines to purchase scarce goods, Elli Schmidt also confronted the inadequacies of the planned economy.

Schmidt may have experienced the effects of these contradictions on a grand scale. While her role as head of the commission was a great honor that endowed Schmidt with power and expertise, her appointment to this position also belied the state's marginalization and feminization of consumer concerns. Even though male functionaries like Otto Grotewohl and Heinrich Rau also spoke out at the Central Committee plenary sessions about challenges to trade and raising the living standard in the GDR, they did not do so in a way that reflected the type of shopping expertise that Schmidt embraced as a woman.[100] Although these men should have been allies with her in her quest to deal with issues that affected consumers, Schmidt still said she felt neglected by her male colleagues, especially Walter Ulbricht. Thus, the story of Elli Schmidt and the State Commission for Trade and Supply offers insight into the gendered dimensions of one of the most important East German inner-party conflicts, the Zaisser-Herrnstadt affair, at the highest level of the state.

Although 1953 marked the end of the State Commission for Trade and Supply and of Schmidt's prestigious career, it was only the beginning of continuing struggles with the issue of consumption in the GDR. The modernization and diversification of consumer opportunities sought in the New Course provided a starting point for even more intensified measures to bring about consumer satisfaction in the second Five-Year Plan starting in 1955.[101] In the second half of the decade more programs emerged that combined ideals of consumer progress and women's emancipation, either through their participation in helping the economy or by producing appliances to relieve them of housework. For example, after the Third Party Conference in March 1956, the Ministry for General Machine Construction set up an Aktiv for Household Technology in which a variety of groups participated, including working women and housewives.[102] The goal of the *Aktiv* was to discuss all new products "above all to hear the opinions of women, on the basis of their long years of practical experience in the household."[103] In 1957 Walter Ulbricht commissioned industry with the task "to study housework scientifically and to maximally relieve working women of housework through new technical household appliances."[104]

Still, the SED's ambivalence toward consumer policy evident in the mixed support for Schmidt's career continued to afflict the consumer economy throughout the history of the GDR. As in 1953, throughout the 1950s the regime seemed consistently confused about how to reconcile socialist ideology and the needs of the consumer to forge a truly alternative consumer culture. These contradictions reached a crisis level again in 1958, when Ulbricht announced the final push to build socialism and instituted stricter policies against private enterprise that made consumption more difficult. At the same time, he promised a higher standard of living for the GDR population that would even rival and surpass the West. The disjuncture between the deleterious effects of building socialism and the goal of a better standard of living was a major factor in the massive flight to the West and the building of the Berlin Wall in 1961. Once again the aggressive push to modernize the socialist economy, as it turned out, clashed with the state's equally modern promise of progress to fulfill consumer desires. The formation of consumer politics in 1953, then, reflected the pattern of the GDR's ongoing struggle to bring about modernity in socialism that would hopefully lift the population out of the deprivation of wartime, provide progress to an affluent future, and help the GDR to rival West Germany and embody an alternative to capitalism. Elli Schmidt's role in this struggle showed how women bore the brunt of the regime's contradictory approaches toward this modernizing transformation of the economy and of gender relations.

NOTES

This is a substantially revised and expanded version of my article "'You as a Woman Will Understand': Consumption, Gender, and the Relationship between State and Citizenry in the GDR's June 17, 1953 Crisis," *German History* 19, no. 2 (2001): 218–52.

1. Grit Bühler, *Mythos Gleichberechtigung in der DDR. Politische Partizipation von Frauen am Beispiel des Demokratischen Frauenbunds Deutschlands* (Frankfurt and New York: Campus, 1997), 22.

2. Donna Harsch, "Squaring the Circle: The Dilemmas and Evolution of Women's Policy," in *The Workers' and Peasants' State: Communism and Society in East Germany under Ulbricht, 1945–71,* ed. Patrick Major and Jonathan Osmond (Manchester: Manchester University Press, 2002), 151–70.

3. Arnold Sywottek notes, for example, that prior to economic stabilization around 1953, the population was skeptical toward the Federal Republic. Arnold Sywottek, "Wirtschafts- und sozialpolitische Entwicklungen als Legitimationsbasis im deutsch-deutschen Systemgegensatz," in *Deutsche Vergangenheiten—eine gemeinsame Herausforderung. Der schwierige Umgang mit der doppelten Nachkriegsgeschichte,* ed. Christoph Kleßmann, Hans Misselwitz, and Günter Wichert (Berlin: Ch. Links Verlag, 1999), 167.

4. A number of monographs on the rationing period have been written, including Rainer Gries, *Die Rationen-Gesellschaft. Versorgungskampf und Vergleichsmentalität: Leipzig, München und Köln nach dem Kriege* (Münster: Verlag Westpfälisches Dampfboot, 1990); Paul Erker, *Ernährungskrise und Nachkriegsgesellschaft: Bauern und Arbeiterschaft in Bayern 1943–1953* (Stuttgart: Klett-Cotta, 1990); Gabriele Stüber, *Der Kampf gegen den Hunger 1945–1950: Die Ernährungslage in der britischen Zone Deutschlands, insbesondere in Schleswig-Holstein und Hamburg* (Neumünster: Karl Wachholtz Verlag, 1984); Karl-Heinz Rothenberger, *Die Hungerjahre nach dem Zweiten Weltkrieg: Ernährungs- und Landwirtschaft in Rheinland-Pfalz 1945–1950* (Boppard am Rhein: Harald Boldt, 1980); and Michael Wildt, *Der Traum vom Sattwerden: Hunger und Protest, Schwarzmarkt und Selbsthilfe* (Hamburg: VSA, 1986).

5. For an examination of the impact of war on the East German economy, see Christoph Buchheim, ed., *Wirtschaftliche Folgelasten des Krieges in der SBZ/DDR* (Baden-Baden: Nomos, 1995).

6. See the discussion in Tony Judt, *Postwar: A History of Europe since 1945* (New York: Penguin, 2005), 6.

7. Belinda J. Davis, *Home Fires Burning: Food, Politics, and Everyday Life in World War I Berlin* (Chapel Hill: University of North Carolina Press, 2000). For a discussion of the American influence on the concept of a "standard of living" in Europe, see Victoria de Grazia, *Irresistible Empire: America's Advance through Twentieth-Century Europe* (Cambridge, MA: Belknap/Harvard University Press, 2005), 75–129.

8. Lizabeth Cohen examines this development in the American case in *A Consumers' Republic: The Politics of Mass Consumption in Postwar America* (New York: Alfred A. Knopf, 2003). See the discussion of how America spread its patterns of consumption and concepts of consumer citizenship to Europe in de Grazia, *Irresistible Empire.*

9. Walter Ulbricht, "Planmäßige Wirtschaft sichert die Zukunft des deutschen Volkes. Referat vor dem Parteivorstand der SED am 29. Juni 1948," in *Der Deutsche Zweijahrplan für 1949–1950* (Berlin [East]: Dietz Verlag, 1948), 20.

10. Amt für Information der Regierung der Deutschen Demokratischen

Republik, ed., *Gesetz über den Fünfjahrplan zur Entwicklung der Volkswirtschaft der Deutschen Demokratischen Republik 1951–1955* (Berlin [East]: Deutscher Zentralverlag, 1951), 65.

11. Peter C. Caldwell, *Dictatorship, State Planning, and Social Theory in the German Democratic Republic* (Cambridge: Cambridge University Press, 2003), 15.

12. Katherine Pence, "Building Socialist Worker-Consumers: The Paradoxical Construction of the *Handelsorganisation*-HO, 1948," in *Arbeiter in der SBZ-DDR*, ed. Peter Hübner and Klaus Tenfelde (Essen: Klartext Verlag, 1998), 497–526. On Soviet trade see Julie Hessler, *A Social History of Soviet Trade: Trade Policy, Retail Practices, and Consumption, 1917–1953* (Princeton: Princeton University Press, 2004).

13. This concept was based on the Soviet development of "cultured trade" that emerged in 1931. See Hessler, *Social History of Soviet Trade*, 198ff.

14. Schi, "Wir bauen: 'Stumme Verkäufer,'" *Konsumverkaufsstelle* 6 (1949): 80.

15. Mark Landsman, *Dictatorship and Demand: The Politics of Consumerism in East Germany* (Cambridge, MA: Harvard University Press, 2005), 92.

16. Judd Stitziel, *Fashioning Socialism: Clothing, Politics and Consumer Culture in East Germany* (Oxford: Berg, 2005), 33.

17. Barbara Einhorn, "Socialist Emancipation: The Women's Movement in the German Democratic Republic," in *Promissory Notes: Women in the Transition to Socialism*, ed. Sonia Kruks, Rayna Rapp, and Marilyn B. Young (New York: Monthly Review Press, 1989), 285.

18. Donna Harsch, *The Revenge of the Domestic: Women, the Family, and Communism in the German Democratic Republic* (Princeton: Princeton University Press, 2007).

19. Leonore Ansorg and Renate Hürtgen, "The Myth of Female Emancipation: Contradictions in Women's Lives," in *Dictatorship as Experience: Towards a Socio-Cultural History of the GDR*, ed. Konrad H. Jarausch (New York: Berghahn Books, 1999), 175.

20. Dagmar Langenhan and Sabine Ross, "The Socialist Glass Ceiling: Limits to Female Careers," in *Dictatorship as Experience*, ed. Jarausch, 178.

21. Ibid., 188–89.

22. For an examination of the mixed messages about gender that proliferated in the GDR media, see *...und Du, Frau an der Werkbank: Die DDR in den 50er Jahren* (Berlin: Elefanten Press, 1990). See also the essays in Gisela Helwig and Hildegard Maria Nickel, eds., *Frauen in Deutschland 1945–1992* (Berlin: Bundeszentrale für politische Bildung, 1993).

23. Donna Harsch, "Approach/Avoidance: Communists and Women in East Germany, 1945–9," *Social History* 25 (May 2000): 162.

24. Jeffrey Kopstein, *The Politics of Economic Decline in East Germany, 1945–1989* (Chapel Hill and London: University of North Carolina Press, 1997), 35.

25. Andreas Pickel, *Radical Transitions: The Survival and Revival of Entrepreneurship in the GDR* (Boulder, CO: Westview, 1992), 36–37.

26. Corey Ross, *Constructing Socialism at the Grass-Roots: The Transformation of East Germany, 1945–1965* (London: Macmillan, 2000), 60ff; Jonathan

Osmond, "From Junker Estate to Co-operative Farm: East German Agrarian Society, 1945–1961," in *Workers' and Peasants' State,* ed. Major and Osmond, 130–50.

27. Burghard Ciesla, ed., *Freiheit wollen wir! Der 17. Juni in Brandenburg* (Berlin: Ch.Links, 2003), 28.

28. Peter Hübner, *Konsens, Konflikt und Kompromiß: Soziale Arbeiterinteressen und Sozialpolitik in der SBZ/DDR 1945–1970* (Berlin: Akademie Verlag, 1995), 149.

29. Manfred Hagen, *DDR—Juni '53: Die erste Volkserhebung im Stalinismus* (Stuttgart: Franz Steiner Verlag, 1992), 25.

30. "Fettaufruf für März 1953," *Nacht-Express* 50 (February 28, 1953), reprinted in Peter Jung, ed., *Verordneter Humor: DDR 1953* (Berlin: Edition Hentrich, 1993), 41.

31. Ciesla, *Freiheit wollen wir!* 24.

32. Kopstein, *Politics of Economic Decline,* 35.

33. Arnulf Baring, *Uprising in East Germany: June 17, 1953* (Ithaca: Cornell University Press, 1972), 20.

34. Since 1948 countries throughout the Eastern bloc cleansed the leading cadres of the governments with purges like those held by Stalin in the 1930s, and the most infamous of these was the Slánský trial in Czechoslovakia in 1952.

35. Peter Joachim Lapp, *Der Ministerrat der DDR: Aufgaben, Arbeitsweise und Struktur der anderen deutschen Regierung* (Opladen: Westdeutscher Verlag, 1982), 169; Landsman, *Dictatorship and Demand,* 80.

36. Min. HuV, H.V.-H.O./IV/52as, November 3, 1952, Versorgungslage Ende 1952, Vertrauliche Verschlußsache, SBZ-Archiv 23/24—1952, 363f., reprinted in Ilse Spittmann and Gisela Helwig, eds., *DDR-Lesebuch: Stalinisierung 1949–1955* (Köln: Edition Deutschland Archiv, 1991), 169; Wolfgang Kiessling, *Der Fall Baender: Ein Politkrimi aus den 50er Jahren der DDR* (Berlin: Dietz, 1991), 80ff.

37. Hübner, *Konsens, Konflikt und Kompromiß,* 150.

38. Lapp, *Der Ministerrat der DDR,* 267.

39. "Staatliche Kommission für Handel und Versorgung gebildet: Elli Schmidt Vorsitzende/Außerordentliche Sitzung des Ministerrates," *Nacht-Express* 28 (February 3, 1953), reprinted in Jung, *Verordneter Humor,* 30.

40. Elli Schmidt's powerful position is underscored by the fact that in the history of the GDR only three women—Hilde Benjamin, Margarethe Wittkowski, and Margot Honecker—held full ministerial positions. Ute Gerhard, "Die staatlich institutionalisierte 'Lösung' der Frauenfrage. Zur Geschichte der Geschlechterverhältnisse in der DDR," in *Sozialgeschichte der DDR,* ed. Hartmut Kaelble, Jürgen Kocka, and Hartmut Zwahr (Stuttgart: Klett-Cotta, 1994), 395. As the historian Gabriele Gast has emphasized, Schmidt's political position in this period was not limited to that of a marginalized representative of women but was central within the Party. Gabriele Gast, *Die politische Rolle der Frau in der DDR* (Düsseldorf: Bertelsmann Universitätsverlag, 1973), 125.

41. Cited in Harsch, "Approach/Avoidance," 163. See also Protokoll, Parteivorstand der SED Nr. 5, Sept. 18–19, 1946, cited in Harald Hurwitz, *Die Stalinisierung der SED: Zum Verlust von Freiräumen und sozialdemokratischer Identität*

in den Vorständen 1946–1949 (Opladen: Westdeutscher Verlag, 1997), 120. The Soviet Military Administration (SMAD) didn't eliminate the "hunger card" as a category until February 1, 1947, when housewives were placed in category III.

42. Stiftung Archiv der Parteien und Massenorganisationen der DDR im Bundesarchiv (hereafter SAPMO BArch) NL 4106/23 Nachlaß Elli Schmidt, Sonderseite Hohenfichte, spring 1953, 29–30.

43. She noted that the commission received 165 letters in only a few days after announcing decisions to improve trade. SAPMO BArch DY 30 IV 2/1/115 13. Tagung des ZK der SED, May 13–14, 1953. Speech by Elli Schmidt, 159.

44. Felix Mühlberg, "Wenn die Faust auf den Tisch schlägt … Eingaben als Strategie zur Bewältigung des Alltags," in *Wunderwirtschaft: DDR-Konsumkultur in den 60er Jahren,* ed. Neue Gesellschaft für Bildende Kunst (Köln: Böhlau Verlag, 1996), 175. See also Jonathan R. Zatlin, "Ausgaben und Eingaben: Das Petitionsrecht und der Untergang der DDR," *Zeitschrift für Geschichtswissenschaft* 10 (1997): 902–17.

45. Ina Merkel and Felix Mühlberg, "Eingaben und Öffentlichkeit," in *"Wir sind doch nicht die Meckerecke der Nation": Briefe an das Fernsehen der DDR,* ed. Ina Merkel (Berlin: Schwarzkopf & Schwarzkopf, 2000), 17.

46. Bundesarchiv (formerly in Postdam, now in Berlin: hereafter BArch) DC 6/1, Regierung der DDR, Min HuV, StK HuV, Versorgungsschwierigkeiten: Beschwerden und Eingaben der Bev. 1953. Letter from Frau Moser, Pankow, March 5, 1953, 72.

47. BArch DC 6/14, Regierung der DDR, Min HuV, StK HuV, Schriftwechsel Versorgung mit Textilwaren, 1–61, February 12, 1953, To: Frau Elli Schmidt Berlin.

48. BArch DC 6/14, Regierung der DDR, Min HuV, StK HuV, Schriftwechsel Versorgung mit Textilwaren, 1–61, Letter from Christel Horn Ballenstedt/Harz, Wallstr. 26, June 6, 1953, To: Liebe Genossin Schmidt! Signed: Christel Horn, Hausfrau.

49. BArch DC 6/14, Regierung der DDR, Min HuV, StK HuV, Schriftwechsel Versorgung mit Textilwaren, 1–61, From: Dr. Paula Mothes-Günther, Leipzig, Platz des Friedens, February 6, 1953, To: die Staatl. Komm. für Handel und Versorgung beim Ministerrat der DDR. Berlin, Frau Elli Schmidt, Sehr geehrte Frau Schmidt.

50. Ina Merkel, *Utopie und Bedürfnis: Die Geschichte der Konsumkultur in der DDR* (Köln: Böhlau, 1999), 44.

51. For example, such protest was articulated by the labor unions in the general strike of 1948. Gerhard Beier, *Der Demonstrations- und Generalstreik vom 12. November 1948: Im Zusammenhang mit der parlamentarischen Entwicklung Westdeutschlands* (Frankfurt am Main and Cologne: Europäische Verlagsanstalt, 1975). Later housewife activists such as Fini Pfannes called for greater price controls from the Federal Republic's Economics Ministry. Elke Schüller and Kerstin Wolff, *Fini Pfannes: Protagonistin und Paradiesvogel der Nachkriegsfrauenbewegung* (Königstein/Taunus: Ulrike Helmer Verlag, 2000).

52. BArch DC 6/1, Regierung der DDR, Min HuV, StK HuV, Versorgungsschwierigkeiten: Beschwerden und Eingaben der Bev. 1953, Letter from VEB

Energieverteilung Salzwedel Frauenausschuß, to Vorsitzende des DFD Frau Elli Schmidt, March 7, 1953, 51.

53. BArch DC 6/2, Regierung der DDR, Min HuV, StK HuV, Versorgung von Schwerpunktbetrieben: Beschwerden und Eingaben von Betrieben, Arbeitern, Presseorganen. 1953. Letter from Franz Gräbner, Coswig, May 19, 1953, To Zentralkomitee Berlin, Elly [*sic*] Schmidt, 12.

54. BArch DC 6/2, Regierung der DDR, Min HuV, StK HuV, Versorgung von Schwerpunktbetrieben: Beschwerden und Eingaben von Betrieben, Arbeitern, Presseorganen. 1953. Letter from BGL d.Fa. Brauerei Richzenhain Waldheim, March 25, 1953, to Kreisrat Döbeln, Handel u. Versorgung, 4.

55. Parenthetical in original. BArch DC 6/14, Regierung der DDR, Min HuV, StK HuV, Schriftwechsel Versorgung mit Textilwaren, 1–61, From: Christel Horn Ballenstedt/Harz, Wallstr. 26, June 6, 1953, To: Liebe Genossin Schmidt! Signed: Christel Horn, Hausfrau.

56. Mühlberg, "Wenn die Faust," 178–79. See also the discussion in Judd Stitziel's essay in this volume.

57. BArch DC 6/10, Regierung der DDR, Min HuV, StK HuV, Lebensmittelkarteneinstufung. Anfragen und Beschwerden der Bevölkerung, March–July 1953, Letter from Elisabeth Barke, Dresden, May 10, 1953, to Die Vorsitzende der Staatlichen Kommission für Handel und Versorgung Frau Elli Schmidt, 15.

58. BArch DC 6/14, Regierung der DDR, Min HuV, StK HuV, Schriftwechsel Versorgung mit Textilwaren, 1–61.

59. BArch DC 6/4, Regierung der DDR, Min HuV, StK HuV, Schriftwechsel, Briefe der Werktätigen, 1–193, Buchstaben F-P, Glauchau, July 11, 1953, To: Liebe Genossin Elli Schmidt! Mit sozialistischem Gruß! From Hildegard Köppen. Glauchau/So. Pestalozzistr. 83.

60. BArch DC 6/2, Regierung der DDR, Min HuV, StK HuV, Versorgung von Schwerpunktbetrieben: Beschwerden und Eingaben von Betrieben, Arbeitern, Presseorganen. 1953. Letter from Franz Gräbner, Coswig, May 19, 1953, To Zentralkomitee Berlin, Elly [*sic*] Schmidt, 12.

61. BArch DC 6/14, Regierung der DDR, Min HuV, StK HuV, Schriftwechsel Versorgung mit Textilwaren, 1–61, From: Christel Horn Ballenstedt/Harz, Wallstr. 26, June 6, 1953, To: Liebe Genossin Schmidt! Signed: Christel Horn, Hausfrau.

62. BArch DC 6/4 Volksrat, Regierung der DDR, Min. HuV, StK HuV, Schriftwechsel, Briefe der Werktätigen, 1–193 (Buchstaben F-P), To: die Vorsitzende des DFD Frau Elli Schmidt, Ministerium Handel und Versorgung-Berlin, Dresden February 17, 1953, Mit Bundesgruß, From: Frida Jommernegy.

63. BArch Potsdam DC 6/14, Regierung der DDR, Min. HuV, StK HuV beim Ministerrat der DDR. Schriftwechsel Versorgung mit Textilwaren, 1–61, June 26, 1953, To: Frau Gertrud Wolfrum, Karl-Marx-Stadt, signed Bäger.

64. BArch Potsdam DC 6/14, Regierung der DDR, Min. HuV, StK HuV beim Ministerrat der DDR. Schriftwechsel Versorgung mit Textilwaren, 1–61, April 27, 1953, To: Frau Elly Voigt [*sic*], letter not signed in file.

65. Landsman, *Dictatorship and Demand,* 92.

66. Christoph Kleßmann and Bernd Stöver, eds., *1953—Krisenjahr des Kalten Krieges in Europa* (Köln: Böhlau Verlag, 1999).

67. Hope Harrison, *Driving the Soviets Up the Wall: Soviet-East German Relations, 1953–1961* (Princeton: Princeton University Press, 2003), 22–25.

68. SAPMO BArch DY 30 J IV 2/2/280 Sitzung des Politbüros des Zentralkomitees der SED. Anlage Nr. 1 zum Protokoll No. 26–53, May 12, 1953, "Beschluß zur Verbesserung der Versorgung der Bevölkerung mit Massenbedarfsgütern," 11–20.

69. Ibid.

70. Eric D. Weitz, *Creating German Communism, 1890–1990: From Popular Protests to Socialist State* (Princeton: Princeton University Press, 1997), 350.

71. SAPMO BArch, NL 106/22, Nachlaß Elli Schmidt, "Die neuen Aufgaben auf dem Gebiet von Handel und Versorgung," Referat Elli Schmidt, gehalten auf der 13. Tagung des Zentralkomitees, May 13 and 14, 1953.

72. Ibid.

73. Ibid.

74. SAPMO BArch DY 30 IV 2/1/115 13. Tagung des ZK der SED, May 13–14, 1953, Speech by Elli Schmidt, 156.

75. "Volle Offenheit bei allen Schwierigkeiten: Elli Schmidt sprach zu Versorgungsfragen," *BZ am Abend*, May 18, 1953, reprinted in Jung, *Verordneter Humor*, 76–77.

76. Harrison, *Driving the Soviets Up the Wall*, 29; Baring, *Uprising in East Germany*, 24.

77. There are a number of studies on the June 1953 uprising, including Torsten Diedrich, *Waffen gegen das Volk: Der 17. Juni 1953 in Brandenburg* (Munich: Oldenbourg, 2003) and Hubertus Knabe, *17. Juni 1953: Ein deutscher Aufstand* (Munich: Propyläen, 2003). For a review of recent books on this subject, see Jonathan Sperber, "17 June 1953: Revisiting a German Revolution," *German History* 22, no. 2 (2004): 619–43.

78. David Childs, *The GDR: Moscow's German Ally* (London: G. Allen & Unwin, 1983), 33.

79. Hagen, *DDR—Juni '53*, 61.

80. Ibid., 62.

81. S. J. Ball, *The Cold War: An International History, 1947–1991* (London: Arnold, 1998), 92.

82. Childs, *The GDR*, 33.

83. Hübner, *Konsens, Konflikt und Kompromiß*, 157.

84. "Regierung trifft Sofortmaßnahmen: Verbesserung der Versorgung mit Nahrungsmitteln, Arbeitsschutzkleidung und Industriewaren, Löhne nach Normen von 1.4.53, Verordnung über Rentenerhöhung," *BZ am Abend*, June 26, 1953, reprinted in Hagen, *DDR—Juni '53*, 99.

85. Harrison, *Driving the Soviets Up the Wall*, 39. According to Otto Grotewohl, this promise for additional imports included 27,000 tons of butter, 8,500 tons of animal fat, 11,000 tons of vegetable oils, 15,000 tons of oil seeds, 20,000 tons of meat, 1,500 tons of fatty cheese, and 7,000 tons of cotton, as well as 231 million rubles of credit. SAPMO BArch IV 2/1/119 Stenographische Niederschrift, 15. Tagung des ZK der SED, July 24–26, 1953, in Berlin, Haus der Einheit. Comments by Grotewohl, file p. 25.

86. Hübner, *Konsens, Konflikt und Kompromiß,* 157.

87. See Rudolf Herrnstadt and Nadja Stulz-Herrnstadt, *Das Herrnstadt-Dokument* (Reinbek bei Hamburg: Rowohlt, 1990). See also Mary Fulbrook, *Anatomy of a Dictatorship: Inside the GDR 1949–1989* (Oxford: Oxford University Press, 1995), 34.

88. Quoted in Baring, *Uprising in East Germany,* 106–7.

89. Quoted in Peter Grieder, *The East German Leadership, 1946–1973* (Manchester and New York: Manchester University Press, 1999), 79.

90. Catherine Epstein, *The Last Revolutionaries: German Communists and Their Century* (Cambridge, MA: Harvard University Press, 2003), 160.

91. Fulbrook, *Anatomy of a Dictatorship,* 34.

92. SAPMO BArch NY4106/23 Nachlaß Elli Schmidt, Gen. Elli Schmidt speech 15. Tagung Z.K. über Handel, 7, file p. 88, and SAPMO BArch DY 30 IV 2/1/120 15. ZK Tagung der SED, July 26, 1953. Comment by Elli Schmidt, file p. 155.

93. SAPMO BArch NY4106/23 Nachlaß Elli Schmidt, Gen. Elli Schmidt speech 15. Tagung Z.K. über Handel, 7, file p. 89, and SAPMO BArch DY 30 IV 2/1/120 15. ZK Tagung der SED, July 26, 1953. Comment by Elli Schmidt, file p. 156.

94. SAPMO BArch DY 30 IV 2/1/120 15. ZK Tagung der SED, July 26, 1953. Comment by Elli Schmidt, file p. 154.

95. Ibid., 153.

96. SAPMO BArch NY4106/23 Nachlaß Elli Schmidt, "Der neue Kurs und die Aufgaben der Parteiorganisation," Referat von Genossin Elli Schmidt, gehalten auf der Sitzung der Betriebsparteiorganisation der Staatlichen Kommission für Handel und Versorgung, August 4, 1953.

97. SAPMO BArch NY4106/23 Nachlaß Elli Schmidt, Elli Schmidt, Vorsitzende der Staatlichen Kommission für Handel und Versorgung, Rundfunkkommentar zu Fragen des Handels, August 11, 1953.

98. SAPMO BArch DY 30 J IV 2/2/316 Politbüro des ZK der SED. Protokoll Nr. 62/53 der Sitzung des Politbüros des Zentralkomitees, August 18, 1953.

99. Ilse Thiele, Schmidt's successor as head of the DFD, denounced her for lack of party loyalty with the following words: "In her appearance in several factories she partly reiterated provocative demands, took on a capitulating stance, assimilated to the situation, and didn't set herself against the provocation with full force. Elli Schmidt thereby represented the interests of women and mothers badly. She took this position above all in discussions in the Politburo of the SED, where through her wavering she supported the defeatist and capitulating line of the Party's enemy, the Zaisser-Herrnstadt faction. . . . Elli Schmidt placed herself not decidedly on the side of the solid core of the SED leadership and thereby favored the position of the enemies of unity." From Ilse Thiele's speech at the Eighth DFD-Bundesvorstandssitzung, September 10–11, 1953, in Berlin (DFD-Archiv), cited in Rita Pawlowski, "Elli Schmidt," in *Frauenpolitik und politisches Wirken von Frauen im Berlin der Nachkriegszeit 1945–1949,* ed. Renate Genth et al. (Berlin-Trafo Verlag, Dr. Wolfgang Weist, 1996), 325n2.

100. SAPMO BArch IV 2/1/119 Stenographisches Niederschrift. 15. Tagung des ZK der SED. 24.–26. Juli 1953 in Berlin, Haus der Einheit. TO: "Die Gegenwärtige Lage und der Neue Kurs der Partei." Remarks by Otto Grotewohl.

101. Walter Ulbricht, "Aus dem Rechenschaftsbericht des Zentralkomitees," in *Über den weiteren Aufschwung der Industrie, des Verkehrswesens und des Handels in der Deutschen Demokratischen Republik. Aus dem Rechenschaftsbericht des ZK, den Diskussionsreden und dem Schlußwort des Genossen Walter Ulbricht auf dem IV. Parteitag der Sozialistischen Einheitspartei Deutschlands, Berlin, 30. März bis 6. April 1954* (Berlin [East]: Dietz Verlag, 1954), 9.

102. "The Aktiv contained representatives of trade, the DFD, the specialist divisions of the central committee (ZK), the working group for women in the ZK, the FDGB, working women, representatives of the Women's Committees, housewives and a row of representatives of factories, as well as constructors, engineers, who are active in the area of household technology." SAPMO BArch SED ZK Abt. Frauen IV 2/17/33, Information der Arbeitsgruppe Frauen über die Probleme der allseitigen Erleichterung der Hausarbeit, 1957.

103. Ibid. See also the discussion in Karin Zachmann, "A Socialist Consumption Junction—Debating the Mechanization of Housework in East Germany, 1956–1957," *Technology and Culture* 43 (2002): 75–101.

104. SAPMO BArch SED ZK Abt. Frauen IV 2/17/33, Information der Arbeitsgruppe Frauen über die Probleme der allseitigen Erleichterung der Hausarbeit, 1957.

Alternative Rationalities, Strange Dreams, Absurd Utopias
On Socialist Advertising and Market Research

Ina Merkel

The most beautiful things in the world were never in the German Democratic Republic (GDR); they were always elsewhere—the country next door, for example, the other Germany, much reviled because of its capitalism; or the great Soviet empire, much praised for its revolution. In the GDR, by contrast, it was never so great; it was a small, provincial, scrawny land. And it also never had a "golden age" that all other surrounding countries had—perhaps it had just some "best years," as one exhibit called it. After the desperate experience of the postwar era, the time of awakening and renewal, of visibly improving life, was remembered as years of prosperity. But even these years—if we assume that the 1960s were really such a period—were not free of contradictions and opposing developments.

The idea of a golden age is a vision of the future that takes place in the past. But even the more distant past couldn't be appropriated into heroic memories in the GDR. For example, the 1920s were a time of inflation and mass unemployment for East Germany's working class, petty bourgeois, and rural citizens. They didn't gain anything from this. And they basically lost the war twice—both as Germans and as members of the lower class or, more precisely, as part of the sub-bourgeois classes. So the new German Republic offered much in the way of upward mobility and encouraged all children to study. Many among the so-called reconstruction generation enjoyed remarkable careers that enabled them to move from new GDR teacher to government minister, from working girl to professor, and so on. What is more, the GDR offered social security, peace, and growing prosperity. Nevertheless, this GDR is not the subject of wistful recollection, even in the face of Germany's ongoing deindustrialization and mass unemployment. Neither its secure workplace, state child care, nor subsidized cultural undertakings are the stuff of nostalgia, since they mainly served the state's economic interests and added too little sparkle to everyday existence. The *Ostalgie* wave that has recently suffused the media cannot obscure this fact. In this way, Ostalgie is not to be confused with nostalgia proper, because it is not about a misty-eyed longing for a harmonious past but is rather a form of identity politics that is better understood as a protest against the way in which dominant interpretations of GDR history have robbed the GDR past of its subversive potential.

To be sure, the GDR was a country of common people (*kleine Leute*). It was mostly concerned with work and sometimes a bit of enjoyment. But just because the people were common does not mean that they didn't harbor dreams. Littler dreams, perhaps, but dreams nonetheless—of little cars, vacations on a cold little sea, snowless little mountains, little rivers, and perhaps a little love on the side as well. None of this has much to do with sparkle or even gold. Gold was the stuff of fairy tales or cinema or the glittering dresses beautiful women wore on their skin. Most would probably not have known where to begin with such a thing.

As little as the GDR wanted to be a truly consumer society, and no matter how absurd it is in the end to accuse it of *not* being one, it was certainly no golden age. Communism was never intended to be the fulfillment of individual desires but instead was based on the ideal of rational needs and the centrality of labor as the greatest need of all. And as for consumption, one imagined that once everyone could have everything that he or she really needed, the desire for symbolic distinction would disappear of its own accord. "Each according to his needs" was not a slogan based on the "all you can eat" principle but in fact presupposed rational consumers. However, rationality has little of the same luster as gold.

Perhaps it is precisely the different logic at work in this society and the reason why it didn't come undone for so long that needs explaining. In a peculiar way, consumer culture serves as a good explanatory field of investigation in this regard. On the one hand, it is connected to popular fantasies of living in excess or, put differently, prosperity for all; on the other, it is here where the contradictions between ideal and reality emerged in a dramatic experiential context. The following discussion will attempt to explore socialism's alternative rationality by focusing on two paradigmatic aspects of consumer culture—advertising and market research.

Closely connected to this is the question of why socialist utopian ideals were never fully abandoned in policy or in everyday consumer behavior.

Anthropological Approaches

At first the topic of consumer culture, advertising, and market research in the GDR seems almost absurd, since socialist societies are considered societies of shortage based on an elementary level of provisioning that departed dramatically from consumption in a modern sense. Historians still disagree as to whether one is dealing with consumer cultures as such when analyzing socialist societies. In these debates about the very definition of consumer culture, the abundance of goods produced by industrial society, and in particular the surplus "decencies" on offer from which "sovereign" consumers can choose "freely," serves as the main yardstick of evaluation. Socialism's conspicuous lack of competitive advertising ends up only perpetuating this long-standing preconception.

The standard investigation of GDR consumer culture as a history of dictatorial control based on systemically produced shortages—planned economy, command structures, and "dictatorship of needs" still parade as favorite catchphrases—has all but answered the questions about this society way before any new archival file has been opened. That is a great pity, for hasn't the unrestricted opening of virtually all archives—something still unimaginable in West European societies, by the way—made it possible to cast new light on the inner logic of socialist society and in turn to call into question received explanations by discovering new horizons of understanding?

An anthropological perspective that strives to understand the inner logic of the cultures and societies promises finer analyses and broader explanations. Its merit lies in reconsidering differing paths of modernization and alternate modes of development rather than disqualifying the GDR tout court as a dead end of research. From this perspective the study of consumer culture in the GDR is inseparable from the more general problems affecting all industrial societies: growing social differences, the squandering of scarce resources, the mismatch between supply and demand, and so forth. Even if many of the devised solutions ultimately failed to win over the citizenry, they still deserve to be taken seriously as alternative enterprises in themselves.

The field of cultural practice is all the more important in this regard, not least because of its breadth and interdisciplinary nature and because it doesn't examine the GDR as simply a closed chapter, as some of the more specialized political or institutional areas of contemporary history might approach it. The complete rupture after 1989 in institutions, the political system, economic life, and the work world stands in marked contrast to the continuities in lived experiences, mental patterns, and cultural practices. In the sphere of consumer culture, the dialectic of transformation and tradition is especially visible and is laden with symbolism and rich cultural meaning. The question of consumption in the GDR is thus no mere by-product of the *Wende* but attracted a great deal of public and political attention from the very beginning.

Official public discourse always put a premium on the theme of "de-differentiation" of GDR society by its equitable distributive principles and the uniformity of supply. Consumer choice in the GDR appears thus to be largely shaped by societal pressures and state directives that allowed only limited room for individuality ("niches") and decision making. Usually such developments are described in terms of collectivism versus individualization or homogenization versus plurality of lifestyles and thereby are commonly interpreted as part and parcel of the GDR's insoluble contradiction between norm and need. Typically the point of departure for these appraisals is the collapse of the GDR, whose causes are often attributed to deficits in the consumer sphere together with constraints on mobility, such as the freedom to travel. Invariably the blame is assigned to either the central administration of the planned economy or the "primacy of politics," wherein all economic questions were systematically subordinated to socialism's overarching political imperatives. Underlying this thesis is the assumption that consumer shortages could have been avoided under different political or economic conditions, in this case one of private property and market competition.

However, shortage does not exist in and of itself but is always a relational concept linked to a specific historical context. Similarly, the concept of a "society of shortage" is misleading in that it is based on the logical misconception that shortage necessarily limits possibilities of behavior and inevitably leads to frustration, envy, stinginess, and covetousness. Yet it is precisely in shortage economies or in times of shortage that individual consumer behavior is often marked by a remarkable ability to improvise and seek outlets for hedonistic pleasures. Both these forms of behavior can bring deep satisfaction, underlining the point that the cultural practices

DIY

associated with shortages can be—and are—unexpectedly diverse. As such they go well beyond the experience of restriction, moderation, and the rational use of resources to include experiences of pleasure and creativity as well.

The term *shortage society* still serves as a controversial concept in East-West discourse, one in which Western cultural criticism often ignores the problem of "surplus society" altogether. The West becomes a colorful normative foil against which the GDR appears in bland black and white. Admittedly, this was often reflected in the attitudes of many GDR citizens, who measured their own lives against perceived notions of West Germany. From this perspective the East-West conflict was seen as primarily a clash of economic systems viewed as polar opposites, as consumer culture under socialist conditions was subjected to derision and dismissal. Yet the concept *shortage society*—despite its admitted value in describing particular developments—fully misses the self-understanding of the GDR, which never sought to become a Western-style consumer society but rather saw itself as embarking on the path toward a more civilized, humane "culture society" (*Kulturgesellschaft*). There is no reason why this shouldn't be another yardstick with which to measure real-existing socialism.

The departure point of socialist consumer policy was the communist ideal of satisfying needs (leisure time, rich relationships, and cultivated individuality instead of material wealth) that were only able to flourish in partial and fragmentary ways under the conditions of real-existing socialism. Indeed, it is precisely the contradiction between communist utopia, socialist policy, and popular hedonistic desires that accounts for the peculiarities of GDR consumer culture. If one investigates the GDR's consumer culture with this contradictory character in mind, then one cannot help but arrive upon a surprising phenomenon: the Party and state leadership were put under enormous pressure by the consumer demands of its citizenry. In fact, consumer culture was the Achilles' heel of the system, a field of public debate on which the Socialist Unity Party (SED) and state leadership knew that they could win or lose popular approval. Granted, there was broad agreement between the leadership and the people about specific utopian ideals such as notions of just distribution and social leveling. Over the decades these ideals served as the cement that—despite deep problems—nonetheless held the society together. For this reason, mine is a plea for approaching GDR everyday life and cultural patterns in the GDR without presuming the overwhelming influence of the economic system and political events. Rather, what we need to do is to delve into the world of individual subjects, their longings, values, and possibilities for agency in concrete conditions, and to show that GDR society existed for so long because there was—alongside the conflicts and opposition—general consensus about key goals and ideals. And it was precisely the fact that these ideals were only partially and unconvincingly translated into reality—the long farewell to utopia that the Party leadership completed in the 1970s—that prompted GDR citizens in 1989 to demand substantial reforms. One cannot understand today's problems—what Jürgen Kocka summarizes with the term *unification crisis*[1]—if one does not grasp this interface of politics and culture, utopia and reality, or, for that matter, state tutelage and individual subjectivity.

In this sense, the study of consumer history of the GDR is best developed and pursued from three perspectives: communist utopia, real-socialist politics, and cultural practice. The first theme of utopian ideals touches on the reconstruction of cultural values that were closely connected to ideas of socialist consumerism. They constituted an important starting point for understanding not only the state's consumer policies but also the people's expectations, demands, and perceptions of normality. As such the formative moments of utopia in terms of consensus and legitimacy are of special interest. What must be investigated secondly is how consumer policy dovetailed with original communist ideals and to what extent it was either partially realized, suppressed, forgotten, revalued, or eventually abandoned. On the one hand, consumer policy in the GDR can be seen as a paternalistic politics of provisioning; on the other, democratic forms of consumption developed over the course of GDR modernization, making a heterogeneous consumer culture possible. Third, the history of GDR consumerism must address the practices of consuming, individual acquisitive strategies, differentiated lifeworlds, as well as the transmission of particular mentalities. This raises an important question of what relationships individuals developed with the surrounding "world of goods" under these circumstances and what changes they experienced in their consumer mentality and consumer behavior over the decades.

The following essay will address these three levels by focusing on two key instances of consumer culture: consumer research and advertising. Despite the absence of competition in the GDR, they were both widely practiced and formalized in institutions, albeit with unique characteristics and functions. Both were informed by an ideal conception of consumption within socialism that clashed with the real existing needs of individuals. Both were meant to mediate between production and consumption in the place of an absent market mechanism. Within consumer research, a utopian socialist concept of need was developed and discussed. Advertising was supposed to spread this consumer ideal and to influence the development of needs through education. However, the very logic of the medium complicated such a policy, since advertising is designed to entertain and incite pleasure. Therefore it inevitably opened up a Pandora's box of symbolic meanings that far exceeded the object and its use value. Policies could not resolve this ambivalence, and consequently the state all but ended advertising in the 1970s. Consumers acted as the starting and end point of both consumer research and advertising, but their cultural practices were not addressed. In the third section, the following question then arises: which diverse forms of individual adaptation developed under these conditions?

Consumption and Reason: The Planning of Needs

One of the basic paradigms of the socialist economic system was the conception that needs, and by extension production, could be planned. Through changed property relations the central state's grip on all economic life was guaranteed. Production output and development costs were supposed to be harmonized with each other. This promised to lead to the salutary effects of rationalization, where resources and capacities would no longer overlap in a way that led to senseless waste. Long-term planning is an elementary component of every complex economy. But in the GDR the claim proved problematic that productivity could be centrally determined and implemented down to the smallest firms.

The consequence was bottlenecks and so-called planning surpluses (*Überplanbestände*), both of which showed how production was neglecting basic consumer needs. Since prices as a regulating instrument were eliminated for ideological reasons—price stability was ultimately the criterion for the superiority of the socialist system—the appropriate solution was seen to lie in the scientific study of needs. One expected from consumer research exact predictions about which consumer goods the population needed in which quantities. In the Ministry for Trade and Supply, the crossing point between production and consumption, two tasks were assigned to the newly created Institute of Needs Research formed in 1961 (later renamed the Institute of Market Research) as key areas of study: influence on production and the education of needs. One of the key goals of socialist production was ostensibly "the greatest possible satisfaction of the growing needs of society." One could only achieve this if "the needs were known in their quantity and quality, when [trade] is informed about need, its development and changes, and thus can influence production accordingly."[2] This was first formulated by the political economist Wolfgang Heinrichs in his 1955 book about the foundations of consumer research. The results of the questionnaires should however "not simply serve as a registry of the expression of consumers' needs with the goal of an appropriate corrective for production and trade, but will simultaneously be made of use for guiding consumer needs in the interest of constructing socialist living and consumer habits."[3] Under capitalist relations of production, market research has a fundamentally different function. It is an instrument of industry, the producer, so as to create a complete market overview "of conditions in general and prices in particular" in order on this basis "to exploit for itself the most favorable exchange possibilities (prices)."[4] Since various producers compete with the same goods, or different goods compete among themselves (motorcycles compete with refrigerators, for example), the payoff was to be the knowledge from market research about which preferences the shoppers gave for one or the other product and for what reasons. This economic interest was lacking in GDR firms, however. What is more, retailers exerted no sort of economic pressure. Rather than free pricing, political pressure was exerted on retailing to lift this pressure completely off of production and to provide no economic stimuli to producers. Therefore, the findings collected by market research in the GDR and the policy suggestions emerging from them all but fell into a void.

Yet these research findings were extremely valuable in another sense in that they served as a unique form of empirical sociology. Today we can thank this agency for amassing unusually rich findings about GDR living standards, income conditions, and consumer preferences across various social groups, in effect making possible a more nuanced picture of historical changes in lifestyles and mentalities. These market research reports are valuable as well insofar as they were not ideologically driven but often chronicled real problems and issues. People and their desires stood at the center of these empirical investigations. The Institute of Market Research was the first—and for a long time the only—establishment in the GDR that could conduct such wide-reaching representative surveys. Surveys often asked about possession of consumer goods at home as well as other consumer wishes. Invariably they were conducted anonymously. Time and

again the consumer researchers praised the great openness of the population. "In one survey of 6000 randomly selected consumers, there were only
2.6 percent refusals to answer."[5] Yet this number rose to 4 percent in 1965
and 8 percent in 1966; and these numbers kept rising. Still, in this short
period of time, thirty-five thousand households or individuals from more
than 440 cities and communities were surveyed, a remarkable sum even if
it is only noted offhand in the literature.

What is particularly interesting is that GDR consumer research systematically extended its objectives and methods far beyond the field of
consumption. Instead, many of the surveys touched on social relations in
the GDR such as youth and leisure, old-age poverty, and discrimination
against women. Alongside income and possessions, budgeting of time was
also investigated. This shift in research interest from consumption to
lifestyles was no coincidence, however, but was a logical result of the
utopian concept of socialist lifestyle that developed shortly after the foundation of the institute. The utopian core of the "Theses on Consumption
in Socialism"[6] presented in 1963 laid down the idea of equality in relation
to the distribution of socially produced wealth for incomes as much as for
produced goods. There were no ideas of consumer policy in this sense,
because they were always expressed as social policy through just distribution rather than in reference to the dubious achievements of the Western
world, such as consumer freedom of choice. Thus the determination "that
the level of consumption of various classes and statuses . . . presently
shows a very strong differentiation"[7] created the demand for an above
average development of monetary income of lower income groups. In this
regard, forms of "prestige consumption" (*Geltungskonsum*) were strongly
criticized, often in the form of unjustifiably rich household possessions, an
overemphasis on personal property, and so forth. All of this was to be
eliminated.[8] According to the utopian communist ideal, the desire to rise
above others would disappear on its own if everyone had the same opportunity to gain access to the same goods. Distinction would then no longer
derive from discrepancies of material wealth but rather from varieties of
individual self-creativity.

A second utopian moment aimed at changing consumer habits. This
didn't have to do just with "prestige consumption" per se but with the
speed of changing fashions, love of shopping, and discarding of things.
"Rational consumer norms" or "reasonable consumption" were opposed
to these attitudes in the name of longevity, functionality, and standardization. To this end designers were asked to deliver classic—and therefore

long-lasting—design solutions for functionally mature products. Third, the concept of socialist consumption was connected with the idea that "the individual framework for consuming goods as personal property . . . , which remains for many consumers the single or dominant form of organizing consumption, would lose its meaning." The social provision of food, laundry centers, and lending services of everything from record players to cars was supposed to offer an attractive alternative to individual consumption.

The ideal of a just distribution of available social wealth was connected to ideas of reducing consumption. This was related to the GDR's difficult economic situation, as well as to the mental makeup of the Party leaders, who had survived the privation and misery of the Weimar and Nazi periods. Conscious reduction to real necessities didn't automatically mean renouncing comfort or fashion, though. The main formula was to provide use value instead of prestige consumption. The desire for mobility was thereby tolerated, but not to the extent that everyone had to own a car. Yet the policymakers did not view consumer opposition as a natural reaction to the planned economy. Rather, they identified the roots of consumer opposition among consumers in which "a large number of habits and remnants from capitalist society are still present. Therefore a constantly active influence on the development of desires of the people is necessary. . . . This will only be successful in the struggle against every form of prestige consumption, manifestations of egoism and the overemphasis of personal interests over the interests of society."[9]

Although a strongly paternalistic streak toward the population is evident, one must not overlook the fact that such values were also held dear among the lower levels of GDR society, especially for that generation that survived the years of privation and misery. Demands to limit consumption in a rational fashion—be it in the development of durable goods, the concentration on use value, and/or the avoidance of symbolic distinction— was very much part of both the long tradition of proletarian self-help (i.e., consumer cooperatives) as well as the educated bourgeois tradition of consumer criticism. It was thus taken for granted that a virtue was being made of necessity; that moderation was compulsory (and temporary) rather than desired and permanent; that an austere lifestyle was the very expression of these specific material conditions; and that consumer desires and longings among the GDR citizenry were often oriented toward the lifestyles of completely different classes and strata.

With the rise of the postwar generation—a new, large, and above all independent consumer group with specific desires and money to spend—it became clear how utopian these ideals were. A 1971 study conducted by the Institute of Market Research cautiously concluded "that the consumer habits of the population in terms of their lifestyles in principle changes very slowly over a long historical period."[10] The ideals were therefore delayed but not set aside completely. This antagonism between socialist goals and the real needs of the masses shaped GDR consumer and social policy. The story of GDR advertising dramatized the homegrown contradictions in which this policy was embroiled.

The Charm of Everyday Life: Leitmotifs in Advertising

West German interaction with East German consumer culture was typically confined to shop windows. Amid the flood of cult books that have appeared since 1989, the curious and weird-looking shop windows were rarely left out. Favorite motifs always cropped up: the forced politicization of the world of goods, featuring busts of Lenin, slogan-laden ribbons wrapped around brassieres, and masses of identical items on display in what were known as "stacked windows." Even the last refuge of advertising—the display window—was dismissed as symptomatic of an impoverished imagination and deep indifference toward the economy. Many authors condemned socialist advertising as utter nonsense.[11] But contrary to memory, there was a lively and diverse advertising culture at least until the 1970s, as noted in posters or advertisements suffusing newspapers, magazines, cinema, television, and radio.

Over the decades, socialist advertising was hotly debated as a controversial cultural phenomenon. On the one side stood the rejection of Western shopping culture; competitive advertising was to be forbidden, since desires that could not be fulfilled should not be whetted. Others countered that advertising was a fitting medium to make new products known, to publicize growing prosperity and economic power, and to propagate new ideals of socialist lifestyle. Still others claimed that advertising offered a certain cultural entertainment value. It could be funny, stir attention, create enjoyment, and better link the viewer's worlds of experience. Advertising, so went the logic, didn't have to do this in a heavy-handed manner; it could also do so satirically and ironically. In each case, though, it was clear that advertising created images that were consciously set apart from reality. It was this very gap between image and reality that created the enjoyment of the advertisement in the end.

Consumers are supposedly seduced into buying goods through images of fun. This is both the hope of manufacturers and the source of criticism among intellectuals, since both sides understand that these goods are often things that aren't "really" needed. Advertising is instrumental in helping create these "false" needs through desire for prestige, the pleasure of possession, and status consciousness. While this was always accepted in the West as a necessary part of the market's need to stimulate consumption, those in the East thought they would remain untouched by it on account of the fact that there was no profit interest at stake. In the West one assumed that advertising always lied, distorted reality, peddled myths, and undermined Enlightenment principles.[12] Under socialism, by contrast, advertising was assigned the didactic function of rational education and consciousness-raising about the virtues of a modest social lifestyle: "Socialist advertising is determined by humanistic principles; it informs the people and enlightens them about that which is useful to them."[13] Advertising in the GDR was thus distinguished from its Western counterpart in its reasoned, enlightened approach to product publicity.

This ideal was scarcely practicable, however. While advertising aimed to propagate socialist lifestyles, in the end its content was severely circumscribed by pressing economic imperatives. This determined the ebb and flow of advertising policy. In the 1940s and 1950s, newspaper announcements and cinema advertising were the dominant advertising media. After 1949 the SED-sponsored advertising agency DEWAG also produced cinema films. In 1954 the Party organ *Neues Deutschland* published a study of print ads in various newspapers and studied differences in the advertising behavior practiced by both private and "people's" firms. Private firms were greatly overrepresented in overall production. In order to change this situation and to ensure that more attention would be devoted to socialist economics, the Ministry for Trade and Supply founded a department devoted to advertising and shop window design.[14] With it the progress and success of the people's economy were supposed to be amply shown to the people. By broadcasting that the GDR too was progressing toward prosperity, the wind could be taken out of the sails of the critics of the planned economy. As a consequence, it is wrong to say that socialist advertising was not competitive; yet its aim was not the hocking of brands or products but rather the legitimacy of the "people's economy" itself.

During the 1960s advertising was increasingly called upon to help regulate the effects of the market. One could not advertise goods that were in short supply, whereas those goods that were plentiful were hyped incessantly. With time, advertising campaigns took on great meaning in connection with the problems of supply. In 1959 the SED Central Committee initiated a concerted campaign for margarine, which was meant to mitigate the shortage of butter. Its central motto—"Valuable, because it's rich in vitamins"—was an appeal to individual health and energy. In 1960 full-page color ads appeared in the *Neue Berliner Illustrierte* magazine that perversely displayed a backdrop of oranges, bananas, grapes, peaches, and peppers, together with abundant vegetable baskets stocked with tomatoes, lettuce, cucumbers, and melons. A small, gray cube of wrapped margarine was placed in the foreground. Margarine was supposed to contain all these good vitamins. Such health propaganda became a standard refrain for pitching basic socialist items. In 1960 there was an advertising campaign for fresh fish; in 1966 the "Goldbroiler" chickens and eggs were peddled with similar messages.

The increasing interest among retailers toward advertising went far beyond the perennial problems of supply and demand. When it was decided in 1959 to broadcast ads on television, the head of the Department of Television Advertising, Hans Lockhoff, justified it thus:

Should we hide our light under a bushel? . . . Life in our Republic has become more beautiful and easier. Energy and industriousness in production have borne fruit. The economy has taken a large step forward. . . . But does everyone see this heartening result, or are there still contemporaries who sit in their comfortable home, chewing on their rich food, all the while praising the unattainable "West" to the heavens? Don't fantastic notions about our life still haunt many West German minds? . . . But what's sure is that we are neglecting to publicize to everyone [our] better life in everyday practice through one of the biggest and most concrete forms of agitation: advertising our economy. Don't [the workers] have the right to experience through interesting ads, colorful posters, and amusing filmstrips all the things that are available to them, how they can live more culturally and more beautifully thanks to the fruit of their labors? Shouldn't one say in a more cheerful form—as opposed to heavy articles and commentary—how one can live more cheerfully? . . . Good advertising is missing as an ingredient in fulfilling our primary economic task, like salt in soup. Where else can one express the optimistic feeling of our better life, the justified pride in our collective achievements, and the solid conviction in our superiority more effectively to the masses, more concisely, or more interestingly than in the colorful palate of advertising?[15]

Apart from the risible claim that advertising would somehow document everyday life, this plea arose from the strong desire to recognize product advertising as a crucial means of political propaganda. Indeed, it was meant to counteract the growing influence of Western advertising. Socialist advertising thus acquired a new function in the ideological battle between the two political camps, conceived as it was as oppositional advertising (*Gegenwerbung*). Yet it was not especially convincing in this respect. When Walter Ulbricht drew attention in a 1962 report to the fact that every year enormous amounts were spent on advertising that had no clear payoff, this had immediate and lasting effects. Now advertising was suddenly considered a total waste. The Council of Ministers then passed a resolution to restrict advertising expenditures by 50 percent, since it had supposedly been proven that the influence of many ad campaigns in the previous months had no relation to their expense. Demands now grew louder that advertising should be eliminated completely, mainly because it contradicted the essence of socialism's social order.[16]

In 1963 there was another twist in connection to economic policy reform. That year's "New Economic System of Socialism" was an attempt to encourage profitability in the economy and to strengthen the individual responsibility of factories. In this context, great meaning was again attached to advertising as a means of regulating supply and demand. Television advertising increased, and sales doubled. The producers of television advertising rejoiced: "With the New Economic System we have overcome the long-standing misperception of the minimal effects of television advertising and the low regard toward its economic usefulness. By making good use of the money-commodity relationship in our national economy, profit will become the decisive criterion for evaluating the performance and management of the economy more generally."[17] For the first time the concept of "consumer freedom of choice" now entered the discussion, and with it the influence upon and education of the consumer was identified as advertising's most important function. "Socialist advertising must be geared toward the fulfilment of socialist consumer standards and lifestyles, along with overcoming capitalist remnants still lingering in the mentality of people. The influence of socialist consciousness must therefore be brought in closer relation with the concrete supply of available goods. . . . From this our populace will see that even within socialism such mental obstacles still exist, and that every effort must be made to free ourselves from their ideological effect."[18]

Yet this hope was never fulfilled, since advertising was prone to constant criticism. Neither could it manage to mediate supply and demand, nor did its proclaimed cultural value of entertainment square very well with broader socialist intellectual principles. Advertising was simply condemned as a senseless waste of precious resources, too closely aligned with dangerous and unwanted Western tendencies.[19] Apart from the difficulty of establishing its political and economic legitimacy, it was really advertising's peculiar media existence as an independent field of symbolic meaning that was its Achilles' heel under socialism. How was a socialist lifestyle supposed to look visually anyway? Smiling families gathered around new refrigerators or televisions? A handsome woman with a vacuum cleaner in hand? How could individual consumption in everyday life be represented as particularly socialist? The advertising leitmotifs of socialist lifestyle tended to cluster around positive images of collective leisure, joyful working women, and health promotion; others focused on idyllic images of youth, family, and couples' happiness. Perhaps the particular charm of viewing GDR advertising today derives from its close relationship to the everyday life and dreams of the time. Little wonder, then, that the main accusation leveled at GDR advertisers was that they tended to reproduce Western consumer images. Consumer asceticism, the self-conscious confinement to use value, and/or functional durability found little resonance in advertising copy.

By the end of the 1960s, SED leaders maintained their conviction that advertising was economically senseless, politically dubious, and culturally damaging. After a long debate in 1975 the Council of Ministers issued a proclamation about the virtues of thrift, which in practice added up to a prohibition on advertising across the land. Permitted were only advertisements for material economy, health care, insurance, cultural policy, production publicity, and the lottery. With it went the end of television advertising, as well as spots in newspapers, radio, and cinema; the advertising industry itself was all but shut down beyond export publicity. In consequence, the campaign to give advertising a new substance and meaning beyond market competition had come to a close. What the very dysfunctionality of socialist advertising paradoxically made clear is that socialist society was also a consumer society shaped by its industrial mass production and urban lifestyle, increasing leisure time and disposable income. And it is primarily this common image of European consumer society that socialist advertising wanted to communicate as well.

The Art of the Consumer: Practices of Appropriation

Consumer conditions under socialism have been a topic among scholars of late. But what does that mean for everyday life, consumer strategies and practices of appropriation? To be sure, the notion of the worker state was the official concept under which all social groups and activities were subsumed. Lifelong salaried labor shaped the daily and weekly rhythm of all workers, and it also structured more personal relationships between the sexes and within families. Nonetheless, the dependence on paid work as the only source of financial gain (since capital and property were absent) provided some room for economic profit, mobility, and social distinction. By means of the mass production of consumer goods, whose standardization severely reduced any variety, all the while making what had been luxury items more and more widely available, the social leveling tendencies of socialist economics were further strengthened. This was intended to lead to a certain similarity of lifestyles, not least because the equalization of salaries and prices was supposed to reflect a shared and equitable world of material conditions.[20]

But how were these broader tendencies toward socioeconomic homogenization received and represented? Is it true, for instance, that what Günter Gaus called the "land of the common people," Dietrich Mühlberg "an underclass society," and Martin Kohli "a society almost without propertied classes" necessarily brought about some sort of cultural homogenization? Did the state's egalitarian crusade really lead to standardized lifestyles? Is, then, the hallowed socialist lifestyle a result of the cultivation and general application of proletariat virtues, or was it rather—thanks to rising general education and material prosperity—more of a "deproletariatization" and "bourgeoisification" of the citizenry despite the state's propaganda to the contrary? Without a doubt all social groups were greatly affected by the dramatic transformations of GDR consumerism and leisure culture, which included the massive introduction of consumer technology into the household and the widespread enjoyment of what were once luxury goods. As the Institute of Market Research studies showed, workers were disinclined toward pursuing social distinctions through consumerism since their incomes were quite modest. In fact, the trendsetters in the world of social distinction were the remains of the entrepreneurial class, artisans, high-ranking functionaries, and the technical intelligentsia. While no precise statistical information is available, it is quite clear that these income groups were the first ones who were able to purchase a television, washing machine, refrigerator, and car; had larger homes; and went often on holiday. Still, it should be noted that they— along with collectivized farmers—had the longest workday in comparison to other groups.

Consumer research on the socioeconomic differentiation of GDR society according to income yields some interesting results. Alongside the occupation categories of workers or employees (*Arbeiter/Angestellte*), intelligentsia, artisans, self-employed workers, and farmers were included retirees and students as distinct social groups. Yet this not only revealed the predominance of "sub-bourgeois" (*unterbürgerlichen*) groups but also indicated further distinguishing elements as noted in table 1.[21] Leaving aside the negligible demographic groups of private entrepreneurs and self-employed workers, what is striking is the income discrepancy according to age, which in this case underlines that certain groups (students and retirees) remained outside the work process. Yet these exceptional groups cannot deflect attention away from the fact that the GDR was clearly a very leveled middle-class society (*Mittelstandsgesellschaft*), with the workers occupying the bottom end of the income scale.

What is more, highly diverse consumer lifestyles also developed among these groups. There are many reasons for this. To the differences in lifestyle among those living in villages, small towns, and big cities can be added the differentiating factors of educational level, gender, age, and

TABLE 1.   Average Net Income According to Specific Social Group

Class/Group	1965	1970	1975	1980
Workers/Employees	105	105	104	106
Intelligentsia	133	143	134	137
Artisans	161	146	165	161
Self-Employed	177	170	186	189
Farmers	120	126	129	129
Retirees	40	47	47	41
Students	30	28	31	29
Total	100	100	100	100

generation. Among people living in rural settings, thriftiness, for example, was generally more pronounced, since they were relatively more self-sufficient and less interested in fashionable clothes, haircuts, restaurants, and holidays than their urban counterparts. Different educational levels could be noted in leisure pursuits and consumer practices: intellectuals read more; constantly sought professional qualifications; watched television moderately; took relatively numerous holidays; developed hobbies such as film, photography, and album collecting; frequented theater; and moved in circles who wrote texts for a living. Intellectuals in the GDR were by and large enthusiastic home improvers: they liked to renovate, build furniture, and tend gardens. Since the 1960s youth became a distinctive consumer group. They were interested in fashion and pursued leisure activities that ensured their cherished generational independence, such as motorcycling, camping, and attending musical events. As soon as young people moved into households of their own, their consumer preferences naturally changed. The financial handicap of the elderly was also extremely noticeable. Retirees lived on the edge of poverty and had little latitude in terms of consumer desires. Gender-specific differences were manifest above all in leisure time. Women had on average over 40 percent less free time than men.[22]

Due to the distribution of privilege, certain groups had access to more resources than others. Older members of the intelligentsia, for example, were given key concessions to entice them to stay in the GDR.[23] Younger members of the intelligentsia, by contrast, had to work harder to attain the same social standards. They also received the short end of the stick when it came to the allocation of decent offices. Young workers were comparatively better off, since they had earlier secured high incomes and could make use of wider social networks for support and provisioning. Those who worked in large export industries were privy to special favors. High-ranking state officials and diplomats, for their part, were able to buy luxury goods in select specialty shops. Single women, and especially those with children, were most neglected among all social groups, while retirees too had to eke out a meager existence at the social margins.

In the 1970s and 1980s the ownership of Western currency acquired increasing importance in East German everyday life, as it seriously transformed income relations. Society became stratified according to "everyone's [Western] aunt's generosity." Access to precious goods and services now was less determined by saved income than by special personal contacts. However one interprets the causes of this development, it did give rise to two contradictory social effects: it accelerated the trends toward both the de-differentiation and re-differentiation (that is, the individualization) of social life. This was especially notable in consumer practices.

For one thing, the broader trend toward income leveling, controlled goods supply, and standardized design inadvertently exerted a strong compensatory pressure toward individualization. Collecting, bartering, bribing, queuing, complaint writing, do-it-yourself projects, moonlighting, home renovation, and general improvisation of all kinds were common expressions of an enormous East German will toward the self-design of life (*Selbstgestaltung des Lebens*). Under the conditions of limited choice, consumerism was a call to creativity, resourcefulness, and individual problem solving. Yet the energy expended on cultural distinction was by no means the quest for social prestige but instead the expression of personality. Despite the severe limitations of real existing socialism, there was always the possibility to make something from what was available, to stylize one's domestic and personal world.[24]

What is more, it was not only GDR goods that were available to individuals. From the very beginning, West German consumer objects and values found their way across the cold war divide. This was especially the case with older citizens, whose own biographical experiences of the "other social system" served as ruptures and dislocation in their everyday lives. As a result, GDR consumer practices were not exclusively determined by the peculiarities of socialism's logic, values, and ideals. They were equally shaped in mosaic fashion by elements from various historical experiences, periods, and social systems.

In this way, consumer culture under socialism shared essential elements with the broader modernization processes found in post-1945 Western Europe and the United States. This was particularly the case with the shortened life span of goods as a result of rapidly changing tastes and styles, the consumer's coming of age in terms of the role of goods in identity formation, as well as the more general rationalization and individualization of lifestyles. What distinguished socialism, however, was the delayed effects of these developments thanks to the GDR's social structure and dominant ideals. Indeed, the very absence of any hegemonic bourgeois class meant that so-called proletariat virtues (such as pragmatism and hedonism) not only were more present culturally but were also ideologically supported. Consumer ideals such as practical use and product durability—as opposed to prestige consumption and fashion—eventually ossified over time. Alongside the dominant everyday images of material prosperity stood other powerful personal ideals: adequate leisure time for the development of individuality and rich social relations became prized values in themselves. In this value system, money carried virtually no symbolic meaning.

Nevertheless, the communist ideals of consumerism in a classless society did not take hold in the GDR. But this was not because of the country's desolate economic situation or because it never succeeded in creating attractive alternatives to individual forms of consumption. It failed because the needs and desires of the people stood in opposition to these ideals. GDR society was faced with a conflict of values that it was ultimately unable to resolve. The socialist utopia promised equality, fair distribution, social security, and communal solidarity. Real-existing capitalism by contrast offered freedom of choice and the possibility of individualization. Banal as it may sound, the GDR couldn't have it both ways.

The GDR, as noted at the beginning of this essay, had no ideal concept of a golden age. Its utopian concept was "geared toward the future," as echoed in the country's national anthem. It believed it had created the preconditions to become the best of all possible worlds. As Gerhard Schulze has recently argued, such an idea is shared by all modern societies.[25] This is a fundamental dimension of the very logic of development and one that stands in a critical relationship to itself. This ambivalence and reflexivity renders absurd the quest for an idealized golden age, historical redemption, and the notion of secular paradise. There can be no imagined happy ending to history and no realized utopian concept in these societies, since this itself would spell the end of the possibility of further development. The GDR then failed in its own utopian aspiration in a double sense: first because it went unfulfilled and second because it remained unreceptive to the dreams and wishes of its own people.

Translated by Paul Betts and Katherine Pence

NOTES

1. Jürgen Kocka, *Vereinigungskrise. Zur Geschichte der Gegenwart* (Göttingen, 1995).

2. Wolfgang Heinrichs, *Die Grundlagen der Bedarfsforschung. Ihre Bedeutung für die Planung des Warenumsatzes und der Warenbereitstellung im staatlichen und genossenschaftlichen Handel der Deutschen Demokratischen Republik* (Berlin [DDR], 1955), 7.

3. Herbert Fischer and Joachim Mayer, "Die Befragung der Verbraucher als Methode der Bedarfsforschung," *Mitteilungen des Instituts für Bedarfsforschung* 2, no. 3 (1963): 63.

4. See the West German publication, Michael Vershofen, "Marktforschung in Deutschland heute," *Zeitschrift für Betriebswirtschaft* 4 (1954): 247.

5. Herbert Fischer, "Die Konsumentenbefragung—eine Form der Einbeziehung der Bevölkerung in die Planung und Leitung der Volkswirtschaft," *Marktforschung* 6, no. 1 (1967): 24.

6. "Thesen zu einigen Problemen der Entwicklung der Konsumtion in der Etappe des umfassenden Aufbaus des Sozialismus," *Mitteilungen des Instituts für Bedarfsforschung* 2, no. 1 (1963): 4–16.

7. Ibid., 7.

8. Ibid., 8.

9. Ibid., 10.

10. "Zur Entwicklung sozialistischer Verbrauchs- und Lebensgewohnheiten bei der Bevölkerung der DDR," 1971, Bundesarchiv Außenstelle Coswig (hereafter BA Coswig), L-102/543, 4.

11. Georg C. Bertsch and Ernst Hedler, *SED—Schönes Einheits-Design* (Cologne, 1990), 12.

12. See Clemens Wischermann, "Der kulturgeschichtliche Ort der Werbung," in *Bilderwelt des Alltags. Werbung in der Konsumgesellschaft des 19. und 20. Jahrhunderts,* ed. Peter Borscheid and Clemens Wischermann (Stuttgart, 1995), 8–19.

13. Margot Kuhle and Paul Schäfer, *Gut beraten—Erfolgreich verkaufen* (Berlin [DDR], 1967), 36.

14. Stiftung Archiv der Parteien und Massenorganisationen der DDR im Bundesarchiv (hereafter SAPMO BA), DY 30/IV 2/610/26, unpaginated, January 16, 1954.

15. Hans Lockhoff (Leiter der Abteilung Werbefernsehen), "Sollen wir unser Licht unter den Scheffel stellen?" *Neues Deutschland,* December 14, 1959.

16. SAPMO BA, DY 30/IV 2/610/33, file page 2, July 17, 1962.

17. Deutsches Rundfunkarchiv, Sammlung Glatzer/Vorbereitung Planmaterialien/Propagandistische und Ratgebersendungen, unpaginated, Jahresplan 1967.

18. Annelies Albrecht, "Die Funktion und Aufgaben der Werbung auf dem Konsumgüterbinnenmarkt, die Verantwortung der einzelnen Organe bei der Lösung dieser Aufgaben und die Vorbereitung und Durchführung der Werbemassnahmen," *Mitteilungen des Instituts für Bedarfsforschung* 3 (1963): 3–8.

19. SAPMO BA, DY30/IV A2/2032/50, unpaginated, August 10, 1970.

20. Wage and tax policy is especially meaningful here, since it led to a broad leveling of wages. Subsidization policies and the achievements of the factories also contributed to a leveling of social differences.

21. The table was put together according to my own calculations from the data of the *Statistischen Jahrbücher.*

22. BA Coswig, L-102/162, file page 73, Horst Scholz, "Die Beziehungen zwischen Umfang und Struktur der Freizeit der Frauen und dem Verbrauch an Waren sowie Dienstleistungen," PhD diss., Hochschule für Ökonomie, Berlin (DDR), 1966.

23. In the 1950s and 1960s, so-called individual contracts were signed with members of the "old" intelligentsia. These contracts secured, among other things, unique financial allotments in the form of special awards, material support in the construction of private homes, and a free choice of schools where their children could study.

24. See the thoughts of Michel de Certeau, *Kunst des Handelns* (Berlin, 1988).

25. Gerhard Schulze, *Die beste aller Welten. Wohin bewegt sich die Gesellschaft im 21. Jahrhundert?* (Munich and Vienna, 2003).

Re-Presenting the Socialist Modern
Museums and Memory in the Former GDR

Daphne Berdahl

In the heart of Leipzig's downtown, on the main street of the city's *Fuss-gängerzone* (pedestrian area) stands a statue called the *Step of the Century*. Completed in the mid-1980s by the renowned East German artist Wolfgang Mattheuer and erected here at this location in 1999, the larger-than-life figure's right hand is extended in the Nazi salute while its left hand is clenched in a worker's fist; it steps forward, half dressed and half in military uniform, with its head hidden and barely visible, into an unknown future. Like many works of art, the statue has been subject to a range of interpretations. Mattheuer has described it as relating to his interest in "the significant tension between conformity and protest, between yes and no, which stimulates and sharpens our vision of the future"; others have read it as an "allegory of totalitarianism" or a "thought-image [*Denkbild*] for the eternal conflict between good and evil."[1] In the German Democratic Republic (GDR), the sculpture was awarded a national prize for depicting the "clash during this century between fascism/Nazism on the one side and Leninism/Stalinism on the other."[2] Yet the statue's placement in front of the Leipzig Forum of Contemporary History (Zeitgeschichtliches Forum Leipzig, or ZGF) in honor of the museum's opening in 1999 has invested it with yet another meaning—now the dominant interpretation—reflecting the museum's mission of portraying the "history of resistance and opposition in the GDR" and its underlying agenda of "comparative dictatorship studies" (fig. 1). According to the museum director, the statue (one of his exhibit favorites) "demonstrates the German people's step away from two dictatorships."[3] Indeed, this or a similar explanation is frequently part of museum as well as Leipzig city tours. In its new context within the cultural landscape of reunited Germany, then, the *Step of the Century* is read as symbolizing the

Fig. 1. *The Step of the Century,* in front of the Leipzig Forum of Contemporary History (ZGF) (Photograph by Daphne Berdahl with the permission of the ZGF.)

new Germany's step *out* of the last century, leaving behind its troubled pasts of Nazism and socialism.

I begin with this image because it illuminates and contextualizes several issues surrounding the politics of memory and museum re-presentations in the former GDR that I address in this essay: the ongoing, often complex and contradictory struggles over the production of East German memory, the contexts of this production, and the ways in which the struggles themselves shed light upon larger social and political processes within reunified Germany more generally. As Pence and Betts point out in the introduction to this volume, the question of the relationship to and representation of the GDR past gained immediate relevance after the fall of the Berlin Wall in 1989 and has been the subject of significant popular as well as scholarly discussion and debate ever since.[4] I am interested here not just in the politics of memory making but also in the various domains in which memory is constructed and deployed and in the cultural implications and effects of such memory-making practices. My aim here, then, is to interrogate the production of historical memory in the former GDR, and I do so by comparing two cases of the "museumification" of GDR history: the state-sponsored and officially sanctioned Forum of Contemporary History in Leipzig and a local association's collection and exhibition of GDR material culture. My discussion is indebted to a large and burgeoning scholarship on museums as critical sites for the convergence of social, cultural, and political forces: as arenas for the production of national identity, national citizens, and national "culture";[5] as objects of the tourist gaze;[6] as part of new disciplines of power;[7] and as spaces of cultural representation and contestation.[8] Yet as the anthropologists Richard Handler and Eric Gable have pointed out, "most research on museums has proceeded by ignoring much of what happens in them."[9] Drawing on ongoing ethnographic fieldwork conducted since 2001 in the city of Leipzig,[10] this essay explores discourses and practices surrounding two radically different re-presentations of GDR history. Both contrasting cases, I argue, reflect ongoing contestations over the meanings of the GDR past as well as the significant power imbalances in which such struggles occur.

Repression and Resistance: The Zeitgeschichtliches Forum Leipzig

The sole satellite branch of the Haus der Geschichte in Bonn (a project initiated by Helmut Kohl in 1982 with a conservative and hence controversial agenda that culminated in the opening of the museum in Bonn eight years later),[11] the Leipzig Forum of Contemporary History is commonly described as the eastern counterpart to the Bonn original. It was opened with great fanfare in a ceremony attended by Chancellor Schröder on October 9, 1999, the tenth anniversary of what is widely believed to be the "turning point" in the peaceful demonstrations of 1989 in Leipzig.[12] The city was selected as the site for the museum because of its role in this history.

As an institution, the ZGF describes itself as a "place of living remembrance." It thus strives to be more than a museum; it is also a memorial and a gathering place for lectures, discussions, and conferences. Indeed, the institution makes a very valuable contribution in this sense to intellectual life and historical work in Leipzig and beyond. Because the explicit focus of the museum is on "the history of resistance and opposition during the dictatorship of the Soviet Occupation Zone and the GDR," it commemorates a critical element of the East German experience as well as the earth-shattering events of 1989. Underlying this focus on repression and resistance is a scholarly interest in and commitment to what is sometimes called "comparative dictatorship studies"—a belief in the historical comparability of the Nazi and socialist regimes, with the latter described in the exhibit catalog as the "second German dictatorship."[13]

These ideological underpinnings are evident throughout the chronologically organized exhibit, where stories and images of suffering, repression, and state violence are foregrounded alongside a narrative of resistance and opposition. Guided tours—frequently given by university students too young to have many memories of the GDR—often privilege the most gruesome or sensational installations, highlighting for visitors a sequential horror of socialist abuses. In addition to key events in political and economic history, exhibits contain several installations on political prisoners as well as the fortification of the inter-German border in the 1950s and the building of the Berlin Wall in 1961 (fig. 2). One display informs visitors of the "burden of the past" in the East, where "former members of the Nazi Party obtained important posts and thus high status in the GDR"—a narrative that is misrepresentative at best for failing to disclose that such practices were in fact more common in postwar West Germany. An entire room, complete with a wall of video footage and a Soviet "division cannon," is dedicated to the uprising on June 17, 1953, while another section focuses on the biographies of political dissidents and the work of oppositional peace and environmental groups. Displays representing GDR consumer culture and material scarcity are sandwiched between depictions of successful escapes and an exhibit devoted to the Stasi (state security police) that includes cases of files, surveillance equipment and paraphernalia (containing, among other items, several odor specimens from regime opponents in canning jars[14] as well as actual Stasi surveillance videos), and a van with a restructured interior to accommodate political prisoners without being recognizable as such on the outside (fig. 3). The narrative culminates in a triumphalist portrayal of 1989, the largest exhibit area in the museum, containing protest demonstration banners, a section of the Berlin Wall, the iconic Trabant car in Western commercial garb (itself a powerful statement), and other artifacts of that eventful period (fig. 4). The last area of the exhibit focuses on post-Wall eastern Germany, with displays on building booms, unemployment, and violence against foreigners that call specific attention to contemporary social issues and economic concerns but also risk naturalizing them in the larger context of the museum's teleological narrative.

Fig. 2.   Images of the Berlin Wall at the ZGF. (Photograph by Daphne Berdahl with the permission of the ZGF.)

Like those of many contemporary museums, the ZGF exhibits draw upon multiple media to invite active visitor participation and engagement. Audio stations, touch screens, video monitors, and interactive hands-on displays abound as part of the Haus der Geschichte's larger objective of enabling visitors to "experience history." A review of the ZGF exhibit after its 1999 opening in the *Frankfurter Allgemeine Zeitung,* for example, praised its "effectively staged tour route" where "not a corner is without a flickering monitor or a chattering loudspeaker."[15] "We present history as an experience, as visitor-friendly and entertaining," the president of the Bonn Haus der Geschichte, Hermann Schäfer, recently asserted.[16] Indeed, in response to a historian colleague's comment that the Bonn museum reminded him of Disneyland, Schäfer reportedly responded, "Thank you very much. But we're not that good yet."[17]

This play with the senses surrounds visitors with images and sounds that can operate on many levels, sometimes eliciting emotional, even visceral, reactions. Upon entering the exhibit area on the Berlin Wall, for

Fig. 3.   The Stasi van and files at the ZGF. (Photograph by Daphne Berdahl with the permission of the ZGF.)

example, one is confronted with videos of attempted escapes, with people screaming, hanging out of windows, or being mangled by barbed wire. The reverberations of tank rumblings and screeching provide the audio background for the June 17 uprising. With the exception of dissident songwriter Wolf Biermann's music, in fact, one's auditory experience of the museum is dominated by the sounds of bullets being fired, churches being blown up, and human cries of alarm. Taken together, these acoustic enhancements are carefully selected to conform to the museum's emphasis on repression and resistance, a narrative described by museum directors and employees as "the Concept."[18]

This narrative concept is stressed repeatedly in the rigorous screening of museum guides. "You must agree with and stand by our concept," one university student was reportedly told firmly during her second round of interviews for a tour guide position. She was not offered the job after expressing reservations about her ability and willingness to comply with the strict guidelines. Indeed, the narrative of repression and resistance not only dominates the museum "Concept" but also can be internalized and reproduced in personal accounts during guided tours. I was told, for

Fig. 4. At the
ZGF, a section of
Berlin Wall and
Trabant painted in
Western commer-
cial style with the
GDR gas company
Minol brand name.
(Photograph by
Daphne Berdahl
with the permission
of the ZGF.)

example, of a visit to the museum by a group of local historians interested in initiating a conversation about representational practices at the exhibit. "Throughout the tour our guide grew increasingly excited and extreme," one of them recalled, "and when we came to the [Stasi van] she claimed that she had sat as a prisoner inside. I thought to myself: Wow! That is really awful. But then a member of our group exclaimed, 'No, Angelika, you sat in the SED district management office!' She turned bright red and just left." Pressure to adhere to the museum "Concept" is allegedly felt very strongly by museum employees, creating an occasional atmosphere of fear and suspicion in the workplace. Most museum employees only wanted to speak off the record, for example, and I was especially alarmed to hear about rumors of wiretapping employee phone conversations.

Rumors and suspicion aside, it seems to me that a more vexing issue is at stake here. While the museum's literature and staff are careful to point out that the focal point of the museum is "dictatorship and resistance" rather than "the history of the GDR," as the sole branch of the Haus der Geschichte national museum in the East (the "little brother" of the Haus der Geschichte in Bonn, I was sometimes told, a description that invoked the diminutive term used in referring to "brothers and sisters in the East"), and the only federally organized and funded museum dedicated exclusively to the GDR, the effect of this emphasis is to re-present GDR history in these terms. Media accounts of the museum's opening heralded it as an "exhibit and information center" that provides "a broad overview of the GDR and the division of Germany"[19] or as containing over "2500 exhibits on the history of the division of Germany and the transition in the GDR."[20] More specifically, the museum was applauded at its opening for its contribution to "the history of democracy in Germany"[21] and for demonstrating the "civil courage" of eastern Germans during the fall of 1989, an "unparalleled enrichment of German history."[22] In his speech at the opening ceremony, Chancellor Schröder asked "not to be misunderstood" when he said that one could be "pleased to be a German today . . . to be proud of the realization of democracy."[23]

This adamant, indeed dogmatic, privileging of resistance at the museum may have as its subtext, it seems to me, the haunted past of the "first German dictatorship" and the question of German guilt. Conceptually and discursively linking the two regimes through the rhetoric of "a second German dictatorship" (a discourse in which comparability may be equated with commensurability, even if that is not its intended effect), the director of the Leipzig ZGF writes in the exhibit catalog:

> We have placed special emphasis on biographical approaches; it was, however, clear that the isolated examples of bravery under the dictatorship stand for the courage of hundreds of thousands of other resisting East Germans.[24]

The privileged narrative here, then, is ultimately one of redemption: a new official history for the new Germany. The national director of the Haus der Geschichte, Hermann Schäfer gestured toward this nationalizing project in describing the mission of the Leipzig ZGF:

> We want to break what the opinion research institutes have diagnosed as the wall of silence between east and west—break it by means

of exhibitions, events and publications produced and sponsored by the new museum in Leipzig, in order to find a historical conception common to all Germans.[25]

Despite favorable ratings in museum visitor surveys (highly touted in the exhibit catalog),[26] local reactions do not reveal that efforts to forge this "common historical conception" have been successful. In informal conversations as well as during interviews on other subjects, I often heard the ZGF described as "victor's history." "It is purely propaganda from the western side," a man in his forties working for the Chamber of Commerce angrily explained. "It disgusts me just when I see the themes portrayed there: 'church in socialism,' 'resistance,' 'opposition.' All of this is a very western perspective." Outside of work, one of the most historically sophisticated of the ZGF tour guides agreed: "The museum conveys to visitors the impression that this is the history of the GDR, but it isn't. It is designed with a western view of GDR history. Many visitors from the east cannot find themselves here." An eastern German historian made a similar suggestion: "Actually I think it is kind of cute," he smiled, continuing that "People in the GDR learned how to read things critically. I hope they apply those skills to this exhibit." In contrast to the positive reviews of most German media following the museum's opening, the leftist daily and former GDR youth publication *Junge Welt* wrote:

> The exhibit on GDR history is not a house of history, but a bazaar that, alongside remnants of the Wall, images of jumping soldiers, original packages from the West [*Westpakete*] and cheap Ulbricht utterances [*Sächseleien*] offers independent publications [*Samisdatszeitschriften*] of oppositional movements and is not much more than a shop of horrors. Special offers for western "*Wendetouristen*" who wish to validate their lack of understanding for the unhappiness and ingratitude of the east.[27]

Another common local reaction—uttered in rage by some while exiting the exhibit area,[28] stated by others as a simple fact in subsequent conversations outside the museum—was "that is not how I experienced the GDR!" "Sure there were people who were imprisoned or who were spied upon," one local merchant told me. "But that was not my experience. I'm sorry, but that was just not my experience." When I asked an artist in her late thirties about the emphasis on dictatorship and resistance exemplified by the Stasi van and border shootings, she answered:

[In GDR times] you spent your days looking for the one detergent that was hard to get that didn't give your kids a rash. And then because you wanted your little ones to have some vitamins, you bought carrots, cleaned them, pressed them together with some apples, because that was how you could get juice. And when there was juice in the store, you took a box to the store and stood in line so that you could go for a while without having to press your own [juice]. THAT was daily life in the GDR.

The social and political context for these reactions is a much more general devaluation of East German histories since reunification. As I have written about elsewhere,[29] such practices have included the selling of East German factories to Western companies, occasionally for next to nothing; the discrediting of the GDR educational system, particularly the *Abwicklung*[30] (restructuring) of the universities; the renaming of schools, streets, and other public buildings; the toppling of socialist memorials and monuments; the trial of Berlin border guards that for many eastern Germans represented a different sort of victors' justice; debates over what to do with and about East Germany's Stasi heritage that have often compared the GDR to the Third Reich; and discourses that ridiculed the backwardness of East German industry and consumer goods while ignoring the social and historical contexts that may have produced it. Although generated and experienced differently in form and content (*Abwicklung* was viewed as an affront and degradation by eastern German academics, for example, whereas the toppling of socialist monuments and memorials was divisive and often done by GDR anticommunists), such practices have generally been grouped together in eastern German discourses of oppositional solidarity against Western hegemony—of which the ZGF has come to be viewed by many as an emblem.

Bearing Witness: The Ostalgie Project

Since the mid-1990s a range of institutional and individual practices have emerged as part of a counternarrative to such hegemonic memory making and devaluations of the GDR. Commonly referred to as *Ostalgie* (nostalgia for the East), the production of countermemories and identities has taken many forms: a self-described "nostalgia café" called the Wallflower (Mauerblümchen) that is decorated with artifacts from the socialist period and serves "traditional" GDR fare; dance parties (Ostivals or Ostalgie Nights) featuring East German rock music, a double of Erich Honecker, and, occasionally, a Trabi or two ("two-stroke techno parties"); numerous publications and trivia games recalling life in the GDR; supermarkets and an annual "OstPro" trade show fair that specialize in East German products, including one store whose name seems to reflect a now common sentiment: Back to the Future.[31] Demand for products through an "Ossi mail order" (*OssiVersand*) Web site that opened in 1998 far exceeded demand, and the 1999 release and box office success of two "Ostalgie films" (*Sonnenallee* and *Helden Wie Wir*) marked the emergence of Ostalgie as a truly mass cultural phenomenon. More recently, the critically acclaimed and top-grossing 2002 film *Goodbye Lenin* unleashed a new wave of Ostalgie, including a flurry of "Ostshows," featuring curiosities of life in the GDR, on at least five major German television networks.

What I want to focus on here, however, is a specific example of a counternarrative to the official histories and memories represented by the ZGF, a collection of East German "everyday objects" by a local nonprofit organization. The collection reflects the privileging of material culture in eastern German historical memory,[32] the most extensive and sophisticated example of which is the Museum for East German Everyday Life Culture in Eisenhüttenstadt, a truly professional undertaking; its mission entails the "museumification of the world of GDR objects as an active and mutual communication that allows for reflective thought in a period of individual and often painful reorientation."[33] The "Zeitzeugen Ostalgie" project (Ostalgie Witnesses to History), however, is representative of more widespread practices of collecting, cataloging, and displaying "GDR everyday life." Voluntary associations dedicated to the documentation and preservation of GDR everyday life, for example, allocate responsibilities among members for collecting everything from East German packaging materials to work brigade medals. Numerous makeshift museums, galleries, and displays in community centers or people's homes similarly contain various objects of the vanished state.[34]

The Zeitzeugen Ostalgie collection is the product of government-subsidized make-work jobs (*Arbeitsbeschaffungsmaßnahmen,* or ABM); the purpose of the organization of which it is a part (whose name is Neue Arbeit—Wurzen) is to generate jobs in the "second labor market" (*zweiter Arbeitsmarkt*), a term referring to the government-subsidized domain of employment. People employed as ABM do not consider themselves to be

working in a "real job," as the man who picked me up from the train station explained immediately after introducing himself: "I am working in the
second labor market," he said. "In capitalism there is a first labor market,
but somehow there is still also a second one." As Angela Jancius has
pointed out in her intriguing study of unemployment in the former GDR,
workers employed in the second labor market perceive themselves as
engaged in "useful but not productive labor."[35]

By any measure, the work of the three ABM staff employed through
the Zeitzeugen Ostalgie project has been a labor of love. With no experience or training in exhibition design, they have painstakingly assembled a
collection of GDR artifacts from the 1960s, 1970s, and 1980s ranging from
food packaging (including some actual food) to electronics to household
furniture. In former classrooms of a vacated school building, the exhibit is
composed of reconstructed domestic living spaces as well as thematic clusters of particular items. A living room features a typical GDR upholstered
sofa, side chairs on silver casters, coffee table, and wall unit displaying
characteristic decorative objects (fig. 5); a kitchen is full of aluminum
cooking pans and utensils, plastic kitchen gadgets and dinnerware, obso-
lescent appliances, and East German foodstuffs (fig. 6). The display items
elicit what the exhibit organizers describe as an "Aha effect," a reaction
that connects personal biographies to collective memory as visitors recognize and tell stories about familiar but forgotten cultural objects. These
East German things are particularly effective *lieux de memoire* for what
Paul Betts has insightfully termed "the aesthetics of sameness. . . . That is,
the very lack of product innovation and repackaging assured that these
objects—however privately experienced and remembered—would function as transgenerational markers of East German culture and identity."[36]
The exhibit's setting in a former elementary school also provides contextual meaning, evoking the radical birthrate decline in the former GDR
after 1989 and a new German state that, in the opinion of many eastern
Germans, is hostile to children.[37] A warehouse of discarded used furniture
for low-income families, the vast majority of which are GDR products,
occupies an adjacent room; a separate ABM project of the Neue Arbeit—
Wurzen, these items represent for many not only the throwaway mentality
of today's consumer society but also the dustbin of history to which the
GDR and its products have been relegated and from which the relics of
Ostalgie have been culled.

The idea for the project came to one of the organization directors one

Fig. 5.   Reconstructed GDR living room (Zeitzeugen Ostalgie). (Photograph by Daphne Berdahl.)

day upon hearing what schoolchildren were learning about the GDR in class:

> I was interested in what the kids were learning about the GDR then, in the year 1997 or 1998. [My young relative] told me that there was nothing to eat, that people couldn't buy anything. Everything was dark and gray. . . . And people weren't allowed to laugh and weren't able to laugh. . . . And I thought to myself, this can't be true. So we brainstormed about how to turn this into an ABM project. . . . what was daily life really like?

As we walked through the exhibit, my hosts repeatedly stressed that they did not want to "glorify the GDR," that this was intended as a completely "apolitical exhibit." As evidence of this, they cited their "strategic decision" not to include political memorabilia like pins, medals, uniforms,

Fig. 6.   Reconstructed GDR kitchen (Zeitzeugen Ostalgie). (Photograph by Daphne Berdahl.)

or Free German Youth (FDJ) scarves. In the kitchen area they described showing schoolchildren how juice was pressed, how fruits and vegetables were preserved, "because you couldn't just go to the store and buy everything." The quaintness of socialist design was particularly highlighted in the electronics room, featuring, among other things, a square phonograph record (fig. 7). "We chose the name 'historical witnesses,'" one of the directors explained when I asked about the project title, "because we didn't want to write simply 'objects of utility' [*Gebrauchsgegenstände*] but also because these [things] really are witnesses."

But to what, we may ask, do these objects bear witness? Part of the answer to this question may lie in the comments and impressions of visitors left behind in the guest book, which overwhelmingly reveals that the exhibit was far from "apolitical." For example:

> One can appreciate the meticulous effort and thoughtfulness that went into this [exhibit], but the strong ideological one-sidedness is very disturbing.

Fig. 7. Colorful display of GDR electronics (Zeitzeugen Ostalgie). (Photograph by Daphne Berdahl.)

Very nice. . . . it recalls memories, above all how the prices remained stabile for years.

Remember this? We used to cook with it. And this we used to wash with. The shampoo wasn't bad either . . . but it was only available under the table.

Because this is also a part of my life, I was very happy to see this exhibit.

Many thanks for taking on the important task of collecting and preserving things from a distant epoch. One shouldn't think of this in terms of Ostalgie, but as a piece of identity preserved.

What emerges in these comments—as in many other practices of Ostalgie—is a sense of a highly complicated relationship between personal histories, disadvantage, dispossession, the betrayal of promises, and the social worlds of production and consumption. As I have argued elsewhere about Ostalgie more generally,[38] such practices must be seen in the context of feelings of profound displacement and disillusionment following reunification, reflected in the popular saying that we have "emigrated without leaving home." As one university student said to me in a conversation about the subject in the spring of 2001:

> Everything simply disappeared. When you leave your past behind, you can normally go home again, look at it—at your *Heimat* and so forth. But in this case everything just disappeared.

The focus on East German things may also recall an identity as producers that has been lost in this transition. In a society where productive labor was a key aspect of state ideology and where the workplace was a central site for social life, the high incidence of unemployment throughout eastern Germany has undermined profoundly many people's sense of self and identity. It is no accident, then, that a collection emphasizing the products of East German labor emerged in the context of the "second labor market," where feelings of disillusionment, devalued selves, and betrayal often prevail. There is something strikingly poignant in this self-validating effort to recall and preserve a distinctive and honorable past, it seems to me—in this work created for and performed by those considered "unemployable" in the "first labor market." "I was born in 1961," one of the project participants told me.

> Those whole years I was a child, youth, adult—school, studies, work. It is a part of my life. The predominant part of my life. This Ostalgie is for me also a piece of my own life, my own identity. . . . Those were formative years, that's how I would see it.

The frequent reference to GDR consumer culture in the guest book comments as well as in the exhibit tour and demonstration is also significant. The fact that East German things have become mnemonics must be viewed in relation to larger historical and political economic processes and contexts. The dominant narrative in the Ostalgie collection is not one of a repressive dictatorship, as at the ZGF, but of a regime that, quite literally, failed to deliver the goods. In this sense, the emphasis on quaint East German things and their scarcity under socialist rule in contrast—explicit or implicit—to the plentiful supply of ever new and improved products in the West affirms and perpetuates a narrative of

Fig. 8.   GDR fashion show at the ZGF in Leipzig, 2001. (Photograph by Daphne Berdahl with the permission of the ZGF.)

"democratization" and national legitimacy in which access to consumer goods and consumer choice is defined as a fundamental right and a democratic expression of individualism. Indeed, many observers have since suggested that the transitions of 1989 were about demands not for political or human rights but for consumer rights.[39] As the historian Ina Merkel has observed: "The struggle between the systems did not take the form of armed conflict, but was rather shifted to the marketplace. And it was here, in the sphere of consumerism, that the battle was won."[40] In the context of this postwar relationship between political legitimacy and mass consumption, such re-presentations of the GDR not only contribute to the production of new (counter) memories and histories; they contribute to the production of citizen-consumers as well.[41]

Conclusion: Fashioning the Past

To conclude, I turn to an event in which these various domains and practices of memory converged: a fashion show of East German clothing styles held at the Leipzig Forum of Contemporary History during the Leipzig "museum night," an evening for promoting city museums with special presentations, exhibits, and extended business hours. The master of ceremonies was an extremely animated local celebrity (and former Socialist Unity Party member), Paul Fröhlich, whose energetic performance enlivened the packed house of onlookers. "Good evening ladies and gentleman," he began. "Welcome to the Zeitgeschlichtes Forum! . . . Here we begin with the slide over there. It is 1951 and the week of German-Chinese friendship! We would like to transport you this evening to the fashion and Zeitgeist of the GDR." While GDR tunes blasted over loudspeakers (ranging from the Puhdys rock band to the 1950s Lispi-Schritt tune to the Oktober Klub's "Sag mir wo du stehst") and period photos were projected onto a nearby screen, models strode down the runway outfitted in exemplary GDR fashion design (fig. 8). The running commentary of the host had the audience laughing and applauding at nearly every example, as Fröhlich drew upon a culturally shared knowledge of socialist products, cultural images, and Party rhetoric. Full of irony, he brilliantly played with the history of socialist industrial design ("Here we have a multifunctional downhill and cross country ski"), often explicitly fetishizing the objects on display: "Please look, with an eye for detail, at these buttons. Look at these, as one says today, 'cool'[42] buttons. These are simply erotic details from GDR designer times!" In another instance, he had the audience in stitches with a demonstration of the sexual eroticism of a GDR vacuum cleaner. (Hint: the vacuum cleaner bag inflates upright.)

The repeated references to GDR consumer culture required a shared and privileged knowledge that excluded any audience member—real or imagined—who had not experienced socialism, creating a strong sense of solidarity among those in the know. It would be easy, therefore, to categorize this performance as another instance of Ostalgie. More than this, however, the show was also a playful appropriation and ironic parody of Ostalgie. In this context, East German things became "camp" rather than objects of nostalgic longing or countermemory. Thus, although one of the ZGF historians described the show as not fitting in with the "Concept," suggesting to me that its presentation was a subversive act because it was an attempt by several staff members to address critiques of the ZGF by bringing in the "everyday" and because the museum director did not approve of the idea, in fact the mocking tone and the focus on the quaint, hopelessly backward, and outdated GDR styles were quite in line with the institutional agenda of creating a "historical conception common to all Germans." Although it did not stress the museum's focal point of dictatorship and resistance, the show not only underscored the relationship between national legitimacy and mass consumption but also belittled and dismissed eastern German critiques of hegemonic memory making contained in many Ostalgic practices. Indeed, poking fun at Ostalgie is fast becoming almost as profitable a cottage industry as Ostalgie itself. Lyrics to a 2001 Leipzig cabaret song, for example, reflect this satirizing sentiment:

Good Federal Republic citizens the Ossis want to be
Yet they buy only eastern products on their chain store
    shopping sprees
Spee and Florena, Rotkäppchen and Fit
How long will the office for constitutional protections
put up with it?[43]

The parodies of Ostalgie in the fashion show and cabaret song reflect one of the latest waves in the ongoing negotiation of memory in the former GDR. Indeed, together with the two cases of "museumification" I have discussed here, they illuminate the multiple, fluid, shifting, complex, and often contradictory forms and domains of memory production—and consumption—in postsocialist eastern Germany. When viewed in this way, the work and the politics of memory can be a window into larger political processes and landscapes of nation building, identity formation, and belonging in a period of social change and discord.

NOTES

This essay is a revised and expanded version of an earlier article, "Expressions of Experience and Experiences of Expressions: Museum Re-Presentations of GDR History," *Anthropology and Humanism* 30, no. 2 (December 2005): 156–70.
    1. "Romantiker im Jahrhundertschritt: Der Maler und Grafiker Wolfgang

Mattheuer wird heute 70." Berlin Online, http://www.berlinonline.de/ . . .
ner_zeitung/archiv/1997/kultur/0002/.

2. http://www.dhm.de/lemo/html/biograpfien/MattheuerWolfgang.

3. In Express Online, wysiwyg://235/http:www.express.de/bonn/museen/
1392214.html.

4. See, e.g., Daphne Berdahl, "Dis-Membering the Past: The Politics of Mem-
ory in the German Borderland," in *A User's Guide to German Cultural Studies,* ed.
Irene Kacandes, Scott Dedham, and Jonathan Petropoulos (Ann Arbor, 1997);
Paul Betts, "The Twilight of the Idols: East German Memory and Material Cul-
ture," *Journal of Modern History* 72 (2000) 731–65; Elizabeth Ten Dyke, *Dresden:
Paradoxes of Memory in History* (London and New York, 2001); Gerd Kuhn and
Andreas Ludwig, eds., *Alltag und soziales Gedächtnis* (Hamburg, 1997); Jost Her-
mand and Marc Silberman, eds., *Contentious Memories: Looking Back at the GDR*
(New York, 2000).

5. Philip Dodd, "Englishness and the National Culture," in *Englishness: Politics and Culture 1880–1920,* ed. R. Colls and P. Dodd (London, 1986); Carol Dun-
can, *Civilizing Rituals: Inside Public Art Museums* (London, 1995).

6. John Urry, *The Tourist Gaze: Leisure and Travel in Contemporary Society*
(London, 1990).

7. Tony Bennett, *The Birth of the Museum: History, Theory, Politics* (London,
1995).

8. Richard Handler and Eric Gable, *The New History in an Old Museum: Creating the Past at Colonial Williamsburg* (Durham, 1997); Christine Mullen Krae-
mer, Ivan Karp, and Steven D. Lavine, eds., *Museums and Communities: The Politics of Public Culture* (Washington, DC, 1992); Ivan Karp and Steven D. Lavin,
eds., *Exhibiting Cultures: The Poetics and Politics of Museum Display* (Washington, DC, 1991); Barbara Kirshenblatt-Gimblett, *Destination Culture: Tourism,
Museums, and Heritage* (Berkeley, 1998); George Stocking, ed., *Objects and Others:
Essays on Museums and Material Culture* (Madison, 1985).

9. Gable, *New History in an Old Museum,* 9.

10. Ethnographic observation, one of the distinguishing features of an anthropological approach, was the primary methodology of my research. Quotations
cited in this essay are drawn largely from taped interviews as well as notes taken
during or after more informal conversations. Following standard anthropological
practice, I have made every effort to conceal the identities of my interlocutors
except in the case of public figures (i.e., the museum directors), whose comments
are part of the public and published record.

11. For a sophisticated discussion of the Bonn museum origins in the context of
wider debates about the politics of German history and memory, see Charles
Maier, *The Unmasterable Past: History, Holocaust, and German National Identity*
(Cambridge, Mass.: Harvard University Press, 1988).

12. Leipzig, known as the "city of heroes," was where the Monday demonstrations of 1989 began. On October 9, over seventy thousand citizens of the city took
to the streets despite warnings of orders to police to shoot; the absence of violence
on this date signaled that the demonstrations against the state could proceed
peacefully, and participant demands and numbers grew after that.

13. Hanna Schissler has pointed to the dangers of perpetuating cold war narratives through such comparisons. See Hanna Schissler, "Introduction: Writing about 1950s West Germany," in *The Miracle Years: A Cultural History of West Germany, 1949–1968,* ed. Hanna Schissler (Princeton: Princeton University Press, 2001) 3–16.

14. One of the many elaborate surveillance practices of the Stasi entailed the collection of scent specimens of regime opponents in preserving jars for use with scent detection dogs.

15. "Die neue Linie 89," *Frankfurter Allegemeine Zeitung,* October 11, 1999, 52.

16. In *General-Anzeiger,* July 5, 2002.

17. Iris Klingehöfer, "Schröder? Findet Uns Richtig Gut." Express Online, http://www.express.de/bonn/museen/1392214.html.

18. This notion of the Concept is consistent with the Bonn museum's agenda and discourse as well. See Maier, *The Unmasterable Past.*

19. *Neue Zürcher Zeitung,* November 19, 1999, 5.

20. Jens Schneider, "Zeitgeschichtliches Forum," *Süddeutsche Zeitung,* October 11, 1999.

21. Rainer Eckert, quoted in *Der Spiegel* 41 (October 1999): 19.

22. Associated Press World Stream—German, October 10, 1999.

23. In Christian Schmidt, "Leipzig: Die Sieger im Freudentaumel," *Junge Welt,* October 11, 1999, http://www.jungewelt.de.

24. Rainer Eckert, "Repression und Widerstand in der zweiten deutschen Diktatur," in *Einsichten: Diktatur und Widerstand in der DDR,* ed. Stiftung Haus der Geschichte der Bundesrepublik Deutschland (Leipzig, 2001), 16.

25. Schäfer quoted in Haus der Geshichte Web site, http://www.hdg.de/Final/eng/oage 141.htm.

26. Stiftung Haus der Geschichte der Bundesrepublik Deutschland, ed., *Einsichten: Diktatur und Widerstand in der DDR* (Leipzig, 2001).

27. "In Leipzig gruselt's einem für der DDR: Das Zeitgeschichtliche Forum ist eröffnet," *Junge Welt,* October 13, 1999, http://www.jungewelt.de.

28. This was reported to me by an employee of the museum shop, located at the exit to the exhibits.

29. Daphne Berdahl, "'(N)ostalgia' for the Present: Memory, Longing, and East German Things," *Ethnos* 64, no. 2 (1999): 192–211.

30. *Abwicklung,* meaning "to unwind" as well as "to liquidate," entailed the restructuring of East German universities through the dissolution departments and institutes, dismissal of East German faculty members (20 percent of professors and 60 percent of *Mittelbau,* or intermediate ranks), the recruitment of West German academics, and the concomitant influx of West German research agendas.

31. See Berdahl, "'(N)ostalgia' for the Present."

32. See also Betts, "Twilight of the Idols."

33. Gerd Kuhn and Andreas Ludwig, "Sachkultur und DDR-Alltag: Versuch einer Annäherung," in *Alltag und soziales Gedächtnis: Die DDR Objektkultur und ihre Musealisierung,* ed. Gerd Kuhn and Andreas Ludwig (Hamburg, 1997); see also Andreas Ludwig, ed., *Alltagskultur der DDR: Begleitbuch zur Ausstellung "Tempolinsen und P2"* (Berlin-Brandenburg, 1996).

34. See also Dyke, *Dresden.*

35. Angela Jancius, "Social Markets and the Meaning of Work in Eastern Germany," in *Culture and Economy: Contemporary Perspectives,* ed. Ullrich Kockel (Hampshire, England, and Burlington, VT, 2002).

36. Betts, "Twilight of the Idols," 754.

37. See, e.g., Daphne Hahn, Irene Doelling, and Sylka Scholz, "Birth Strike in the New Federal States: Is Sterilization an Act of Resistance?" in *Reproducing Gender: Politics, Publics, and Everyday Life after Socialism,* ed. Susan Gal and Gail Kligman (Princeton, 2000).

38. Berdahl, "'(N)ostalgia' for the Present."

39. E.g., Zygmunt Bauman, *Intimations of Postmodernity* (New York, 1992); Betts, "Twilight of the Idols"; John Borneman, *Belonging in the Two Berlins: Kin, State, Nation* (Cambridge, 1992); Slavenka Drakulić, *How We Survived Communism and Even Laughed* (New York, 1991).

40. Ina Merkel, "Consumer Culture in the GDR, or How the Struggle for Antimodernity Was Lost on the Battleground of Consumer Culture," in *Getting and Spending: European and American Consumer Societies in the Twentieth Century,* ed. Charles McGovern, Susan Strasser, and Matthias Judt (Cambridge, 1998), 282.

41. Daphne Berdahl, "The Spirit of Capitalism and the Boundaries of Citizenship in Post-Wall Germany," *Comparative Studies in Society and History* 47, no. 2 (2005): 235–51.

42. The play with words cannot be captured in translation here, as the German term *geil* draws on the word's different colloquial meanings of "cool" and "horny."

43. The text of the song in German is as follows:

Sie möchten gute Bundesbürger sein
Und kaufen in der Kaufhalle Ostprodukte ein
Spee und Florena, Rotkäppchen und Fit
Wie lange macht das der Verfassungsschutz noch mit?

Contributors

Daphne Berdahl was associate professor of anthropology and global studies at the University of Minnesota. She is the author of *Where the World Ended: Re-Unification and Identity in the German Borderland* (1999) and coeditor of *Altering States: Ethnographies of Transition in East Central Europe and the Former Soviet Union* (2000). She was a Guggenheim Fellow in 2007 for work on her second book on the politics of memory in the former GDR. An article based on this research appeared in *Anthropology and Humanism* (2005). In addition, she was working on a project focusing on the relationship between mass consumption; globalization; and changing understandings, visions, meanings, and practices of citizenship in post-Wall Germany. A recent article based on this research appeared in *Comparative Studies in Society and History* (2005). Tragically, she passed away following a struggle with cancer a few months before publication of this book. She will be missed.

Paul Betts is reader in German history at the University of Sussex in Brighton, England. He is the author of *The Authority of Everyday Objects: A Cultural History of West German Industrial Design* (2004) and coeditor (with Greg Eghigian) of *Pain and Prosperity: Reconsidering Twentieth Century German History* (2003). He has also coedited (with David Crowley) a special issue of *Journal of Contemporary History* (2005) titled "Domestic Dreamworlds: Notions of Home in Post–1945 Europe" and is joint editor of the journal *German History*. Currently he is writing a history of private life in the GDR.

Alon Confino is professor of modern German and European history at the University of Virginia. He is the author of *Germany as a Culture of Remembrance: Promises and Limits of Writing History* (2006) and *The Nation as a Local Metaphor: Württemberg, Imperial Germany, and National Memory, 1871–1918* (1997); editor of "Histories and Memories of

Twentieth Century Germany," a special double issue of *History and Memory* (2005); and coeditor (with Peter Fritzsche) of *The Work of Memory: New Directions in the Study of German Society and Culture* (2002). He is now at work on a project entitled "Foundational Pasts: An Essay on the Holocaust, the French Revolution, and Historical Understandings."

Greg Eghigian is director of the Science, Technology, and Society Program and associate professor of modern European history at Penn State University. He is the author of *Making Security Social: Disability, Insurance, and the Birth of the Social Entitlement State in Germany* (2000) and coeditor (with Paul Betts) of *Pain and Prosperity: Reconsidering Twentieth-Century German History* (2003) as well as (with Andreas Killen and Christine Leuenberger) of *The Self as Project: Politics and the Human Sciences in the Twentieth Century* (2007). He is presently writing a history of the science and politics of criminal deviance and incarceration in Nazi, East, and West Germany.

Dagmar Herzog is professor of history and Daniel Rose Faculty Scholar at the Graduate Center, City University of New York. She is the author of *Intimacy and Exclusion: Religious Politics in Pre-Revolutionary Baden* (1996) and *Sex after Fascism: Memory and Morality in Twentieth-Century Germany* (2005), which appeared in German translation as *Die Politisierung der Lust: Sexualität in der deutschen Geschichte des zwanzigsten Jahrhunderts* (2005). She is the editor of *Sexuality and German Fascism* (2004) and *The Holocaust in International Perspective* (2006) and coeditor (with Guenter Bischof and Anton Pelinka) of *Sexuality in Twentieth-Century Austria,* a special issue of *Contemporary Austrian Studies* (2006). She is currently working on the death of God in twentieth-century Europe.

Young-Sun Hong is associate professor of history at State University of New York at Stony Brook. She is currently working on a book manuscript entitled "The Third World in the Two Germanys: Locating Race and Gender in Post–1945 Germany," in which she examines the multiple locations of the Third World and non-European peoples in postfascist politics of difference (race, gender, sexuality) in Germany and the "White Atlantic." Her first book, *Welfare, Modernity, and the Weimar State* (1998), is an important theoretical and methodological intervention in the current German historians' debates on German modernity, and her most recent contribution to this debate is "Neither Singular nor Alternative: Narratives of Welfare and Modernity in Germany, 1870–1945," published in *Social History* (2005).

Thomas Lindenberger, Dr. habil., historian, is project leader at the Zentrum für Zeithistorische Forschung (ZZF) Potsdam and teaches at Potsdam University, Germany. His research on the social and cultural history of twentieth-century Germany focuses on protest and violence, public order, and mass media. He serves on the editorial boards of *WerkstattGeschichte* and *Genèses* and is on the standing committee of EurhistXX: The Network for the Contemporary History in Europe. He is currently directing a research group funded by the German Research Foundation (Deutsche Forschungsgemeinschaft, or DFG) titled "Mass Media in the Cold War" at the ZZF Potsdam. He is the author of *Straßenpolitik. Zur Sozialgeschichte der öffentlichen Ordnung in Berlin, 1900–1914* (1995) and *Volkspolizei. Herrschaftspraxis und öffentliche Ordnung im SED-Staat, 1952–1968* (2003); editor of *Massenmedien im Kalten Krieg. Akteure—Bilder—Resonanzen* (2005); and coeditor (with Konrad H. Jarausch) of *Conflicted Memories: Europeanizing Contemporary Histories* (2007).

Alf Lüdtke is professor of history and chair of the Arbeitsstelle Historische Anthropologie at the University of Erfurt and senior research associate at the Max-Planck-Institut für Geschichte, Göttingen. He is the author of many publications, including *Gemeinwohl, Polizei und Festungspraxis: Staatliche Gewaltsamkeit und innere Verwaltung in Preussen, 1815–1850* (1982) (translated as *Police and State in Prussia, 1815–1850* in 1989) and *Eigen-Sinn. Fabrikalltag, Arbeitererfahrungen und Politik vom Kaiserreich bis in den Faschismus* (1993); editor of and contributor to *Alltagsgeschichte. Zur Rekonstruktion historischer Erfahrungen und Lebensweisen* (1989) (translated as *The History of Everyday Life* in 1995) and *Herrschaft als soziale Praxis. Historische und sozialanthropologische Studien* (1991); coeditor of and contributor to *Akten, Eingaben, Schaufenster: Die DDR und ihre Texte. Erkundungen zu Herrschaft und Alltag* (1997); *Die DDR im Bild* (2004); and *The No Man's Land of Violence. Extreme Wars in the 20th Century* (2006). He is also among the founders and coeditors of the journals *Historische Anthropologie* and *WerkstattGeschichte,* as well as the book series *Selbstzeugnisse der Neuzeit.*

Ina Merkel is professor of cultural studies at Philipps-Universität, Marburg. She is the author of numerous articles and books about GDR consumer culture and gender, including *Utopie und Bedürfnis. Die Geschichte der Konsumkultur in der DDR* (1999) and . . . *und Du, Frau an der Werkbank. Die DDR in den 50er Jahren* (1990). She is the editor of *Wir sind doch nicht die Meckerecke der Nation! Briefe an das Fernsehen der DDR* (2000). Her current research is on the concept of the "popular" in socialism.

Katherine Pence is assistant professor of history at Baruch College, City University of New York. She is completing a book entitled *Rations to Fashions: Gender and Consumer Politics in Cold War Germany.* She has written a number of articles on East and West German consumer culture and gender for publications such as the journal *German History* (2001) and various edited collections. Her most recent article is "Shopping for an Economic Miracle: Gendered Politics of Consumer Citizenship in Divided Germany," in *The Expert Consumer: Associations and Professionals in Consumer Society,* edited by Alain Chatriot, Marie-Emmanuelle Chessel, and Matthew Hilton (2006). Her new research examines German commodity cultures of imports and exports in the transnational context of postwar decolonization.

Judd Stitziel, an independent scholar based in Washington, D.C., is the author of *Fashioning Socialism: Clothing, Politics, and Consumer Culture in East Germany* (2005). He received his PhD from The Johns Hopkins University and has taught at Cornell University and Wesleyan University.

Dorothee Wierling is deputy director of the Research Center for Contemporary History in Hamburg (FfZ) and professor of modern German history at the University of Hamburg. Her latest book is *Geboren im Jahr Eins. Der Geburtsjahrgang 1949 in der DDR, Versuch einer Kollektivbiographie* (2002). Her new research project concerns a family correspondence during World War I, provisionally entitled "'Coffee Worlds': Coffee Trade in 20th Century Hamburg."

Index